AGING AND SOCIETY

AGING
AND
SOCIETY

A CANADIAN PERSPECTIVE

Mark Novak
University of Manitoba

NELSON CANADA

© Nelson Canada,
A Division of International Thomson Limited, 1988

Published in 1988 by
Nelson Canada,
A Division of International Thomson Limited
1120 Birchmount Road
Scarborough, Ontario
M1K 5G4

Canadian Cataloguing in Publication Data

Novak, Mark W.
  Aging and society

ISBN 0-17-603415-3

1. Aging – Canada.   2. Aged – Canada.
3. Gerontology – Canada.   I. Title.

HQ1064.C3N68 1988   305.2'6'0971   C88-093559-6

COVER: CP Laserphoto, 1985
        Senior citizens protested de-indexing of old age
        pensions at Parliament Hill on June 19, 1985.
        The federal government abandoned its
        controversial plan on June 27, after a month of
        public protest.

Cover Design: Falcom Design and Communications

Printed and bound in Canada

4   92 91

I dedicate this book to my family —
Mona, Chris, Jon, Sean, and Daniel

CONTENTS

PREFACE

A few times each year I meet with publishers' representatives to learn about new texts for my courses. Our conversations go something like this:

Rep: What will you be teaching next year, Professor?

Me: My second-year course on Aging and a course on the Life Cycle. Do you have any Canadian texts?

Rep: (Silence) Let me see ... (He or she looks through a large binder that holds book outlines.) Hmmm ... Nothing Canadian, but we'll be coming out with the third edition of Crimpton's [U.S.] text this spring.

Me: No thanks. I already use a different text from the United States. Anything Canadian coming out in the future?

Rep: Not as far as I know.

The representative leaves with an apology for not having a Canadian text. We both agree that someone ought to write a gerontology text for Canadian students.

After more than twelve years of waiting for someone else to write a suitable undergraduate text, I decided to write one myself. I knew what I wanted in a Canadian text.

First, I wanted a readable book — one that students could read without stumbling over social science jargon and dense academic prose. I have defined most technical terms within the text so that students will not have to flip to a glossary or interrupt their reading by looking at footnotes. I also present examples, charts, or graphs to illustrate difficult points. I hope that these techniques will free students to think about what the text says.

Second, I wanted a text that presented aging in the context of Canada's history and social life. In the past I have used U.S. texts in my aging courses, and each year I have to delete large sections of the text from the assigned readings. I cannot see why Canadian students need to know about the number of older people in Arizona, about the U.S. Social Security System, or about the differences between aging U.S. blacks, whites, and Mexican Americans. These are interesting topics, but Canada has its own geographic regions, its own social policies, and its own mix of cultures and ethnic groups. Canadian students should first learn about aging in their own country.

Third, I wanted a text that described Canada's social institutions — its health care, income, and housing systems, as well as its family and community life. Canadian students should know that their health care system, for example, provides free health benefits to all older people and that the retirement income system provides a basic income to older Canadians. These systems create a social safety net for older people and provide the basis for a decent old age today.

Canadian students should also know that their society has problems. Many Canadians hold negative stereotypes about older people (my own children put me down by telling me I am getting old); the fast pace of modern society often pushes older people to the sidelines (try crossing a six-lane city street if you have arthritis in your legs); and some groups of older people (many of them very old women) still live in poverty. Canadian society needs improvement. Students need to know what parts of the social system work for older people and what parts work against them. *Aging and Society: A Canadian Perspective* gives students the facts about aging. It also helps students sort through and understand the issues surrounding aging today.

ORGANIZATION

This book begins by describing large-scale (macroscopic) changes in society. It then shows how these changes affect people and social institutions. It concludes by showing how individuals respond to these changes and how they in turn give new direction to society. The structure of the book reflects a dialectical model of social change.

Part I, Gerontology Today (Chapter 1), introduces the student to the field of aging. It shatters many of the myths people have about aging and shows the range of topics gerontologists study.

Part II, Historical Change (Chapters 2 and 3), looks at the changes in Canada's history and demographic structure that led to population aging (the increased proportion of older people in the population). It also places Canada in a world context.

Part III, Maturational Change (Chapters 4, 5, and 6), looks at individual aging — the biological, psychological, and developmental changes that come with age.

Part IV, Institutional Change (Chapters 7 through 13), looks at Canada's institutions — the health care, social security, and housing systems as well as the family, the community, and the institutions responsible for death and dying.

Part V, Societal Change (Chapters 14 and 15), looks at Canada's political structure, political action, and the effects of aging on Canadian society in the future.

Together these chapters give students a broad understanding of how aging affects the individual and society.

SPECIAL FEATURES

I have included a number of features that make this a more useful book.

First, this text can be used in either a one- or a two-term course. An instructor of a two-term course will be able to use the entire book, but an instructor of a one-term course may want to select specific chapters for reading. These might include chapters that deal with population aging and Canada's social institutions (Chapters 1, 3, 7, 8, 9, 10, and 12).

Second, each chapter starts with an outline of the chapter's contents and an introduction to the chapter's main themes.

Third, in each chapter the text is supplemented with exhibits that include graphs and charts; sidebars; and excerpts from other publications. Some of the sidebars and excerpts present controversies in the literature; others present case studies that show the human side of aging. Most graphs and charts have accompanying explanations describing them and showing their relation to the text.

Fourth, each chapter concludes with a series of main points that summarizes the text. Each chapter also includes an annotated list of several important sources that students can consult for further reading.

Fifth, the book includes a list of organizations and agencies that deal with aging in Canada. This list covers non-governmental and federal and provincial government sources. Students can use these sources to get the most up-to-date information on aging for term papers or reports.

Sixth, the book includes a reference list. This list contains all of the sources referred to in the text, in alphabetical order by author. Each reference has beside it a number (or series of numbers) that correspond to the chapter(s) where the reference appears. A student can use this list when it comes time to do a research paper. All the references cited in Chapter 10 (Housing and Transportation), for example, have a number "10" beside them. A student who wants to do a research paper on housing can quickly look at the chapter numbers to pick out all the references for housing and transportation.

ACKNOWLEDGMENTS

Peter Milroy, Editorial Director of the Academic Division at Methuen Publications, started me on this project. He showed up at my office one day to ask if I would write a gerontology text, and he suggested that I apply to the Secretary of State of Canada for research support. Six months later, the Secretary of State granted me a Canadian Studies Writing Award to write this book. I thank the Department of the Secretary of State for its support. I especially thank Peter Milroy for his belief in this project.

The library staff at the University of Winnipeg helped me almost daily. Allison Dixon ordered books for me from interlibrary loan, Linda Dixon helped me with computer searches, and the Chief Librarian, William Converse, gave me a line of credit so that I could copy documents and microfilm sources. I thank them all for their help.

Two research assistants, Riva Love and Ruth Dowse, helped me gather most of the information for this book. Ruth searched Statistics Canada's published reports since 1980 for data related to aging. She also compiled the list of groups and organizations at the back of this book. Riva borrowed dozens of books from interlibrary loan, sent for hundreds of published and unpublished papers, and kept track of all the sources I used. Both she and Ruth read several versions of this manuscript and made careful comments on each. Riva always made sure I responded to her comments and that I improved a chapter before I went on to other work. I thank her for her keen eye and her goal of perfection. I thank both Riva and Ruth for their hard work and patience.

Many Canadian colleagues in the field of gerontology sent me their papers and research reports. I cannot thank them all here, but they helped make this a better text. A few people deserve special mention. Neena Chappell, my friend and colleague, gave me space at the University of Manitoba Centre on Aging to work for the year. She read early versions of several chapters and made critical, helpful comments. A number of other colleagues also read and commented on the text. Paul Baker read the entire manuscript. He showed me what I had to do and then encouraged me to do it. Victor Ujimoto, C. G. Gifford, and Wayne McVey also commented on specific chapters. Professor McVey kindly supplied me with charts and data on demographic change. These people all took time from their busy schedules to help me with this text. I thank them for their efforts. I alone take responsibility for the text's shortcomings.

I owe special thanks to Leroy Stone, a good friend and a tireless worker, who taught me the importance and the limits of demographic research. Two close friends, John Hofley and Hans Mohr, inspire all of my work. I can never repay them, only thank them, for their support and friendship.

I dedicate this book to my family — my wife Mona and my sons Christopher, Jonathan, Sean, and Daniel. Sean and Chris deserve special thanks for helping me prepare the final draft of this manuscript. The whole family deserves credit for lightening my spirits with their good humour and love.

PART I

GERONTOLOGY TODAY

CHAPTER 1

WHAT IS GERONTOLOGY?

WHY STUDY AGING?

Everyone needs to know about aging. First, all of us are getting older. Some people are past 65 already, and most adults not yet 65 or over will become a part of the older population sometime between now and the year 2030.[1] We will want to make old age as good a time of life as it can be. Second, between now and the time you younger students reach old age, your parents, aunts, uncles, neighbours, and older friends will grow old. You will want to know about aging so that you can help them live the best old age possible.

Third, more people work with the elderly than ever before, and more people will find themselves working with the elderly in the future. Older Canadians make up nearly one-tenth of the population today (9.7 percent in 1981). Experts predict that this figure will grow to between 14 percent and 17 percent of the population by the year 2030 (Health and Welfare

---

[1]The terms "old," "elderly," "aged," and "senior" in this text refer to people aged 65 and over unless another age is given.

Canada 1983). Nurses, social workers, teachers, counsellors, and even travel agents will have more and more older people as clients.

An older population will also put new demands on Canada's social structures. Sociologists define a *social structure* as a relatively stable pattern of social interactions (Abercrombie, Hill, and Turner 1984, 198–99). The family, the education system, and the health care system all fit this definition, and they will all change as Canadian society ages:

- More Canadians will live in three- and four-generation families. And many people will become grandparents while they still have active careers of their own.
- Schools and universities already attract more older students than ever before. These students want flexible schedules. They also need different kinds of teaching methods and different grading schemes than younger students.
- The health care system will also change. The current system favours treatment of acute illness, but older people have more chronic ailments like arthritis, hearing problems, and diabetes. An aging society needs to prevent illness before it happens.

Gerontology is the discipline that systematically studies aging. It looks at aging from two points of view: how aging affects the individual and how an aging population will change society. This chapter describes (1) the goals of gerontology, (2) the history and structure of the field, and (3) the methods gerontologists use in their work.

ATTITUDES TOWARD OLD AGE

People hold many *stereotypes* about old age. Sociologists define a stereotype as "a one-sided, exaggerated and normally prejudicial view of a group, tribe or class of people" (Abercrombie, Hill, and Turner 1984, 209). People who hold a stereotype do not check it to see if it is true. If they meet someone who looks different than the stereotype predicts, they think he or she is an exception. Stereotypes often have some basis in truth, but they exaggerate and distort the truth. Often stereotypes lead to discrimination or unfair treatment.

When it comes to old age we hold both positive and negative stereotypes: the wise old farmer and the kindly grandmother; the dirty old man and the sex-starved spinster. Many of our stereotypes take a negative view of older people and old age (Bassili and Reil 1981).

Gerontologists call prejudice against older people *ageism*. Butler (1969) says ageism comes about because the young and the middle-aged feel distate for aging. They see old age as a time of weakness, sickness, and dying. Ageism also comes about because people know little about old age, and because what they know is based on myth and fear.

In our culture, people learn to be prejudiced against the old. Negative views about older people come from many sources. Towler (1983) ana-

Exhibit 1.1

WHAT IS IT LIKE TO BE OLD?

No one can know the answer to this question until they reach old age themselves. But Professor Paul Baker of the University of Victoria set out, at age 33, to learn about aging first-hand. In the story that follows he describes his experiment with old age.

"You're too young to be a gerontologist. How can somebody who's only 33 know what it's like to be 83?" This reaction from one of the few older students in my course on the sociology of aging bothered me. My first instinct was to haul out my academic/scientific defences and claim that you don't have to be an X to study X's (be they old, female, black, or handicapped).

But I was left with the uncomfortable feeling that maybe she was right, maybe I was missing some of the more subjective and emotional aspects of aging by working only with "hard," "objective" data. Then I ran across John Griffin's classic book, *Black Like Me*, written in 1961. Griffin dyed his skin black and passed as a black man in the southern United States for a month. His book showed how different the world was for a black man, and made a lot of white people realize what racism meant at the human level.

So, how could I become old? The answer was obvious: the same kind of makeup that turned Dustin Hoffman old in *Little Big Man* might work for me, and with the help of a makeup artist in Vancouver, plus some old clothes, a cane, and a gray wig, I made the transformation. The makeup took several hours to apply, and hurt like hell going on and coming off, but it worked.

My main interest was in experiencing society's reactions to an old man. I walked around in Victoria and Vancouver about a dozen times, in different places, at night and during the day. And what I found was pretty much what I expected: a few people go out of their way to help the old, a few turn their backs, and most people simply ignore them.

One "young" woman (my own age) waited patiently for me as I struggled up the stairs at the Victoria Institute of Gerontology, held the door open, and said "have a nice day." I felt very uncomfortable: I was really a young, healthy, male but was masquerading as a decrepit old man; I actually felt like I was a "burden" and almost told her I could open doors for myself, even if I was old.

On the other hand, I was shoved off the sidewalk in front of the Empress Hotel by a large, noisy bunch of tourists. It may have been accidental, but I felt angry and frustrated. On crowded streets I could no longer stride along and know that other people would move aside. I had to be on the defensive, anticipating others' moves. Crossing busy streets became a totally different experience. I hung back so that the crowds could bolt across as soon as the light changed, and then I shuffled along, keeping my eye on the cars, which seemed like racehorses just itching for the gates to open. The lights always started flashing

"DONT WALK" before I was across. What was I supposed to do, the bunny hop?

I experimented with getting in and out of cars and using buses. The basic lesson I learned was that the world gets bigger and faster for an old man, and I was acutely aware of this dramatic change because I was really young, and hadn't gradually accepted the inevitable changes of aging.

I discovered a sense of comradeship of the old, who had the time to sit and talk. I also found a subtle difference between old Victoria and big Vancouver: it seemed easier to be old here, partly because of the size and pace, but maybe also because in Victoria we have so many old people. I think we have learned to be a little more patient.

Would I do it again? Probably not ... pretending to be old hurt my back, my legs, my feet. It was hard to explain to friends and neighbours what I was doing. I think I'll wait for old age to creep up on me slowly, and in the meantime, I think I have gained a better understanding for my old friends.

Source: Paul M. Baker, "Old Before My Time," personal communication, 1983b. Reprinted with permission of the author.

lyzed five hundred of the most popular books for children (kindergarten to Grade 6) and fifty of the most popular TV shows. He found fewer older people than expected and only a shallow development of their characters. He concluded that the media gave children a biased and misleading view of old age.

Other mass media also foster prejudice against older people. Newspaper stories, for instance, often blame older people for the rising cost of health care in Canada. Harding and Neysmith (1984) say that this practice overlooks the deeper reasons for rising health care costs and creates a negative public image of older people.

Even jokes take a negative view of old age and older people. Palmore (1971) studied attitudes to older people in humour. He looked at 264 jokes taken from ten popular joke books. He found that one-quarter of the jokes took a positive view of aging, and about one-fifth took a neutral view, but more than half of the jokes showed a negative attitude to aging or the aged. He also found a double standard in jokes about age: the jokes about women, more often than the jokes about men, portrayed older people negatively.

These jokes project our own fears and doubts about aging onto older people, but do these fears have a basis in fact? Studies of older Canadians show that fears have little basis in fact. Orris (1970), for example, found that 72 percent of the older people he interviewed in Saskatoon thought their income was adequate. Koenig, Doyle, and Debeck (1977), in British Columbia, found high life-satisfaction in a sample of 730 older people. Most of the people in this study said they were pleased with their housing, and four-fifths said they were pleased or mostly satisfied with their health.

Exhibit 1.2

PROFILE: BREAKING THE STEREOTYPE OF OLD AGE

A senior citizen who used his youthful combat training to corner a man who broke into his neighbor's house was awarded a certificate for police service yesterday.

Although the young man threatened to shoot him, "I wasn't afraid of him at all," 65-year-old Evald Asu said.

Asu, an Estonian, said that when he faced the hoodlum, he remembered resistance tactics he learned for use against the Soviet Red Army in the 1940s.

"When it comes to a serious fight, I can fight like the devil," Asu, 5-foot-8, said.

On the afternoon of Feb. 9 [1984], Asu was trying to get his Siamese cat off the roof of his Lipton Street residence when he noticed a man attempting to enter a house next door.

When he saw the man break a side-door window with his fist and go into the house, Asu said he grabbed his metal ice scraper and went toward the home.

"You can just about expect anything from a character like that," he said.

He was unaware that neighbor Evelyn Tolentino and her two young children were hiding in a bedroom inside.

Asu said the hoodlum was 6-foot and half his age.

"I told him to come out with his hands up, the police are here," he said. "You can't fight in a house.

"I think he was embarrassed; instead of police, there was an old man standing there."

Asu said the man swung at him, but he hit him first with his fist.

"I told him to stay," Asu said, saying he just wanted to keep the man there until police arrived.

But the man backed away toward the fence, where he put his hand into his jacket pocket and threatened to pull out a gun and shoot Asu.

Asu said he swung his ice scraper, coming down on the man's hand several times.

"If he had a gun one of us would have been dead and I didn't want it to be me," he said.

The man jumped the fence with his arm bleeding and Asu followed him down the back lanes.

It was then he said he remembered his guerilla training.

"We went barehanded. We learned to fight," he recalled.

As he followed the man between the houses, he said: "I knew exactly what I was doing. I was watching his hands, his feet."

Asu said the man pointed something at him, so he kept his distance.

"At 30 yards (27.4 metres) that kind of creep couldn't kill me," he said.

Meanwhile, the police had arrived in response to Tolentino's call.

Asu returned to meet them and then led the officers along the man's path, shown by a trail of blood.

A 21-year-old man was arrested shortly and has since appeared in court charged with break and enter with intent to steal from the Tolentino residence. ...

"You can't leave it to someone else

to do," [Asu] said. "If we all put in a little bit, we could fight them   (hoodlums) pretty good."

Source: Joscelyn Proby, "Combat Skills Put to Use," *Winnipeg Free Press*, April 10, 1984, 3. Reprinted with permission of the *Winnipeg Free Press*.

Exhibit 1.3

FACTS ON AGING

Try the following quiz to see how much you know about aging in Canada. The quiz is based on Palmore's "Facts on Aging: A Short Quiz" (1977), but it incorporates suggestions made by Canadian researchers who have revised Palmore's work (Matthews, Tindale, and Norris 1985). The correct answers are at the bottom of the next page. You will find the facts to support these answers throughout this book.

True or False?

1. At least 15 percent of the aged are living in long-stay institutions in Canada (i.e., nursing homes, mental hospitals, homes for the aged, etc.).
2. British Columbia has a higher proportion of older people in its population than any other province.
3. Older people today have less contact with their families than older people in the past.
4. Older people stand a higher risk of criminal victimization than people in other age groups.
5. Memory declines with age.
6. A decline in sexual vigour in older men is usually due to hormone deficiencies.
7. Retirees more often feel depressed, bored, and ill than those who keep working.
8. Most older people in rural areas depend on public transportation.
9. The body's systems go into a steady decline from age 40 on.
10. The majority of older people have incomes below the poverty level (as defined by the federal government).

Turn to the bottom of page 10 for the answers.

Northcott (1982) studied 440 Edmontonians and found that older people reported higher life-satisfaction than the young. More often than younger people they said they felt no pressure in life. Northcott concludes that "old age looks far more attractive than stereotypes suggest."

MYTHS AND REALITIES OF AGING

Gerontology has two goals. First, scholars and researchers work to produce accurate knowledge about aging. Second, professionals who work with older people apply this knowledge to create a better life for their clients. Academic gerontologists try to decrease prejudice and stereotyping in society by writing about the facts of aging today. Consider the following myths and the facts that gerontologists have found to replace them.

Myth: People feel lonely and lost in retirement. They often get sick and die shortly after they retire.

Reality: A majority of people enjoy retirement (Atchley 1976, 87). Given the chance and a decent income, most people retire as soon as they can (Health and Welfare Canada 1979, 53). Palmore, Fillenbaum, and George (1984) report that retirement has little, if any, effect on health, social activity, and life-satisfaction or happiness. Streib and Schneider (1971) found that the health of some workers improves when they retire. Many workers start new careers, take up volunteer work, or go back to school.

Myth: People in older age groups face a higher risk of criminal victimization than people in younger age groups.

Reality: Older people report more fear of crime than younger people. Older women who live alone reported the most fear (Kennedy and Silverman 1984–85). Researchers say that loss of social networks due to retirement, widowhood, and staying home leads to increased fear of crime. But this fear of crime does not fit the facts about crime against the elderly.

Studies in Britain, the U.S., and Canada show that older people run *less* risk of victimization than any other age group. A 1981 Canadian survey found that older people made up only 2 percent of victims of personal crimes (Solicitor General of Canada 1985). Older people had only one-sixth the rate of violent and personal victimizations compared to all adults and one-twelfth the rate of the 16–24 age group. *The Canadian Urban Victimization Survey* (Solicitor General of Canada 1983, 3) sums up these findings. It states that "contrary to popular belief, ... elderly people are relatively unlikely to be victimized by crime ... . In fact, the actual sample counts of sexual assault and robbery incidents for those over 60 were so low that estimated numbers and rates are unreliable."

Myth: Most old people live in institutions.

Reality: Only a small percentage of older people live in nursing homes, hospitals, or asylums at any given time — about 8.4 percent nation-wide (Schwenger and Gross 1980). Figures differ by province. Alberta has the highest percentage of people 65 and over in institutions — 9.4 percent in various types of institutions. Provinces like Manitoba and Ontario have closer to 9 percent. Newfoundland has only 5.6 percent of the 65 and over population in institutions. Most institutions house the very old, sick, and frail elderly — people who cannot live on their own.

Exhibit 1.4
Criminal Incident Rates by Age: Seven Cities
(Rates per 1,000 Population)

Type of Incident	16–24	25–39	40–64	65 or older	All Age Groups Combined
Sexual Assault	9	3	1*	**	3.5
Robbery	21	9	5	4	10
Assault	123	62	20	8	57
All Violent Incidents	154	74	25	12	70
Personal Theft	134	73	38	13	70
All Personal Incidents	288	147	63	25	141

*The actual count was low (11 to 20), therefore caution should be exercised when interpreting this rate.
**The actual count was too low to make statistically reliable population estimates.

This table shows a decrease in victimization for each older age group. The trend holds true for each type of crime listed here. It also shows that all people, including older people, experience a higher rate of personal incidents — violence and personal theft — than other kinds of crime. These crimes may make a greater impact on older than on younger people because an older person may have a harder time making up the loss of money or valuables.

Source: Adapted from Solicitor General of Canada, *The Canadian Urban Victimization Survey, Bulletin 6: Criminal Victimization of Elderly Canadians* (Ottawa: Minister of Supply and Services, 1985), 2. Reproduced with permission of the Minister of Supply and Services Canada.

Research shows that stereotypes about old age decrease with increased education. Palmore (1977) devised a "Facts on Aging" quiz (see Exhibit 1.3). He gave the quiz to undergraduates, graduate students, and faculty. He found that undergraduates got the fewest correct answers (65 percent), graduate students came next (80 percent), and faculty got the most correct answers (90 percent).

Matthews, Tindale, and Norris (1985) gave a modified version of Palmore's quiz to public health nurses and also to students and faculty at Guelph University. They found that people with the most knowledge about aging scored best on the quiz. Undergraduate students just com-

---

All of the statements in Exhibit 1.3 are false.

pleting a gerontology course scored highest. Introductory students in a Human Development course scored lowest. Their results suggest that when people learn about aging, their concept of old age improves.

Other research supports this idea. Studies show that education in general, and knowledge about aging in particular, improves people's attitudes toward old age. Gallie and Kozak (1985) found that the more education people had, the better they did on both knowledge of aging and attitude to aging scales. People who had a background in gerontology scored significantly higher than those who did not.

Knox, Gekoski, and Johnson (1984), in a study of undergraduate students, found that positive contact with older people in general leads to better attitudes. So does voluntary, frequent contact between a younger person and an older person they know well. Gfellner (1982) reports that a student placement program for thirty-one undergraduates led to the elimination of negative stereotypes of the aged and more awareness of their own aging. This evidence shows that knowledge about aging can overcome ageism. Knowledge relieves fears and replaces negative stereotypes with facts that give students a more positive view of old age.

The study of aging shows that old age also has its compensations. Older people in Canada have guaranteed incomes, subsidized housing, and free medical care. They get reduced rates on buses, in hotels, and for rental cars. They get tax breaks, free tuition at many universities, and financial support for recreation programs (Palmore 1979). Atchley (1985, 6) declares that in old age the positive results "outnumber the negative by at least two to one." Zarit (1977, 11) says that life for older people is "getting better all the time."

The study of aging shows that social policies and the attitudes of others cause many of the worst problems older people face. Gerontology tries to remove these obstacles to a good old age by learning and publishing the facts on aging.

THE HISTORY OF GERONTOLOGY

Gerontology comes from the Greek words "geron" (old man) and "logos" (reason or discourse). Writings about aging can be found in the scriptures of the Far East, Biblical sources, the Greek philosophers, and medical writings of the Middle Ages. One list of writings on aging before the nineteenth century came to 1,800 titles (Freeman 1979, 81). Freeman describes the early writings about aging (from the first written records to the seventeenth century) as the product of perceptive individuals. These writings reflect their authors' biases and fears as well as the attitudes of their time. Not until the seventeenth century, with the rise of the scientific method, did researchers look at the facts about aging. These researchers came mostly from the natural sciences and from medicine.

Francis Bacon, credited as the founder of the scientific method, wrote one of the best-known early books on aging, *Historia Vitae e Mortis* (The History of Life and Death, 1623). Bacon wanted to use systematic ob-

Exhibit 1.5

CONTROVERSY: DO WE LIVE IN AN AGEIST SOCIETY?

Schonfield (1982, 267) says that introductory gerontology texts often give "the impression that a negative attitude toward elderly people is rampant in the United States and presumably, also, in other western countries." He goes on to say that these texts exaggerate the amount of prejudice against older people in North America. Review articles and studies by well-known gerontologists find little evidence for this supposed prejudice. Studies show that older people maintain good relations with their families, receive many services from the government, and get preferred treatment from restaurants, banks, and airlines.

Schonfield's own research shows that people have both postive and negative attitudes toward old age and aging. He found that between 20 percent and 77 percent of his sample agreed with stereotypes about older people, but many of these same people said that the statement applied to only a portion of the older population. He says that "at most one in five participants could be convicted [of stereotyping]" (Schonfield 1982, 269).

Schonfield (1982, 270) concludes that:

"... some acts portray ageist attitudes, but these are insufficient to justify the generalization that ours is an ageist society. On the other hand, there seems to be ample evidence to contradict the generalization."

Schonfield's research shows the danger of generalizing about attitudes toward older people. Still, his research shows that some proportion of people (as many as one in five) do stereotype older people. More education and information about aging might decrease this proportion.

servation to learn the causes of aging, but his own work echoed the biases of the past. One passage could have come straight from Aristotle 2,000 years before: "Men of age," Bacon says, "object too much, consult too long, adventure too little, repent too soon, and seldom drive business home to the full period, but content themselves with a mediocrity of success" (cited in Freeman 1979, 38).

By the eighteenth century the scientific method began to change the way researchers studied aging. Mathematicians and scientists began to use the mathematical techniques of natural science to study aging. Astronomer Sir Edmund Halley constructed the first table of life expectancy. Quetelet (1796–1874), a Belgian astronomer-mathematician, conducted studies of birth rates, death rates, and how crime and suicide varied with age. He wrote a book titled *On the Nature of Man and the*

Development of His Faculties (1835), in which he described how human traits like strength and weight varied with age (Birren and Clayton 1975, 18).

In the early 1900s scientific interest in old age began to grow. In 1903 Elie Metchnikoff at the Pasteur Institute in Paris first used the term "gerontology" (Freeman 1979, 16). He wrote one of the first modern books on aging, entitled *The Problem of Age, Growth and Death* (1908). In 1912 the Society of Geriatry began in New York — one of the first groups in North America to study aging.

Research and writing on aging grew quickly after 1950. A study of the literature published between 1950 and 1960, for example, found as many publications in those 10 years as in the previous 115 years combined (Birren and Clayton 1975). A bibliography of sources on aging for the years 1954–1974 listed 50,000 entries (Woodruff 1975). Research in gerontology now goes on in many disciplines, including biology, psychology, and sociology.

CANADIAN DEVELOPMENTS IN GERONTOLOGY

Gerontology in Canada grew slowly from 1950 to 1980. In 1950 the government set up the first of a series of committees to study aging. This Committee — the Joint Committee on Old Age Security of the Senate and House of Commons — studied the effects of aging on Canadian society and on individuals. The Committee focused on income security, but also collected information on housing, health, and welfare services (Health and Welfare Canada 1982b, vii).

In 1963 the Senate of Canada appointed a Special Committee to study the services, facilities, and preventive programs available to older people. At that time Canada had no national body devoted to research on aging, so the Committee had to gather its own facts. It used Dominion Bureau of Statistics (now Statistics Canada) census data, research reports published by the Department of National Health and Welfare Canada, and submissions by scholars, researchers, and agencies across the country. The Committee collected the most up-to-date information on aging, and its report gives a good overview of aging in Canada at that time. The Committee refers again and again to the lack of social scientific research on aging. The Committee found gaps in many fields (like the study of retirement in Canada) and poor-quality research in others. A questionnaire sent by the Committee to government departments, universities, and voluntary organizations across the country found a lack of co-ordinated gerontological study. Only 78 out of 118 organizations answered the questionnaire, and less than one-third (24) reported any research on aging from 1950 to 1963. The Committee learned of only 129 research projects started in Canada from 1950 to 1963 — 71 by universities, 38 by voluntary organizations and 20 by provincial and federal government — an average of only 10 research projects per year throughout the country (Senate of Canada 1966, 170–73).

The Committee traced the slow rate of growth in Canadian research to a lack of research funds. Federal Health Grants to support aging research averaged less than $75,000 per year for the ten-year period 1955–1965. Only four provinces (Quebec, Ontario, Saskatchewan, and British Columbia) received these funds, and three institutions in Quebec received more than 77 percent of the total (Senate of Canada 1966, 173).

Other groups — Canada's Department of Labour, the Department of Veterans Affairs, and a number of voluntary agencies — supported research in the 1950s and '60s. The Ontario Department of Public Welfare, for example, started a "Longitudinal Study of Male Workers, Ontario, 1959–78." This study focused on social, economic, and health changes in male workers and offered a rare chance to look at changes in workers over time. It also looked at the adjustments to aging and the kinds of services men used as they aged (Senate of Canada 1966, 75).

Canadian research activity increased during the 1960s and 1970s. In 1971 Manitoba began a province-wide survey of the needs of the elderly. The researchers set out to measure the needs of older people and to measure how well present resources met, or failed to meet, these needs. They questioned 3,558 people who lived in the community and 1,247 older people who lived in long-term care facilities — a total of 4,805 people over the age of 65 (Government of Manitoba 1973). The province repeated this survey in 1976 and again in 1983. This is the largest, most complete longitudinal study of aging in Canada.

In 1973 the Canadian Council on Social Development (CCSD) sponsored a nation-wide study of elderly persons' housing. The Council's report, *Beyond Shelter* (Canadian Council on Social Development 1973), shaped housing policy in Canada for at least the next decade. The government also formed a Special Senate Commission on Retirement Age Policies. The Commission's report, *Retirement Without Tears* (Senate of Canada 1979), described the major issues facing retired Canadians and suggested social reforms.

In 1971 Canadian researchers and scholars started the Canadian Association on Gerontology (CAG). The CAG presents position papers to the government on issues related to aging, keeps track of research activities across the country, and sponsors a yearly "Scientific and Educational Meeting." The CAG also publishes proceedings from these meetings (Canadian Association on Gerontology 1977–85). It has a computerized data base of 2,000 resource persons in Canada and publishes a "Running Bibliography" on aging research by Canadian scholars. Dr. Norman Blackie, Executive Director of the CAG since 1982, says that the CAG also plans to set up an electronic bulletin board. "Researchers or practitioners will be able to ask questions of one another and share the latest information and insights into aging in Canada" (Blackie 1986).

In 1976 the Quebec Department of Health set up one of the first Canadian gerontology centres (the Laboratoire de gerontologie sociale) at the Université Laval. In 1980, recognizing the need for more stable support for gerontology research, the Social Sciences and Humanities

Research Council of Canada (SSHRC) for the first time awarded over $1 million to researchers through its Strategic Grants Division program on Population Aging.

The Council also set aside funds to sponsor five new Gerontology Centres in Canada. Today these Centres exist at the University of New Brunswick, the University of Guelph, the University of Toronto, the University of Manitoba, and Simon Fraser University. The Centres conduct and encourage research, keep local researchers informed about national and provincial research activities, and sponsor forums and seminars on aging (Hancock 1984).

By 1980 Canadian gerontology had begun to come of age. In that year Victor Marshall (1980a) published the first collection of gerontology writings by Canadian scholars, *Aging in Canada*. The collection includes papers on varied topics from demography to health care to housing. The collection includes articles that take a sociohistorical view of aging and articles that look at intergenerational conflict. These articles show Canadian gerontology's links to European and British traditions of critical social science. Other articles show Canadian gerontology's links to U.S. research. Marshall (1980a) noted in his introduction that Canada still lacked basic research on aging — research on family life, biological research, and studies of mental functioning in later life. He spoke of the small number of Canadian researchers as pioneers, many of whom "have worked, of necessity, virtually alone, without the benefit of colleagues who share their research interest in gerontology" (Marshall 1980a, 6).

During the 1980s research activity in gerontology has increased steadily. In 1982 the Canadian Association on Gerontology published the first issue of the *Canadian Journal on Aging*. That year the program of the CAG's 11th Annual Scientific and Educational Meeting contained 129 abstracts (these included media presentations, symposia, and discussion groups, as well as papers). By 1985 the Annual Meeting sponsored over 100 research papers and 84 sessions (including symposia and discussion groups). The Meeting also included 45 technical, educational, and media exhibits.

Gerontology in Canada has grown quickly in the past few years, but more research on aging needs to be done. A review of the CAG Annual Meetings from 1982 to 1985 showed that researchers presented more papers on health-related issues than on any other subject. We still know too little about healthy older people, even though most older people live healthy, active lives. We also need to know more about the social conditions that lead to good aging. What do people of different ethnic backgrounds need as they age? Do the needs of people in rural areas differ from those of people in cities? Do older people have unique educational needs? How do they learn best? And what do they want to know? Researchers have begun to turn to these and other questions about aging. Later chapters in this book will report the latest Canadian research findings on these topics.

CONCEPTUAL ISSUES AND RESEARCH METHODS

Three Dimensions of Research on Aging

In 1980 the Gerontological Society and the Association for Gerontology in Higher Education set out to define the discipline of gerontology (Foundations Project 1980). They asked 111 scholars, researchers, and professionals in the field to describe a basic education program in gerontology. These experts came from disciplines as different as biomedicine and economics, and they differed in how they described the exact content and boundaries of the field. But they did agree, as their most significant conclusion, that three broad areas of study should make up the core of a gerontology curriculum — biomedicine, psycho-social studies, and socioeconomic-environmental studies.

The first area, biomedicine, looks at the changes in physiology and health that come with age. This area includes studies of the biochemical causes of aging, studies of reaction time and stress, and studies of dementia. Experts disagreed least about the curriculum content for this area; this may be due to the long tradition of biomedical research on aging.

The second area, psycho-social studies, looks at the changes that take place within individuals and between individuals and groups. This includes psychological studies of memory, learning, and personality, as well as studies of friendship and recreation.

The third area, socioeconomic-enviromental studies, looks at the effects of aging on social structures like health care and education; it also looks at the effects of social structures on the aging individual. It includes the study of income policies, health care systems, and formal social supports.

Social gerontology includes both psycho-social and socioeconomic-environmental research. It looks at aging from the point of view of the individual and from the point of view of the social system. When social gerontology looks at biological or physical change in old age it asks how these changes affect the individual or society as a whole. A social gerontologist, for example, will want to know how diseases in old age affect hospital costs or how changes in lung capacity affect a person's ability to work. A social gerontologist will also want to know how a social norm like retirement affects the older person's health or how changes in family life in Canada affect the psychological well-being of the elderly. Social gerontology has grown in importance from the 1950s onward in Canada.

Research Issues

Hendricks and Hendricks (1981) say that studies done on aging in the 1960s supported many of the negative stereotypes of aging. These studies often focused on sick and institutionalized older people. They also had many conceptual and methodological problems. A whole line of research,

Exhibit 1.6

TIME-LINES

This series of time-lines shows three dimensions of aging. Line A refers to the biomedical changes that take place with age. Biomedical aging takes place at different rates for each person, and at different rates for each system of the body. Still, we can describe the aging process in terms of some general trends that take place in the physiology over time.

A

1 — 18; peak of sexual vigour
2 — 30 onward; decline of 1 percent per year on average
3 — 40; physical decline shows up as greying hair, wrinkled skin, balding, loss of stamina
4 — 47; menopause
5 — 70; high risk of heart disease and stroke
6 — 71.88; (1981) life expectancy at birth for males
7 — 78.98; (1981) life expectancy at birth for females
8 — 120; (estimated) life span

Line B refers to psychosocial and socioeconomic-environmental changes that take place with age. Most psychologists and social psychologists agree that human beings develop through a series of stages (though different psychologists list different stages and different patterns of aging). Sociologists say that culture (societal values, norms, and expectations) all play a role in shaping the individual's development. This time-line lists some of the basic events in the life course in Canada today.

B

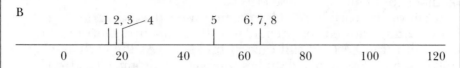

1 — 16; legal driving age
2 — 18; legal voting age
3 — 18; fluid intelligence high (e.g., ability to visualize objects in space)
4 — 20; first marriage
5 — 50; last child leaves home
6 — 65; crystallized intelligence high (e.g., ability to define words)
7 — 65; pensionable age (under rules of most pension plans)
8 — 65; person may begin a second career

Only time-line A shows aging as a constant decline with age. Line B shows aging as a complex series of changes — some abilities like fluid intelligence decrease, others like crystallized intelligence may increase. Also, a person may experience declines on one dimension (e.g., physical stamina), but increases in another (e.g., more involvement in recreation in retirement). Some changes that come with age, like a second career, can only develop in later life.

Line B also reflects the social structures of society. These structures can change, and they are changing today. The Canadian government, for example, has begun to allow a choice of retirement ages for people who get benefits from the Canada Pension Plan; this will allow people to retire before or after age 65 if they choose.

---

for instance, concluded that intelligence decreases as people age. This research supported the view that people get "simple-minded" as they get older. Later studies (Schaie and Labouvie-Vief 1974) showed that this research confused *age differences* (differences between people of different ages) with *age changes* (changes due to aging). Baltes and Schaie (1977) found that younger cohorts (groups of people born at the same time) had more education than older cohorts, and more education may have led to higher intelligence scores. Educational level, they said, accounts for a large part of the intelligence difference between younger and older people.

This example shows the problems gerontologists face when they try to describe changes due to aging. Schaie (1968, 560) describes three kinds of effects that can confound findings on age changes: (1) *maturational changes* — changes due to aging; (2) *cohort differences* — the fact that younger cohorts may differ genetically from older cohorts (in strength, height, etc.); and (3) *environmental effects* — changes in culture like the increase in formal schooling, historical events like a war, or changes in the quality of life like cleaner water and air. Researchers have developed methods to disentangle these effects.

Much of the early research on aging used the *cross-sectional* method. This method allowed researchers to gather data in a short time at a low cost, but it caused (and still causes) problems. As the early intelligence studies show, cross-sectional studies confound environmental effects (lower education levels in older cohorts) with age changes (changes in intelligence due to increasing age). The findings from cross-sectional studies cannot tell us whether aging (maturation) leads to changes in intelligence, health, or any other variable that changes over time.

Longitudinal research designs overcome this problem. A longitudinal study looks at a sample of the same group of people at two or more points in time. A longitudinal study follows a single group of people through time. A longitudinal study of how aging affects intelligence would test the same group of people at, say, ten-year intervals. The results give a truer picture

---

Exhibit 1.7

LONGITUDINAL VS. CROSS-SECTIONAL DESIGNS

The chart below shows the difference between cross-sectional and longitudinal designs. The cross-sectional study took place in 1930. It studied three age groups (10-, 20-, and 30-year-olds) at that one point in time. The longitudinal study also began in 1930. But it measured the 1930 birth cohort three more times (in 1940, 1950, and 1960) at three different ages (10, 20, and 30 years old). The time-lag study measured 30-year-olds at four different points in time (1930, 1940, 1950, and 1960).

Cohort	Time of Measurement				
1900	1900	1910	1920	1930	Cross-Sectional
1910	1910	1920	1930	1940	Time-Lag
1920	1920	1930	1940	1950	
1930	1930	1940	1950	1960	Longitudinal
	0	10	20	30	

Age

Source: Adapted from P.B. Baltes, H.W. Reese, and J.R. Nesselroade, *Life-span Developmental Psychology: Introduction to Research Methods* (Monterey, California: Brooks/Cole, 1977).

of the effects of age on intelligence, because this kind of study avoids the problem of trying to compare different cohorts (people with different educational backgrounds). Gerontologists use longitudinal studies when they want to learn about age changes (Birren 1968, 549; Hultsch and Deutsch 1981, 37), but this method also creates problems. Environmental changes — historical events, changes in the economy, or changes in political values — can confound changes due to aging.

A third type of method, time-lag comparison, tries to overcome the problems raised by simple cross-sectional and simple longitudinal designs. Time-lag studies look at different groups of people of the same age at different points in time (e.g., 70-year-olds in 1960, 1970, and 1980). This type of study tries to measure differences between cohorts. Like cross-sectional and longitudinal methods, the time-lag method also faces problems. It confounds cohort effects with environmental effects. If a research study finds that 70-year-olds in 1980 visit doctors less often than 70-year-olds did in 1960, this may be due to the better health of 70-year-olds in

1980 (a cohort effect) or it may be due to some change in the health care system like higher costs to users (an environmental effect).

Each type of study creates problems when it comes time to interpret results. In addition, longitudinal and time-lag studies pose practical problems. First, they often take many years to complete — years that researchers must wait before they can show results to granting agencies or the public. Second, they are expensive to set up and to maintain. Third, subjects in longitudinal studies drop out (or die), biasing results in later rounds of the study (Birren 1968, 549).

Gerontologists have solved some of these problems by turning simple cross-sectional and simple longitudinal designs into sequential designs. Birren (1968) describes a sequential design as a series of periodic cross-sectional studies during a longer longitudinal study. The cross-sectional studies allow for quick data collection. The longitudinal study provides a check on cross-sectional findings. These two methods together also provide time-lag data on the sampled members of same-aged groups at different times.

The Aging in Manitoba study (Government of Manitoba 1973) offers this kind of option to researchers. The study offers comparable data on health and health care needs among older people for a random sample of older people in the province at different points in time. This type of study allows researchers to compare the needs of different age groups in a given year (e.g., 66–75-year-olds; 76–85-year-olds in 1971) (Havens 1980). It allows researchers to study the changes in these groups' needs over time (whether the needs of the sample of 76–85-year-olds have changed in the ten years from 1971 to 1981). It also allows researchers to see whether social changes have affected all age groups (e.g., whether all groups of older people use hospitals more in 1971 than in 1981). Researchers can then separate *period effects* — effects due to social change (e.g., new medical care policies) — from effects due to aging (the need for more medical care as a person ages).

Botwinick (1984) shows that these complex designs still do not unconfound time of measurement, age, and cohort effects, though they do give researchers more information about the group under study. He concludes that unconfounding variables takes a great deal of time and effort. Without the effort, the researchers could make a fundamental error in understanding, but even with the effort, the researcher still has to explain, for example, what specific historical events led to changes in health care use or how these events translated themselves into different behaviours. "Separating the confounds," he says, "is not the end of the line, it is but the beginning" (1984, 400). Whatever method the researcher chooses, Botwinick's final comment on methods still holds: "Common sense and logic," he says, "must accompany the analysis separating the confounded variables" (1984, 403).

Types of Research Methods

Gerontologists use psychological tests and surveys to study aging, but they also use other research methods. Researchers in each dimension of aging (biomedical, psychosocial, socioeconomic-environmental) have their preferred methods.

Exhibit 1.8

RESEARCH METHODS MOST OFTEN USED IN EACH DIMENSION OF GERONTOLOGY

Biomedical research
    Laboratory experiments
    Controlled studies
    Field trials (e.g., of medications)

Psychosocial research
    Performance tests
    Paper-and-pencil tests
    Questionnaires
    Participant observation field work

Socioeconomic-environmental research
    Questionnaires
    Census and other archival data
    Documents

Pharmacologists, chemists, and neurophysiologists, for example, use laboratory techniques and controlled experiments to study aging; historians use libraries, archives, diaries, and even paintings (Fischer 1978; Aries 1962); literary scholars use plays, novels, and poetry (de Beauvoir 1978; Berman and Sobkowska-Ashcroft 1985). Some studies require more than one method — a questionnaire survey of a large population, for example, may include a psychological test; and an anthropological field study may include the study of a society's literature and history as well as a measurement of the people's physical condition. Researchers use the method or methods that will best answer their questions.

GERONTOLOGY TODAY

Research on aging in Canada has increased in the last ten to fifteen years, and it will continue to increase as the population ages. This research can help governments, social service agencies, and professionals to plan better programs for older people.

Chappell (1982b, 65) suggests five strategies for improving communication between researchers and practitioners: (1) researchers and practitioners should talk and listen to one another, (2) researchers should teach more research courses designed for practitioners (and practitioners should take them), (3) organizations that fund research should set up meetings between researchers and service delivery staff, (4) agencies should meet with graduate students to let them know about data sources for their research, and (5) researchers should present their findings at public forums to shape policy for the elderly.

This collaboration between researchers and practitioners will also open researchers to new research questions. Practitioners can tell researchers about their concerns and the concerns of their organizations. This can lead to co-sponsored research projects. Older people themselves should also have more input into the research process. They can serve on advisory boards to research centres, they can attend research forums, and they can encourage governments to sponsor more research to meet their needs.

Universities, colleges, and technical schools have begun to add gerontology courses to their programs. Many universities also sponsor certificate programs in gerontology. These programs allow professionals who work with the elderly — nurses, social workers, dentists, policy planners — to learn more about the latest research on aging. Nearly all provinces also have a social services division that directs programs for the elderly and a provincial gerontologist or a gerontology consultant who helps create new programs based on the latest research (Health and Welfare Canada 1982b, 161). All of this activity makes gerontology one of the fastest-growing and most exciting fields today.

SUMMARY

1. The growth of the older population in Canada has made aging a major social issue — one that will affect all of us.
2. Gerontology has always had two goals: first, to increase our knowledge about old age and, second, to improve the quality of life in old age. Today in Canada these goals take the form of scholarly research and the practical application of research findings.
3. Modern gerontology has grown in three overlapping phases: a natural-scientific phase that focused on biomedical knowledge (1900–present); a psychosocial phase that focused on personal relations and psychological development (1940–present) and a socioeconomic-environmental phase

that focused on social structures (1960–present). These three approaches to the study of aging form the three dimensions of modern gerontological knowledge.

4. Gerontologists have developed methods to disentangle age effects (changes due to age) from changes in groups due to differences in cohorts, historical events, and the effects of repeated testing. Gerontologists also use methods borrowed from traditional disciplines to study the history, philosophy, and anthropology of aging.

5. Gerontology today is one of the fastest-growing fields of study. It can make old age a better time of life by increasing knowledge about aging and by modifying or creating social structures that meet the needs of older people.

SELECTED READINGS

Health and Welfare Canada. *Canadian Governmental Report on Aging.* Ottawa: Minister of Supply and Services, 1982b.
   The government wrote this report for the United Nations Conference on the Elderly in 1982. It gives a good overview of the services and programs for older people in Canada up to about 1980.
Canadian Association on Gerontology. *Canadian Gerontological Collection, Vols. I–V.* Winnipeg: Canadian Association on Gerontology, 1977–85.
   Collections of papers presented at annual meetings of the CAG. Varied papers on topics like dementia, leisure, memory, and ethical issues.
Marshall, Victor W., ed. *Aging in Canada, 2nd ed.* Toronto: Fitzhenry and Whiteside, 1986.
   A collection of recent writings by gerontologists from across Canada. Some excellent reviews of the Canadian literature on topics like population change, health care, and the family.

PART II

HISTORICAL CHANGE

CHAPTER 2

AGING THEN AND NOW

INTRODUCTION

In Laurel Creek, West Virginia, old men retire to the porch. They watch the traffic go by, they talk to friends and neighbours, and they arrange for part-time work. Life on the porch in the early years of retirement allows a man to keep in contact with the community. When a man gets older and his health fails, life on the porch allows him to draw on his social credit. People stop to check on him, and they make trips to the store to get his groceries. If bad health keeps him indoors, his absence from the porch alerts people that he may need extra help. When a man nears death he may come out to the porch to receive last visits from friends and neighbours. Life on the porch keeps a man part of the community until he dies (*Human Behavior Magazine* 1977, 23).

Life on the porch matches an ideal we have of late old age. It reminds us of another time — a time when people grew up and died in the same town, when neighbours knew one another well, and when the young respected the old. Today many people feel that old age has become worse. We push old people aside in retirement, advertisers tell everyone to "think young," and even birthday cards make fun of aging. One card reads, "Roses are red, violets are blue, thank goodness I'm not older than you."

It seems that in the past people enjoyed old age, but that in modern society older people get little respect or attention.

Has old age become worse over time? Did simpler societies offer a Golden Age to the old? Or do we just like to believe things were better in the past?

Social gerontologists try to answer these questions. They take two approaches: some gerontologists study ancient societies to see how such societies viewed and treated older people; other gerontologists study modern societies to see how different social structures lead to different experiences of old age. This chapter will examine both points of view. It will look at: (1) how aging differs in different types of societies, (2) how social structures affect aging, and (3) how aging today differs from aging in the past.

THREE TYPES OF SOCIETIES

This chapter will look at aging in three distinctly different types of society: (1) hunting and gathering, (2) agricultural, and (3) industrial. These societies range in order from the simplest to the most complex kinds of social structures and from the most ancient societies to the most modern. They give a picture of how aging has changed over time.

Hunting and Gathering Society

Humans lived in hunting and gathering bands for a million years or more and only settled into agriculture between ten and twenty thousand years ago (Bronowski 1976, 50, 59). People in a hunting and gathering society survive by gathering wild plants and by stalking or trapping wild game. These groups (sometimes as few as twenty people) move constantly from place to place in search of food. Hunting and gathering societies resemble an extended family. They have simple technology (bows, spears, fire) and no permanent settlement.

Archaeologists estimate that people in hunting and gathering societies had a maximum life expectancy of 40 years and a normal life expectancy of about 18 years (Lerner 1970; Cutler and Harootyan 1975, 32; Howells 1960). Cowgill and Holmes (1972) report that these societies define a person as old by age 45 or 50, and Simmons (1970; 1960), in a study of seventy-one contemporary simple societies, says that people in these societies are old at 50 or 60 years of age. He estimates (on the basis of scarce data) that these societies rarely have more than 3 percent of their people over age 65. The terms "old" and "elderly" in this section (and in other sections on simple societies) refer to people 50 to 60 years old.

Amoss and Harrell (1981, 5) describe a single condition that leads to a good old age in primitive society. They say the old have high status when their contribution to subsistence outweighs their cost to the group. Older people do well when they still have a valued role to play in the culture. Their ability to give to the group depends on two things: first, the culture must offer alternate roles for older people to play as they lose their strength, and, second, the older person must have good health.

The Inuit (Eskimo) of Canada serve as a good example of a hunting and gathering society. The Inuit live in a climate that demands physical strength to survive, but they love and respect their elders and allow their older members to take part in social life as long as they can. Men, for example, "retire" slowly from work. As a man loses his strength, younger male members of the community or household do more of the winter hunting. The older man may then take shorter hunting trips or teach the young how to hunt. Older Inuit women have an easier time moving into old age than do men (this is true of women in most nomadic societies). They pass the heavy work on to younger women and spend more time taking care of the children.

Older men and women find personal ways to adapt to decreases in their strength. Older men will start to hunt early in the spring in order to stockpile food for the winter. They may also strike a bargain with a young hunter — the older man fixes the gear and the younger man hunts. Older women sometimes adopt children. The Inuit allow their elders to play new roles in society as their health and strength decline. For example, the Inuit value their old as much for their knowledge and wisdom as for their work. A person still gives something to the group when he or she recalls and passes on the knowledge of Inuit lore. This social role makes the old person useful to the group and improves their status and treatment in the community.

Not all groups make these arrangements for older members. The Chipewyan, who live in Canada's northern prairies, have no roles for older men to play. The Chipewyan do not value knowledge of tribal lore or craftwork. A man has status when he succeeds at hunting, but when he stops hunting he loses respect and power in the group — people label him "elderly." Men will do anything to avoid the label. Some men continue to hunt even when their health fails. Sharp (1981) reports the case of a man who had just recovered from a heart attack and had emphysema, but still went into the bush alone. His wife worried that he would kill himself through overexertion, but he risked his life rather than be called old. The Chipewyan offer fewer options to older men than do the Inuit.

Researchers report that hunting and gathering societies distinguish between two different stages of old age. In the first stage a person retires from the heavy work of middle age, but he or she still has good health. In the second stage the older person gets sick or becomes demented or frail. Simmons (1960, 87) calls people in this second group the "overaged."

In Inuit society, for example, older people keep their status as long as they do some useful work for the group. Their status drops if illness makes them dependent. People make fun of the frail elderly, say nasty things to them, or ignore them. The "overaged" get the worst cuts of meat, have little money, and have to do without trade goods. A stranger may take in an Inuit who outlives his or her spouse, children, and close relatives, but the old person will get no respect and will have to do the worst work (Guemple 1977).

Exhibit 2.1

DO NOMADIC PEOPLE ABANDON THEIR ELDERS?

In any nomadic society, if people live too long and become decrepit or demented, the group may abandon or kill them.

Jacob Bronowski (1976) shows this in his film *The Harvest of the Seasons*. In Iran (Persia), he follows a nomadic group called the Bakhtiari on their yearly journey to their summer pastures. The tribe climbs over six mountain ranges, through high passes and snow, until it reaches the Bazuft river.

Bronowski says the test for the group comes at the river. The Bazuft, a trickle in summer, swells each year with melting snow and spring rain. The group — men, women, and animals — must swim across. For the young, crossing the Bazuft stands as a test of adulthood. For them, life begins, but for the old, Bronowski says, life ends.

The camera records in detail the struggle to cross the river. The current batters horses, donkeys, sheep, goats, and people. The young men swim for their lives and help the animals get across. But then the camera pulls back to focus on two figures among the rocks — a dog and an old man. The dog races back and forth looking from the man to the group below. The man sits silently with his back against the rocks watching the tribe cross the river. No emotion shows on his face. He no longer has the strength to cross the river, and the tribe will go on without him. "Only the dog is puzzled to see a man abandoned," Bronowski says. "The man accepts the nomad custom; he has come to the end of his journey ..." (1976, 64).

Life in many nomadic cultures demands this kind of choice. The tribe must move on to survive. The old, who cannot keep up, get left behind. This man accepts his fate. He probably left his own parents to die in the same way. This dramatic case shows the dark side of life in primitive society. "In a vigorous community," Turnbull (1961, 35–36) says, "where mobility is essential, cripples and infirm people can be a handicap and may even endanger the safety of the group."

A study by Maxwell and Silverman (1977, 37) found that 80 percent of the societies that devalued the elderly lived as nomads for at least part of the year. The harsher the environment, the greater the chance a group will kill or abandon its aged. Killing the aged shows up most often in societies that have irregular food supplies, move often, and live in severe climates (Simmons 1970, 240).

The Inuit also abandon their aged when the older person becomes a liability to the group. They do this as a last resort, and they encourage the older person to make the decision (Guemple 1980), but sometimes the group will withdraw its support rapidly, thus hastening death (Glascock and Feinman, 1981, 27).

Glascock and Feinman found this same ambivalence to old age in fifty-seven simple societies they studied. They found that in 35 percent of the societies younger people treated older members well, and in 80 percent young people showed respect for the aged (1981, 27). Many of these same societies abandoned and killed their elderly (Koty 1933; Maxwell and Silverman 1977, 38). Glascock and Feinman (1981, 25) found non-supportive treatment (abandoning and killing the aged) in some form in 84 percent of the simple societies they studied. This, they say, contradicts the idea that all simpler societies support the aged. Research shows that simpler societies vary in how they treat the aged and that treatment of the aged often depends on how much an older person contributes to or takes from the group.

Agricultural Society

People in agricultural societies live on food produced from farming the land. These societies have more complex technologies than hunting and gathering societies. They also have more complex social structures, including social classes and bureaucracies.

Humans settled into villages and cities for the first time — in the Middle East, China, and India — about 10,000 years ago at the end of the last Ice Age. For the first time in human history, societies gathered a surplus of food. In these societies older people often owned property, and they used property rights to get support from the young. "Property rights," Simmons (1970, 36) says, "have been lifesavers for the aged. ... The person who controlled property was able to get more out of life and to get it much longer. Indeed, the importance of property for old age security can hardly be overrated."

As a general rule, in agricultural societies, those with land command the most respect, those without land the least. All over the world, property rights create a legal dependence of the young on the old (Amoss and Harrell 1981, 10). Old people among the Gwembe Tonga of Zambia today, for example, get power by owning livestock and land (Colson and Scudder 1981, 139–41). Older people among the Etal Islanders of Micronesia gain respect when they own property. The Etal look down on old people who hold on to all their land, but they think of a person as foolish if he or she gives it all away. The land serves as an inheritance bribe (Nason 1981, 168).

Americans in the past also used property to hold power in old age. Fischer (1978) studied aging in the United States from 1607 to the present. He found that young men had to wait to inherit their father's land before they could start a family. In the seventeenth and eighteenth centuries that meant a son might reach age 40 before he owned the farm. Fischer (1978, 52) calls the land "an instrument for generational politics"; parents used it to ensure good treatment in their old age.

Fischer (1978) also found that coercion like this bred hostility. The diaries of Colonel Landon Carter, for example, report signs of growing anger between the younger and older generations. One night in 1776, Colonel Carter reports, his son, Robert Wormeley Carter, invited friends over for gambling with cards. When the enraged Colonel ordered the game to stop, his son exploded and called his father a tyrant. The two men almost came to blows. After that the Colonel carried a pistol with him in the house. He wrote in his diary, "Surely it is happy our laws prevent parricide. ... Good God! That such a monster is descended from my loins!" (Greene 1965, 250, 310, 315, 713, 763, 1004, 1102, cited in Fischer 1978, 75).

Other agricultural societies in the past also expressed their dislike for the aged, some more openly than the Americans. Aristophanes mocked the old in his plays, Aristotle derided the way most people grow old (though he thought a philosopher could live a good life even in old age), and Machiavelli, during the Renaissance, portrayed the old man as a lecherous fool in his play *La Clizia*. Tension between the generations sometimes surfaced in song. An Austrian folksong (Berkner 1972, cited in Fischer 1978, 69) says:

Papa, when will you give me the farm?
Papa, when will you give me the house?
When will you finally move to your little room
And tend your potato patch?

Studies of English Canadians in the late nineteenth century show the same tensions between the young and the old. Historical accounts show that parents gave a great deal of thought to how they would pass their land down to their children (Gagan 1983b; Mays 1983), and the children, who worked to improve the family farm, sometimes into their thirties, expected to get it as a reward for their work. In 1853 Susannah Moodie wrote that "death is looked upon by many Canadians more as a matter of ... a change of property into other hands, than as a real domestic calamity" (Moodie 1853, cited in Gagan 1983b, 185).

Ontario farmers kept intergenerational tension low by passing the land down before they died. Synge (1980) says that the older people stayed on the land with the inheriting child and his family. The young or the old couple built a new house nearby. "They [my parents-in-law]," one woman says, "stayed on in the house till they built a place out back for them" (Synge 1980, 138). Getting the land early in life must have reduced some tensions between the generations, but it created others. Selling the land to the young risked the older generation's old-age security. Parents, when they did sell the land to their children, often kept a few acres for themselves to maintain their independence in old age (Mays 1983, 220–21).

The content of farmers' wills also suggests some worry about future security. Wills stated exactly what the inheriting son was to do for his parents. One will describes in detail the kind of food ("flour, pork and butter and milk, potatoes and other vegetables"), the kind of firewood ("plenty of good wood ready for use"), the transportation ("a horse and buggy") and the cash ("$100 a year") that a son had to give his mother for the rest of her life (Gagan 1983b, 186).

Inequality in Old Age in Agricultural Society

Treatment of the aged in agricultural societies differed by social class. The elderly who owned land in these societies could keep power until they died. For this reason, older people who owned land commanded the greatest respect in societies from Canada to traditional China (Ikels 1981). The poor and landless lived less well and got little respect.

"To be old and poor and outcast in early America," Fischer (1978, 60) says, "was certainly not to be venerated but rather to be despised. ... Old age seems actually to have intensified the contempt visited upon a poor man. A rich old man was the more highly respected because he was old, but the aged poor were often scorned." A New Jersey law in 1720 ordered police to search ships for old people and to send them away. In one case the crew of a ship placed a poor, sick old man on a barren island and left him there to die (Fischer 1978).

Fischer describes drunk, crippled old men who hid in cellars and roamed the wharves at night looking for food. Poor old widows also held low status. Their womanhood made old age and poverty worse (as it did in most countries). Without money a woman was degraded and left to depend on others for support. Neighbours sometimes forced old widows to move away to keep poor rates down. Even their children sometimes turned them away. "If the aged poor were only a small minority [in early America]," Fischer (1978, 61) says, "their misery was great."

Laslett (1976) reports that in Elizabethan England the Poor Law of 1601 made children responsible for their aged parents — but only their parents. This excluded other relatives from aid by law. The existence of a law that spells out the relations between the generations suggests that custom bound children to their parents less than we think. Laslett says that in some cases a parent who lived with his or her children got listed in offical records as a "lodger, receiving parish relief" (1976, 95). In other cases the children moved into the family cottage and left their widowed mothers and sisters in poorhouses.

Stearns, in a study of France, says that "older women were treated horribly in the popular culture of traditional society" (1977, 119). Villages expected widows over age 45 to stay single, and literature made fun of older women. Even the grandmother role got little prestige. Other historians have also documented the suffering of the aged poor in the past

(Hufton 1975). The large numbers of poor people and their misery argue against the idea of a Golden Age in pre-industrial society.

Agricultural society, in its treatment of older people, looks like a mirror image of primitive society. In the simplest societies the old had no wealth, but they received respect as long as they gave to the group. The !Kung San, for example, roam the Kalahari desert throughout their lives and have little property. The young revere their elders as storytellers, spiritual leaders, and healers (Biesele and Howell 1981). In agricultural societies the elderly get the most respect if they own property and keep it from their children until late in life or until they die. In agricultural society "a firm hold on the strings of a fat purse," Simmons (1970, 46) says, "was one effective compensation for declining physical powers" (see also Cowgill 1986, 108). The old may be respected in this kind of society, but often they are not loved by the young (Fischer 1978).

Modern Industrial Society

The agricultural revolution created a new form of society. Agriculture produced a surplus of food and gave rise to the first cities. It created social classes and based status on ownership of property. This kind of society lasted until the middle of the eighteenth century, when three interrelated changes began to reshape social life: (1) industrialization, (2) urbanization, and (3) the demographic transition.

These changes took place over two hundred years, and they still affect society today. They began at different times in different places, and sometimes one type of change — economic change, demographic change, a change in values — had more influence on a society than another. Scholars still argue over what change came first in what society, but taken together these three changes revolutionized social life and led to a new age for aging.

Industrialization

By the nineteenth century most of Europe had begun to industrialize. Industry began to use steam and water power to increase productivity, the factory system gathered workers and raw materials in cities, and transportation systems spread the production of factories to all classes and countries. Some countries industrialized before others, and some more quickly than others, but by 1850 industrialization had changed the shape of European society (Stearns 1967, 69–73).

Industrialization both caused and resulted from the breakup of rural life. Cottage industry (small groups of workers in villages producing mostly for local needs) failed as the factories produced more and cheaper goods. At the same time parents could no longer keep their sons on the farm through the promise of future inheritance. As death rates declined, families had too many sons who wanted the land. The younger sons had to move to the city to find work, and the city welcomed them as a cheap source of labour. The new pace of work and life in the city freed young people from traditional ties and beliefs (Stearns 1967, 75ff, 111).

Industrialization also decreased the status of older people in another way. In North America in the twentieth century, the establishment of retirement rules forced older workers out of work. In North America both labour and management supported the idea of retirement. Management liked it because it allowed them to release costly workers who had seniority. Unions supported retirement because in return they won seniority rights (first hired, last fired rules) from management (Haber 1978). In short, unions traded older workers' right to work for younger workers' job security. Retirement expressed in a formal rule the decline of the older person's status in industrial society.

Urbanization

Canadian society changed from a rural society to an urban society between 1851 and 1950. During the nineteenth century both men and women migrated to the cities. Cross (1983) found that Montreal attracted large numbers of young women from the crowded countryside. Bradbury (1983) describes Montreal in 1871 as a city in transition from pre-industrial to industrial life. Accounts of this time say little about the elderly.

Katz (1975) gives one of the few reports on what life was like for older people in a Canadian town. He studied Hamilton, Ontario, between 1851 and 1861. In a report on 597 land-owning men in 1851, he counted only 26 men aged 60 or over out of 597, or about 4 percent of the population. (Men among the poorer classes died younger and probably made up a smaller proportion of the population than the land-owners.) Men who owned land had the most security in old age, and men aged 60 and over had the highest proportion of land-owners compared to other age groups. After age 60, Katz shows, a man's power began to decrease, and men over 60 had a greater chance of having less land from one year to the next than any other group. Men 60 and over also showed the least chance of having a servant (a sign of wealth). After age 60, Katz (1975, 163) says, men often "decline[d] into difficult circumstances."

Synge (1980) says that in small businesses and on farms older people could adjust their work to suit their health and strength, but in industrial cities older people had to meet the demands of the workplace or quit. No public pensions existed in the nineteenth century, and many older people in the cities had no private savings. Older people in the cities, especially those without children, often had to take the lowest forms of work, move into public homes for the aged, or live in poverty.

In North America, urban life undermined traditional society in another way. The cities supported a market system in which individuals could accumulate wealth outside the family structure. Inequality in society began to grow as some individuals gathered wealth for themselves through trade. Successful individuals turned from public affairs to private concerns. This focus on the self broke the individual's communal bonds, including the bonds of one generation to another (Fischer 1978).

Synge (1980), who studied working-class families in Ontario in the early twentieth century, found that city life made old age an uncertain time. Young people earned their own wages and gave money to their parents while they lived at home as young adults, but when these children grew up they moved out and parents lost this income. Few social services existed for older people, and an unmarried daughter often looked after her parents as they aged. Families sometimes passed the job of care from one child to the next. Synge reports the case of one old woman who moved from one child's house to another's for her last 25 years.

Katz (1975) found that few older people in Hamilton lived with their married children, and the poorest households were least likely to house an older relative. Only 8 percent of households in 1851 and 10 percent in 1861 had adults of two or more generations. "Only when old age and loneliness were combined," Katz (1975, 254) says, "would a parent move in with her children."

Katz (1975) found that 58.8 percent of women aged 60–69 were widowed (almost double the rate of men). Women of the poorest social class (Irish Catholic women) faced an eight times greater chance of widowhood than women of the highest class (Canadian-born Protestant women). Poor widows had little or no savings and no pensions from their husbands. The poorest women, especially those without children, would end up on charity (a special charity, the Ladies Benevolent Society, grew up to help them) or in a "house of refuge and industry" (Katz 1975; Synge 1980).

On the surface the new freedom and equality in urban industrial Canada made all people more alike, but for the old they meant a decrease in status. "A really democratic ethic," Cowgill (1986, 51) says, "is incompatible with any system of stratification based on ascribed statuses ... . You cannot have gerontocracy [rule of the eldest] and democracy at the same time."

The Demographic Transition

The *demographic transition* refers to the changes in population that led the developed nations (of Europe and North America) to have a high proportion of older people. The demographic transition took place in North America at the end of the nineteenth century along with industrialization and urbanization. The "demographic transition" refers to a three-stage process of change that explains how European and North American societies shifted from a youthful to an older population structure.

Stage 1: 1300–1750. Before the eighteenth century, population remained relatively stable. Populations had high birth rates (many children born), but they also had high death rates (many deaths). French studies of the seventeenth century estimate that there were about eight children

Exhibit 2.2

DEMOGRAPHIC TRANSITION THEORY

The Demographic Transition

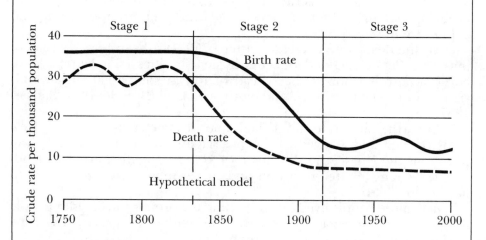

Stage 1: Demographic transition theory says that before industrialization, societies had high birth rates and high death rates. Population size stayed small because of the high (though variable) death rates. The proportion of old and young in society also stayed stable.

Stage 2: Industrialization led to a decrease in death rates. Birth rates stayed high, and the population grew in size. These societies had a growing proportion of young people.

Stage 3: Further into industrialization the birth rate dropped. Death rates stayed low, and population size stayed stable. The birth rate sometimes fluctuated (as with the Baby Boom of 1946–1964). Society has a growing proportion of older people.

Source: Chart based on McVey 1987, personal communication. Reprinted with permission of the author.

to a normal marriage and that about 70 percent of the households had children. Children made up 45 percent of the population at that time (compared to half that figure in industrial societies today) (Laslett 1965).

Only a small number of people lived to old age in pre-industrial society. Figures exist only for scattered populations before 1800, but they give some idea of the proportions of people 65 and over. A national census in Iceland in 1703, for example, reported 4.6 percent of the population 65 and over; Belgrade in 1733 reported 2.1 percent; and Nishinomiya, Japan, in 1713 reported 6.6 percent. A listing of counties in England from 1599 to 1796 showed proportions of people 65 and over between 1.4 percent and 6.4 percent of the population. Rarely in any of these places did the 65 and over population top 10 percent, and Laslett (1976) cautions that past the age of 60 people tended to exaggerate their age.

Stage 2: 1750–1850. A series of events caused rapid population growth in Europe from 1750 on. It also changed the proportion of young and old people in society.

First, the death rate decreased after 1750. Deaths in wars decreased, the cycle of epidemics ended, better hygiene in cities led to better health, border controls stopped the spread of disease, and food supplies increased due to better climate and more open land (Braudel 1981; Stearns 1967, 60).

Second, the birth rate stayed high and in some cases increased. New lands opened and allowed earlier marriage in the countryside. Young people in the cities, who did not have to wait for their parents' land, married young. Better nutrition and more opportunity led people to have more children.

Third, more people lived to old age, and the proportion of older people in the population began to grow. In France, the first society in Europe to show population aging, the proportion of the elderly rose from 7.3 percent of the population in 1776 to 10.1 percent in 1851 (Laslett 1976).

Stage 3: 1850–Present. The birth rate and death rate in Western Europe had both declined by 1900. This completed the transition to an aging population. The biggest change in death rates came from improvements in the general standard of living. Diet and hygiene in the cities improved. Clean underwear, soap, coal for heat, and glass in the windows all helped people stay healthier. Improved housing and more efficient treatment of water and sewage decreased disease. As the standard of living rose, the virulence of disease — and so the death rate — declined.

These changes led all social classes to decrease the number of children per family (Stearns 1967, 62). Middle-class families led the way. They had smaller families to ensure that their children would have the money needed to enter the middle class themselves. Rural families followed later, to ensure that each of their children would get a good portion of land. Children had a different meaning in agricultural and industrial societies. In an agricultural society children are an economic asset; they help produce food, care for the farm, and increase a family's wealth. In an urban society children are an economic liability. They cost the individual family money to raise, but the family gets little economic benefit from children. These facts led to a decreased birth rate.

From 1850 onward the proportion of older people in the developed nations grew. Longer life expectancy meant that more people lived into old age. *But more than anything else, the decrease in the birth rate after industrialization led to a higher proportion of older people in society.*

The three trends mentioned above — industrialization, urbanization, and the demographic transition — put an end to almost all of the following conditions, each of which supported the high status of older people:

1. Ownership and control of property
2. A monopoly on special knowledge
3. Ancestor worship and a high value placed on tradition (where the old provide a link to the gods)
4. Society organized around kinship and extended family
5. Small stable communities
6. High mutual dependence of group members
7. Small numbers of older people
8. Special roles for the aged (Rosow 1965; Eisdorfer 1981)

In the past two centuries the economy, the structure of family life, and the relations of the old to the young changed. Old age became more common, but it also lost its privileged status (Fischer 1978).

MODERNIZATION THEORY

Cowgill and Holmes (1972) refer to the shift from agricultural to urban society as a process of *modernization*. Modernization is "the transformation of a total society from a relatively rural way of life based on animate power, limited technology, relatively undifferentiated institutions, parochial and traditional outlook and values, toward a predominantly urban way of life based on inanimate sources of power, highly developed scientific technology, highly differentiated institutions matched by segmented individual roles, and a cosmopolitan outlook which emphasized efficiency and progress" (Cowgill (1974, 127). Cowgill and Holmes (1972) theorized that the status of older people decreases with increases in modernization. They reviewed studies of fourteen contemporary societies from around the world. These ranged from a study of the Sidamo of Southwest Ethiopia to two studies of Israeli society (one of a kibbutz) to a study of the aged in the USSR. They found that small numbers of older people, ancestor worship, low social change, extended families, a value system that emphasized the importance of the group, stable residence, and low literacy (where the group values the old for their knowledge) all lead to high status in old age. In modern societies, where the reverse holds true, older people have low status (Cowgill and Holmes 1972, 322–23). Cowgill and Holmes (1972) concluded that these trends support modernization theory.

Some recent research also supports this theory. Palmore and Whittington (1971) studied the change in status of the elderly in the United States between 1940 and 1969. They used a "similarity index" to compare the status of the aged (65 and over) and the non-aged (14–64 years old) and found a decrease for the aged in the weeks and hours worked as well as a decrease in income and education level compared to younger people. They found improvements only in the health status of the elderly. They conclude that even with improvements in health and health care, the elderly have lost status relative to the young over the thirty years they studied.

A later study by Palmore and Manton (1974) also supported the idea that status drops in old age in modern society. Palmore and Manton compared people 65 and over to people 25–64 in thirty-one countries. They used an "Equality Index" (EI) to compare these groups. This index measured employment status (employed or not employed), occupation for those employed, and years of education completed for each group. The researchers then computed the similarity of the young and the old in each country. EI scores ranged from the 90s for underdeveloped countries like Iran to the 50s for developed nations like the United States or Canada. (A score of one hundred means perfect equality.) "This indicates," the researchers write, "that the socioeconomic status of the aged is almost equal that of younger adults in some under-developed countries, but has apparently declined to about one-half of equality in some of the modernized countries" (Palmore and Manton 1974, 207). Bengtson and his colleagues (1975) studied more than 5,000 men in six developing countries and found that negative views of aging increased with increased modernization.

Other writers, many of them historians, have criticized modernization theory. Laslett (1976) says that the theory compares the problems of the present to an idealized past and longs for "a world we have lost." He shows that the treatment and status of the aged varied from time to time and from place to place before modernization (as it varies today among simpler societies). Even in a single society, researchers often find ambivalent feelings toward the aged.

Most people think of Japan, for example, as a country that reveres its aged. Traditional tenets urge respect and honour for the elderly, and the Japanese try to follow this rule (Plath 1972). But Plath found a second view of aging in Japanese culture — *Obasute* or "discarding granny." This theme of abandoning the old, he says, runs through Japanese literature from the sixth to the twentieth century. Even within industrial societies the treatment and status of the aged has differed from class to class and between women and men (Achenbaum and Stearns 1978; Quadagno 1980).

Some of the latest research describes a middle ground between the pro- and anti-modernization camps. Cohn (1982) found that the status of the old does drop at the start of modernization. Changes in education and more professional and technical jobs cause this drop, but, as modernization increases, the educational and occupational gap between the old and the young decreases (Palmore and Manton 1974). New cohorts of people move into old age, and the status of the aged improves. Their findings (based on thirty-one countries) show a J-shaped curve — the status of the aged drops with the start of modernization but improves as time goes by. Improved retirement benefits, more adult education, and job retraining, they say, will raise the status of the aged in the future.

Exhibit 2.3

THE DEGA AND THE NACIREMA: THEN AND NOW

About 30 years ago, an anthropologist named Horace Miner described some of the peculiar body rituals among a tribe called the Nacirema. Most of his writing concerned the repressive sexual attitudes and primitive medical practices of that culture. Very little was said about the position of older people among the Nacirema. However, an unpublished manuscript was recently discovered which describes the relationship between the Nacirema and another tribe called the Dega. This manuscript was written in 1958 by Dr. L. N. Rekab of Adanac University, and portions of it are presented ... below.

I believe this material is vitally important because it gives us an eyewitness account of the abuses inflicted upon the Dega by the Nacirema culture, and because it offers a historical baseline by which we can judge the progress which has been made since that time.

For some time now, members of the Dega tribe have been migrating into the village occupied by the Nacirema. Relations between the two cultures are far from cordial. Perhaps the best way to describe the situation is that the Nacirema treat the Dega like visiting relatives who have overstayed their welcome. The Nacirema prohibit the Dega from taking any active part in the economy, except for some child-care work, or tending the sick and the lame among their own group. This work is called *gnireet-nulov* and is never rewarded with pay or goods. The Nacirema explain that the Dega refuse to accept compensation because that would take away the honor of *gnireet-nulov* and turn it into mere labour. The Dega told me they had never been offered any pay.

The Dega appear to be slaves to the Nacirema, although neither group seems aware of the relationship. The Dega are not subjected to long days of hard labour, but are kept in a state of enforced idleness. They are given a meagre allowance for food and clothing, called a *noisnep*, which gives them a standard of living not much better than the poorest Nacirema. Some of them are permitted to live in their own individual huts, but many of the Dega are forced to live in group quarters called *gnisrun* homes. They are confined to small rooms, usually shared with another Dega, all their personal possessions are taken away from them, and they are tended by apprentices of the village witch doctor.

The daily life of the Dega is occupied mainly by sedentary activities. The Nacirema encourage them to play children's games and to do some weaving, but the articles they produce are given away, not sold in the market. A favorite pastime of the Dega is a sport called *flog*. Small white rocks are hit with a stick, over a large area of long grass, sand pits, and ponds. The aim of the game is to find the rock after you hit it. Each player has to buy a dozen special rocks from the Nacirema who makes them, who is called the *orp*. The player who returns at the end of the day with the most rocks is given free drinks by the other players. Sometimes the wealthy Nacirema also play *flog*, but never on the same day as the Dega. The Nacirema complain that the Dega take too long to finish the game. One of the Dega told me that the reason they played so slowly was that they had nothing else to do anyway, so enjoyed the company and the fresh air. ...

The temple is the major gathering place for the Dega. They attend the religious ceremonies regularly, but conversations with the priest and the Dega revealed a curious discrepancy. While the priest was sure that they believed fervently in the religious teachings, most of the Dega said that they did not really believe, but like to see their friends and listen to the music.

The temple is also used for activities which are a major source of excitement for the Dega. The most popular activity is a game of chance called *ognib* which consists of chanting by the priest and the creation of magic geometric shapes by the Dega. At the end of each chant, one of the players shouts the name of the game and jumps up and down with great excitement. The priest inspects the magic shape to see if it has been done correctly, and if it was, presents a clay pot to the winner.

... The sexual practices of the Dega are either nonexistent, or are very well-hidden. No births have ever been observed among the Dega, so it may be inferred that they are beyond their reproductive years. However, there seems to be no sexual activity at all. I asked one Nacirema warrior if he had ever heard of such activity among the Dega, but he just laughed loudly, saying 'that would be like two rocks trying to lay an egg!' When I asked if any Nacirema had sexual relations with the Dega, he turned pale, spat on the ground, and told me he would rather sleep with a wild pig. Even though some of the Dega are very good-looking, the Nacirema consider them all as sterile, sexless individuals.

What will become of the Dega? Their future looks bleak, but I observed that new members arrive almost daily from the forest outside the village. Because of this immigration, there seems to be an increase in their numbers each month. When food was scarce, there was some talk among the young Nacirema warriors of attacking the Dega, but this was discouraged by the older warriors, who seemed more sympathetic to them.

The total population in the village seems to be kept in check by the disappearance of the Nacirema warriors after the ceremony of the gold sundial. This ceremony occurs only among the oldest of the Nacirema, who are given a small sundial and sent off into the forest to rest before they battle with the great spirits. Only one warrior ever returned while I was in the village, and he had gone crazy. He came back and began embracing the Dega, crying out 'Brother! Sister!' He was put out of his deluded misery by a young warrior.

What has happened in the quarter century since Dr. Rekab wrote this account? Well, the Dega have not died out. In fact, their numbers have increased dramatically since then, and most of the abuses put upon them by the Nacirema have disappeared. The *gnisrun* homes have been improved, the *noisnep* plans are providing a better standard of living for the Dega, and the Dega themselves are taking on a more active role in Nacirema society. To be sure, there are still some problems that need solving. However, it is a sure bet that the Dega will never again be second-class citizens.

Source: Paul M. Baker, "The Dega and the Nacirema: Then and Now," personal communication, 1987a. Reprinted by permission of the author.

POST-INDUSTRIAL SOCIETY

Today some people in the developed nations still live badly in old age — they have poor housing, poor nutrition, bad health, and little money. Studies also show that some people still hold negative attitudes toward the aged. Baker (1983a) found, in a study of attitudes toward various ages, that the youngest and oldest ages received the lowest ratings. He found that middle-aged people were rated highest. He describes the findings as an inverted U with status low early in life, rising to mid-life, and falling in old age.

A study of Canadian novels over four decades found both positive and negative views of old age. Matthews and Thompson (1985) studied forty novels — half of them winners of the Governor General's Award for Fiction. They found that most older characters had high self-esteem and high life-satisfaction, but they also found that more recent novels treated the aged as comic figures. They see this as a possible sign of growing negative attitudes to the old.

These studies show that in modern society people still feel ambivalent about old age. Kastenbaum and Ross (1975) call this an "approach–avoidance dilemma." They say that limited resources and the physical decline that comes with old age make it unattractive in all societies. On the other hand most people know and like older individuals and at all times in history some younger people cared for and loved their aged relatives and friends.

Today, in spite of some negative attitudes toward old age, older people as a group in North America live materially better lives than older people at any time in history. Schulz (1980) reports "major breakthroughs" in private and public programs to deal with economic problems in old age.

He cites as proof the increase of private pensions, property tax relief and an increase of almost 100 percent in U.S. Social Security benefits from 1970 to 1980. He could also have included in his list improvements in Canadian Old Age Security benefits, the Canada Pension Plan, and Canada's free nation-wide health care coverage for the elderly. All these programs increase older people's independence and freedom (Schulz 1980, 5).

Some writers predict an age-irrelevant society in the future (Fischer 1978; Neugarten 1980). This kind of society will react toward individuals on the basis of what they can do, rather than on the basis of sex, race, or age. This fits with the trend in North America to eliminate racism and sexism today. Fischer (1978) points to the end of mandatory retirement as a sign of this trend, and Atchley (1980) cites better treatment of old age on television as a sign of improved attitudes toward and treatment of the elderly in industrial nations.

AGING IN THE WORLD TODAY

In the year 2000 about 18 percent of the population of the developed nations (like the U.S. and Canada) will be over age 60 (Salas 1982). This will result mostly from a decrease in birth rates and to a lesser extent from increased longevity. These nations make up only a small proportion of the countries of the world.

The developing nations (like the Latin American, African, and Middle Eastern countries) make up three-quarters of the world's population and have relatively young populations. The death rates in these countries have begun to fall as they did in Europe in the nineteenth century, but in many of these countries the birth rates have stayed high and these societies have grown in size. They have large numbers of children and proportionately few older people — some with as few as 2 percent of the population aged 65 and over (e.g., Ivory Coast and Afghanistan).

The low proportion of people aged 65 and over in the developing nations, compared to the developed nations, tells only part of the story of aging in these countries. Many of these countries still face a crisis due to the large numbers of older people in their societies. In South Asia, for instance, the older population will grow 174 percent from the year 1980 to 2000. In Japan the older population is expected to grow from 15 million people in 1980 to 33 million people by 2025 — from 12.7 percent to over 25 percent of the total population in forty-five years (Salas 1982). Also, the less-developed nations make up nearly 75 percent of the world's population (Population Reference Bureau 1980). The greater number of people surviving to old age in these societies today due to improved health and medical care and the high percentage of older people in developed nations have already begun to swell the world's aged population.

In 1950 about 200 million people in the world were aged 60 or over. By 1975 that population had grown to 350 million, and projections estimate that there will be 1 billion people aged 60 and over by 2025. This population will have grown 224 percent in about fifty years, while the total world population will have grown by only about 102 percent. By 2025 the world population of the elderly (60+) will be about 14 percent of the total world population (Salas 1982).

Sixty percent of the world's elderly (60+) will live in the developing nations by the year 2000, and by 2025 that figure will climb to almost 75 percent. For these poorer nations, which lack the resources and the social machinery to meet older people's needs, these changes will create problems never seen before (Salas 1982).

When nations develop, the young often move to the cities. This leaves the aged in rural villages with little family or social support. These villages lack communications, transportation, supplies, and services that the elderly need. Older workers sometimes return to their home countries after years of working in another country. They have no work, no skills, and no pensions. They will grow old in poverty.

Solutions that fit Western industrialized countries do not necessarily fit the developing nations (Gillin 1986). These countries have neither the social services nor the economic resources to help the elderly poor. These countries also cannot afford the housing, health, or welfare services for the old that Western nations have set up. One case shows the kinds of problems people in these countries face. The *Globe and Mail* (1983, B8) reported that:

After 35 years as a farm labourer, Feliciano Rodriguez has retired. The Peruvian Social Security system is giving him a pension equivalent to 10 cents (U.S.) a month. All is not lost, however ... . He gets an extra 2 cents a month because he is married.

Gerontologists need new theories of aging to explain the changes taking place in these countries (see Exhibit 2.4) and new plans for social change that fit the needs of an aging world.

CONCLUSION

Did older people live better lives in the past than they do today? Can we learn something about aging from past societies? Will aging in the future differ from aging today?

Older people's status in the past differed from time to time, from place to place, and from class to class. Some societies treated their aged badly, some treated them well, but all of these societies had fewer older people than societies today. We cannot look to the past for ways to create a good old age today. The large number of older people in the world today "remains irreducibly novel," Laslett (1976, 96) says, and "it calls for invention rather than imitation."

In the future, as in the past, aging will differ from society to society. The wealthier nations will have the best chance of creating a materially satisfying old age for their people. The poorer societies will struggle under the burden of more people — old and young. One thing seems certain: aging populations will challenge all countries in the world. The economy, the political system, the culture, the level of development, and

---

Exhibit 2.4

CONTROVERSY: MODERNIZATION VS. DEPENDENCY THEORY

Modernization theory views developed industrial societies as the model for less-developed nations and proposes that less-developed nations set up policies for older people like those used in developed countries (Neysmith and Edwardh 1983). But developed nations' solutions often do not fit the needs of developing societies.

Some theorists propose a new theory of aging — dependency theory. Dependency theory uses a critical Marxist approach to study aging. It says that the social and economic structures in a society create the status of the old and that to understand aging in the developing world gerontologists have to understand the economic relations between nations. Dependency theory looks at "the dynamic process involved in societal transformation" and at the societal and world-wide forces that decide the fate of older people (Hendricks 1982).

Dependency theory begins with the fact that structured inequality exists between developed and less-developed societies. Less-developed or peripheral nations now depend on the developed or core nations for their economic well-being. The peripheral nations of Latin America, Africa, and Asia produce raw materials, crops, and manufactured goods for the core nations. The core nations decide what a peripheral country should grow or make for its markets. This keeps the peripheral country dependent and poor, and it disrupts the country's economic, familial, and political life.

Younger people move off the land to work in the cities. Also, the gap between rich and poor people in the peripheral country grows. Families, for example, grow less food for their own use. They begin to grow cash crops for export. This makes it harder for them to support large families that include older members (Gillin 1986). Older people also lose status in these societies because their knowledge does not serve the core nation's needs (Hendricks 1982). "Old people do not simply become out of date," Hendricks (1982, 343) says, "they are made obsolete. If one goal of gerontology is to upgrade the quality of life for older people in any given society, then it must first understand the structural imperatives that have shaped their control over potential resources." Dependency theory adds this understanding to the study of aging and society.

the age structure of a society will all affect how a society responds to this challenge.

Canada cannot copy past societies in its treatment of older people, but it can learn something from the past and from simpler societies. The !Kung San elders heal the sick through dance and music. In Chinese culture the older woman works as matchmaker. Among the Coast Salish tribe of British Columbia the old serve as ritual leaders. Wherever older people have had valued roles to play in their societies they have lived respected and purposeful lives. Canada can make this a goal of its policies for older people.

SUMMARY

1. Culture, custom, and the economic life of the group all influence how a society treats its older members. A study of three types of societies — hunting and gathering, agricultural, and industrial — shows that treatment of the aged differed in the past from time to time and from place to place. None of these societies in the past created a Golden Age for older people.
2. Like most societies, past and present, modern Western societies show an ambivalence toward the aged. Negative stereotypes exist, and some discrimination against the aged takes place. Modern societies also offer older people independence, a high standard of living, and many opportunities for life-satisfaction.
3. The developed nations have a high percentage of older people. They will have to shift resources to serve the changing needs of their populations.
4. Modernization theory predicts a decline in the status and treatment of the aged in modern society when compared to societies in the past. Some studies that compare developed and developing nations today support modernization theory, but critics of the theory argue that it oversimplifies life in the past, that it ignores differences in treatment of the elderly within a society, and that it undervalues the opportunities for a good old age and the life-satisfaction of older people today.
5. The developing nations have large numbers of older people, even though older people make up a small percentage of their populations. This increase in the numbers of older people poses service delivery, economic, and health care support problems for developing nations. Dependency theory says that the economic exploitation of these nations by the developed nations of the West deepens the misery of older people in these societies.
6. Population aging has become a world-wide challenge. Dependency theory places the process of aging in the context of international economic relations. The response a nation makes to the challenge of aging will depend on its traditions, its culture, its level of development, and its economic strength.

SELECTED READINGS

Amoss, P.T., and S. Harrell, eds. *Other Ways of Growing Old: Anthropological Perspectives.* Stanford, California: Stanford University Press, 1981.
This book of readings shows the varied ways people grow old around the world. It removes some of the romantic ideas we have about aging in simpler societies. It also shows how social and economic conditions shape old age.

Cowgill, Donald O., and Lowell D. Holmes, eds. *Aging and Modernization.* New York: Appleton-Century-Crofts, 1972.
The book of readings that set off a major controversy about aging today and in the past. The articles themselves, studies of other cultures, make good reading. They show how aging differs from culture to culture.

Laslett, P. "Societal Development and Aging." In *Handbook of Aging and the Social Sciences*, ed. R.H. Binstock and E. Shanas. New York: Van Nostrand Reinhold, 1976.
A fascinating look at aging in Europe in the past. Laslett challenges the myth that past society offered older people a Golden Age. He shows that treatment of the aged varied from time to time and from place to place. A good read for history buffs.

Synge, Jane. "Work and Family Support Patterns of the Aged in the Early Twentieth Century." In *Aging in Canada: Social Perspectives*, ed. Victor W. Marshall. Toronto: Fitzhenry and Whiteside, 1980.
A close look at intergenerational relations in Ontario in the early 1900s. One of the few studies of aging in Canada in the past.

CHAPTER 3

AGING IN CANADA

INTRODUCTION

When people think about aging they think of wrinkled skin, grey hair, and false teeth. But societies age too. From 1901 to 1981 Canada's population grew four and a half times. During this same period the older population grew *nine* times — twice the rate of the general population. From 1971 to 1981 the total population grew by 13 percent, while the population 0–14 *decreased* by 14 percent and the older population *grew* by 35 percent. The proportion of people aged 65 and over rose from 5 percent of the total population in 1901 to almost 10 percent of Canada's population in 1981. This makes Canada's population one of the oldest in the world, and demographers expect Canadian society to age even more in the next fifty years (Statistics Canada, 1984b).

   This chapter will look at: (1) why Canadian society has aged, (2) the

49

population structure of Canada today, and (3) the impact of population aging on health care and pension programs.

AGING AROUND THE WORLD

The United Nations groups societies by the proportion of their populations aged 65 years old and over. It defines a country as "young" if it has less than 4 percent of its population aged 65 and over, as "mature" if it has between 4 percent and 7 percent of its population 65 and over, and as "aged" if it has more than 7 percent of its population 65 and over (United Nations 1956; 1975). Exhibit 3.1 presents the proportion of older people in a sample of countries from around the world.

The European countries that went through demographic transitions first have the largest proportions of older people. Almost a century ago France and Sweden had more than 7 percent of their populations aged 65 or over (France had 8.2 percent 65+ in 1900; Sweden had 8.4 percent

Exhibit 3.1
Percent of Population 65 and over, Canada and
Selected Regions and Countries

Country	Percent 65 and Over
World	5.8 (1980)
Developed Nations	11.1 (1980)
Developing Nations	4.0 (1980)
Sweden	16.3 (1980)
England and Wales	15.1 (1980)
France	13.5 (1982)
United States	11.3 (1980)
U.S.S.R.	10.2 (1980)
Canada	*9.7 (1981)*
Japan	9.0 (1980)
China	6.0 (1980)
Mexico	4.0 (1980)
Pakistan	3.0 (1980)
Guatemala	3.0 (1980)
Afghanistan	2.0 (1980)

Source: Adapted from Health and Welfare Canada, *Fact Book on Aging in Canada* (Ottawa: Minister of Supply and Services, 1983) and Donald O. Cowgill, *Aging Around the World* (Belmont, California: Wadsworth, 1986). Reproduced with permission of the Minister of Supply and Services Canada.

65 + in 1900). England and Wales, along with Germany, became old societies around 1930; both had 7.4 percent 65 + in 1930 (Laslett 1976). The high death rates for young men and the low birth rates during World War II speeded up societal aging in these countries. By 1982 France had 13.5 percent of its population over age 65, and by 1980 England and Wales had 15.1 percent and Sweden had 16.3 percent over age 65 — the highest percentage in the world (Health and Welfare Canada 1983).

Canada is a young nation when compared to these European nations. Until 1900 Canada still had less than 5 percent of its population aged 65 and over. Canada aged gradually through the first part of this century and became an old nation by UN standards (with 7.8 percent 65 +) in 1951 (Statistics Canada 1984b). By the year 2021 Canada's population aged 65 and over will make up between 14 percent and 17 percent of the population (Health and Welfare Canada 1983) — at least triple the proportion of older people in 1900 (see Exhibit 3.2).

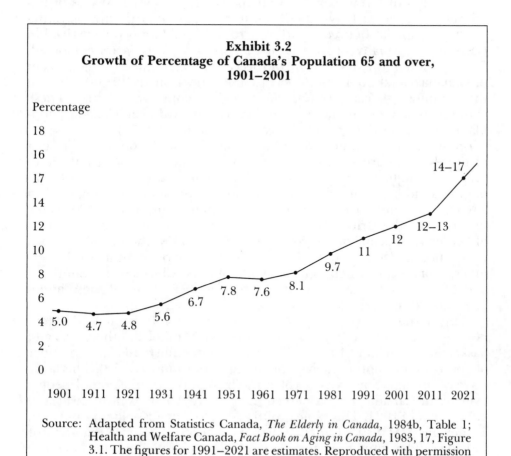

Exhibit 3.2
Growth of Percentage of Canada's Population 65 and over,
1901–2001

Source: Adapted from Statistics Canada, *The Elderly in Canada*, 1984b, Table 1;
          Health and Welfare Canada, *Fact Book on Aging in Canada*, 1983, 17, Figure
          3.1. The figures for 1991–2021 are estimates. Reproduced with permission
          of the Minister of Supply and Services Canada.

What caused Canada to age in the twentieth century? What will keep it aging in the years ahead? And what effect will population aging have on Canadian society? A look at Canada's population — past and present — will answer these questions.

CANADA COMES OF AGE

Demographers study three conditions that affect a population's size and structure — the birth rate, the death rate, and immigration. Each of these demographic forces caused the Canadian population to age from the mid-1800s to the present (Beaujot and McQuillan 1982).

Immigration

Of the three demographic forces — birth, death, and immigration — immigration played the smallest part in aging Canada's population. It also affected different parts of Canada in different ways. Waves of immigration in the early twentieth century brought new groups of young adults to Canada. Between 1901 and 1911 1.5 million people arrived in Canada — as many people as in the previous forty years combined. Immigration in the first decade of this century accounted for 44 percent of Canada's total population increase (Statistics Canada 1981a). Most of these immigrants came to Canada in their twenties and thirties. These young people (and the families they raised) helped keep Canada's population young at the start of this century (see Exhibit 3.2).

Immigration continued to add to Canada's population until the start of the Great Depression. From 1901 to 1931 successive waves of immigration brought from 3.5 to 4.5 million people to Canada. These immigrants did more than increase the number of people in Canada, they also changed the face of Canadian society. Immigrants before 1900 came mostly from the British Isles, but Leacy (1983) reports that Canadians of "other European" origin rose from 37 percent of the European-born population in 1881 to 43 percent of the same population in 1911. Germans, Norwegians, Mennonites, Doukhobours, Chinese, and Southern and Eastern Europeans arrived in large numbers. Most of these immigrants were young males.

Many of the Eastern European groups, along with Icelanders and Mennonites, settled in the Prairies. Provinces like Manitoba in the 1880s and Saskatchewan around 1911 had high birth rates due to the large number of young immigrants in their populations (Henripin 1972, 18). This large wave of immigration partly explains a drop in the proportion of people over 65 in Canada from 5 percent in 1901 to 4.7 percent in 1911 and 4.8 percent in 1921. This same group added to Canada's older population as they aged. Statistics Canada (1981a) estimated that more than half of Canada's older immigrant population had immigrated to Canada before 1929. Older immigrants made up 16 percent of Canada's older population in 1981 (Statistics Canada 1984b).

Population projections show that the proportion of immigrants in the older population will grow in the years to come. A major wave of immigrants to Canada in the early 1950s accounts for about 6 percent of Canada's growth from 1946 to 1978. These young immigrants lowered the median age of Canadians and added children to the Baby Boom of the 1950s and 60s. They will add to the older population in the next century.

Death Rates

By the late nineteenth and early twentieth century, death rates began to drop across the country. The best figures on death rates come from Quebec. Henripin and Peron (1972, cited in Beaujot and McQuillan 1982) say that the crude death rate in Quebec dropped by half from 24 per 1,000 in 1871–75 to 12.9 by 1921–25. These figures probably overestimate the drop in death rates for Canada as a whole. Historians say that Canada's large cities still suffered from high death rates (Gagan 1983a; Cross 1983; Torrance 1981; Artibise 1977), but a steady, if not dramatic, decline in the death rate did take place. Life expectancy at birth rose from 41.9 years for men and 44.2 years for women born in 1851 to 62.8 years for men and 70.2 years for women in 1931. Life expectancy at age 65 also increased 2.6 years for men and 5.4 years for women in the same eighty years. This meant that more people, especially women, lived longer and that more people lived into late old age (Legare and Desjardins 1976, cited in Beaujot and McQuillan 1982).

Death rates declined steadily for men and women at all ages between 1951 and 1976, but infants gained the most (see Exhibit 3.3). Infant mortality rates (the death rates of children less than a year old) decreased by about 60 percent for both males and females from 1951 to 1976. By 1978 only about 1 percent of children died before their first birthday.

Control of childhood disease, better pre-natal care, and better nutrition account for most of this change. Deaths from scarlet fever and diptheria dropped from a rate of 47 (per 100,000) in 1921 to only 1 death (per 100,000) in 1981. Smallpox no longer shows up at all as a cause of death in Canada (Statistics Canada 1981c). As a result of these changes in disease rates, infant mortality fell during the fifty years from 1931 to 1981 from 96 to 10.8 (deaths per 1,000 live births) for males and from 76 to 8.4 for females — a decrease by a factor of 9 for both sexes (Leacy 1983; Statistics Canada 1981c). Life expectancy at birth increased from 1931 to 1981 by 12 years (from 60.0 to 71.9) for men and by 17 years (from 62.1 to 79.0) for women.

Maternal mortality dropped more than 100-fold in fifty years from 5.8 deaths (per 1,000) live births in 1930 to .06 in 1981 (Leacy 1983; Statistics Canada 1981c). In this century tuberculosis, bronchitis, influenza, and pneumonia (once known as "the old man's friend") have almost disappeared as causes of death. Canada since 1971 has even seen a drop in

Exhibit 3.3
Evolution of Life Expectancy by Age and Sex,
Canada, 1951–81

Year	At Birth		At Age 60		At Age 80	
	Males	Females	Males	Females	Males	Females
1931	60.0	62.1	16.3	17.2	5.6	5.9
1941	63.0	66.3	16.1	17.6	5.5	6.0
1951	66.3	70.8	16.5	18.6	5.8	6.4
1961	68.4	74.2	16.7	19.9	6.1	6.9
1971	69.3	76.4	17.0	21.4	6.4	7.9
1981	71.9	79.0	18.0	22.9	6.9	8.8

Source: Adapted from Wayne McVey, personal communication, 1987, based on
Statistics Canada, Vital Statistics: Vol. 3, *Deaths* (Ottawa: Information Can-
ada, 1973b). For the Years 1931–1971 — Life Tables, Canada and Prov-
inces, 1975–1977, Cat. No. 84–532 (Ottawa: Supply and Services 1979c).
Figures for 1981 derived from Statistics Canada, Life Tables, Canada and
Provinces, 1980–82, Cat. No. 84–532 (Ottawa: Minister of Supply and
Services 1984d). Also, Dhruva Nagnur, Longevity and Historical Life Ta-
bles 1921–1981 (Abridged) Canada and the Provinces, Statistics Canada,
Cat. No. 89–506 (Ottawa: Minister of Supply and Services, 1986). Reproduced by permission of the Minister of Supply and Services Canada.

This table shows a steady increase in life expectancy at birth and at ages
60 and 80 from 1941 to 1981 for both sexes. Note that women gain proportionately more in life expectancy at all these ages than do men. This
may be due to differences in lifestyles, habits, or environmental conditions
(like working conditions).

ischemic heart disease, one of the most common causes of death in adulthood (McWhinnie and Ouellet 1981). People in the oldest cohorts, aged
85 +, show some of the greatest improvement (Beaujot and McQuillan
1982). In 1951 there were five people 85 years old or over for every one
hundred people 65 and over; by 1981 there were eight people 85 or over
for every one hundred people 65 and over (Statistics Canada 1984b).

As a result of these changes, the standardized death rate (that takes
into account the aging of Canada's population) fell for both sexes by
almost 30 percent from 9.0 in 1951 to 6.4 in 1976 (Beaujot and McQuillan
1982). Women show the greatest gains in this death rate decrease. This
shows up as greater gains in life expectancy compared to men, especially
at later ages (see Exhibit 3.3).

Better medical care, a safer environment, and a higher standard of
living mean that today 98 percent of all children born in Canada can
expect to live through infancy, 90 percent can expect to live to age 50,

66 percent to age 70, and 40 percent to age 80 (Statistics Canada 1981a). This gives Canada — along with Sweden, Denmark, Norway, and the United States — one of the highest life expectancies in the world. This also means that more people than ever enter old age.

Birth Rates

A population ages when the proportion of younger people declines. Quebec in the 1700s, for example, had a young population and one of the highest birth rates ever recorded. From 1700–1730 women averaged one child every two years until they reached age 30. Women who reached the age of 50 averaged 8 to 9 children. In the middle of the eighteenth century married women averaged thirteen children apiece (Henripin 1972). During this time the birth rate ran two to six times higher than the death rate, and Quebec's population grew twenty times from 1608 to 1765 and by one and a half times again by 1851 (Kalbach and McVey 1979). Death rates in Quebec began to decline after 1780, but even with this decline Quebec's birth rate was still high and the population stayed young (Kalbach and McVey 1979; Henripin 1972).

Frontier regions in Ontario also had high birth rates. McInnis (1977) and Henripin (1972) report rates similar to Quebec's in rural Ontario in the mid-nineteenth century. A writer of the time reported that children "in Canada [are a man's] greatest blessing, and happy is that man who has a quiver full of them" (Philpot 1871, cited in Gagan 1983b). McInnis says that Upper Canada at the time "had one of the highest birth rates in the world" (1977, 202). Gagan (1983b) estimates that settled Ontario families in Peel County had eight to nine children. New immigrants to Canada before 1830 often had more.

Around 1850 Canada began its demographic transition when the birth rate decreased. Henripin (1972) shows that the birth rate in Canada as a whole dropped by about 30 percent from 1851 to 1951 (with a sharp drop during the 1930s). The provinces each showed the same trend. The Quebec birth rate dropped least, about 20 percent from 1851 to 1921; Ontario showed a sharp drop of about 50 percent during this same time; Manitoba between 1881 and 1921 showed a drop of more than 60 percent; and Saskatchewan showed a similar drop between 1901 and 1921 (Henripin 1972). *This drop in the birth rate, more than any other demographic change, led to the aging of Canadian society.*

Baby Boom and Baby Bust

Two changes in the birth rate — the Baby Boom and the Baby Bust — account for the greatest changes in Canadian population from 1951 to the present.

First, from 1946 until about the early 1960s Canada went through a Baby Boom. Between 1941 and 1961 the total fertility rate ("the average

Exhibit 3.4
Median Age* of the Population, Canada, 1881–1971
(Excluding Newfoundland)

Year	Median Age	Year	Median Age
1881	20.1	1941	27.0
1891	21.4	1951	27.8
1901	22.7	1961	26.5
1911	23.8	1966	25.6
1921	23.9	1971	26.4
1931	24.7	1976	27.8
		1981	29.6

*Half the population is older and half is younger than the median age.

Canada's median age rose 9.5 years from 1881 to 1981. This table shows a jump in the median age of 3.7 years between 1931 and 1941. This reflects the sharp drop in the birth rate during the Depression years. The table also shows a steady rise in the median age throughout this century until 1961, then a drop from 1951 to 1966. During these years the rise in the birth rate (the Baby Boom) led to a decrease in the median age by 2.2 years to 25.6. In 1976 the median age rose again to its 1951 high of 27.8. By 1981 almost half the population was over the age of 30.

Sources: Dominion Bureau of Statistics *Census of Canada* (1961 Census), Bulletin 7:1–4 (Ottawa: Queen's Printer, 1964); Statistics Canada, *1966 Census of Canada*, Vol. 1 (1–11) (Ottawa: Queen's Printer, 1968); Statistics Canada, *Census of Canada, Bulletin 1:2–3* (1971 Census) (Ottawa: Information Canada, 1973a); Statistics Canada 1978b, cited in Warren E. Kalbach and Wayne W. McVey, *The Demographic Base of Canadian Society*, 2nd ed. (Toronto: McGraw-Hill Ryerson, 1979), 161, Table 6:3.

number of children that would be born alive to a woman during her lifetime if she were to pass through all her childbearing years conforming to the age-specific fertility rates of a given year") rose from 2.83 to 3.84 (Beaujot and McQuillan 1982, 220–21). The age-specific birth rate (the number of births in a given age group per 1,000 women in that age group) nearly doubled for 15- to 19-year-olds from 30.7 to 58.2 (Statistics Canada 1978d, cited in Beaujot and McQuillan 1982). Total births soared from 264,000 in 1941 to almost 476,000 in 1961 (Statistics Canada 1978d, cited in Beaujot and McQuillan 1982). The Baby Boom reversed a general trend of decreased fertility rates that began in the nineteenth century (Henripin 1972). It also reversed a century-long trend in population

Exhibit 3.5

HOW TO READ A POPULATION PYRAMID

Population pyramids graphically portray a society's population structure at a certain point in time. They allow researchers to compare societies at a glance. Most pyramids have the same design:

The title: The title contains the name of the country and the year this "snapshot" was taken. The title should answer the questions: What? Where? When?

The centre line: The centre line divides the pyramid by sex — males on the left, females on the right.

The base: The horizontal axis can represent absolute numbers or percents. Pyramids typically use percents because they allow cross-cultural comparisons. On the pyramids for Canada, 1986–2001, the centre line marks 0 percent, and each point on the baseline marks 2 percent of the population (males to the left of centre, females to the right).

The tiers: Each tier or layer of the pyramid stands for an age cohort (conventionally a five-year group). The lowest tier stands for the youngest age cohort (0–4 years old), and as one moves up the pyramid the cohorts get older. The top cohort (65 + in the Canada pyramids) contains everyone over a certain age.

Pyramids allow a viewer to compare age cohorts within a country (e.g., the size of young cohorts can be compared to the size of older cohorts), to compare sex differences within cohorts (by comparing the size of a tier to the right and left of the centre line), and to see unusually large or small cohorts at a glance. Gerontologists use population pyramids to compare countries for different years, to study population change over time, or to compare countries with one another for the same year.

aging (taking aside the years 1911 to 1931) that began in the late nineteenth century.

Second, after 1961 Canada went into a Baby Bust cycle. The total fertility rate dropped from 3.84 in 1961 to 2.81 in 1966 — a rate below that of 1941, to the present (1985) rate of 1.7 (McVey 1987; Beaujot and McQuillan 1982). The crude birth rate (the number of live births per thousand population in a given year) dropped from 26.1 in 1961 to 22.2 in 1981 to 14.8 in 1985 (below the rate of the 1930s) (Beaujot and McQuillan 1982, 220; Statistics Canada 1975; McVey 1987).

This has led to a sharp drop in the number of young people in Canada. Between 1976 and 1981, for example, the population of young people 0–17 years old decreased from 7.3 million to 6.8 million, or a 4 percent decrease from 32 percent to 28 percent of the population. Children under

Exhibit 3.6
Four Population Pyramids:
Projected Population Distributions for Selected Years,
Canada, 1986–2001
(Series 1, Low Growth Scenario, Total Fertility Rate = 1.40,
Net Immigration = 50,000 per year)

Projected Population, Canada: 1986

Age Group   [1984 Projection Series 1]

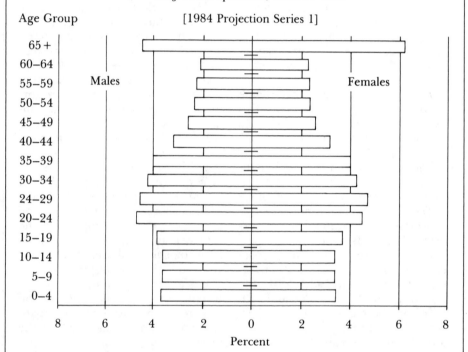

These pyramids show at least three important trends: first, the growth in size (from earlier pyramids) of the oldest age cohorts (aged 65 +); second, a growing proportion of women compared to men in the oldest cohorts; and third, the movement of the Baby Boom cohorts into old age. The 2001 pyramid now looks top-heavy, with small younger age groups below a large older population.

15 showed a 7 percent decrease (Statistics Canada 1983). Statistics Canada projects a further decline in the younger population into the next century. If these projections are right, the younger population (under age 20) will fall to less than 20 percent of the population, while the older population will grow to 25 percent of the population (Romaniuc 1984).

This decrease in the birth rate, especially the sharp drop since the

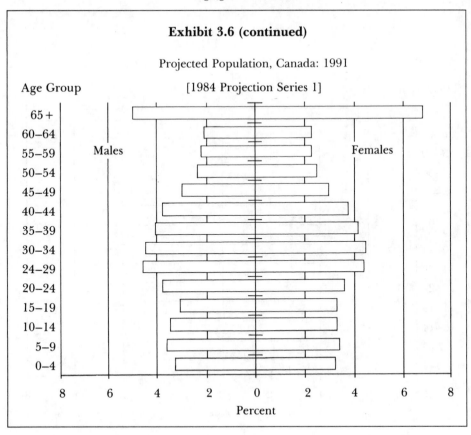

Exhibit 3.6 (continued)

Projected Population, Canada: 1991

[1984 Projection Series 1]

1960s, speeded up the rate of population aging in Canada. Between 1961 and 1981 the population aged 65 and over rose two percentage points from 7.6 percent to 9.7 percent of Canada's population (Statistics Canada 1984b). The older population will increase sharply again in the first decade of the twenty-first century when the Baby Boom generation moves into old age.

Summary of Population Aging in Canada

Canada's demographic transition took place from before 1850 to the present in three stages. In the first stage, before 1850, Canada had a high death rate, a high birth rate, and, for Ontario and the Maritimes, a high rate of immigration. These forces kept the average age of Canadians low. Gagan (1983a) says that in Ontario in the mid–nineteenth century half the population over the age of 15 was made up of men under the age of 30. Kalbach and McVey (1979) put the average age of Canadians in

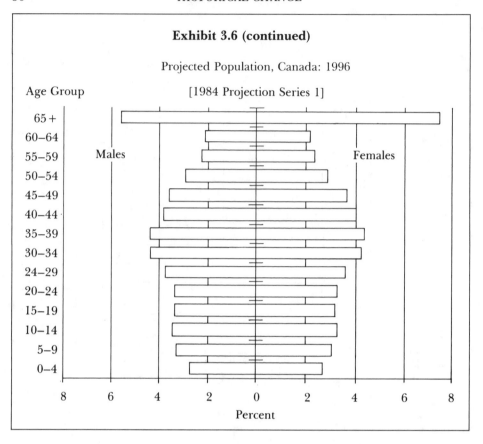

Exhibit 3.6 (continued)

Projected Population, Canada: 1996

[1984 Projection Series 1]

the mid–nineteenth century at around 20 years (compared to a median
age of almost 30 in 1981).

The second stage of the transition began after 1850 as major declines
in birth and death rates took place (Kalbach and McVey 1979). This
second stage differed from the second stage in Europe's demographic
transition. In Europe death rates declined and birth rates stayed high
for some time before they dropped to complete the transition. In Canada
both birth and death rates dropped (with some important fluctuations in
birth rates) until the present. These changes transformed Canada from
a young nation (under 4 percent 65+) in the late 1800s to a mature
nation (with about 7 percent of the population 65+) by 1950.

In the third stage of the transition, today, Canada has low death rates,
low birth rates, and an aging population. Canada's population pyramid
has changed in the past 150 years from a wide-based, triangular pyramid
to a more rectangular shape today (See Exhibit 3.6.).

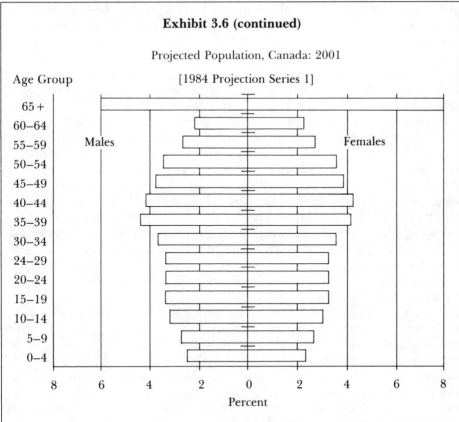

Exhibit 3.6 (continued)

Projected Population, Canada: 2001

[1984 Projection Series 1]

Source: Adapted from M.V. George and J. Perreault, *Population Projections for Canada, Provinces and Territories 1984–2006*, Statistics Canada Cat. No. 91–520 (Ottawa: Minister of Supply and Services, 1985), cited in Wayne W. McVey, personal communication, 1987. Reproduced with permission of the Minister of Supply and Services Canada.

AGING IN CANADA TODAY

Older people differ by age, sex, marital status, and health. They come from different ethnic backgrounds, they have lived through different historical events, and they live in different parts of the country. These differences make older people one of the most diverse age groups in the country.

The Old-Old and the Young-Old

The older population itself has aged in the past eighty years. In 1901 people aged 80 and over made up about 15 percent of the older population, by 1981 they made up about 19 percent of the older population, and Health and Welfare Canada (1983) estimates that by 2001 this group will make up 24 percent of the older population. The old-old (people aged 75+) show more health impairment than the general population, and those 75 and over show the highest proportion of disabilities among those 65 and over (Health and Welfare Canada and Statistics Canada 1981). This group will need more institutional supports and more house-hold maintenance, medical care and community health care supports than young-old people. At the same time that the oldest cohorts grow in size, the younger cohorts 65 and over will also get larger. Projections show approximately a doubling in the population aged 65–74 from 1986 to 2021 (McVey 1987). These large cohorts of young-old Canadians will make new demands on society. The young-old will change retirement patterns by retiring early or by staying on at work past age 65. This group will want more recreational and educational opportunities. Services like job bureaus, schools, and counselling programs will be needed to serve these people.

All of these programs, for the young-old and the old-old, will cost taxpayers more money. In 1976, for example, Canada's social security system cost 14 percent of the gross national product. A larger proportion of this money went to older people than to any other age group (Health and Welfare Canada 1982b). If the population of older people doubles in the next fifty years as expected, will the public be willing to pay out even more of the country's income for older people? Or will the costs lead to resentment and a crisis in Canadian society? We will discuss these issues in more detail later in this chapter under the topic of dependency ratios.

Ethnicity

In 1981 people of British background made up half (49.3 percent) of Canada's older population, people of French background made up a quarter (23.0 percent) of the older population, and the rest of Canada's older population came from a wide variety of backgrounds including non-French and non-British European, African, and Chinese cultures (Statistics Canada 1984a). Compared to younger people, a higher pro-portion of older people spoke a language other than English or French at home (11 percent of people aged 65 and over compared to just over 6 percent of people under age 50) (Health and Welfare Canada 1983).

This reflects the high immigration rates of the early 1900s. These people, who learned a language other than English in their native coun-tries, continued to use this language at home. They have now reached old age, and they make the older population today an ethnically diverse group. This diversity shows up in a comparison of the old-old (people over 75 years old) and younger age groups. Younger age groups show smaller proportions of people with British background. Sixty-two percent of people aged 80 and over claimed British background, compared to

Exhibit 3.7
The Elderly and Non-Elderly Populations by
Ethnicity, Canada, 1981

Ethnicity	Per 100 of Age Group	
	0–64	65 +
Total	100.0	100.0
British	39.3	49.3
French	27.1	23.0
British/French*	1.9	0.8
Jewish	1.0	2.0
Polish	1.0	1.7
Ukrainian	2.1	3.3
German	4.7	5.4
Dutch	1.7	1.4
Chinese	1.2	0.9
Italian	3.2	2.3
Native peoples	2.2	0.8
All other	14.7	9.2

*Multiple response.
　Note: This table includes British, French, and British/French, plus the eight
　　　ethnic origins (single response) with the largest counts for the total
　　　population.
Source: Adapted from Statistics Canada, *The Elderly in Canada* (Ottawa: Minister
　　　of Supply and Services, 1984b), Table 8. Reproduced by permission of
　　　the Minister of Supply and Services Canada.

only 54 percent of people aged 65 and over and 44 percent of people
under age 65. These figures reflect the increased numbers of people
who came to Canada from Eastern and Southern Europe early in this
century as well as the numbers of more recent immigrants from Asia,
South America and Africa (Health and Welfare Canada 1983). Exhibit
3.7 shows the proportion of older people from Canada's largest ethnic
groups.

Some ethnic groups have a higher proportion of older people than
others. Exhibit 3.8 shows the proportion *within each ethnic group* of people
aged 65 or over. Note that more than 16 percent of people claiming
Jewish ethnicity and almost 15 percent of people claiming Polish ethnicity
are aged 65 or older. These are two of the "oldest" ethnic groups in the
country. At the other extreme, only about 7 percent of people claiming

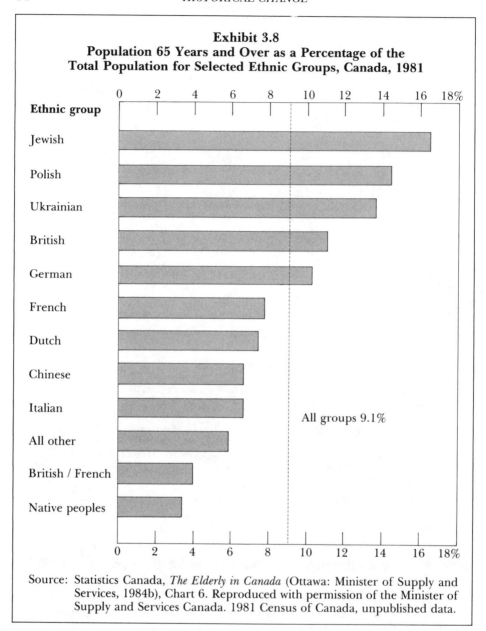

Exhibit 3.8
Population 65 Years and Over as a Percentage of the
Total Population for Selected Ethnic Groups, Canada, 1981

All groups 9.1%

Source: Statistics Canada, *The Elderly in Canada* (Ottawa: Minister of Supply and Services, 1984b), Chart 6. Reproduced with permission of the Minister of Supply and Services Canada. 1981 Census of Canada, unpublished data.

Chinese or Italian ethnicity are aged 65 or over. Native peoples have a very "young" population with less than 4 percent of their population aged 65 and over. The high proportion of Jewish older people shows the effect of low fertility rates on the aging of the Jewish population. The small proportion of older Natives shows the effect of high fertility rates on their population (Statistics Canada 1984b).

Gerber (1983) reports that both the size of an ethnic group and the proportion of older people in the group determine the institutional supports that older people can expect from their group. A large group with a moderate proportion of its population aged 65 and over can provide a more complete community life for its elderly. A small group with a high proportion of older people may be able to offer little support. Also, the concentration of the group (how near one another members live), their location (urban or rural), the proportion of old-old to young-old, family size, and cultural values all affect the number of supports older people can draw on. People of Finnish background, for example, tend to live in rural areas and have small families. This can lead to hardship in late old age if a person needs health care services or informal (family) supports. As these people age, spouses and friends die, and their social networks get smaller. This can lead to a lack of care and support in late old age. People of Italian background, on the other hand, have large families, tend to live in cities, and tend to live with their children. Older Italians have more access than members of smaller groups to community resources and family support in old age.

This brief look at ethnicity and aging shows that ethnic groups vary in their size, their location, their proportion of older people, and their institutional completeness (how much community support they offer their older members). For this reason Driedger and Chappell (1987, 75) say that "ethnicity can have significant implications for care and supportiveness in old age," and so policies for older people from different types of groups (large, small, rural, urban) will have to vary. Driedger and Chappell say that planners and policy makers should take ethnicity into account, along with socioeconomic status and physical mobility, when designing programs for specific groups.

Regional Distribution

Seventy-four percent of older people lived in Ontario, Quebec, and British Columbia in 1981, but Manitoba, Saskatchewan, and Prince Edward Island had the highest *proportion* of older people in their total populations — 12 percent for each. P.E.I. had the highest proportion of people aged 80 and over in its population — 3.3 percent. Manitoba, Saskatchewan, and Nova Scotia came next with between 2.2 and 2.6 percent (Health and Welfare Canada 1983).

These figures tell only part of the story of where older people live in Canada. Some regions within the provinces have much higher proportions of older people than the overall figures indicate. Northcott (1984) shows that migration patterns influence the proportion of older people in a province's population, especially migration of the young. "Where nonelderly net out-migration is heavy," he says, "as in Saskatchewan and Manitoba, such provinces tend to have a high and an increasing proportion of aged residents." Some small towns in Saskatchewan and Manitoba, for example, already have more than 17 percent of the population over age 65 — a proportion Canada may reach only in the next century. These shifts in the population due to migration (largely the effect of non-elderly migration) have important policy implications. As younger people leave an area to find jobs or get training and education, the older people who remain may need more formal social supports.

Older people make up only about 9.4 percent of the population in large urban centres, even though many of them live in big cities. They make up a larger percentage (13 percent) of the population in small urban centres between 1,000 and 5,000 population. Areas with some of the highest proportions of older people include Vancouver (11.5 percent), St. Catharines–Niagara (11.5 percent), and Victoria (17 percent) (Statistics Canada 1984b). People aged 65 and over make up only 5.4 percent of the population in rural farm areas, and people aged 80 and over make up less than 1 percent of these areas. Older people tend to move from rural areas to urban centres as they age (Statistics Canada 1984b).

Internal Migration

Older people follow internal migration patterns similar to those of younger people, but they are less mobile than the non-aged (Northcott 1984). Between 1976 and 1981 half of all Canadians under age 65 moved, but only about one-quarter of those 65 and over moved (Health and Welfare Canada 1983). Most older movers (60 percent) moved within their local area. Shulman (1980) reports a peak in migration around retirement age. Some older people return to their home towns after years of working somewhere else. People who moved out of their locality most often moved from farms to cities, from Quebec to Ontario or from almost anywhere to British Columbia. The Atlantic provinces had the smallest proportion of older movers (Health and Welfare Canada 1983; Statistics Canada 1984b). Shulman says that some cities and provinces will have populations older than the rest of Canada. "For these provinces — and some specific cities within them — preparation to meet the changing needs of the population will have to occur quite soon" (Shulman 1980, 34). (See Exhibit 3.9.)

Increased Numbers and Proportion of Older Women

The death rates for older women have decreased faster than for older men through most of this century. Between 1921 and 1976 the death rate of Canadian women aged 70–74 decreased by 50 percent, while men in this age group showed only a 10 percent decrease (Statistics Canada 1979a). In 1931 the life expectancy for a 60-year-old woman was 17.15 years, in 1961 it was 19.90 years, and in 1981 it was 22.85 years. (For a

---

Exhibit 3.9

VICTORIA: PREVIEW OF AGING IN CANADA?

The elderly currently are outnumbered nationally by more than four to one by those 24 and under, but because of a falling birth rate, the declining immigration of young adults and longer life expectancy the over-65s are catching up. In Victoria they already have — with consequences that make the B.C. capital like no other city in Canada. Said [Mayor Gretchen] Brewin: "We have to respond to kids who want to skateboard on the sidewalks and to seniors with frail bones who would just as soon the kids didn't." But the city administration, she concedes, faces far more complex problems that one day will test every major centre in the country: ...

Youth employment. As more and more of the city's resources are diverted to serving the elderly, said Brewin, the number of jobs outside the service industries steadily decreases. She added, "We somehow have to find enough exciting opportunities to keep our young people here." ...

Nursing homes. Victoria already has about eight times as many nursing homes and homes for the aged per capita as Toronto, five times as many as Montreal and nine times as many as Halifax. But it needs more to shelter the 10 per cent of those 65 and over who need some form of institutional care. Brewin said that it is becoming harder and harder to find locations for nursing homes that do not arouse opposition from other age groups in the neighborhood but are, at the same time, within walking distance of stores and bus stops. ...

Political power. ... Said Brewin: "Grey power is growing. People retiring today are in better health and have a lot of political smarts. They know what they want, and they lose no time in telling you what it is. If you ignore them in this town, you are absolutely in trouble, and politicians across the country had better realize that they are facing the same situation." ...

Mayor Brewin added: "A lot of people entertain this image of Grandma sitting on the front porch in a rocking chair with a blanket wrapped around her knees. Well, let me tell you: Grandma doesn't do that any more. Today she's downtown shopping for a trip to Hawaii."

Source: Rae Corelli, *Maclean's*, "A Matter of Care," October 6, 1986, 51. Reprinted with permission of the publisher.

---

man it was only 16.29 years in 1931, 16.73 years in 1961, and 17.96 years in 1981.)

As a result of these changes, the proportion of older women in the population has grown. At the turn of the century there were 105 men

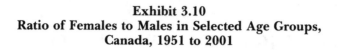

Exhibit 3.10
Ratio of Females to Males in Selected Age Groups,
Canada, 1951 to 2001

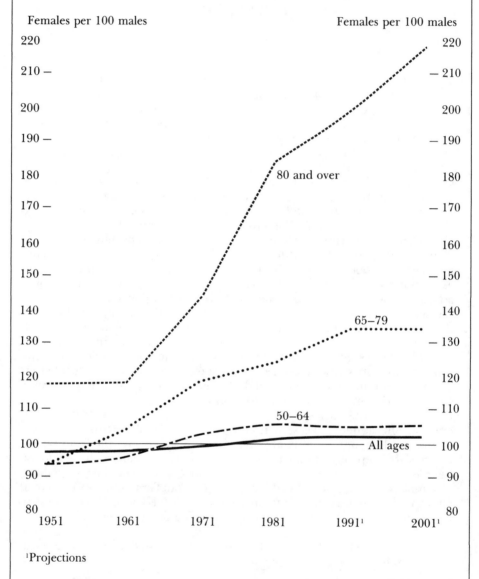

¹Projections

Source: Health and Welfare Canada, *Fact Book on Aging in Canada* (Ottawa: Minister
of Supply and Services, 1983), Figure 3.3. Reproduced with permission
of the Minister of Supply and Services Canada.

for every 100 women aged 65 and over, and in the mid-1950s older men still outnumbered older women, but by the 1960s the pattern reversed itself. By 1981 there were 124 women for every 100 men aged 65–79 and 184 women for every 100 men aged 80 and over (Health and Welfare Canada 1983; Stone and Fletcher 1980).

Projections show that the gap between the number of men and the number of women in the older population will level off at about 134 women to 100 men aged 65–79, but the gap will get wider for the group aged 80 and over. Projections show that by 2001 women aged 80 and over will outnumber men 218 to 100 — or better than two to one (Health and Welfare Canada 1983). (See Exhibit 3.10.)

This means that policies and programs for older people will have a greater impact on women than on men, simply because more women will live longer to be affected by them. This is especially true of health care, housing, and income support programs. We will study these programs in detail in the chapters ahead. For now, we will look at the overall impact of population aging on Canada's economy.

THE IMPACT OF POPULATION AGING

The Dependency Ratio and the Cost of an Aging Population

The concern about the increasing numbers of older people typically pits the old against the young. The Science Council of Canada (Auerbach and Gerber 1976, 3) calls an older population of between 13 percent and 15 percent "a significant social burden." Statistics Canada (1979a, Introduction) reports that old age creates problems that "are the nation's concern," and some writers say that an older population could lead to intergenerational conflict (Tindale and Marshall 1980). These sources assume a high dependence of older people on the young and suggest that the young will rebel or resent the burden of a large older population.

Gerontologists use a figure called the *overall dependency ratio* to gauge the burden the old and the young place on people in middle age. Experts arrive at this ratio by adding the number of people under age 18 to the number of people aged 65 and over. They then compare this figure to the population 18–64:

$$\frac{\text{(the no. of people aged 0–17)} + \text{(the no. of people aged 65 and over)}}{\text{(the no. of people aged 18–64)}}$$

(Some writers use 0–14 or 0–20 as the age span for the younger group).

Denton and Spencer (1980) used the dependency ratio to look at dependency in Canada. They found that while the ratio of people 65 and over to those 20–64 will nearly double from 1976 to 2031, the proportion of young people will decline. When they combined these projected changes in the young and old populations, they found that this led to "a somewhat

Exhibit 3.11
Dependency Rates for Canada, Selected Years 1901 to 1986;
Two Projections for Selected Years 1991 to 2031
(Percent)

Year	65+/18–64		0–17/18–64		Overall Dependency	
1901	9.3		74.9		84.2	
1921	8.7		72.6		81.3	
1941	11.2		56.5		67.7	
1961	14.3		72.8		87.1	
1976	14.4		52.8		67.2	
1981	15.6		45.2		59.8	
1986[1]	16.8		40.8		57.6	
	A	B	A	B	A	B
1991[2]	18.7	18.6	38.0	39.9	56.7	58.5
2001	21.4	20.7	31.6	41.6	53.0	62.3
2021	33.4	27.6	25.7	40.7	59.1	68.3
2031	45.3	33.5	25.5	43.5	70.8	77.0

[1]Census data 1986. Cat. No. 91–101.

[2]Assumptions of Projections A and B: Projection A is the "most plausible course of events in the short term." It is a low-growth scenario. It assumes a fertility rate (the number of children per woman by 1996) of 1.4. Projection B assumes "a complete reversal in fertility ... trends." This is a high-growth scenario. It assumes a fertility rate (the number of children per woman by 1996) of 2.2. Both projections assume that life expectancy at birth will increase to 74.9 years for men and 81.6 years for women by 1996.

Source: Figures for 1991 and 2001: Statistics Canada, *Population Projections for Canada, Provinces and Territories.* 1984–2006, Cat. No. 91–520 (Ottawa: Minister of Supply and Services, 1985, p. 41); Figures for 2021 and 2031: Statistics Canada Demography Division, unpublished data provided to Statistics Canada, Health Division, Social Security Section, September 1987. Reproduced with permission of the Minister of Supply and Services Canada.

lower overall dependency ratio for the remainder of this century and throughout the first decade of the next, as compared with 1976, and then a pronounced increase in the following two decades or so" (Denton and Spencer 1980, 24–25). In spite of this increase, in 2031 (when the Baby Boom will create large increases in the over 65 population) the overall dependency ratio may not be much higher than in 1976. Exhibit

3.11 shows recent Statistics Canada dependency projections based on two sets of population assumptions. Assumptions A lead to a relatively modest increase in the overall dependency ratio in 2031. Assumptions B lead to a more dramatic increase in the overall dependency ratio in 2031, but still a rate lower than 1961.

The Ontario Ministry of Treasury and Economics says that the "crude dependency rates" presented in Exhibit 3.11 tell only part of the story. Crude dependency rates tell us little about the economic burden of an older population (Stone and Fletcher 1980). A study by Canada's Treasury Board Secretariat (1977) estimated that in 1976 government expenditures for people aged 65 and over came to two and a half times the costs for people aged 0–17.

The Secretariat found that education costs for the young came to about the same amount as Old Age Security costs for the old. But medical care costs for people aged 65 and over came to twice the costs for people aged 0–14; Canada Assistance Plan costs for the old came to triple the costs for the young, and hospital costs for older people came to more than ten times the costs for the young (Treasury Board Secretariat 1977).

The Ontario Ministry of Treasury and Economics (1979) calculated "effective dependency rates" based on these differences in the costs for older and younger age groups. They conclude that with a total dependency ratio of 66.7 in 2031 (about the same crude rate as in 1976), but with more older people and fewer younger people in the population, the effective dependency rate for 1991 goes above the 1976 rate. And by 2031 the effective dependency rate exceeds the 1976 rate by 43 percent (see Exhibit 3.12) (Ontario Ministry of Treasury and Economics 1979, 15).

These figures look gloomy, but Myles and Boyd (1982, 259) say that "alarmist exercises in futurology ... have produced more oversight than insight" when it comes to the issue of dependency in the future. Even small changes in Canada's economy and social norms, for example, could lead to large decreases in the effective dependency rate. The Ontario Ministry figures (see Exhibit 3.12), for example, assume a traditional retirement age of 65 (the age when people can get Old Age Security payments), but government policy could raise this age. Also, more middle-aged workers today have private pension plans, so when they reach old age they may rely less on government pension supplements than do pensioners today. More flexible retirement plans will allow some people to work full- or part-time after age 65. The Canada Pension Plan recently changed its rules to make both early and late retirement more attractive. All of these trends will change current dependency patterns and alter future projections.

A stronger economy would also ease the dependency burden. Even a small improvement in the income for middle-aged people, compared to costs for services to the old, would significantly decrease the effective dependency rate. The Ontario Ministry of Treasury and Economics (1979)

Exhibit 3.12
Projected Dependency Rates Relative to 1976

	1976	1981	1991	2001	2011	2021	2031
1. Relative Crude Dependency Rates							
Total	1.00	0.89	0.86	0.82	0.78	0.89	0.99
Aged	1.00	1.03	1.16	1.22	1.30	1.74	2.20
2. Relative Effective[1] Dependency Rates							
(a) Equal Growth							
Total	1.00	0.98	1.02	1.01	1.02	1.20	1.43
Aged	1.00	1.14	1.40	1.48	1.59	2.11	2.72
(b) 1% Growth Differential							
Total	1.00	0.94	0.89	0.82	0.78	0.86	0.96
Aged	1.00	1.08	1.23	1.23	1.24	1.56	1.85

[1]Assuming 1.8 fertility rate and net immigration of 100,000.

Source: Ontario Ministry of Treasury and Economics, *Issues in Pension Policy: Demographic and Economic Aspects of Canada's Ageing Population* (Toronto: Ontario Ministry of Treasury and Economics, 1979), p. 15, Table 4.

found that if income for working people increases even 1 percent faster than dependency costs, then the effective dependency rates will be less than in 1976.

In a strong economy higher costs for services to the elderly may not create a burden for the middle-aged. Also, higher birth rates in the future or higher rates of immigration would alter the effects of dependency. A higher birth rate and more immigration would mean more young people to support the older population. Weller and Bouvier (1981) point to one of the greatest weaknesses of using dependency rates to project into the future. They say that dependency rates focus too narrowly on the costs of having more older people in society. They remind us that an older population will also bring benefits. An older population will have a lower crime rate and a lower auto accident rate, and it will show more concern for fitness, diet, and disease prevention. These trends will all reduce the waste of social resources and create a higher quality of life for people of all ages.

McDaniel (1986) says that demographic trends do not determine social change. Demography shapes individual experience and social life. The Baby Boom generation, for example, had to fight harder for schooling, jobs, and housing because of their large numbers. Smaller generations that follow may find life less stressful. Demography also shapes social institutions like schools, income distribution policies, and health care. The future will see a shift in services to older people. But demographers still need to study the connections between demographic facts and social change. How much choice do countries have in how they will respond to demographic change? What determines the choices a country makes? Are there models of preferred adaptation to an aging population?

Countries like Sweden and Norway could serve as models for Canadian policy. These countries already have more than 14 percent of their populations over age 65, and they have not faced crises due to their aging populations. They have tax structures similar to Canada's and progressive programs to serve older people. These countries show that the transition to an older society can come about without social conflict and distress (Myles 1982), and Canada can use these models as a guide. But Canadian society has its own mix of ethnicity, age/sex ratios, economic institutions, and values, so it will have to discover new responses to population aging. The Science Council of Canada says that the change to an older society "can be done" — and done without social upheaval (Auerbach and Gerber 1976, 3). This change will take planning, thought, and creative social action, and all of us will play a part in this societal transformation.

SUMMARY

1. Canada has a younger population than most of the other developed nations. It had about 10 percent of the population aged 65 and over in 1981. Demographers project that this population will double by 2021 and will equal between 14 percent and 17 percent of the total population.
2. Canada went through a demographic transition between 1850 and 1950. During this time immigration increased, the death rate decreased, and, most important of all, the birth rate decreased. Between 1850 and 1950 the older population grew from about 4 percent of the population to over 7 percent.
3. Canada today has a diverse older population. Older people differ by ethnicity, sex, income, education, and marital status. They also differ by age. Longer life expectancy in old age has given rise to at least two groups of the elderly — the old-old and the young-old. Each group has its own lifestyles, resources, and needs.
4. The growth of the older population (and the decrease in the younger population) have led some people to predict an economic crisis due to the large numbers of dependent older people. Gerontologists measure the dependence of young and old people on people in middle age. They call this measure the overall dependency ratio (or rate).
5. Experts look at dependency rates to project the future costs of an aging society. Future dependency rates depend on the assumptions made by the researcher. A weak economy in the future, low birth rates, low immigration rates, and a rise in costs of services for the old

(compared to per capita income for the middle-aged) will increase the burden on middle-aged people. A strong economy, higher birth rates, more immigration, and a rise in per capita income for middle-aged people (compared to costs in services for the old) will mean less burden on middle-aged workers. Changes in social values and retirement ages and better preparation for old age by middle-aged people today could also decrease effective dependency rates.

6. Dependency rates focus on the costs of an aging society. But an aging society may have a lower crime rate, a lower accident rate, and more concern for lifelong health and fitness. These changes would decrease the waste of social and economic resources and improve the quality of life in Canada.

7. Canada can grow old without upheaval and conflict; most of the developed nations have done so. But the transition to an aging society will take planning, thought, and creative social action.

SELECTED READINGS

Kalbach, Warren E., and Wayne W. McVey. *The Demographic Bases of Canadian Society*, 2nd ed. Toronto: McGraw-Hill Ryerson, 1979.
A basic demographic text that covers topics like the demographic transition; the basic themes of immigration, mortality, and fertility; and Canada's age and sex structure. The book also looks at other non–age-related topics including ethnicity and race. A well-written text with helpful references at the end of each chapter.

McDaniel, Susan A. *Canada's Aging Population*. Toronto: Butterworths, 1986.
A good overview of aging and demography in Canada. The book covers basic demographic concepts like the dependency ratio, population pyramids, and population age/sex structure. The book also examines current issues in population aging, including aging in a world context, policy implications of population aging, and the future of aging in Canada. Well written, and the author uses up-to-date sources throughout the text.

PART III

MATURATIONAL CHANGE

CHAPTER 4

THE BIOLOGY OF AGING

INTRODUCTION

Mr. Shigechiyo Izumi died at the age of 120 years on the island of To-kunoshima, Japan, in February 1986. He was the world's oldest man whose age could be verified. He attributed his long life to "the daily cup of *shochu* [sugar-cane liquor] and keeping a simple diet" (*Time* 1986b). Other centenarians attribute their long life to regular sex, walking five miles a day, or drinking a shot of whiskey before bed. One 100-year-old man claimed that eating a pound of peanuts a day led to his long life.

Scientific research supports some of these methods for longer life. Moderate drinkers, for example, live longer than teetotalers (though no one knows why) (Woodruff 1982); a simple diet low in fats, salt, and sugar can decrease disease; exercise leads to good health and possibly a longer life. But even with good habits, a good diet, and a good environment, physiological aging takes place. Older people on the covers of health and nutrition magazines beam good health — but they still have white hair, brown spots on their skin, and wrinkles like older people all over the world.

Gerontologists distinguish between the life span (the maximum number of years a species can live) and life expectancy (the number of years at birth an average member of a society can expect to live). Scientists think that the human life span of somewhere between 110 and 120 years has stayed the same for the past 100,000 years. Human life expectancy at birth, on the other hand, has increased in the past 2,000 years from an average of 22 years in ancient Rome to around 70 years today. Technology and biomedical science continue to extend life expectancy (Stone and Fletcher 1986b), and if this trend continues, most people in the future will live close to the maximum human life span (Botwinick 1984). This means that more people will live to old age and more people will live longer in old age than ever before.

The study of biological aging has two goals: to understand biological aging and to apply this knowledge to extend and improve human life. This chapter will look at (1) why people age, (2) what effects aging has on health, behaviour, and everyday life, and (3) how older people cope with physical change.

THE CAUSES OF AGING

Strehler (1977) divides the intrinsic processes of aging (*determinate processes*) from the effects of culture, habits, and the environment (*ancillary processes*). Intrinsic aging includes the loss of lung elasticity, the accumulation of debris in aging cells, and the slowing of a person's reaction time. Environmental aging includes the effects on a person's physiology of smoking, pollution, and a calcium-poor diet. Biologists try to separate intrinsic from environmental aging in order to understand the biological causes of aging. Strehler lists four criteria that define intrinsic aging.

1. True aging occurs *universally*. All members of a species will show age changes if they live long enough, though the rate of change will vary from culture to culture. People exposed to the sun, for example, will show signs of aging skin — wrinkles and stiffness — early in life, while people who stay covered from the sun may wrinkle at a later age. Still, all people will show some decreased elasticity in the skin, if they live long enough.
2. True aging is *intrinsic* to the organism. A person cannot change or manipulate the rate of this process. Until recently scientists considered atherosclerosis (thickening of the interior of the artery due to fatty deposits) to be a sign of intrinsic aging, but today scientists view it as a disease that may or may not occur as underlying processes of aging

Exhibit 4.1

CONTROVERSY:
THE LONG-LIVED
PEOPLE OF ABKHAZIA

"Work hard and never worry," say the Hunza people of Pakistan. The Hunza claim to produce some of the longest-living people in the world. They say they live such long lives because they have good water and a good climate and they stay happy. The Vilcambambans of Ecuador also claim long lives. About 1 percent of them claim to live past the age of 100 (compared to about 1 in 10,000 in North America). The Abkhazians, one of the best-known and most-studied of the long-lived peoples, live in the Caucasus mountains of the Soviet Union. The Soviet census reports that 70 percent of Soviet citizens 110 years old or over live in this region (Benet 1976, 7).

Some of the Abkhazians (like the Hunzas and Vilcambambans) claim to be 120, 130, or even 160 years old. Pitskhelauri, a Soviet researcher, reports that the oldest man in one district of Abkhazia is 139 years old. This man, he says, works as a farmer and has "150 children, grandchildren, great-grandchildren, and great-great-grandchildren" (1982, 53).

Stories like this have led journalists, television crews, and researchers from all over the world to study and visit the Abkhazians, but few scientists outside the Soviet Union believe their claims. Hayflick (1974, 43) says that researchers have "reported these claims without sufficiently emphasizing the meager evidence for the allegations. ... Claims of super-longevity should be taken with as much skepticism as any claim unsupported by proof."

Careful studies of the Abkhazians' ages, for example, reveal that "only 38 percent of the 115 [people] thought to be over 90 were actually verified as being over 90. ... Furthermore, *none* of those reevaluated were found to be actually over age 110" (Palmore 1984, 95). A recent study of the Soviet census by Bennett and Garson (1986) found that the data exaggerate the ages of these people and that only a small fraction of the number of people who claim to be over 100 years old have actually reached that age. Recent studies have put an end to the myth that a long-lived people exists, but the latest research leaves open two important biological questions: First, why do so few humans in any society live past 100 years of age, if humans have a potential life span of 110 to 120 years? Second, what are the causes of biological aging?

take place. Smoking, a fatty diet, and high blood pressure can all increase the risk of atherosclerosis. Decreased lung elasticity, on the other hand, seems like a true sign of aging.

3. True aging is *progressive*. It takes place gradually and leads to a cumulative decline in function. Strokes, heart attacks, and tumours — major killers in old age — come on quickly, and therefore they probably do not represent unchangeable parts of the aging process. These diseases may develop as a result of many gradual changes in molecular and cell function. Biological research will have to look to the molecular level of the body, at the aging cell, to understand many of the diseases of old age.

4. True aging is *deleterious*; it leads to functional decline that makes death more likely. True aging or *senescence* leads to a gradual decline in a person's ability to cope with environmental demands.

Disease, accidents, or social conditions do not cause intrinsic aging. Eating yogurt, jogging, or massaging the skin will not stop it. Scientists base the latest theories of aging on research in genetics, cell biology, and human anatomy. A complete study of these theories would require a course in biology or human physiology, but we can at least look at the basic findings on physiological aging.

THEORIES OF BIOLOGICAL AGING

Biologists study aging in simpler organisms (unicellular animals, plants, and insects) and in human body systems (the circulatory, reproductive, and endocrine systems). They study pathology (hypertension, nutrition, and drug use) and cell biology. They study aging and evolution, and methods of life extension (low-calorie diets and hypothermia). But none of these approaches have produced a unified theory of aging. Hayflick (1985) says that current theories reflect as much the methods and models of the researchers' disciplines as they do the underlying processes of aging. This chapter will describe a few of the most promising biological theories of aging. Each of them gives some insight into the aging process.

Cellular Theory

Some of the most active research has focused on the biochemistry of the cell. These changes lead to aging in all parts of the body — in the cells, tissues, organ systems, and behaviour. Human life begins with a single fertilized cell. That cell divides, and then the new cells divide again and again to form the human body. Some cells stop dividing in youth. Neurons that make up the brain and spinal cord, for example, stop dividing early in life; this explains why the body cannot repair damage to the spinal cord (Goldstein 1984).

Other cells, like intestinal cells and blood cells, divide throughout life. Until the 1960s, researchers thought that cells like these could go through unlimited divisions, but research by Hayflick and Moorhead (1961) found that there was a limit to cell division and that this limit differed from species to species. Tortoise cells, for example, divide 90–125 times before they die, chicken cells 15–35 times, and human embryo cells 40–60 times. Hayflick and Moorhead also found that the older the cell donor, the fewer the divisions before the cells died. They found that cells from adult humans could divide only about 20 times before death (versus 50 times for cells from younger people).

These findings led to the idea that cells have built-in limits and that an organism's life span depends on the number of divisions its cells can undergo before death. Based on these findings Hayflick and Moorehead (1961) calculated the human *life span* (the maximum number of years humans can live) at 110–120 years.

This theory explains why tortoises live longer than humans and why humans live longer than chickens, but it does not explain why so few humans reach the maximum life span of 110 years. Hayflick and Moorhead took their research a step further. They looked inside the cell to see why people live less than their full life span, and they found that after a year of active multiplication in the lab, cells show signs of aging. "These cells demonstrate an increased doubling time (normally 24 hours), gradual cessation of mitotic [dividing] activity, accumulation of cellular debris and ultimately total degeneration of the culture" (1961). Before cell division stops and the cells die, the structure and function of cells change (Hayflick 1970). Cells produce less energy, they make enzymes more slowly, and they allow waste to fill up inside them. Biologists call this the *"Phase III" phenomenon*. A closer look inside the cell will show the causes of these changes.

Cells consist of organic molecules — sugars, fats, proteins, and nucleic acids. These molecules each play a part in cell life: sugars give the cells energy; fats and proteins make up part of the cell membrane. Proteins also form enzymes that speed up reactions within cells. The cell nucleus in the centre of the cell contains nucleic acids — DNA (deoxyribonucleic acid) and RNA (ribonucleic acid). These long ribbons of molecules govern cell activity and reproduction. DNA creates RNA, and RNA in turn oversees the creation of proteins that structure the cell. Scientists have traced some of the slowdown in cell activity to changes in the DNA and RNA within cells.

Molecular Theory

Molecular biologists study the chemistry of the cell — the DNA, the RNA, and the cell wall. A DNA molecule looks like a spiral staircase (see Exhibit 4.2, Illustration A). Chemical base pairs bond across the two sides of the staircase to form stairs. When the DNA molecule splits, as it does in cell division, it splits along the base pair bonds into two strands. Each strand then synthesizes a new strand to create two new identical strands, one in each new cell. Biologists suggest that *cross-linkages* — foreign chemical links between the strands — stop the strands from dividing (see Illustration B). Normal by-products of metabolism can cause cross-links, and so can pollutants like lead and smoke. More and more cross-links occur over

Exhibit 4.2

CROSS-LINKING DAMAGE TO DNA

Illustration A

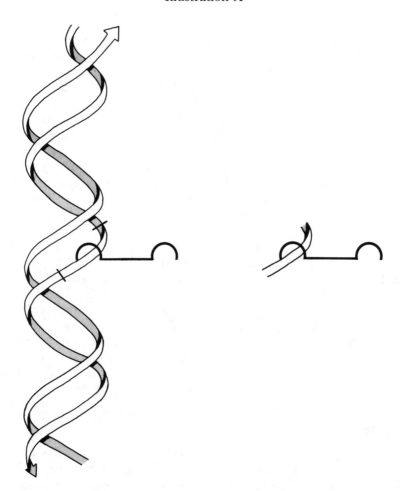

Sometimes (see Illustration A) the cross-linking molecule attaches to only one strand. The body can loosen this link and repair the damage using the other strand as a model.

Infrequently (see Illustration B), the repair takes too long and the linking molecule is able to attach itself to both DNA strands. Then the body faces a dilemma. (1) If it cuts out this cross-link, it cuts out parts of both DNA strands. Then the DNA stays damaged because neither strand has a base

Exhibit 4.2 (continued)

Illustration B   Illustration C

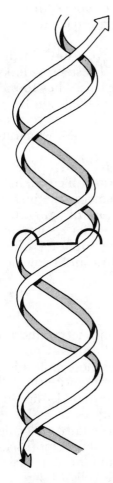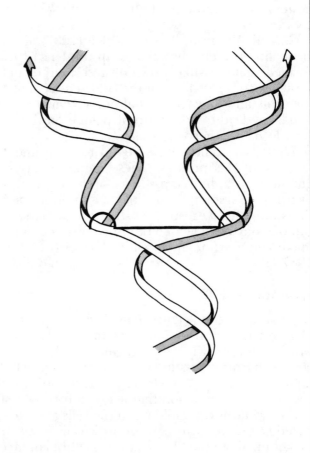

on the other side to use as a template for repair. (2) If the body leaves the cross-link in place, the DNA starts to divide, but the cross-link stops the process. This leads to a Y-shaped error (Illustration C).

Source: Adapted from J. Bjorksten, "Crosslinkage and the Aging Process," in *Theoretical Aspects of Aging*, ed. M. Rockstein, M.L. Sussman, and J. Chesky (New York: Academic Press, 1974).

time, and as they accumulate they become harder for the body's defences to remove. Also, as people age, their repair systems may become less efficient. The accumulation of cross-links in the body ultimately leads physical systems to break down.

Recent research lends support to the cross-linkage theory of aging. Cerami, Vlassara, and Brownlee (1987) have found that the non-enzymatic addition of glucose to protein and nucleic acids causes a series of age-related changes in the body. Normally, enzymes attach glucose to proteins or nucleic acids at specific sites for specific purposes, but non-enzymatic attachment of glucose occurs haphazardly and often forms irreversible cross-links. Cerami, Vlassara, and Brownlee report "that the nonenzymatic addition of glucose to nucleic acids may gradually damage DNA" (1987, 90).

Cerami, Vlassara, and Brownlee (1987) also found cross-links in the crystalline protein that makes up the lens of the eye. These cross-links formed a cataract-like browning and clouding of the eye lens. They found evidence for cross-links in the collagen sac that separates the brain from the skull, and they found that non-enzymatic glucose attachment to proteins may lead to a buildup of plaque on the walls of arteries, which in turn leads to atherosclerosis.

These researchers have begun to experiment with methods to delay or prevent this process. These methods include a drug called amino-guanidine to inhibit cross-links, and a method for enhancing the body's own repair system. Cross-links may not be the only cause of aging, but the study of how to prevent them raises "the possiblity that treatments can one day be developed to prevent some of the changes that too often make 'aging' synonymous with 'illness' " (Cerami, Vlassara, and Brownlee 1987, 96).

Free Radical Theory

Free radicals are molecules that have an unpaired electron, a large amount of free energy, and a tendency to bond with other molecules (Gordon, Ronsen, and Brown 1974). Normal metabolism produces these molecules. They can cause cross-links and can damage cells by bonding with the cell membrane. They also release new free radicals when they bond, and this creates a chain reaction that leads to further cell damage.

Free radicals can build up in the cells and create a large fatty molecule called *lipofuscin* — the basis of brown "liver spots" on the skin. Lipofuscin makes up about 6 to 7 percent of the human myocardium (heart muscle) and nearly 75 percent of the volume of some nerve cells by age 90 (Strehler 1977). Gordon, Ronsen, and Brown (1974) say that as lipofuscin takes up more room in the cell it may interfere with the cell's ability to create enzymes, release energy, and get rid of wastes. This leads to more sluggish cell performance — a sign of aging.

Selective Inhibition Theory

Cross-links and free radicals damage the cell or genetic material, and this leads to cell breakdown, inefficient body function, and signs of aging. But the selective inhibition model says that the DNA itself causes aging.

Scientists know that some cells stop dividing early in life. "Off switches" stop cell division in certain parts of the body (for example, the brain and spinal cord), and this allows for the body's selective growth and development. These same switches, though, keep the body from renewing itself later in life. No one knows for sure how this happens. Strehler (1977) suggests that genetic programs may switch off the cell's ability to divide by inhibiting the cell's ability to translate genetic messages. Also, some genes may serve a positive function early in life and then damage the system later. Williams (1957) called these *pleitropic* genes. He described a hypothetical pleitropic gene that led to calcification of bones early in life, but then led to calcification of arteries in old age. Some evidence for these genes now exists (Rose and Charlesworth 1981a; 1981b). If further research bears out this hypothesis, then this will mean that aging occurs as a by-product of normal human development.

Another theory, one that focuses on the immune system, supports the idea that the body's own systems turn against it with age. Autoimmune theory says that the body has fewer antibodies to protect it as it ages (Walford 1969). The body also loses its ability to tell its own healthy cells from foreign cells. Scientists call this an autoimmune response. The immune system contains two kinds of white blood cells — B cells and T cells. B cells release antibodies to attack bacteria and viruses, while T cells directly attack cancer cells and transplant cells. With age, T cells fail to attack cancer cells and instead attack the body's healthy cells. This could explain the rise in cancer, rheumatoid arthritis, and diabetes in older adults.

These theories and studies describe only some of the explanations for why aging takes place. Other theories and studies look at the endocrine system that regulates the body's inner chemistry, at neurotransmitters, and at the brain. Each theory has something to tell us about aging, but no theory gives a complete explanation. Future study will have to explain the Phase III phenomenon, changes in genetic material, and changes in cell and tissue function that occur with age. Research will also have to explain how and why the organization of cells in the body and the body's inner environment change with age (Weg 1974). A complete theory of aging will also have to account for differences in the way individuals age. Some people show little decline in function even in late old age, while others show signs of decline in late middle age. Researchers continue to look at the structure and function of the cell and genetic material for a single explanation of aging.

THE EFFECTS OF AGING ON BODY SYSTEMS

Current models of aging propose that intrinsic changes in the cells cause aging and that over time these changes compound one another and lead to changes in the body's systems. This section will describe some of the changes that take place in the body's systems as a person ages — it will look at changes in bone structure, in the cardiovascular system, and in system integration. Many changes take place in other body systems as well, but these examples will give some idea of what happens to the body with age.

Changes in Bone Structure

The body loses bone mass with age as mineral salts take the place of solid bone. Bones get more porous and brittle, and this leads to a higher risk of fracture, to stooped posture, and to loss of height. These changes take place in both men and women from age 35–40 on, but women more often than men suffer from an extreme loss of bone mass called *osteoporosis*. This shows up as widow's or dowager's hump, stooped posture, and compressed or collapsed vertebrae. In some cases the spine bows so much that the lower ribs sit on top of the pelvis. Loss of bone mass can make bones so weak that they cannot support a person's weight. Research shows that in some cases when an older person fractures a hip during a fall, the femoral neck (near the hip bone's ball joint) fractures first and then a person falls, rather than the other way around. Kart, Metress, and Metress (1978) report that 75 percent of people with a broken hip show some osteoporosis of the femoral neck.

Scientists do not know the cause of osteoporosis. Research suggests that lack of calcium in the diet, poor absorption of calcium as a person ages, or hormone loss may play a role in the onset of the disease. A decrease in activity with age may also bring on (or accelerate) loss of bone mass. Some treatments for osteoporosis include estrogen treatment to halt the process (though this may increase the risk of cancer), increased calcium intake, and exercise.

Changes in the Cardiovascular System

The heart also changes with age. The heart's weight increases due to fat and calcium deposits, and it also loses resiliency and beats fewer times per minute on average as a person ages (Shock 1962). Cardiac output (the amount of blood pumped by the heart in a single beat) decreases on average by 0.7 percent per year from age 20 on (Rockstein and Sussman 1979), so that by age 75 a man's cardiac output is only 70 percent of a 30-year-old's at rest, and blood flow to the brain has dropped by 20 percent (Shock 1962). The blood vessels also get stiffer with age; this is called hardening of the arteries or arteriosclerosis. (Atherosclerosis, or ischemic heart disease, on the other hand, refers to the growth of fatty plaques on the walls of the arteries. These can close off the free flow of blood and lead to a heart attack.) Arteriosclerosis shows up in people in all societies and gets worse with age. A decrease in arterial flexibility leads to reduced blood flow, slower oxygen transport, slower nutrient uptake, and slower waste elimination. These changes can lead to decreased energy and activity as a person ages.

Changes in System Integration

Studies of bone structure or the cardiovascular system (or any of the other body systems) focus on changes in one part of the body at a time. Research on reaction time (RT) suggests that the relations between the body's systems also causes functional decline. *Reaction time* refers to how fast a person responds to a demand from the environment. This includes how fast a driver responds to a red light, how fast an airline pilot responds to an emergency signal, or how fast a person reacts to a visual test in a laboratory. Laboratory studies of reaction time show that people respond more slowly as they age (Birren 1964, 107; Botwinick 1970; Cerella, Poon, and Fozard 1981; Cerella, Poon, and Williams 1980; Welford 1977).

Why does reaction time decrease? Researchers have studied several reasons for the decline, among them decline in the senses (the older person perceives the stimulus less clearly), decline in neuro-muscular action (the muscles respond more slowly), and changes in the central nervous system (the brain processes the need for a response more slowly). Botwinick (1984) concluded, after an extensive review of the literature on RT decline, that none of the above reasons explains slower RT in older subjects.

He suggests, instead, that a decrease in RT comes about when the central nervous system (CNS) and the autonomic nervous system (ANS; the system that regulates body activity like heart rate) lose their integrated style of functioning. A study by Thompson and Marsh (1973), for example, showed that younger people with high-speed RT show simultaneous heart rate changes and changes in the CNS. Older people, who responded more slowly, showed unrelated heart rate and CNS changes. Botwinick (1984, 235) says that "evidence for central control of speed loss with age may yet be found if CNS activity is investigated concomitantly with ANS activity." This research suggests that the disintegration in the relationships between physical systems, rather than a decline in any one physical system, causes a decline in physical function.

Decreases in bone strength, declines in cardiovascular efficiency, and slower reaction time point to a general decline in physical functioning with age, but how much do these declines affect the older person's health and social life? Does physical decline lead to a decline in the older person's well-being?

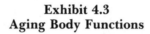

Exhibit 4.3
Aging Body Functions

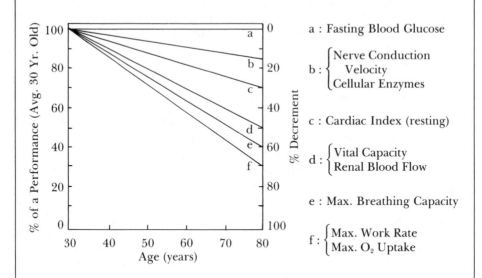

Age decrements in physiological functions in males. Mean values for 20- to 35-year-old subjects are taken as 100%. Decrements shown are schematic linear projections: (a) fasting blood glucose, (b) nerve conduction velocity and cellular enzymes, (c) resting cardiac index, (d) vital capacity and renal blood flow, (e) maximum breathing capacity, and (f) maximum work rate and maximum oxygen uptake.

Source: Diagram from N.W. Shock, "Systems Integration," in *Handbook of the Biology of Aging*, ed. C.E. Finch and L. Hayflick (New York: Van Nostrand Reinhold, 1977), 640. Orig. N.W. Shock, "Energy Metabolism, Calorie Intake and Physical Activity of the Aging," in *Nutrition and Old Age*, ed. L.A. Carlson (Uppsala: Aluiquist and Wiksell, 1972). © Swedish Nutrition Foundation.

Strehler (1982) says that from age 30 onward the body shows an average decline in function of about 1 percent per year, though different functions decline at different rates in any one person, and some people show more decline in functions than other people. Shock (1977) says that the more a function requires the integrated work of many body systems the greater the decline in that function over time.

Changes in Health

Researchers have asked two questions about the effects of physiological aging on the older person's well-being. First, do health problems increase with age? Second, does physiological aging limit the older person's activities?

Changes in Health Status

The 1978–79 Canada Health Survey (CHS) (Health and Welfare Canada and Statistics Canada 1981) asked a random sample of community-dwelling Canadians about their health. The sample included members of nearly 12,000 households from across Canada (not including Indian Reserves, the Territories, and certain remote areas). The survey compared the health status of children under age 15, adults (15–64 years), and older people (65+). The survey found that 86 percent of respondents aged 65 and over reported at least one acute or chronic health problem (14 percent reported no health problem). Also, older respondents reported more chronic conditions than younger adults (aged 15–64). Older people reported arthritis, rheumatism, hearing problems, hypertension, limb and joint problems, heart disease, and sight disorders as their most common problems. Among people aged 75 and over, 36 percent of men and 55 percent of women reported having arthritis and rheumatism (compared to only 7 percent and 14 percent for men and women of all ages). For the 75+ age group, 34 percent of men and 18 percent of women reported hearing problems (compared to only 5 percent and 4 percent of men and women of all ages) and 22 percent of men and 43 percent of women reported hypertension (compared to only 5 percent and 8 percent of men and women of all ages). Twenty-six percent of both men and women aged 75 and over reported heart disease, compared to only 4 percent of both men and women of all ages (Health and Welfare Canada 1983).

The Canada Health Survey (Health and Welfare Canada and Statistics Canada 1981) figures also showed that specific groups among the older population — women and very old people — may need more help as the population ages. Women, for example, reported more chronic health conditions than did men. The Canada Health Survey found that 21 percent of men compared to only 15.3 percent of women aged 65 and over reported no chronic conditions. At the same time, 36.8 percent of women compared to only 27.6 percent of men reported three or more chronic conditions. Women "have more days per year of restricted activity, more days of bed disability, more doctor's visits, higher expenditures for health care and higher rates of institutionalization than men" (Chappell, Strain, and Blandford 1986, 44). These figures may reflect a continuation of a pattern from their middle years, a denial of health problems by men, or the fact that more men than women are married and have someone to care for them so that they stay out of institutions.

Studies also show that the oldest age groups among people aged 65

Exhibit 4.4
Percent of Population in Each Age Group
Self-Reporting Selected Health Problems, Canada,
1978–79*

Health Problem	Less than 15	15–64	65+
Chronic			
Arthritis and Rheumatism	<1%	10%	42%
Hearing	2%	3%	17%
Hypertension	<1%	6%	29%
Heart Disease	<1%	3%	20%
Vision	2%	5%	16%
Acute			
Headache	<1%	6%	4%
Acute Respiratory	6%	3%	2%
Influenza	4%	3%	2%

*These figures include both acute and chronic problems mentioned at the time of the interview. Note that the older group shows much higher rates of illness than the younger group for chronic problems like arthritis and rheumatism.

Source: Adapted from Health and Welfare Canada and Statistics Canada, *The Health of Canadians* (The Canada Health Survey) (Ottawa: Minister of Supply and Services, 1981), 115. Reproduced by permission of the Minister of Supply and Services Canada.

and over have more health problems than the younger groups. Gerontologists often divide the older population into two age groups: the young-old (aged 65–75) and the old-old (aged 75 and over). Some researchers (Chappell and Havens 1980) divide the older population further according to differences in their health status. For women they describe three groups: young-old (aged less than 75), middle-old (aged 75–84), and old-old (aged 85 and over); for men they describe two groups: the young-old (aged less than 80) and the old-old (aged 80 and over). The Canada Health Survey (Health and Welfare Canada and Statistics Canada 1981) divides the older population into two age groups, 65–69 and 70 and over. The survey reports that chronic conditions increase with age. Slightly more than 20 percent of the group aged 65–69 reported no chronic conditions, but this proportion dropped to only 16.5 percent for the group aged 70 and over. Almost 35 percent of the 70+ group reported three or more chronic conditions compared to only 29 percent of the group aged 65–69.

These figures show that chronic conditions increase with age and that some groups — the old-old and women — suffer the most from these conditions. These groups may need special attention as the population ages and as these groups grow in size.

Limits on Activity Due to Physical Decline

Gerontologists measure *functional disability* as well as the number of illnesses a person has. Chappell, Strain, and Blandford (1986, 36) define functional disability as a "functional limitation on the *performance of normal daily role activities* as a result of illness or injury" (emphasis added). This measure looks at the effects of illness on a person's everyday life.

The Canada Health Survey (Health and Welfare Canada and Statistics Canada 1981) reports that functional disability increases with age; 23 percent of the group aged 65 to 69 reported a limit to their major activity. This figure rose to 29 percent for the group aged 70 and over. Chappell, Strain, and Blandford (1986) say that the use of age 75 or 80 as a cutoff would produce even greater differences between the oldest and younger age groups. The Canada Health Survey (Health and Welfare Canada and Statistics Canada 1981) reports that people aged 65 and over spend more time than younger adults (aged 15–64) in bed due to illness. Older people also report more *annual disability days* per person than younger people (annual disability days are days a person had to spend in bed or had to stop or decrease their major activity due to illness).

The Canada Health Survey (Health and Welfare Canada and Statistics Canada 1981) found that most older people (61.8 percent) manage their daily activities on their own, but more than 26 percent of people aged 65 and over reported that poor health limited their major activity compared to less than 7 percent of adults aged 15 to 64. Almost 9 percent of people aged 65 and over reported that they could not do their major activity due to illness compared to only 2 percent of adults aged 15–64.

Chappell, Strain, and Blandford (1986, 37) compared the rate of chronic illness with the influence of illness on daily activity. They found that "both the number of chronic conditions and the extent of functional disability tend to increase with age. However, chronic conditions do not necessarily translate into functional disability. ... That is, while over three-quarters of elderly persons have at least one chronic condition, only about half experience some functional disability. Even fewer, about one-fifth, require assistance with basic activities." Most older people cope with declines in their health. They accept the health changes that come with age, adjust their expectations about their activities, and gradually make changes in their lives to cope with physical decline (Chappell, Strain, and Blandford 1986, 43).

COPING WITH PHYSICAL CHANGE

The research on physical functioning, reaction time, and health makes old age seem like a time of loss and suffering. But older people vary on these measures. Studies show that 80 percent of old people live without functional handicaps on their basic activities and with a positive view of their health (Branch and Jette 1981; Riley and Foner 1968). Cape and Henschke (1980, 299) report that "only beyond the age of 80 does this picture begin to change significantly."

Studies of reaction time, for example, show that groups of older people make more varied responses than groups of younger people (Botwinick and Thompson 1968), and some older subjects do just as well as younger subjects on these tests. A study by Surwillo (1963) found that age accounted for only about 4 percent of the variance in reaction time. Studies show that exercise (Botwinick and Thompson 1968), practice (Murrell 1970) and motivation (Botwinick, Brinley, and Robbin 1958, 1959) all decrease the differences in reaction time between young and old people (though they do not entirely eliminate age group differences).

Older people can also make up for declines in the senses, muscles, and organs as they age. They can wear glasses and hearing aids to improve their senses, they can hire homemakers to help with heavy housework, and they can change their diet to make up for slow digestion and poor food absorption. Three responses to aging can decrease the effects of physiological decline: changes in a person's environment, changes in their lifestyle, and improvements in technology.

Changes in the Environment

Sense thresholds (the point where a person can begin to perceive a stimulus) begin to increase as early as age 30, and by age 60 most people notice changes in their senses. Compared to people 15–64 years old, people 65 and over in Canada report about five times the rate of trouble hearing without a hearing aid (Health and Welfare Canada and Statistics Canada 1981). Likewise, among people who reported some health problem in Canada in 1978–79, people 65 and over had three times the rate of reported sight disorders as people 15–64 (Health and Welfare Canada and Statistics Canada 1981).

Hearing aids and glasses can help correct some of these problems, but hearing aids amplify all sounds, even background noises. In one case an elderly man with a hearing aid in a university class showed up to take the course a second time. Surprised, the professor asked him why. The man said that students talking behind him, a bus depot across the street, and a noisy heating system all made his hearing aid useless. Some days he left it at home or shut it off and tried to read the professor's lips. "I only got half of what you said last time," he told the professor. "So I've come back to get the rest."

This man needed a quieter classroom setting.

Changes in the environment — including changes in the way other people speak to or treat an older person — can help a person cope with physical decline.

Exhibit 4.5

GOOD SETTINGS TO LIVE IN

The Manitoba Health Services Commission, in 1980, published a *Planning Guide for Personal Care Homes in Manitoba*. The Commission based the *Guide* on years of informal research in more than one hundred rural and urban personal care homes in the province. It suggests environmental changes that help older people cope with sensory loss.

Lighting

The Commission recognized that older people on average see less well than younger people. The Commission warns against pockets of light that create an uneven effect on walls and floors of hallways. This can lead a person to misjudge the floor's height or the distance to a wall. This can also increase a person's fear of falling and can thereby decrease the older person's movement in the home. The Commission also suggests soft indirect lighting at entrances. Direct lighting can create too great a contrast between the outside and the entry of the home.

Sound

Sounds from TVs, radios, and intercoms can blend into an audio mush that can distract and tire residents. The Commission warns against "a constant source of

meaningless sound in social areas." Designers can use rough textures, pile carpets, and soft drapes to dampen background noise. This will make it easier for people to hear one another. Also, small lounges or quiet areas allow people to communicate.

Other studies show that simple techniques for talking with older people who have a hearing problem can make up for their hearing loss. Speaking louder, for example, makes things worse. It raises the pitch of the speaker's voice (making it harder for the older person to understand) and it puts the older person on the defensive. Instead, speak "low and slow." Speak in a lower tone with distinct enunciation, speak slowly and find other words to say the same thing if you have to repeat yourself. Someone with a hearing loss often gets meaning from the context. Barrett (1972) found that people with a hearing loss fill in the gaps when they listen to familiar music. People also do this when they listen to someone speak. Take your time when you talk to someone with a hearing loss.

A speaker should also keep in mind that a person's vision can compensate for hearing loss. Face the older person who has a hearing problem and, when speaking, let the light in a room fall on your face (not behind you and in the older person's eyes).

Older people with a hearing loss often read your lips without knowing they do it. Get a person's attention by touch or gesture first so they get what you say from the start.

Decoration

Designers should avoid rough surfaces on walls. These can cause skin abrasions. Patterned carpets or vinyl blocks can lead to optical illusions. Zigzags or stripes can give the illusion of movement. Sharp contrasts in colours can give the illusion of a change in depth. People may try to step up or down and lose their balance. This can also cause people to avoid public space and withdraw to their rooms.

Personal care homes house only a small percentage of older people — people too ill to care for themselves. But these principles of design and communication can improve life for many older people.

Changes in Technology

Benjamin Franklin invented bifocals in the eighteenth century by cutting his glasses in half when he found he needed to watch the speakers' expressions at the French court. Today technology helps older people cope with aging in dozens of ways. Some people wear electronic pace-makers to regulate their hearts, people with severe arthritis can have joint replacement surgery, and in some cases a person can have a childhood problem corrected in old age. One woman lived for her first 60 years with her hip bones outside their sockets. Her muscles and ligaments allowed her to walk, but she limped and tired quickly. Her muscles weakened as she aged, and her doctor said she would have to spend the rest of her life in a wheelchair. She searched for and found a doctor who agreed to operate on both of her hips. He told her it would endanger her life, but she decided to try the operation. She now has both hips in place in their sockets and she stands two inches taller than in her youth.

Technological aids to older people range from the simple (e.g., a thick piece of rubber tubing that fits over a wooden spoon handle to help a person with arthritis or a weak grip) to the complex (e.g., a Century tub with a crane-like lift and a swing-like seat that lifts an immobilized or frail older person into a stainless steel tub. Water and pre-measured amounts of soap come out of jets in the side of the tub. The person sits up to their chest in the water, while it swirls them clean). Technological aids range from the common (e.g., a colour television) to the unusual (e.g., a chair with a seat that lifts a person to a standing position when they press a button). In the future computers may also allow housebound older people to order groceries, get their mail, or play Scrabble with a grandchild across town.

Haber (1986) says that in the future robots may help older people with their daily chores. Robots might help bathe and feed people in nursing homes. Voice-activated robots will pick things up or move things around for a person. Robots can also help patients do passive exercises, help a person walk, or bring a person something they need. Haber argues that robots could free staff from unpleasant work and give them more time to spend with patients. He says that voice-activated robots would give aware but immobilized older people a feeling of control over their environment. This, in turn, will increase their life-satisfaction. Research will have to be done to see whether robots further dehumanize institutional settings, whether older people (or institutions) can afford complex machines, and whether people will use high-tech equipment if they have the chance.

Changes in Lifestyle

People can also change their habits to cope with biological aging. Heavy smoking and drinking put wear and tear on the body, overeating can increase a person's risk of heart disease and diabetes, and long exposure to the sun increases the risk of skin cancer. A person can cut back on activities and habits that speed the process of aging.

A study by Smith, Reddan, and Smith (1981), for example, found increased mineral content in the bones of older women who exercised. The researchers studied thirty women who averaged 84 years old. Twelve of these women took part in an exercise program; eighteen did not. The researchers matched the two groups for age, weight, and how well they could walk. The experimental group exercised for thirty minutes a day, three times a week, for three years; the control group did no exercise. The researchers found that the control group had more than a 3 percent loss in bone mineral in three years, while the exercise group showed more than a 2 percent gain in bone mineral over the same time. The researchers say that the exercise program accounted for more than 96 percent of the difference between these two groups. A study at Stanford University supports these findings. Lane et al. (1986) found that runners had 40 percent higher bone density than non-runners (*Time* 1986a, 68).

Men can also benefit from regular exercise as they age. A study of 17,000 male Harvard alumni showed that men who exercise regularly can expect to live a year longer than those who do not (Paffenbarger et al. 1986). Paffenbarger, chief researcher for the study, says that "for each hour of physical activity, you can expect to live that hour over — and live one or two more hours to boot" (*Time* 1986a, 68).

The study also found that exercise could lessen the risk of illness for smokers and for people with high blood pressure. The study found that "men who walked nine or more miles a week (burning off at least 900 calories), for example, had a risk of death 21 percent lower than those who walked less than three miles a week" (*Time* 1986a, 68). The researchers say that exercise could extend the lives of some men ten to twenty years. This study looked only at white upper-middle-class men. Future studies will have to see whether the same conclusions apply to women, minorities, or people with low incomes.

These studies point the way to a new view of aging. Science cannot stop or reverse the process of aging, but individuals can improve their environment and can delay chronic problems through lifestyle changes and exercise. Leo and Blonarz (1981) report on one medical expert who says that "the body is now felt to rust out rather than wear out." Over time organs lose their reserve capacity (the amount of work they *can* do even though the conditions may never demand this amount of work). But "if loss of reserve function represents aging in some sense, then exercising an organ presents a strategy for modifying the aging process" (Leo and Blonarz 1981).

SCIENTIFIC PROSPECTS FOR LONGER LIFE

People have tried to reverse or stop the process of aging at least since Ponce de Leon set out to find the fountain of youth. Drug companies have looked into the effects of animal glands, sex hormones, and chemical therapy on aging. One company that sells skin cream includes in its formula "proteins from the placentas of black sheep (because they are so resistant to disease)" (Toufexis 1986, 51). These methods can make the skin softer or add water below the skin to temporarily smooth out wrinkles, but they do nothing to increase life expectancy or reverse aging.

Still, the search goes on. Scientists have explored many methods for increasing life span and extending youth. They have found that certain drugs, calorie-restricted diets, and lowered body temperatures (during hibernation) extend the lives of some animals in the laboratory (Schneider and Reed 1985). Will any of these methods lead to a longer, healthier life for humans in the near future?

Neugarten and Havighurst (1979) asked the leading biological researchers about extensions in human life span. All but two of the researchers they spoke with predicted only small changes in life expectancy in the near future. Most researchers predicted a slow increase in life expectancy in the next few years due to better health care, healthier lifestyles, and new medical technology. An end to cancer, for example, would increase life expectancy at birth by about 2 years, an end to cardiovascular disease would add about 17 years, and an end to diseases like pneumonia, influenza, and diabetes would add a little more than 2 years at birth (Rockstein and Sussman 1979).

These changes would raise life expectancy from about 70 years to about 90 years at birth, but this would still not change the human life span of 110 to 120 years. The life span depends on intrinsic processes of aging — possibly the slowing of cell metabolism, increases in collagen due to cross-linkages, and pleiotropic genes. It may also depend on other physiological processes as yet unknown to science. At the moment, it seems, humans will have to make the best of the 110 to 120 years they have.

SUMMARY

1. Human aging is universal, intrinsic, progressive, and deleterious. Heredity, culture, habits, and the environment all influence the rate of aging.

2. No single theory ties together all the facts about aging. Most theories today focus on changes in the cell. Research shows that cell metabolism declines with age, and this allows waste to accumulate in the cells. Researchers call this the "Phase III Phenomenon." Studies also show that cross-links can damage DNA, leading to faulty cell reproduction. Also, free radicals attack DNA and the cell walls. This too leads to cell breakdown.

3. Breakdown in the cells leads to a decline in physical functions. The body's systems break down or decline in efficiency. Reaction time slows, and the risk of chronic illness increases.

4. People can cope with changes in physical function, reaction time, and health. Changes in lifestyle can improve or at least slow the rate of physical decline. Training can make up for some of the loss in reaction time. Eyeglasses, hearing aids, and a supportive environment can make up for losses in the senses.

5. Technology can help people cope with declines in health. Designers can adapt simple objects like spoons for people with arthritis, computers can increase a person's contact with others, and in the future robots may help people bathe, exercise, and do daily tasks.

6. Research shows that changes in diet and exercise can slow the aging process. People can even improve their lung capacity and bone density through exercise. This can lead to a longer and healthier life.

7. Many older people stay healthy and active as they age. They live without handicap and without special help. In the future, science may find a way for people to live past the current limits of the human life span. For the moment, though, research shows that people can extend the number of years they live in good health.

SELECTED READINGS

Health and Welfare Canada and Statistics Canada. *The Health of Canadians*. Ottawa: Minister of Supply and Services, 1981.
  Good summary statistics and discussions about the health habits, illnesses, and mental condition of Canadians.

Neugarten, B.L., and R.J. Havighurst. "Aging and the Future." In *Dimensions of Aging: Readings*, ed. J. Hendricks and C.D. Hendricks. Cambridge, Massachusetts: Winthrop, 1979.
  Two well-known gerontologists review the future of aging in North America. They predict more young-old, more old-old, and more government supports for older people. You may or may not agree with what they say, but this article will make you think about physical aging and its effects on society.

Strehler, B. *Time, Cells and Aging*, 2nd ed. New York: Academic Press, 1977.
A thorough look at the cellular theories of aging. More than most social science students will need, but Strehler writes clearly and presents a wealth of ideas and information.

CHAPTER 5

THE PSYCHOLOGY OF AGING

INTRODUCTION

A few years ago, one of Canada's leading geriatric specialists gave a talk on memory to a group of seniors. He told the group that, in the absence of disease, memory stays about the same in old age as in youth. Young people and old people both forget things, but older people notice it more, because they expect memory loss to come with age. A man stood up at the end of the talk and said, "I respect your views, Doctor. But I know my memory has gotten worse with age. What I want to know is what I can do about it." This response fits with two things research has found out about older people and memory: first, older people believe their memories are getting worse (Dixon and Hultsch 1983), and, second, memory failure upsets them, even if they forget something unimportant (Cavanaugh, Grady, and Perlmutter 1983).

Many people, older people included, accept the stereotype that cognitive decline is a normal part of aging. But recent research on memory, intelligence, and creativity questions this myth. Studies show that people can learn and grow intellectually in old age as well as in youth. On some measures mental ability may even improve with age. Dramatic declines in mental functioning are due to physiological disorders or distress, not to normal aging.

This chapter will look at: (1) memory and intelligence in later life, (2) creativity, and (3) the psychological problems some older people face.

NORMAL CHANGES IN PSYCHOLOGICAL FUNCTIONING

Learning and Memory

Memory is the recall of information after learning has taken place. Most measurement of memory takes place in psychological laboratories. Psychologists in the field of aging have spent more time on the study of memory than on any other topic. Poon (1985) reports that between 1964 and 1974, 72 percent of the papers in the psychology sections of gerontology journals dealt with memory. Between 1979 and 1980, 58 percent of all papers dealt with memory. Psychologists show a strong interest in memory and aging for a number of reasons. First, popular stereotypes about aging and early psychological research on memory predict a decline in memory with age. If this is true, studies of memory can trace the causes of this decline. Second, psychologists can study memory in the laboratory under controlled conditions. This makes research on memory relatively easy to do. Third, studies of memory have produced testable models of how the mind works. These models attempt to explain complex processes like learning, forgetting, and the storage and retrieval of information. For all of these reasons, and because research on memory may lead to remedies for memory decline, the study of memory has dominated the study of psychological aging.

Much of the research on memory and aging points to some decline in memory with age (Waugh and Barr 1982; Arenberg 1977). Welford (1958), for example, referred to the decline in learning ability in old age (the decline in retention of information) as an established fact. Many studies show that older people take longer to learn new information, longer to search for it in memory, and longer to use it when they need it. But not all studies agree with these findings. Some research shows that the design of memory tests, the content of memory tests, and the use of cross-sectional designs (which compare older and younger people at one point in time) may all lead to exaggerated estimates of memory decline in older people. Hundreds of studies have tried to sort out the effects of age on memory. Researchers have taken three major approaches to the study of memory and learning (Hultsch and Deutsch 1981): (1) the associative approach, (2) the information processing approach, and (3) the contextual approach.

The Associative Approach

The associative approach views memory as a response to a stimulus. Subjects are said to remember when they associate the right response with the right stimulus. A person forgets when the bond between the stimulus and the response is broken. This can happen because the connection between the stimulus and the response weakens over time or because something (like other information) interferes with the response.

Researchers in this tradition treat the mind as a "black box." Information goes in, and researchers measure what comes out. By comparing the outputs of younger and older subjects on the same test, researchers attempt to assess how much memory declines with age. A common method used in this tradition is *paired associate* learning. The researcher presents subjects with word pairs like arrow–storm, iron–harp, and pipe–whale. The subjects learn the list of paired words, then the experimenter presents the subject with one word of each pair and asks the subject to recall the other word.

Most studies find that younger subjects do better than older subjects on association tests (Arenberg and Robertson-Tchabo 1977; Witte 1975; Canestrari 1963). Early research in this tradition (Cameron 1943; Welford 1958) assumed that memory declined because the human organism deteriorated over time. More recent research using association tests suggests that external conditions, not inner psychological changes, may explain some of the declines in older subjects' scores.

First, most association studies use a cross-sectional method — researchers study two or more different age groups at one point in time. This method confounds age and cohort effects. For example, does memory decline with age, or do older people lack skills at memorizing that younger people learn in school today? Many of these tests compare university undergraduates with older volunteers from the community, and most of these older people have less than a university education. Does memory decline with age, or does a person's educational level or vocabulary influence their ability on memory tests? Longitudinal or sequential research would sort age from cohort effects, but researchers have not pursued this issue.

Second, some research suggests that the tests themselves favour younger learners. Associative tests often require a fast answer to a stimulus. These speeded tests lead to lower scores for older subjects, and the faster the pace, the worse older people do compared to the young (Arenberg and Robertson-Tchabo 1977; Witte 1975). Canestrari (1963) slowed down the pace of an association experiment. This study found that both older (age 60–69) and younger (age 17–35) learners made fewer mistakes at a slower pace, but older learners' scores improved the most. Canestrari found that, when given the chance, older people took more time to respond than younger people. Also, older people scored more errors because they failed to answer (rather than because they gave a wrong answer). These results suggest that the older person's memory may work as well as the younger person's, but older people need more time to retrieve information.

Third, association tests ask people to recall unusual pairs of words (like whale–tea). Established verbal habits may stand in the way of recall on this kind of test (Kausler and Lair 1966; Lair, Moon, and Kausler 1969). Researchers find that when they use word pairs that have a high association of one word with another (for example, bread–butter, seed–tree) older subjects improve their scores (Hultsch and Deutsch 1981).

Fourth, older people may take a different approach to the test setting than younger people. Some studies find that older subjects are more cautious in giving an answer (Canestrari 1963). A study by Okun, Siegler, and George (1978) found that increased cautiousness in older subjects leads to more errors and that cautiousness and not memory decline led to lower scores.

Biological decline may explain older learners' need for more response time. But this research also suggests that the type of test used, the test-taking skill of the individual, and the past experience of the learner contribute to the lower memory scores of older subjects. A closer look at the learning process and at ways to improve learning in older people supports this view.

The Information Processing Approach

The information processing approach to the study of memory has dominated memory research since the 1960s. Researchers in this tradition often use the same methods (paired-associate laboratory tests) to study memory, but they do not treat the mind as a black box. The information processing approach assumes that: (1) the person plays an active part in the learning and retrieval of information, (2) researchers can study memory both quantitatively (in terms of output) and qualitatively (in terms of how the process works), and (3) researchers can trace the flow of memory through a series of stages (Poon 1985).

The information processing model makes an analogy between the mind and a computer. It says that memory takes place in four stages:

First, a person sees or hears something. This leads to a memory trace that lasts only a few moments. Psychologists call this sensory memory.

Second, this information goes into a short-term or primary memory store. Poon (1985, 431) says that primary memory is an "ephemeral, limited-capacity store in which information is still 'in mind,' as it is being used." Primary memory lasts longer than sensory memory, but can hold only a few bits of information — a few words or a telephone number.

Third, the mind moves information from primary to secondary memory for storage. To do this the mind processes or transforms the information. This model says that the mind stores information in meaningful patterns so that it can retrieve the information quickly.

Fourth, long-term storage of information takes place in tertiary (or remote) memory. Tertiary memory holds information like childhood recollections.

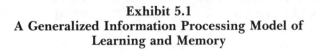

Exhibit 5.1
A Generalized Information Processing Model of
Learning and Memory

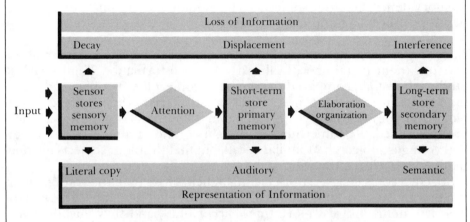

This diagram includes the main components of memory (except tertiary memory) according to the information processing model. Information moves from left to right into more permanent memory stores. Each stage has its principal method of retaining information (bottom bar), and at each stage information can be lost (top bar).

Source: David F. Hultsch and Francine Deutsch, *Adult Development and Aging: A Life-Span Perspective* (New York: McGraw-Hill, 1981), 143. Reprinted with permission of the publisher.

Hundreds of research studies in the past twenty years have looked for decrements in each of these memory stores. Researchers have found relatively little difference between younger and older people in either sensory, primary, or tertiary memory (Walsh 1976; Walsh, Till, and Williams 1978; Fozard 1980; Craik 1977). On the other hand, researchers have found relatively large differences between younger and older people in secondary memory. For this reason, most of the research in the past few years has concentrated on secondary memory.

Researchers asked where, in the processing of data into secondary memory, a loss of information occurs: during learning, storage, or retrieval? Few researchers think that the storage of information leads to memory deficits (Hartley, Harker, and Walsh 1980), and a review of recent research suggests that retrieval problems explain only some of the memory deficit in older subjects (Smith 1980). Most of the differences between younger and older subjects seem to be due to learning (acquisition) differences between these groups. Psychologists now believe that retrieval and acquisition are closely related. How someone retrieves information (how they search for and find information in memory) depends on how they acquired it (the methods they used to organize and store the information).

Psychologists have looked at several acquisition processes that explain memory deficits in older subjects: (1) encoding, (2) organization, and (3) depth of processing and elaboration.

Encoding. Encoding requires that a person take new bits of information and put them together with already stored information (Smith 1980). Studies show that, compared to younger people, older people need more time to learn something new. Hulicka and Weiss (1965) arranged for older and younger subjects to learn paired words to a set criteria (each group learned the same number of pairs). They found that the older and younger subjects had similar recall, but that the older subjects needed more trials to learn the word pairs.

Speeded trials increase the learning deficit. More than the young, older subjects miss verbal and pictorial items presented at a rapid rate. They miss late items in a list more than earlier ones, and they encode some items at the expense of others. Waugh and Barr (1982, 190) say that "the older the subject, the less efficiently and the more selectively he encodes — perhaps because ... he simply lacks the time to encode efficiently and comprehensively."

Studies also show that older subjects do not integrate separate events or non-related pieces of information as well as younger subjects. They also fail to register or hold on to as many trivial details as the young. This makes it harder for them to tell one test problem from a similar but different problem on a future test (Winocur 1982). Older people may also use typical ways to encode an event rather than new ways. This may make it harder for them to learn difficult material. McCormack (1982) reports that the more difficult the material to learn, the more poorly older people do.

Organization. Research shows that older people use fewer *mediation strategies* to process information, or they use them less effectively than do the young. (Mediation strategies include memory aids like picturing a word or finding a rhyme to help recall a memorized pair.) Hulicka and Grossman (1967) compared older and younger subjects' approaches to taking a memory test. They found that older subjects less often used mediators on their own. Hultsch (1971) found that when researchers gave older people mediators to use, older subjects' scores improved. Hulicka and Grossman (1967), in a paired-associate word study, gave simple mediation instruction to older and younger subjects like "form an image of the pair." They found that older people improved more than younger people. A study by Poon, Walsh-Sweeney, and Fozard (1980) also found that older people benefit more from organizational techniques than younger people. This may be because younger people already perform well on these tests or because they already use mediators. Studies show that older people can use mediators, if they are encouraged to use them, but they do not develop and use them spontaneously (Kausler 1982). Older people may lack the practice at using these techniques. Again, educational differences between younger and older subjects may account for the differences in the use of mediators.

Depth of Processing and Elaboration. Craik and Lockhart (1972) say that deeper processing of information and elaboration of information both improve recall. Depth of processing refers to the type of processing done: conceptually reworking some information (semantic processing, for example) is thought to be deeper than, say, writing out new information (orthographic processing) or reciting that information (phonemic processing). Elaboration refers to the amount of work done on the information at a particular level. Teachers assign essays, for example, so that students will elaborate (semantically) on concepts taught in class. Sanders et al. (1980) studied younger (aged 29–47) and older (aged 63–85) learners. They asked some members of each group to rehearse word lists out loud. The researchers found that older people took an inactive and non-strategic approach to memorizing their lists, while the younger people actively organized and categorized their lists as they memorized them. Other studies report similar results (Howard, McAndrews, and Lasagna 1981). Most of the research on processing reports that older people fail "to engage in deep semantic elaborational and organizational processing of the material" (Hultsch and Deutsch 1981, 151).

This research suggests that memory declines in older adults may be due to the use of inefficient processing techniques rather than to biological decline, and that these differences may be due to differences between younger and older subjects in educational background and verbal ability. Cavanaugh (1983), for example, studied the recall of TV show content. This study found that older subjects with low verbal ability recalled less than younger subjects. When Cavanaugh compared younger subjects to older subjects with high verbal ability, the study showed no difference between the two groups' scores. Taub (1979) found that the better a person's vocabulary, the greater their ability to retain pieces of prose in memory. Bowles and Poon (1982) found significant age differences in memory between young and old samples with a low vocabulary, but no age differences in high-vocabulary samples.

These results suggest that older people can improve their memories through instruction or alternative test conditions. If older people can improve their memory scores, then this calls into question the idea that memory inevitably declines with age. A number of studies support a more optimistic view of memory. Ross (1968), for example, found that a supportive context improved older subjects' ability to learn paired words. A challenging setting, where the instructor said that she would test the students' intelligence, led to the least efficient learning. A supportive setting, where the instructor asked for help, led to the most efficient learning. Older subjects did not learn as quickly as younger subjects under any conditions. But this study and others show that older people have more mental potential than laboratory studies report (Erber and Botwinick 1983; Leech and Witte 1971). Poon (1985) found, for example, that when older people could control the pace of their learning they showed less decrement in memory (Poon 1985). Finally, most studies show that older people learn familiar and relevant material better than new and irrelevant material (Smith 1977; Canestrari 1963). Barrett and Wright (1981), for example, found that older people did less well than younger people on a list of words unfamiliar to them, but they showed a better rate of recall than younger people on a list of familiar words. All of these studies show that laboratory tests and experiments put the older learner at a disadvantage. In some cases the research methods themselves produce the memory deficits that older people display.

All laboratory studies raise an important question: how well do the results of memory studies predict an older person's ability to remember details in everyday life? The answer: not very well. Memory studies done under laboratory conditions have poor ecological validity (the transferability of knowledge from lab to life). Older people rarely learn or recall well under pressure, and research shows that they remember best when they learn information relevant and useful to them.

The Contextual Approach

The contextual view of memory sums up much of the research on memory in old age. This view begins with the insight that memory takes place in a social context and that many conditions influence memory, including "the physical, psychological, and social context in which the event was experienced, the knowledge, abilities, and characteristics the individual brings to the context, [and] the situation in which we ask for evidence of remembering" (Hultsch and Deutsch 1981, 153). The previous review of the literature supports this view. Research shows that different types of older people (with more or less education), under different conditions (supportive or non-supportive), exposed to different types of materials to learn (relevant or irrelevant) vary in their ability to remember.

Only a few studies have looked directly at what older people remember about the world around them. These studies have found little of the memory deficit reported in laboratory studies. A study of memory of recent public events, for example, found no difference between younger and older subjects (between ages 20 and 80) on recent events (Poon et al. 1979). When the researchers asked about events that occurred from the 1920s to the 1970s, they found that older subjects scored better than younger subjects. Lachman and Lachman (1980) studied the "actualization of world knowledge," subjects' ability to recall information about the world around them, like the price of food, current events, or geography. Their research showed either no age differences in memory on this kind of test or a slight difference that favours older people (Perlmutter 1978; Lachman, Lachman, and Thronesbery 1979; Botwinick and Storandt 1980). Poon (1985, 435) concludes a review of the research on memory by saying that "in general, evidence to date shows minimal differences in memory for familiar discourse materials that may be found in the everyday environment." The research reported to date, Poon says, should end the stereotype of older people as forgetful. The current literature shows that older people may have different learning styles and a different attitude toward laboratory tests than younger people. These differences show up as deficiencies on specific types of tests in the laboratory. But they may not be deficiencies, only differences in the way older and younger people use their minds.

Summary

Studies disagree about the effects of aging on memory. Some studies show that memory decline takes place with age, but other studies show that the types of tests given, the test setting, and past experiences affect test scores as much as or more than age.

Intelligence

The research on intelligence in old age parallels the research on memory. Early studies assumed that intelligence decreases in old age as the body declines. More recent research questions this simple connection between senescence and intelligence.

Psychologists use at least two definitions of *intelligence*. First, they take a global view of intelligence. They refer to it as the "ability to negotiate environmental demands successfully" (Labouvie-Vief 1985, 506). Second, they take a pragmatic view of intelligence. They refer to it as "that which intelligence tests measure" (Labouvie-Vief 1985, 506) or "what the test-taker can do now" (Botwinick 1984, 250). Psychologists most often use this second (more limited) definition when they conduct research on intelligence and aging. The use of intelligence tests to measure intelligence again raises the question of "ecological validity" (as it did for studies of memory). How well do these test scores predict a person's performance in everyday life? The answer, once again, is: not very well. But the use of tests does allow psychologists to measure and analyze specific kinds of intellectual performance. It also allows them to connect intellectual performance on tests with changes due to aging.

The results of hundreds of studies of intelligence have produced a generally accepted pattern of change due to aging. Early research, during the 1930s, reported a decline in intellectual ability after age 20 (Miles and Miles 1932; Jones and Conrad 1933; Wechsler 1939). These findings supported the idea that mental ability declines along with the body, and all IQ tests build this expectation of decline into their design. They assume that older people will score less well than younger people, and they correct for supposed age declines in their formulas for calculating IQ. The most recent Wechsler Adult Intelligence Scale (WAIS–R) Manual uses this approach. It puts the peak of intelligence at between 20 and 34 years (Wechsler 1981) and assumes that each later age group will show a decline in scores.

The actual scores on WAIS–R scales support this assumption of decline with age, but they also show that decline does not take place uniformly. Scores on the WAIS–R Verbal Scale, for example, decrease steadily from a mean score of 61.42 at ages 25–34 to a mean of 51.50 at ages 70–74 (84 percent of the younger group's score). Scores on the Performance Scale drop earlier and more sharply from 51.14 at ages 20–24 to a mean score of 30.62 at ages 70–74 (60 percent of the younger group's score) (Wechsler 1981, 26). Other cross-sectional studies of intelligence show a similar pattern of decline in some abilities and less decline in others (Schaie and Labouvie-Vief 1974). Few researchers contest this pattern of change. Instead, researchers argue over the meaning of these findings. Researchers disagree on at least three issues: (1) the concept of intelligence as a single structure, (2) the methods used to produce these findings, and (3) the potential of cognitive functioning in later life.

Intelligence as Multidimensional

Tests like the WAIS–R consist of a number of subtests (the WAIS–R has eleven). Six of the tests measure Verbal abilities including Information, Vocabulary, and Comprehension. Five of these tests, including the Digit Symbol test and the Block Design test, measure Performance abilities. (The Digit Symbol test, for example, asks a subject to match a symbol to one of nine digits written across the page. The subject must then write the symbol next to the appropriate digit when it appears in the test. The subject's score depends on how many symbols he or she writes correctly during the time allowed for the test.) The test's design assumes that these subscales measure parts of a single underlying entity: intelligence.

More current research on intelligence questions this view. This research supports a multi-dimensional view of intelligence. The WAIS–R scales themselves point to this multidimensionality. They show what Botwinick (1984) calls the "classic aging pattern." The Performance Scale scores show a much greater decrease with age than the Verbal Scale scores (40 percent vs. 16 percent). "This classic aging pattern, relative maintenance of function in Verbal skills as compared to Performance skills, has been seen many times with a variety of different populations" (Botwinick 1984, 254). These findings give support to the idea that "both decrement and stability — or even growth — over the adult period [are] the rule" (Labouvie-Vief 1985, 502).

Horn and Cattell have developed a model of intelligence that explains these results. They describe two types of intelligence, which they call *fluid intelligence* and *crystallized intelligence* (Horn and Cattell 1966; 1967; Cattell 1963). Fluid intelligence refers to reasoning, abstracting, concept formation, and problem solving. It makes little use of knowledge gained through reading, schooling, or work. According to Horn and Cattell, fluid intelligence relies on how well the physical and nervous systems function. Performance tests that demand the use of fluid intelligence ask subjects to mentally manipulate unfamiliar material in new ways, and they sometimes require physical skill at manipulating objects. Verbal tests that demand the use of crystallized intelligence depend more on stored information, acculturation, and learning (Horn 1978, 221–22).

This two-part model helps explain the empirical results on intelligence. Number and verbal skill problems measure crystallized intelligence; spatial and reasoning questions measure fluid intelligence. Fluid intelligence may follow the decline of the biological system from the teen years on, while studies of crystallized intelligence show stable intelligence scores and even *increases* in scores with age (Schaie, Rosenthal, and Perlman 1953; Schaie and Strother 1972).

A single universal decline (for all people on all types of intelligence measures) does not fit the evidence. Charness (1982), for example, reviewed the literature on mental ability and found that older people do less well than younger people on novel problem-solving tasks, but they perform about as well as younger subjects on familiar tasks that older subjects know well, like chess or bridge. Botwinick (1984) reports that chronological age accounts for only about one-quarter of the variance in IQ scores. This means that age alone is not a very sound predictor of a person's intelligence score. Baltes and Willis sum up the current research: "The striking feature of descriptive aging research," they say, "is one of much variablity, both between persons and within persons for distinct abilities" (1982, 355).

Longitudinal vs. Cross-Sectional Methods

Few studies of IQ have looked at the variability among *individuals* (differences like educational level, social class, personal experience) in their samples. For one thing, most of these studies (like studies of memory) use a cross-sectional method to draw conclusions about age changes. These studies ignore the fact that older and younger cohorts differ on more variables than just age. Age cohorts differ in education, test-taking ability and vocabulary. These differences depend on when a person was born and what they did during their lifetime. These differences only partly depend on the effects of aging on intelligence. When intelligence tests are used to compare age groups they confound cohort differences with age changes.

Longitudinal and sequential studies of intelligence try to overcome this problem. These studies measure the same groups of people at more than one point in time. Most longitudinal studies find less decline in intelligence with age than do cross-sectional studies. Some studies find no decline or even some improvement on some measures with age. Owens (1972), for example, used a longitudinal approach to study changes in intelligence over time. This study looked at Army Alpha test scores of ninety-six men aged 19, 50, and 61. Owens found that some scores decreased as his subjects aged, but other scores increased. He found more decline in his subjects on the last test than on the first two tests, but not the amount of decline expected if intelligence declined steadily in all subjects from middle age on.

Schaie and Strother (1972) studied changes in intelligence over seven years in a stratified-random sample of 500 people. They used two tests: the Primary Mental Abilities Test (PMA) and the Test of Behavioral Rigidity (TBR). First they did a cross-sectional analysis of the test scores. They found that intelligence decreased with age — the same result found in other cross-sectional studies. They then compared test scores of each cohort at the two points in time (a longitudinal method). They found steady declines in test scores for only three variables. They conclude that "the cross-sectional differences for all other variables" measure the differences *between generations* — education differences, test-taking skill differences, or life-experience differences — not changes in intelligence due to aging.

Schaie and Labouvie-Vief (1974) took this study a step further. They returned to this group for a third test in 1970. They gave tests to 301 people tested in 1956 and 1963. They added new groups to their study to make up for people who dropped out of the first sample. Again, they found that the younger groups scored better than the older groups. But they also found that the older groups got roughly the same scores as they did seven years before. The researchers concluded that cohort differences accounted for most of the differences in test scores between younger and older subjects.

Botwinick (1984) takes a less optimistic view of intellectual functioning in old age. He reviewed the Schaie and Labouvie-Vief (1974) longitudinal study and found that decline set in by about age 53. Earlier cross-sectional research by Schaie (1959) showed declines around age 55. "Thus, the longitudinal sequences and the cross-sectional data are not very different" (Botwinick 1984, 262). Declines in intelligence occur regardless of the method used.

Botwinick also says that longitudinal studies play down the effects of age on intelligence because people with low intelligence scores drop out of the studies. This leaves more intelligent people at older ages. The longer the study and the more times the researchers test the subjects, the more dropouts affect the results (1984, 262). A study by Botwinick and Siegler (1980) controlled for dropouts and found that both longitudinal and cross-sectional analyses showed declines in intelligence with age. Labouvie-Vief (1985) responded to Botwinick and Siegler (1980) by noting that they studied people aged 60 and over. She says that cohort differences showed up in Schaie and Labouvie-Vief (1974) mostly for groups aged 60 and under. For subjects past age 70, Schaie and Labouvie-Vief

Exhibit 5.2

NEW TESTS FOR OLDER PEOPLE

Some researchers point to age co-hort differences other than educa-tion that may account for differences in intelligence scores. Older people report less desire to do well on stan-dard intelligence tests (Baltes and Schaie 1982), they say these tests ask irrelevant questions (Demming and Pressey 1957, 46), and sometimes they refuse to take the tests. Also, the tests ask about things that younger cohorts have learned (new terms or concepts), but that older cohorts may not have heard of or care about (Read 1984). Some re-searchers feel that these test condi-tions and attitudes of older people bias scores on intelligence in favour of the young.

Demming and Pressey (1957) de-signed a group of intelligence tests to overcome these problems. They designed tests to measure a person's ability to meet everyday demands. These questions come from one of their tests:

Find the word that has been changed [the word that does not fit] in the sentence below:

1. "He disappeared behind a crude mahogany door at the rear of the shack."

Answer the following questions:

1. "Where in the yellow pages of the telephone directory would you look if you wanted to buy an Airedale? Under heating equip-ment, kennels, shoe stores, real estate, dairy equipment?"
2. "The person to baptize a baby is a naturalist, notary public, nur-seryman, magistrate, clergyman."

Demming and Pressey (1957) gave their tests to a number of adults of different ages along with some stan-dard intelligence tests. They found that on the standard tests in most cases the older groups had lower scores. But on their tests they found that all of the older groups (except the 50+ group on one of their tests) scored better than the 20–24 groups.

Demming and Pressey (1957) con-clude that adults become better in-formed as they age and that when intelligence tests ask questions rele-vant to adult life, older people do better than standard tests predict.

(1974) also found steady declines in intelligence with age. Labouvie-Vief (1985, 505) concludes that decline in intelligence does occur late in life, but that current research at least calls "attention to the fact that significant decrements are considerably delayed into the far end of the 60- to 70-year-old spectrum."

The debate over the effects of age on intelligence continues in the literature. Future research will focus on the causes of differences in intelligence within different age groups and between different cohorts.

Studies of educational differences among cohorts, for example, tries to explain the differences in older and younger people's intelligence scores. Green (1969) conducted the most careful study of education's effect on intelligence and aging. He gave intelligence tests to four age groups — with subjects ranging from age 25 to 64 — and controlled for education. He found that before controlling for age, the groups showed the classic aging pattern — Verbal scores stayed stable, while Performance scores and Full (or total) scores declined. When he controlled for education, he found that Verbal skills rose with age and Performance skills (except for the Digit Symbol test) remained stable. The Full WAIS–R also stayed stable. This study suggests that cohort differences in intelligence scores may be due to educational differences between group members. Birren and Morrison (1961), describing the effects of education on IQ in old age, say that statistically education explains as much of a person's general intelligence score on the WAIS–R as do any of the eleven subtests that measure specific abilities. Future cohorts of older people, with higher levels of education, may show little or no difference compared to younger people in intelligence scores on crystallized intelligence tests.

Improvements in Cognitive Functioning in Later Life

Some of the latest research on intelligence explores ways to improve older people's intellectual functioning. This research shows that older people can improve their performance on intelligence tests. Instruction in test-taking methods and problem-solving strategies, for example, can improve the cognitive performance of older subjects (Labouvie-Vief 1977; Baltes and Willis 1981; Denney and Palmer 1981). Some of these studies (Sanders and Sanders 1978) show long-term effects. After one year Sanders and Sanders (1978) found that trained subjects performed better than untrained subjects or subjects who simply practised the similar problems. Still, these studies show that "the old, like the young, have more potential than is typically measured by the tests" (Botwinick 1984, 271).

Summary

Studies show that people who have good health and who live in a challenging environment score better on intelligence tests than those who do not (Schaie 1975). People who read books and newspapers and who travel and talk with friends keep their minds fresh. Researchers now think of the individual as modifiable. Baltes and Willis (1982, 120–21) conclude that "people can learn to make better use of their minds at any age. The logical approach [to observed decrements in mental functioning in later life] might be the development of compensatory education programs at about the time of retirement ... ." Chapter 12, on education, will discuss some of these programs in detail.

Creativity

The large body of psychological research on memory and intelligence focuses on decline in psychological functioning with age. But comparatively few studies have looked at creativity in later life. At least three different measures of creativity exist in the literature (Botwinick 1984). First, some studies measure creative achievement by evaluating the greatness of a work or by counting the number of creative works by an individual. Second, some studies use psychological tests to measure creativity. These tests take place in the laboratory. They allow for comparisons of old and young people on a number of test dimensions. Third, some studies use a more global definition of creativity. They define creative activity as activity that brings fulfilment to the individual and possibly even to others (though it might not reach world-historical importance). Studies done from each point of view have looked at whether creativity declines with age.

Exhibit 5.3

CAN OLDER PEOPLE
BE CREATIVE?

Henry Wadsworth Longfellow thought so. His poem *Morituri Salutamus* salutes creative older people of the past.

> Cato learned Greek at eighty; Sophocles
> Wrote his grand Oedipus, and Simonides
> Bore off the prize of verse from his compeers,
> When each had numbered more than four score years.
> And Theophrastus, at four score and ten,
> Had just begun his *Characters of Men.*
> Chaucer, at Woodstock with the nightingales,
> At sixty wrote the Canterbury Tales;
> Goethe at Weimar, toiling to the last,
> Completed Faust when eighty years were past.

Creativity as Measured by Great Work

Lehman (1953) studied the ages at which scientists, philosophers, mathematicians, painters, inventors, and other creative people produced their greatest works. He selected for his sample people who had already died (because someone still alive could still produce a great work). Lehman found that past and present scientists produced their greatest creative work between the ages of 30 and 40. Most great writers produced their greatest works before the age of 45, with most poets producing their greatest works in their late 20s and early 30s. Painters peaked between ages 30 and 45. In most fields Lehman found that achievement steadily decreased after age 45.

Lehman (1968) went on to study athletes, chess champions, orators, politicians, businessmen, and atomic scientists. He found that still-living atomic scientists, for example, showed a peak in achievement between ages 25 to 29 and a sharp drop in achievement from age 35 on. He also found that older atomic scientists (aged 60 to 64) made only one-tenth the number of contributions as the younger (25- to 29-year-old) scientists. Lehman found the same pattern for still-living astronomers, mathematicians, and botanists.

Lehman's research set off a wave of controversy. Dennis (1968), for example, challenged Lehman's conclusions about the decline in creativity with age. First, he said, Lehman's research combined people with different lengths of life. Fewer people live to old age, so there will be fewer people to create great works in later life. Lehman's findings might reflect a demographic fact of life rather than a decline in creativity. Second, Dennis questioned Lehman's approach to the study of creativity. Lehman used the works of critics, historians, and experts to decide on the quality of his subjects' work. Dennis argued that experts may favour the early, groundbreaking work of great people. Experts may also find it harder to judge more recent work by a great master.

Dennis (1968) conducted his own research on creativity. He used a measure different from Lehman's to compensate for these errors. First, while Lehman studied the age when creators produced their *greatest work*, Dennis studied the *creative output* (the number of works produced) of 738 people. Second, he selected long-lived subjects to control for the effects of mixed longevities. All of the people in his study had lived past age 78.

Dennis measured the output of people in a variety of disciplines — artists, scientists, scholars, dancers. He found that each group produced the least amount of work in their 20s. In almost all fields, creativity (measured by output) peaked between ages 40 and 49 (about a decade later than Lehman's finding). Dennis, like Lehman, found that people in different fields peaked at different ages. Artists (dramatists, librettists, architects) peaked earliest and showed the sharpest decline in their 70s. Dennis found that scientists also decline in middle age, but they showed a sharp decline only after age 60. Scholars showed little decline with age. They produced as much in their 70s as in their 40s, and they added to their former number of books by 25 percent between ages 70 and 79.

Dennis's (1968) research findings differ from Lehman's in the following ways. First, Dennis found that creativity peaked in middle life for many people, but this peak came later than Lehman's research showed. Second, he found a less dramatic decline with age than did Lehman. Third, he found that some creative people show little or no decline in creative output with age.

Dennis's work expands rather than contradicts Lehman's. Dennis shows

Exhibit 5.4

PORTRAITS OF THREE CREATIVE OLDER CANADIANS

Barker Fairley

Barker Fairley began teaching German at the University of Toronto in 1915. He wrote a book of poems and five books on Goethe during his academic career. When he retired he turned to painting for creative fulfilment. A biography of Fairley by Hubert de Santana in *Today* magazine describes his career as a painter.

He remembers vividly the day he took up painting. "I was in my 45th year and had never made a drawing in my life. My friend, the painter and poet Robert Finch, said that I ought to paint and arranged for us to go on a field trip the following day. I was reluctant and said to my wife, 'I hope it rains tomorrow.' It didn't rain, and we went out and painted, and I did a little watercolor which has the characteristics of my later work. It was all there immediately."

For lack of encouragement Fairley stopped painting for 10 years.

He began again in his 60s and has painted ever since. His shows now sell out and the cost of his paintings rose from a few hundred to a few thousand dollars in the three years since he turned 90 (he was 93 in 1980). How does he sum up his long and extraordinary life? ... "Like Goethe, I never toed the line professionally or in any way. I followed my nose, I remained a lover, a *Liebhaber*, in that sense an amateur. I just did what I chose and liked from first to last."

Hubert Evans

Edith Iglauer, Hubert Evans's friend and neighbour, wrote a short biographical sketch about him in 1980. He was 88 at the time. Hubert Evans wrote "more than 200 published short stories, 60 serials, 12 radio plays for the CBC and seven books of fiction" from the 1920s to 1954. When his wife died he stopped writing from 1960 to 1976. Then "... he broke the long silence ... to produce two new volumes of poetry — *Whittlings* and *Endings*. The poems were so well received — Margaret Laurence, the writer, has called them 'sheer wisdom in a lunatic age' — that Evans, regaining confidence, completed a novel that had been simmering on what he refers to as 'the back burner' for almost 50 years. *O Time in Your Flight*, published [in 1979], was acclaimed across the country ..."

" 'People are going back to what they can read and enjoy,' [he says], 'but I am writing to please myself and nobody else. I love my subject, and I like writing. I've got this thing about writers being creative people, that creativity came in a package the night I was conceived. Maybe it was something my mother had for supper. If writers don't write, they'll be like the adipose fin on the salmon. At one time it was quite a big thing, but the salmon didn't use it, and now it's no bloody good to him.' "

Elisabeth Hopkins

Elisabeth Hopkins held her first painting exhibition at age 80. Ann Rhodes described Ms. Hopkins's career and life in a feature for *Chatelaine*.

Her first exhibition was held when she was 80. Today her paintings sell for up to $1,150. She still lives alone, as she always has. She [was] 89 in April [1983]. ... Painting had been a purely private pleasure until, in her mid-70s, she suggested to a Galiano [B.C.] gift-shop owner that her greeting cards might sell for a nickel apiece. For a full-size painting her price was $5, the sum paid for one that came to the attention of the Bau-Xi Gallery in Vancouver, which has shown her work ever since. ...

"Sometimes," [she says], "I've no idea what I'm going to do. The animals and the flowers just appear. I think you might say it is a joy to me." There's joy too in the letters and visits from admirers of her work. ...

Pinned up in Elisabeth Hopkins's home is a cartoon clipped from *The New Yorker*. It shows two older women, one clearly weighed down by her years, the other sprightly. The line reads: "Well, I tried old age, but it wasn't my cup of tea."

Sources: Edith Iglauer, "The Unsinkable Hubert Evans," *Today Magazine*, December 20, 1980: 16–18; Hubert de Santana, "Portrait of the Artist as an Old Man," *Today Magazine*, November 29, 1980: 12–14; Ann Rhodes, "Five Women Who Defy the Stereotypes of Aging," *Chatelaine*, February 1983, 57 and 166. By permission of the author.

that differences in the peak age of creativity may depend as much on the social structure of a discipline as it does on a creative person's age. Scholars, for example, reach a peak later than artists and stay productive longer. Dennis explains that the arts depend more on individual creativity. An artist's output declines if he or she loses strength or gets sick. Think of a dancer who injures his or her back or strains a knee. Dancers (and athletes) peak early in their work, and they retire early because of the wear on their bodies. Scholars and scientists can get younger colleagues (like graduate students) to help them with their work. They can stay productive even if their strength declines (Dennis 1968).

Later studies by Simonton (1977) on great composers partly supported the idea that creativity declines with age. Simonton found that total productivity peaked between ages 45 and 49 and then declined. Total themes (musical ideas) in composers' works also decreased after ages 30 to 34, though they did not decrease to a point below the totals of the composer's younger years. Studies of Nobel Prize winners (Zuckerman 1977) and high-level chess players (Elo 1965) also report peaks in creativity for people in their mid-30s.

Why does creativity decline with age? A decline in health, a decrease in energy, changes in a profession, and different goals and motivations later in life all lead to some decline in creative output as a person ages. But not all people show a decline in creativity as they age. Sophocles, Michelangelo, Goethe, Picasso, Winston Churchill, Grandma Moses, and Georgia O'Keeffe, to name only a few great individuals, all remained creative past the age of 80. Lehman, for example, reported many cases of creativity in old age. He found that 20 percent of still-living atomic physicists made contributions to their field after age 65 (1968, 100).

Lehman might argue that most of these people had created their greatest works at younger ages. Still, they continued to contribute to society and culture as they aged. And some types of creativity, like comprehensive historical studies, may be possible only in old age. It may take a great historian a lifetime to amass the knowledge and gain the perspective needed to make a great contribution.

Pressey and Pressey (1967) argue that the contributions great older people make may have a more global impact than the narrow creative contributions of these same people in their youth. These contributions may look less exciting than a breakthrough in science or art by the same person earlier in life, but Pressey and Pressey say that people in their later years bring experience, wisdom, and a concern for humanity to their work. These virtues get overlooked in discussions of quantity and quality of creative works.

Creativity as Measured by Psychological Tests

Lehman (1953; 1968), Dennis (1968), and Pressey and Pressey (1967) studied unique groups of people — people famous enough to have their work noted in history. But what about "average" people? Does creativity change with age? Studies of average people often rely on psychological tests of creativity. These tests suffer from the same problems as tests of memory and intelligence because they measure educational background and test-taking ability as much as creativity. Like memory and intelligence studies, many creativity studies show a decline in test scores with age.

Bromley (1956) studied 156 men and women aged 17–82 and found a decline in creative thinking with age. He controlled for intelligence and still found that creativity declined with age. Bromley found that the youngest group, with a mean age of 27, showed the highest quality and quantity of creative response. Alpaugh and Birren (1977) found the same trend in a study of 111 working and retired teachers aged 20–83. They found a decline in creativity starting around age 25 on one test and between ages 30 and 40 on another test.

A recent study by Jacquish and Ripple (1981) found a less clear decline in creativity with age. They studied 218 men and women 18–84 years old. They found that the oldest group (61–84) had lower fluency and flexibility scores, but scored as well as the youngest group (18–25) on originality. The middle group (40–60) scored best on all measures.

A recent study by Crosson and Robertson-Tchabo (1983) compared two groups of women. One group included 271 women artists and writers aged 23–87. A second group included 76 women aged 26–74 with no career in the creative arts. The study found that the non-creative career subjects over 60 years old scored significantly lower than the non-creative career people under age 50. But the study found no significant correlation between age and creativity in the creative group. Crosson and Robertson-Tchabo suggest that continued creative work may help a person stay creative longer.

Creativity as Personal Expression

Creativity can refer to a great achievement, a test score, or a form of personal expression. This last perspective treats creativity as a source of individual satisfaction regardless of how other people judge the works produced.

Kenneth Koch, a professional poet and teacher, reports on the value of creative expression for personal well-being. Koch agreed to teach poetry writing to twenty-five people in a nursing home in New York City. He reports that on the first day the people looked "old, sick, tired, uncomfortable. Some seemed to be asleep or almost so" (1982, 210). Other people in the class gazed around the room or showed signs of pain. Koch began with a collaborative poem, one where each person in the group contributes a line. In this case he asked each person to contribute a line about their childhood. Some people refused to contribute, but most did, and Koch put their lines together into a poem. He reports that the group members became "excited at the unaccustomed pleasure of hearing what they said read aloud, and excited at hearing it admired by me and by other students" (1982, 211). Koch (1977) eventually collected these poems in a book titled *I Never Told Anybody*. These poems represent the first formal creative works produced by these people. But it only hints at the joy that poetry writing brought to their lives. Koch's (1977) report shows that older people often lack an opportunity to express themselves creatively. Older people may show low creativity scores partly because they have little chance to use their creative talents.

Crosson and Robertson-Tchabo (1983) support this view. Based on their research, they say that more opportunity to express their creativity would lead to more creativity in older people. Butler (1974) says that today older people have to become *autodidacts* — self-teachers. These kinds of people take charge of their own learning, they transform their world in response to their own concerns, and in the process they create something new. This view of creativity makes later life a time of potential discovery and self-renewal rather than a time of decline.

PSYCHOLOGICAL DISORDERS: ABNORMAL AGING

Studies of memory, intelligence, and creativity describe the normal changes that come with aging, but some people show abnormal changes as they age. They may suffer from psychological problems such as paranoia, anxiety neuroses, and schizophrenia. Experts call these *functional disorders* because they interfere with how a person functions. These problems have no clear organic cause, and some older people have suffered with them throughout their lives. Other people suffer from *organic disorders*, diseases of the brain such as Alzheimer's disease, Parkinson's disease, or stroke. All of these illnesses arise from a deterioration of the brain.

Organic Brain Disorders

Organic brain syndrome, senile dementia, or dementia are general terms used to describe a variety of organic brain disorders. Organic disorders lead to confusion, forgetfulness, and sometimes anti-social behaviour. Some demented individuals wander, strike out, or resist help from their caregivers. Dementia cases create stress for both professional care providers and family caregivers.

Hendricks and Hendricks (1986, 238) report that 4–6 percent of the young-old (aged 65–84) suffer from organic brain disorder, but that 20 percent of people 85 + suffer from these illnesses. Canadian studies say that dementing illnesses will show up in greater number as more people live into late old age. "Those managing to stay on till well beyond 85 will form a group with very much higher than average risk of severe dementia (i.e. a prevalence rate in the neighborhood of 25 percent)" (Stone 1986, 31). A study by Robertson, Rockwood, and Stolee (1982) in Saskatchewan supports this estimate. They found moderate to severe dementia in 2.4 percent of people aged 65–69, but 29.9 percent dementia in the 85 and over group. Nursing homes and hospitals in the future will have to care for more and more demented patients. The increased numbers of dementia cases in the future will make care for these people a major challenge for the health care system.

A number of brain disorders can cause dementia, including multi-infarct dementia (dementia due to a series of strokes), Parkinson's disease (a degeneration of the brain stem), and Alzheimer's disease (a degeneration of the parietal-temporal cortex). Alzheimer's disease is the most common form of dementia. A look at this illness will show some of the characteristics of these organic diseases.

Alzheimer's Disease: A Case Study of Organic Disorder

Health and Welfare Canada (1984) reports that 100,000 to 300,000 Canadians suffer from Alzheimer's disease, and more than 10,000 people die from the disease each year. Until a few years ago few people knew about Alzheimer's disease. Experts called it "pre-senile dementia" — a disease of middle age. Often doctors diagnosed the disease as hardening of the arteries, and for many years experts thought that the signs of Alzheimer's disease — forgetfulness, bizarre behaviour, incontinence — came as a normal part of aging. Today researchers know that Alzheimer's is not a normal part of aging. Alzheimer's disease ranks as the fourth or fifth most common cause of death in Canada, after cancer, heart disease, and stroke.

Two types of lesions (abnormal structures) in the cerebral cortex or outer layer of the brain define Alzheimer's disease. The first type of lesion is called "tangles" because the white nerve cell fibres look like twisted bits of thread. The second type of lesion is called "neuritic plaque" — bits of degenerated nerve cells gathered around a fibrous core (Leroux 1981; Butler and Emr 1982). Amyloid, a protein not normally found in the brain, forms these plaques (Health and Welfare Canada 1984). One neuropathologist describes plaques as "mothholes in fabric ... if you were inside an Alzheimer brain, it would look like someone had been loose with a shotgun in there, but really it's more akin to someone taking a hatchet to telephone cables. The flow of information around inside the brain is disrupted" (Leroux 1981).

Both tangles and plaques show up in healthy older brains, but Alzheimer's patients have more of them. Research shows that the more plaques and tangles there are, the more memory loss and mental decline will occur. The older the person, the greater the chance of getting Alzheimer's disease. It shows up in 2 to 3 percent of people over age 60 and in more than 20 percent of people over 80. One estimate says that 60–70 percent of nursing home patients have some degree of Alzheimer's.

No one knows the cause of Alzheimer's disease, but researchers have found a number of clues about the disease's origins. One line of research suggests a genetic cause. Health and Welfare Canada (1984) reports that family members have a one in six chance of getting the disease if a parent has had Alzheimer's and a one in twelve chance if a brother or sister has had the disease. Heredity may increase a person's chance of getting the disease, but the fact that family members share a common environment may also play a role.

Another line of research has studied the chemistry of the brain for clues to the disease's origins. Researchers have found ten to thirty times the normal amounts of aluminum salts in parts of the brain with Alzheimer's lesions. Aluminum salts injected into rabbits or cats leads to neurofibrillary tangles common in Alzheimer's. Researchers at the University of Toronto have shown that tangles appear when aluminum levels reach those found in Alzheimer's patients (Wurtman 1985).

Other researchers have found low levels (as little as 10 percent of the amount found in normal brains) of the enzyme choline acetyltransferase (CAT) in the hippocampus and cerebral cortex of Alzheimer's patients. The loss of CAT results from the loss of cholinergic or acetylcholine-releasing nerve terminals in these parts of the brain (Wurtman 1985).

Exhibit 5.5

THE STAGES OF DECLINE DUE TO ALZHEIMER'S DISEASE

Health and Welfare Canada (1984) describes three stages that an Alzheimer's patient goes through. Some people may go through these stages in a few months; others may take years. The changes that come with Alzheimer's disease begin slowly. Often family members recognize the first signs only when they look back over a year or two of caregiving.

Stage I: A person first shows changes in memory. They forget their keys or their wallet. They may also forget recent events or forget that they did a job around the house. This gets worse in time. The person forgets more often, takes longer to do simple jobs, or begins to recheck work already done.

One woman recalls that her husband, an engineering professor, would spend three or four hours writing a fifty-minute lecture that used to take him an hour to write. Another woman recalls that she first thought her husband, a physician, was ill when he lost his way home from work one night. He planned to stop at a patient's house for a short house call around 5:00 P.M. The patient lived only a few blocks from their house, so his wife expected him home around six. She began to worry at eight o'clock when she still hadn't heard from him. An hour later he came in exhausted. He had spent the last three hours driving around their neighbourhood looking for their house.

Stage II: The second stage of the disease includes more memory de-cline, loss of speaking ability, and an end to normal daily activity. The ill person may wander at night, lose control of his or her bowel and bladder, and threaten others. One woman left a knife in her garden after she used it to weed the flower bed. Her husband picked it up and stalked through the bushes into a neighbour's yard, saying to the neighbour, "I'm going to kill you." The neighbour ran inside and called the police. When the sick man's wife came outside to finish weeding, she found the police wrestling her husband into a squad car.

In another case a man walked into a new car dealer and signed a contract for a $20,000 car. His wife found out only after the salesman called her to check on the financing. The owner of the dealership agreed to void the contract, but only after she pleaded and explained about her husband's illness.

This stage of the disease can put stress on the family. Caregivers — most often spouses or children of the ill person — can feel tense, trapped, and exhausted. Members have to take on new roles — wives become chauffeurs or nurses, children become parents or police, husbands become homemakers (Novak and Guest 1985). Mace and Rabins (1981, 63) report one case of a burdened husband who had to bathe his wife. "She screams for help the whole time I am bathing her. She'll open the windows and yell, 'Help, I'm being robbed.' " One man confessed to

Mace and Rabins (1981, 179), "There was a time when I considered getting a gun, killing my wife, and then killing myself ... ."

Stage III: The person in the last stage of Alzheimer's disease needs institutionalization and often twenty-four-hour nursing care. The person can no longer speak or communicate. They may wander or move constantly unless restrained. Seizures may occur. Death occurs between two and nineteen years after the disease starts (Health and Welfare Canada 1984). Because diagnosis often comes late, Alzheimer's victims sometimes live only five to eight years after diagnosis. Death often comes from an illness like pneumonia or heart disease. Death certificates rarely mention Alzheimer's disease as a cause of death. This makes it impossible to know the exact number of deaths caused by Alzheimer's.

Not all Alzheimer's patients show all these symptoms. Some show other symptoms of confusion like depression and crying. But these stages give a general picture of the disease. They also give only a faint idea of the stress that Alzheimer's disease puts on the primary caregiver.

Some studies have used lecithin (a food rich in choline) to increase CAT in Alzheimer's patients, but with little success.

None of the research so far has produced a method to treat Alzheimer's disease. Physicians cannot even make a certain diagnosis of the disease. A doctor can only rule out other causes of confusion and personality decline like brain tumours, blood pressure problems, or hyperthyroidism. Doctors have to rule out dozens of other illnesses before they can label the illness Alzheimer's. Caution prevents doctors from diagnosing Alzheimer's when a person might have a treatable illness or a problem like overmedication or infection. The inability to diagnose Alzheimer's quickly leaves families in limbo and forces patients to go through dozens of tests.

The absence of a cure for Alzheimer's disease or a way to arrest its progress leads to many years of declining function, stress on family caregivers, and, in the end, institutionalization.

Organic disorders pose problems for the diseased individuals and for their families. They also pose problems for health care workers, social service workers, and public housing managers. Service workers will care for more and more clients with these illnesses in the coming years. They will need to understand the basis of the illness and how to treat these clients.

Functional Disorders

Functional disorders disrupt normal life. They include emotional upset, depression, and anxiety. Hendricks and Hendricks (1986) say that 25–60 percent of older people in and out of institutions in the U.S. report mental distress and that 10–15 percent have emotional problems that need mental health attention.

The Canada Health Survey (Health and Welfare Canada and Statistics Canada 1981) asked a sample of more than 23,000 people from all over Canada to report health problems they had. The study found that compared to the population 15–64, people 65 and over had more than two and a half times the rate of self-reported mental disorder (12.3 percent of 65 and over compared to 4.5 percent of people 15–64), and that older women reported mental disorders at almost twice the rate of older men (15.4 percent of women 65 and over compared to 8.5 percent of men).

The Canada Health Survey found that the proportion of an age group reporting frequent symptoms of anxiety and depression goes up slightly throughout adulthood. More than 4 percent of males 65 and over and nearly 8 percent of females 65 and over (7.7 percent) report frequent symptoms of anxiety and depression. This comes to slightly more than the proportion of males and females 45–64 who report these problems (3.8 percent for males and 6.9 percent for females). But more than 9 percent of the older group did not respond to this question, two to three times higher a proportion of "unknowns" than the 45–64 age group. Health and Welfare Canada and Statistics Canada (1981) estimate that these unknowns would probably add to the proportion of older people feeling distress. Including the unknowns, the distressed group comes to 14–17 percent of people 65 and over. This fits with other studies in the U. S. that put the percentage of depressed elderly at 13–15 percent (Gurland and Toner 1983; Murrell, Himmelfarb, and Wright 1983).

Anxiety may contribute more than depression to the increased proportion of distress in older age groups, because not all studies agree that depression increases with age. Hirshfield and Cross (1982), for example, reviewed the research on depression and found that young adults had the highest incidence of this problem. A Canadian study by Chappell and Barnes (1982) found that the amount of depression in the population goes down as age increases.

This does not mean that policy makers and health care professionals can ignore depression in old age. A close look at the findings on mental well-being show that some people stand a greater chance of anxiety and depression than others in old age. Research shows that anxiety, depression, and unhappiness depend on a person's health and social life and not just on their age. The "unhappy" Canadian, the Canada Health Survey reports, is likely to be old, female, widowed, low-income, in poor health, and with not much education (Health and Welfare Canada and Statistics Canada 1981). The inability to get out and the loss of social supports can also lead to unhappiness or depression. This puts the mental health of many infirm older Canadians at risk.

Treatment and Intervention

Butler (1975) says that often mental health experts ignore the needs of older people. Most psychiatrists, he says, like to treat young, well-educated, successful people. A study by Gibson (1970) found that many

Exhibit 5.6

PET THERAPY

One of the newest forms of therapy — pet therapy — offers older people companionship and relief from loneliness. Some experts say it can lead to better health and longer life.

A year ago Dolores Kohler, 36, an Edmonton housewife and long-time SPCA volunteer, pioneered the city's first "visitation program" by loading her part-Husky, Max, and her two cats, Snow Prince and Cricket, into her station wagon and driving them over to the Venta Nursing Home. That visit, and each of her subsequent monthly visits to the home, were a resounding success. The old folks, says Venta recreation director June Berrisford, "brighten up the minute Dolores walks in the room. They look forward to her coming — it's a big day." Last month, Elva McCartney, the SPCA's education director, decided to expand the program, taking on six more pet owners and scheduling three more homes for regular visits.

Such success, however, is hardly news to Calgary's Humane Society (SPCA), which started a similar program two years ago and now has about 170 volunteers leading more than 200 cats and dogs through nine institutions for the elderly on a regular basis. Pet therapy is booming, according to Calgary program chairman Wendy Betts, 43, for one simple reason: "Animals give patients something to live for." ...

Besides providing elderly widows, widowers and invalids with uncritical friends, says Calgary program director Betts, such visits can also have concrete medical benefits, such as the temporary relief of minor aches and pains. As well, recent studies have shown that talking to an animal, petting one, or even just staring into an aquarium can be sufficiently strong an emotional outlet to reduce blood pressure. At a 1982 symposium on pet therapy in Toronto, Dr. Aaron Katcher, an associate professor of psychiatry at the University of Pennsylvania, revealed that of 93 victims of coronary disease surveyed in a Philadelphia hospital, there were 3 percent fewer deaths among those who went home to pets. "Considering the number of people that suffer coronary disease," observed Dr. Katcher, "a 3% improvement in the survival rate can mean a significant contribution to the nation's health."

Source: Gail Herchak and Brian Wilford, "The Therapy of Pets," *Alberta Report*, November 28, 1983. Reprinted with permission of the publisher.

psychiatrists believe that older people will not improve from therapy. Studies also show that community clinics and therapists in private practice see only a small number of older people (Eisdorfer 1972; Butler 1975). A study in Alberta found that in 1980–81, with 7.5 percent of the

Alberta population over age 65, older people made up only 3.9 percent of cases in community mental health clinics (Alberta Senior Citizens Bureau 1982). The report does not say why so few older people come to clinics for help. Transportation problems, lack of familiarity with psychotherapy, or the stigma of visiting a clinic may keep older people away. Alternatively, older people may prefer other methods for coping with their problems. Still, these figures point to a potential unmet need among older people for professional psychological help.

A whole range of treatments can help older people cope with psychological problems. Chemical therapies exist to treat some reversible organic brain syndromes. Physicians can treat alcoholics in the early stages of Wernicke-Korsakoff's dementia — a neurological disease — with large doses of thiamine. Many more therapies exist for older people with functional problems — problems related to a person's personality or social life. Drug therapy can help older people cope with functional problems like depression, psychotherapy can help a person with a personality disorder, and milieu therapy can help a person to change their environment. New programs for older people with psychological disorders (LeBlanc 1985) will offer older people more options for treatment in the future. Some of these alternatives will need to take forms — such as day centres or hospital adult day care programs — that older people feel comfortable using.

CONCLUSION

Psychological well-being means more than coping with problems, stress, and loss. It means growth, learning, and a sense of purpose. The research on the psychology of aging shows that older people in good health stay alert, intelligent, and able to learn. They face stresses unique to later life, but they can get through these crises themselves or with the help of others. Sometimes the biggest block to older people's well-being comes from the prejudices and stereotypes other people have about old age. The research on the psychology of aging has begun to remove the basis for these stereotypes. More research and knowledge about old age and new cohorts of older people will teach us more about mental potential in later life.

SUMMARY

1. Early research supported the myth that intellectual ability declines with age, but more recent research questions these findings.
2. Studies show that younger people do perform better than older people on some memory and intelligence tests, but the pace of testing, the types of questions asked, and the way older people learn can all decrease their performance.
3. Early studies used cross-sectional methods to study the effects of aging on intelligence. The results confused cohort differences with age

changes. Longitudinal methods show declines in fluid intelligence (problem-solving skills). But they show little change and possibly some increase in crystallized intelligence (skills based on acquired knowledge).

4. The abilities to encode, search for, and retrieve information all decline with age. But older people may not try hard on tests because they see them as meaningless. This decreases their motivation and lowers their performance. Tests that study knowledge actualization show that older people learn and use information as well as younger people in everyday life.

5. Research shows that older people can improve their scores on intelligence tests through training.

6. Studies of both the quality and quantity of creative production show a decline in creativity with age. Comparisons of older and younger people on psychological tests also find greater creativity among younger subjects. Both of these approaches to the study of creativity emphasize the products of creative work. Reports of subjective creative development show that people can create and learn to create at any age. Education, opportunity, and an interest in a subject can all lead to increased creativity in later life.

7. The number of cases of organic brain disorders like Alzheimer's disease will increase as more people live to late old age. These disorders place a heavy burden on families, and the people with these diseases often need professional health care support at the end of their lives.

8. Functional mental disorders (e.g., anxiety and depression) show up less often than most people expect. Older people with these problems can benefit from drug therapies, psychotherapy, or milieu therapy.

9. The research on the psychology of aging presents a balanced view of aging. Some mental faculties may decline, but others remain stable as long as a person is in good health. More research and knowledge about old age will teach us more about mental potential in later life.

SELECTED READINGS

Baltes, P.B., and K.W. Schaie. "The Myth of the Twilight Years." In *Readings in Aging and Death: Contemporary Perspectives*, 2nd ed., ed. Steven H. Zarit. New York: Harper and Row, 1982.
This essay shows how longitudinal research has changed the way psychologists think about intelligence in later life. The authors summarize the main findings in a few easy-to-read pages.

Health and Welfare Canada. *Alzheimer's Disease: A Family Information Handbook.* Ottawa: Minister of Supply and Services, 1984.
A good basic review of Alzheimer's disease — what it is, how it affects victims and their families, and what families can do to get help.

Hultsch, David F., and Francine Deutsch. *Adult Development and Aging: A Life-Span Perspective.* New York: McGraw Hill, 1981.
A good summary of the research on memory and intelligence. Readable and filled with sources to follow up.

THE SOCIAL PSYCHOLOGY OF AGING

INTRODUCTION

What is a good old age? This question has guided research in the social psychology of aging for more than fifty years. Researchers have found that many patterns of good aging exist. Here are three cases that show the variety of forms a good old age can take.

Joe Willis, 70, worked as an engineer for an oil company until he retired in 1975. Now he spends January and February playing golf in Florida, and he spends the summer at his cottage in the Muskokas. His company calls him back two or three times a year as a consultant, he serves on the Board of Directors of a senior centre, and he volunteers as a nursing home visitor. "I visit the old folks once a week," he says. "At Christmas I take them to a show or out shopping." Joe does not see himself as old. He works less now and has more leisure time, but he feels the same as before he retired. He stays active and involved, and has found new ways to give meaning to his life.

Birdie Caldwell's husband died fifteen years ago. She moved out of their house and into a two-bedroom apartment a year after his death. She also went back to work as a secretary — work she had not done since her teens. Now, at age 65, she still lives on her own. She has two daughters who live less than an hour away by car. She visits them a few times a month and sometimes stays for the weekend. She travels, belongs to a bridge group, and enjoys her freedom.

Rose, 73, also lives by herself in her own apartment. Her husband died three years ago. She has a bad case of arthritis in her legs which keeps her indoors most of the year. On warm days she walks a few blocks to the local shopping centre. Most of the time she watches TV, knits, or talks to friends on the phone.

Rose feels content and happy in her old age. She sometimes talks to ten or fifteen friends or relatives in a week. Nieces and nephews call her from all over the country on her birthday or on holidays, her daughter lives two and a half hours away by car, and her son lives across the country. She has five grandchildren; their pictures fill her walls and table tops.

Three different portraits of old age. Birdie stayed active; Rose lives a quiet life without social demands; Joe found new roles to replace ones that he had lost. Each of these people show a different response to the challenges of aging, but they all report high life-satisfaction. These cases show only a few of the patterns of successful aging today.

This chapter will look at: (1) how personality changes as a person ages, (2) how social structures influence a person's development, and (3) how older people can overcome some of the problems they face in society today. The chapter ends with a discussion of good aging.

PERSONALITY DEVELOPMENT

Psychologists who study the individual in society focus on personality development. A number of researchers describe this development as a series of stages. Erik Erikson (1963) has created one of the best-known stage models of the life cycle. He calls his model the "Eight Ages of Man." His model describes eight stages of ego development. At each stage, he says, the person faces a crisis with two possible outcomes. If a person gets through the crisis successfully, growth comes about, and the person reaches a new stage of development. If not, the person experiences some psycho-pathology that inhibits further development.

Erikson (1959) describes five stages that occur during childhood and youth, and he devotes the last three stages of his model to adult life (see Exhibit 6.1). These adult stages correspond roughly to early, middle, and late adulthood. Each stage offers the person a specific challenge. The

---

Exhibit 6.1

ERIKSON'S STAGES OF EGO DEVELOPMENT

Childhood Stages
Stage 1:   Basic Trust vs. Mistrust
Stage 2:   Autonomy vs. Shame, Doubt
Stage 3:   Initiative vs. Guilt
Stage 4:   Industry vs. Inferiority

Adolescence
Stage 5:   Identity vs. Role Confusion

Adulthood
Stage 6:   Intimacy vs. Isolation
Stage 7:   Generativity vs. Stagnation
Stage 8:   Ego Integrity vs. Despair

Source: Adapted from Erik Erikson, *Childhood and Society*, 2nd ed. (New York: W.W. Norton, 1963).

---

sixth stage, Intimacy vs. Isolation, requires a specific task, "to lose and find oneself in another" (Erikson 1959, Appendix). Love is the virtue of this stage: the young adult will marry or make some other permanent or semi-permanent bond with another person. The crisis of this stage focuses on the experience of "intimacy." If the person fails to achieve intimacy, then he or she will face "isolation."

The task of the middle adult years, Erikson says, is "to make be, to take care of" (1959, Appendix). Here the person's concern turns to what he calls "generativity" and its opposite, "stagnation." This includes the generation of products and ideas as well as having children (Erikson 1976, 7). This stage has its unique virtue: care for oneself, but also care for others and for the world as a whole. In mid-life the person becomes concerned with the "maintenance of the world" and with passing the culture on to the coming generations (Erikson 1976, 15, 27).

The task of late adulthood, Erikson says, is "to be, through having been: to face not being" (1959, Appendix). "Wisdom" is the virtue of this last stage; it comes when the person achieves "integrity" and overcomes the threat of "despair and disgust" (1959, 98). Like other psychoanalytic thinkers (Buhler 1951; Jung 1976), Erikson describes old age as a time of inwardness, a time for the person to reflect on the past and to bring

Exhibit 6.2

PECK'S STAGES OF PSYCHO-SOCIAL DEVELOPMENT

Middle Age

1. Valuing Wisdom vs. Valuing Physical Powers. After the late twenties a person needs to shift from dependence on physical power to the use of good judgment to get things done.
2. Socializing vs. Sexualizing in Human Relationships. With the climacteric (menopause), people learn to value one another for their personalities rather than their sexuality.
3. Cathectic Flexibility vs. Cathectic Impoverishment. Cathexis refers to emotional investment. When children grow up and move away or when a spouse dies, a person has to build new relationships.
4. Mental Flexibility vs. Mental Rigidity. A person can get closed-minded and rigid when they reach middle age. They have achieved some success, and they may feel they have the answers to life. A person needs to find new answers and to ask new questions at this time of life.

Old Age

5. Ego Differentiation vs. Work-Role Preoccupation. A person's career often defines their identity in middle life. Retirement forces a person to redefine who they are. This is a time for the expansion of activities and self-definition.
6. Body Transcendence vs. Body Preoccupation. Physical decline can lead to a preoccupation with the body and a sense of despair. Peck says that people can occupy themselves with pleasing relationships and activities.
7. Ego Transcendence vs. Ego Preoccupation. Death can threaten the meaning of a person's life as well as their physical existence. Death loses some of its sting when a person sees that their culture will go on and that future generations will benefit from what they have done.

Source: Robert Peck, "Psychological Developments in the Second Half of Life," in *Middle Age and Aging*, ed. Bernice L. Neugarten (Chicago: University of Chicago Press, 1968).

closure to life. At this point, he says, people with a healthy personality accept their life as the product of their own actions within a particular culture. This last stage sums up the seven earlier stages, and when a person achieves integrity, Erikson says, it brings a wholeness to life. A person who displays integrity inspires the young to trust in the culture and to follow its prescriptions for action (Erikson 1982, 63; Erikson 1963, 269). A number of studies support Erikson's model of adult stages. They find the same order of stages he describes, and they find that the stages follow one another as he predicts (Constantinople 1969; Boyd and Koskela 1970; Ciaccio 1971).

Some writers have expanded on Erikson's outline of middle and later life. Erikson began as a child psychologist, and his life cycle model reflects his interest in children. In his classic paper "Growth and Crises of the Healthy Personality" (1950), for example, he spends forty-five pages on the first twenty years of life. He devotes only five pages to the next fifty to sixty years. Peck ([1955] 1968) modified Erikson's model five years later, adding more stages to it.

Erikson's last stage, Peck said, "seems to be intended to represent in a global, nonspecific way all the psychological crises and crisis-solutions of the last forty or fifty years of life" ([1955] 1968, 88). Peck divided this last stage of life into two periods — middle and old age. He found seven crises a person had to overcome within these periods. At each stage the person gives up the narrow commitments — to the body, to people, to concepts, and finally to the self — that dominated earlier stages of life. Peck's work shows that middle and later life are complex and active periods of development.

Levinson (1978) and his co-workers at Yale also found more stages in mid-life than Erikson described. Levinson based his conclusion on the study of forty American men between the ages of 35 and 45. Ten men worked as executives, ten as hourly workers, ten as academic biologists, and ten as novelists. Levinson and his team conducted in-depth interviews over many weeks with each man.

Levinson (1978) found that a series of age-linked "shifts" took place for all these men in mid-life. He found that men alternate between stable, structure-building periods and transitional, structure-changing periods. Structure-building periods last six to eight years. During a structure-building period a man makes important choices and works to achieve specific goals. Transition periods last four to five years. During transition periods a man evaluates his present life structure, explores new possibilities, and makes choices that will move him toward a new structure. The move from home to university or from university to a first job, for example, takes place in the "early adult transition." A young man builds his first life structure as he enters the work world, gets married, and has children. Levinson described nine periods that men pass through between the ages of 17 and 65. Levinson could study only the stages up to the "Entering Middle Adulthood" period, because of his subjects' ages. He proposes that between ages 50 and 55 a man can modify the life structure set down in his forties. Then, between ages 55 and 60, a man settles into middle adulthood, and from age 60 to 65 he begins the transition into late adulthood. These later stages follow a pattern of breakdown and structure-building characteristic of early stages in life.

Levinson's (1978) study has some obvious drawbacks. First, he studied

Exhibit 6.3

LEVINSON'S DEVELOPMENTAL MODEL

Age	Period
17–22	EARLY ADULT TRANSITION
22–28	Entering the Adult World
28–33	Age 30 Transition
33–40	Settling Down
40–45	MID-LIFE TRANSITION
45–50	Entering Middle Adulthood
50–55	Age 50 Transition
55–60	Culmination of Middle Adulthood
60–65	LATE ADULT TRANSITION

The stages in capital letters refer to periods where a person ends a life structure and starts a new one. A person in one of these transitions appraises their present life, explores possible changes, and makes choices that lead to a new structure.

Source: Adapted from D. J. Levinson, *The Seasons of a Man's Life* (New York: Knopf, 1978).

only a small, homogeneous group of people (forty middle-class, white, male subjects) in a specific society (the United States) at a specific time in history (the 1970s). Only future work can say how well Levinson's model and his specific stages will apply to women, the poor, non-Anglo ethnic groups, other cultures, and other times in history.

Gould (1978) clinically observed and gave a questionnaire to 524 men and women between the ages of 16 and 50 years. He found, like Erikson, Peck, and Levinson, that people faced a series of predictable crises in adulthood. He also found that in order to grow to a new stage of development a person had to shed a "network" of false assumptions that they carried with them from childhood. "Adulthood *is not a plateau*," Gould (1978, 14) says, summing up his findings, "rather it is a dynamic and changing time for all of us."

These studies all propose that a stage model of development best describes middle and later life. But other studies question whether a set of universal stages exists. Surveys of large numbers of people, for example, have not found the stages these models predict. Lacy and Hendricks (1980), for example, looked for attitude changes predicted by Gould's work. They used data from a survey of over 9,000 people, but they could not find attitude shifts to support Gould's stages.

Braun and Sweet (1983–84) reviewed data from four large surveys to see if passages from one stage of life to another existed. They compared personality differences within and between age groups. They did find personality differences between age groups, but they found that in studies done at different times and in different countries (the U.S. and Canada) the characteristics of each age-stage differed. They also found that after a passage around age 19, little developmental change took place in people's attitudes as they aged. These data fail to support the stage model of adult development.

Butler (1975) has criticized the stage model of development for another reason. He challenges the idea that a person in old age can only accept who they are and what they have been. "People are locked in by such a theory," he says. They may look healthy from Erikson's point of view, but they suffer because they are trapped by their work, marriage, or lifestyle. "Excessive or exaggerated identity, seems clearly to be an obstacle to continued growth and development through life and to appreciation of the future. ... Human beings need the freedom to live with change, to invent and reinvent themselves a number of times throughout their lives" (Butler 1975, 400–401). Blau (1973, 185) warns that adults can "become *too well adjusted* to society's expectation and insufficiently attuned to their own nature and needs" in old age.

One of the newest perspectives in the social psychology of aging — the life-span developmental perspective — sees the individual as continually changing from birth to death (Baltes and Goulet 1970). Unlike stage models, it does not describe an end point or goal of development (like integrity or ego transcendence). Instead, the life-span developmental model treats crisis and change as a constant part of life. "At the very moment when completion seems to be achieved," Riegel (1976, 697) says, "new questions and doubts arise in the individual and in society." The life-span developmental model sees development as a dialectical process in which the individual changes in response to societal demands and society changes in response to individual action and adaptation (Riegel 1975). Life-span developmental theorists find many patterns and stages of aging. They say that different people have different personalities, use different coping styles, and have different resources to use in coping with the world. People live in different social classes and come from different cohorts. All of this creates varied patterns of aging. The life-span developmental model also turns the researchers' attention to the social context to explain the differences in the time of onset, direction, and duration of developmental stages (Novak 1985–86).

PERSONALITY AND SOCIAL CONTEXT

Life-span development researchers study three types of environmental effects: (1) non-normative events (unexpected events such as illnesses, layoffs, and accidents), (2) normative, history-graded events (historical events that shape a person's life, such as the Great Depression or World War II), and (3) normative age-graded events (socially sanctioned events that occur most often at a certain age like marriage or retirement) (Riegel 1975; Baltes, Cornelius, and Nesselroade 1979).

Non-Normative Events

Sociologists define *norms* as "shared rules or guidelines" that prescribe right behaviour under certain conditions (Ian Robertson 1981, 60). Every society has *age norms* that prescribe how a person of a certain age should act. University students, for example, can hitchhike across the country with backpacks each summer, travel to Europe with Eurail passes, and sleep in railway stations or open fields. People accept this behaviour from the young, and they even expect students to take time off to travel. Social gerontologists call this a normative life event.

People can also go through non-normative events, including accidents, sudden changes in health, or divorce. Social psychologists call them "non-normative" because society does not prescribe that everyone go through these events and because people cannot plan for them.

Non-normative life events or life crises — such as the death of a close friend, widowhood, or illness — can lead to shock and fear. Novak (1985) studied the response to life events in a sample of twenty-five healthy, middle-class, community-dwelling, older people in Winnipeg. These people all scored high on a standard test of self-actualization (a measure of personality development). Most of them had gone through at least one major non-normative life event — early retirement, loss of a spouse, or an illness.

Sometimes these events came about because a person felt an inner urge to change (one subject retired early so that he could devote himself to writing and to reading philosophy). Sometimes change came from outside: widowhood or illness forced a person to rethink their mid-life roles. Many of these subjects found the process of change painful and frightening.

Novak (1985) reports that these non-normative events took a common pattern. First, a person faced a problem or moment of crisis — a "challenge." These challenges included widowhood, early retirement, and illness. Second, they "accepted" the challenge. They interpreted the challenge as a demand for some response. Third, they responded to or "affirmed" their lives in spite of the challenge. This allowed them to enter a new phase of life beyond the roles and responsibilities of middle age.

These people were studied after they had passed through this life event. Did they succeed in affirming their lives because of their self-actualizing, integrated personalities, or did the life events they faced lead these people to a new integrated stage of adulthood? Studies of coping styles suggest that people bring their coping methods with them into later life (Lawton and Nahemow 1973; Lieberman 1975).

Exhibit 6.4

THE SOCIAL READJUSTMENT RATING SCALE

Holmes and Rahe (1967) published one of the best-known measures of life events — the Social Readjustment Rating Scale (SRRS). Their scale includes normative and non-normative life events. The scale gives the highest score (100) for "death of a spouse" and the lowest score (11) for "minor violations of the law." A high total score of events predicts a decrease in life-satisfaction and higher risk of illness (Chiriboga 1984). Researchers have used the scale with many age groups, including older people.

Here is the Holmes and Rahe scale with each item ranked and given its average Life Change Unit score.

Social Readjustment Rating Scale

Rank	Life Event	Mean Value
1	Death of spouse	100
2	Divorce	73
3	Marital separation	65
4	Jail term	63
5	Death of close family member	63
6	Personal injury or illness	53
7	Marriage	50
8	Fired at work	47
9	Marital reconciliation	45
10	Retirement	45
11	Change in health of family member	44
12	Pregnancy	40
13	Sex difficulties	39
14	Gain of new family member	39
15	Business readjustment	39
16	Change in financial state	38
17	Death of close friend	37
18	Change to different line of work	36
19	Change in number of arguments with spouse	35
20	Mortgage over $10,000	31
21	Foreclosure of mortgage or loan	30
22	Change in responsibilities at work	29

23	Son or daughter leaving home	29
24	Trouble with in-laws	29
25	Outstanding personal achievement	28
26	Wife beginning or stopping work	26
27	Beginning or end of school	26
28	Change in living condition	25
29	Revision of personal habits	24
30	Trouble with boss	23
31	Change in work hours or conditions	20
32	Change in residence	20
33	Change in schools	20
34	Change in recreation	19
35	Change in church activities	19
36	Change in social activities	18
37	Mortgage or loan less than $10,000	17
38	Change in sleeping habits	16
39	Change in number of family get-togethers	15
40	Change in eating habits	15
41	Vacation	13
42	Christmas	12
43	Minor violations of the law	11

Source: T. H. Holmes and R. H. Rahe, "The Social Readjustment Rating Scale," *Journal of Psychosomatic Research 11* (1967): 213–18.

History-Graded Events

Non-normative events describe sudden changes in a person's personal life, but history-graded events change the lives of many age cohorts. The term "cohort" describes a group of people born at the same point or within the same period (usually five or ten years) of time (Schaie 1968, 559; Marshall 1983, 52).

Older people who were between the ages of 75 and 85 in 1985, for example, were born between 1900 and 1910. These people share the experiences of two world wars and the Great Depression of the 1930s. If you talk to one of these people about their past, you will almost always hear stories about the Depression and the World Wars. These historic events left their mark on this cohort, shaping their family lives, their work lives, and their values.

Tindale (1980) studied a group of poor old men in a large Canadian city. Most of them lived through the Depression as teenagers, rode the rails as hobos, and picked tobacco or fruit for twenty-five cents an hour. They have little education and few family ties.

Their lives today show the effects of their past. "They were poor before the depression," Tindale says, "poorer still during it, and only a little less poor after it" (1980, 91). These men now live alone on government pensions. They eat and sleep in the downtown missions and Salvation Army shelters. They never had much, and they do not expect much now.

The cohort born between 1945 and 1955 (30- to 40-year-olds in 1985) expect different things from life and from society, based on their experiences. These people belong to one of the largest cohorts in Canadian history. Canada built elementary schools for these people when they were children in the 1950s and 1960s, universities for them in the 1960s and 1970s, and housing for them in the 1980s. They have lived through a relatively peaceful, affluent time in Canada's history, and they expect more from society than do older age groups.

As cohorts age (and members die) cohorts replace one another in society's age structure. Riley, Johnson, and Foner (1972) call this *cohort flow*. As cohorts flow through the age structure they change the size of particular age groups (e.g., the size of the group 20–30 years old will differ in 1940 and 1970). New cohorts also bring new values with them as they age. Older people today, for example, have less education than younger cohorts. The 1981 Canada Census reports that almost 60 percent of the cohort born between 1897 and 1906 had less than a Grade 9 education (Statistics Canada 1984b). Younger Canadians have more schooling: 80 percent of the population under 65 had more than Grade 9, and almost 40 percent had between nine and thirteen years of school (Statistics Canada 1984b). Younger, more educated groups will probably demand more educational opportunities when they reach old age.

Riley, Johnson, and Foner's (1972) model of aging omits a few important concepts about aging and age-grading. Historical events, for example, also get filtered through the *age stratification system*. This refers to the system of age grades a society uses (e.g., child, adolescent, young adult). The 1900–1910 cohort went through the Great Depression of the 1930s in young adulthood, and the Depression affected their decision to marry as it did the early years of their careers. The Depression also affected the cohort born between 1920 and 1930, but it had a different effect on these people. They lived through the Depression as children. Some of them may not remember the Depression at all; others may simply have accepted the hard times as "the way things are."

Gerontologists use the term *generation* to describe people who share an awareness of their common historical or cultural experiences, but who may come from more than one cohort. The Baby Boom cohorts born between 1945 and the early 1960s form a generation; they have all lived under the threat of nuclear war, and they have lived in a relatively affluent time in Canadian history. This generation of Yuppies (Young Urban Professionals) in the 1980s will become the Gruppies (Greying Urban

Professionals) of the 1990s and the Ruppies (Retired Urban Professionals) of the 2020s.

Braun and Sweet (1983–84) found that a "generational event" theory of personality better explained the differences between age groups than a theory of life stages. Generational event theory says that attitudes form for a generation in their teens. People who grow up at the same time in the same society share the same attitudes. These attitudes stay fairly stable throughout life because of what Neugarten (1964, 198) calls the "institutionalization of personality." People expect themselves to respond in the same ways to life's demands, others expect the same responses, and people choose their friends and contacts to support a stable sense of self.

These studies all show the effect of social and historical events on individual personality. Like non-normative events, history-graded events happen without warning, and sometimes the changes they bring about do not show up until years later. Society also shapes personality growth more directly through normative age-grading.

Normative Age-Graded Events

Anthropologists report that all societies (Linton 1936) move people through a series of *age grades*. Age grades define certain rights and responsibilities for their members. They give order to the life course and help people judge their own development (Cain 1964).

Males of the Nandi tribe in Kenya, for example, belong to one of seven age groups — two for boys, one for warriors, and four for elders. These groups give males their status and allow them to play certain roles at given times in their lives. Likewise, pre-industrial societies recognized three stages of life — infancy–childhood, mature adulthood, and old age. Industrialized society today includes the stages of infancy, childhood, adolescence, young adulthood, middle age, and old age. Some writers have now added a new stage, the young-old, after middle age and before late old age. This last stage makes sense in a society where people can expect to live in good health for ten or fifteen years after age 65.

Neugarten, Moore, and Lowe (1968) say that people internalize the age-grade system and know the proper time for a life event to occur. A Canadian middle-class girl today who falls in love at the age of 14 will feel it is too early to marry. A woman graduate student in her early twenties may also feel it is too early to settle down. A single career woman of 40 who wants to get married may feel she is late.

Someone for whom major life events come early or late — a teenaged mother or a newlywed octogenarian — may feel out of sync with the age-status system. Gerontologists call this *age-status asynchronization.*

Neugarten and Moore (1968) say that a person can be on time in certain ways and late or early in others. They can feel on time when they choose to marry, but late in advancing in their profession. Research shows that occupation, ethnic background, and social class affect the timing of life events.

The lower a woman's social class, for example, the earlier she tends to go through life events like marriage or having her first child (Neugarten and Moore 1968). Neugarten and Moore found that women professionals had their first child an average of six years later than unskilled working-class women. The researchers also report that women go through different life events than men. They found, for instance, that women enter a new phase of life in their late forties. The last child leaves home, menopause occurs, and many women enter the labour market. This produces "an increasingly accentuated transition period in the lives of women," one that men do not face (1968, 13).

Neugarten and Moore (1968) conclude that the social groups we belong to regulate our life cycle. Groups expect certain behaviours from their members, and members rely on these expectations to guide their actions.

Summary

The life-span developmental model accepts the idea that maturation and psychological change affect human development, but it says that a more complete picture of human development requires knowledge of a person's life events and social context. It shows that society and history play important parts in shaping individual development. This means that maladjustment and psychopathology can have social roots.

THE SOCIAL ROOTS OF PROBLEMS IN OLD AGE

Some maladjustment in later life comes about because society gives older people fewer guides to define correct behaviour than it gives the young. Rosow (1976) says that older people occupy a *tenuous* status — a status or position in the social structure that does not have a role associated with it. A retiree, for example, occupies a status (retired person), but does not have a role to play in society (retirees are expected *not* to work, but nothing else is expected of them). The loss of roles in later life (through retirement or children growing up) excludes older people from taking part in society. It also signals a problem older people have today: finding meaning in later life.

Loneliness

The absence of social roles for older people creates new social-psychological problems in old age. Some studies link loneliness to social isolation (Wood and Guest 1978). Wood (1978) describes loneliness as the loss of *social identity* — the identity people get from interaction with others and from holding social positions. Loneliness comes about when a person feels a "relational deficit" or gap between the number of relationships desired and the number they have (Weiss 1973; Sermat 1978). Wood (1978) found greater loneliness among older women than older men, greater loneliness among unmarried than married older people, and greater loneliness for older people with no university education. Other studies find that older people feel they can do little about their loneliness (Lopata 1969; Abrahams 1972; Gordon 1976).

Perlman, Gerson, and Spinner (1978) suggest two ways to combat loneliness. First, older people should maintain their social contacts with friends and neighbours. Second, since social resources can help older people make these contacts, better transportation, well-designed housing, and more recreational facilities give older people more choice and a stronger sense of control over their lives. Most studies agree that a good old age means more than just adaptation of older people to what in some cases is an inhospitable environment. Older people also need a more supportive social setting to grow old in.

Suicide

Who commits suicide in old age and why? A report by Health and Welfare Canada (1977c) says that loneliness and isolation, widowhood or divorce, retirement, and serious illness all increase the risk of suicide. Jarvis and Boldt (1980) did one of the first studies of suicide among older Canadians. They studied the social backgrounds of the 154 people aged 60 and over who committed suicide in Alberta from 1968 to 1973. Their findings support the Health and Welfare (1977c) report. They found that poor health leads many older people to suicide. A large number of the older suicide cases had chronic diseases — heart disease, diabetes, and lung disease. These people also saw doctors more often, they more frequently took drugs for health problems, and they spent more time in hospitals than did younger suicides. Illness, Jarvis and Boldt (1980) found, leads to suicide more often in men than in women. Older women who commit suicide tend to have a mental rather than a physical disorder.

Men also choose different means to kill themselves than do women. Sixty-four percent of older men used firearms to kill themselves, but 46 percent of older women hanged themselves. Both older men and older women use lethal methods, which means that when they try, they intend to succeed.

Studies (Miller 1979; Jarvis and Boldt 1980) also show that older suicide victims often have poor social lives. Jarvis and Boldt (1980) found that older suicides tended to live alone and to have little communication with others. As the population ages, the rate of suicide in old age may increase, especially among certain groups — lonely people, people with chronic illness, and widows.

Miller (1979) suggests some direct ways to prevent suicide among older people. He says that family doctors should know the clues to suicide in old age and what to do to help an older person at risk. Older people should have better access to psychiatric services, should they need them. The media should make people more aware of the signs of suicide in older people. Prevention should also include broader changes in society — such as changes that help older people stay involved in social life. The next section discusses a model for understanding the social causes of individual breakdown. It also describes some of the ways that breakdown can be avoided or reversed.

Social Breakdown

Kuypers and Bengtson (1973) say that older people often suffer from psychological breakdown due to inadequacies in the social environment. They call this a social breakdown syndrome, and they describe this syndrome as a seven-step process (see Exhibit 6.5).

1. Role loss, lack of norms to guide behaviour, and the loss of friends and relatives to use as reference groups (groups that support one's values and behaviour) all make a person susceptible to breakdown.
2. The person begins to depend on external labels for a sense of self. In Canada these labels sometimes have negative connotations (e.g., widow, retiree).
3. Society may view the older person as incompetent. Middle-aged children may begin to take responsibility away from an aging parent. Insititutions often leave the older resident with nothing to do for him or herself.
4. The older person may assume a dependent role in response to this treatment.
5. The older person develops skills that fit the dependent role. People learn to live down to the expectations others have of them.
6. The person loses previous skills. People in a nursing home setting may lose the ability to make their bed or to chop vegetables because they never get the chance.
7. People label themselves as sick and inadequate. This fulfils the prophecy of the social definition of older people as incompetent and creates a further turn in the cycle of breakdown. It makes the older person more susceptible to negative labelling.

A case study will show how this syndrome can lead to breakdown.

Carl Teicherow, 71, worked for Canada Manpower until 1979. He took early retirement at age 63. He says he retired because in the mid-1970s his department began to hire college graduates to fill new jobs. Carl had only a high-school diploma and felt that his new co-workers looked down on him. As his older co-workers retired and more young people joined his division, he felt increasingly isolated. He began to feel that the young workers got all the credit and the promotions. "Those young people they hired didn't know as much as they thought," he says. "Sure they had university degrees, but they had no common sense. They didn't know anything about people. I said, 'The hell with it, if the government doesn't care about this department why should I.' So I quit as soon as I had the chance."

Carl still feels bitter about work and the young people who joined his

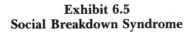

Exhibit 6.5
Social Breakdown Syndrome

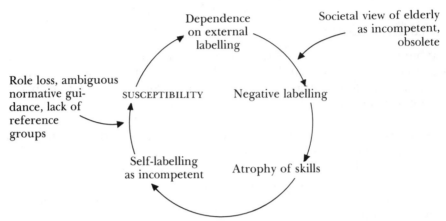

A systems representation of SBS as applied to old age with negative inputs from the external social system.

Kuypers and Bengtson (1973) propose a way to reverse the social breakdown syndrome. They propose a reorganization of the social system to provide older people with new ways to feel worthwhile. This approach includes (1) a new value system that bases social worth on a person's basic humanity, not on what he or she produces, (2) greater self-reliance, (3) a strong internal sense of control, (4) learning new problem-solving strategies, (5) better-quality services like housing and transportation, and better income, (6) maintaining coping skills, and (7) a reduced susceptibility to external judgments. An improvement on any of these items would increase the older person's quality of life.

Source: J.A. Kuypers and V.L. Bengtson, "Social Breakdown and Competence: A Model of Normal Aging," *Human Development 16* (1973): 181–201. Reprinted with permission of S. Karger AG, Basel.

department. He doesn't work now, or do much of anything else. He had leadership skills during his working years: his wife says he got elected president of any group he joined. But he quit most of those groups after he retired. Now he watches TV or reads, but these activities give him little pleasure. He had a bad bout of depression a year ago and threatened suicide. His doctor gave him some pills and told him to find something

**Exhibit 6.6
A Possible Social Reconstruction Syndrome**

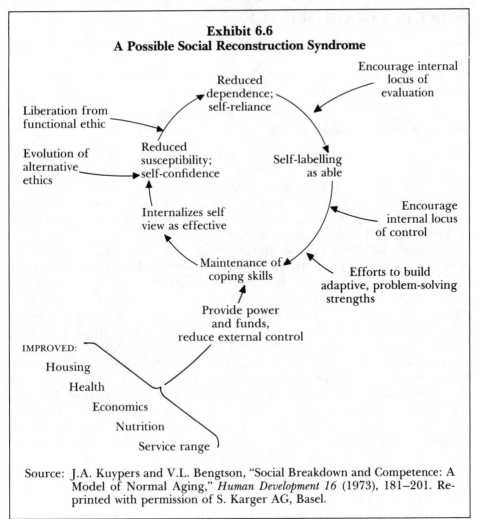

Source: J.A. Kuypers and V.L. Bengtson, "Social Breakdown and Competence: A Model of Normal Aging," *Human Development 16* (1973), 181–201. Reprinted with permission of S. Karger AG, Basel.

to keep busy. His wife worries about his depression, but she does not know what else to do.

Kuypers and Bengtson (1973) propose a way to reverse the social breakdown syndrome. They propose a reorganization of the social system to provide older people with new ways to feel worthwhile. This approach includes: (1) a new value system that bases social worth on a person's basic humanity, not on what he or she produces, (2) greater self-reliance, (3) a strong internal sense of control, (4) learning new problem-solving strategies, (5) better-quality services such as housing and transportation, and better income, (6) maintaining coping skills, and (7) a reduced susceptibility to external judgments. An improvement on any of these items would increase the older person's quality of life.

WHAT IS A GOOD OLD AGE?

Social-psychological theories describe more than one pattern of good aging. These theories take into account the person's social context and the *roles* people play in society. Rosow (1976, 458) defines a role as a "pattern of activity intrinsic" to a social position.

Disengagement Theory

Cumming and Henry (1961) describe old age as a time of disengagement — a time to withdraw from social roles and to decrease activity. They based their theory on a study of 279 people aged 50 to 70 years old in Kansas City. The study focused on people in good health and with enough money to live comfortably. They found that in this sample social roles and emotional ties decreased with age.

Cumming and Henry (1961) describe disengagement as inevitable, universal, and satisfying to both the person and society. Disengagement, they say, serves an important psychological function. It allows older people to reduce their activity naturally as their strength declines. Disengagement also serves a useful social function. It allows older people to leave social roles before the final disengagement — death. This creates a smooth transfer of power and responsibility from one generation to the next.

Critics attacked disengagement theory almost as soon as it appeared. First, disengagement theory supports the stereotype of old age as a time of weakness and decline. Second, the theory assumes that the old perform less well than the young. It supports the existence of mandatory retirement based on age, rather than a person's ability to do the job. Third, the theory assumes that all older people respond to the world in the same way — that they all disengage from social roles.

Activity Theory

Neugarten, Havighurst, and Tobin (1968) describe a second major theory of aging: activity theory. This theory is just the reverse of disengagement theory. It says that as people lose social roles in old age they stay happiest when they replace lost roles with new ones. This theory blames society for the process of disengagement. Modern society, it says, pushes older people out of social roles. This theory fits the North American view that happiness comes from work and activity.

Research by the Chicago team found support for activity theory. Neugarten, Havighurst, and Tobin (1968) found three types of active people who reported high life-satisfaction. One group started new activities to fill in for lost social roles. The researchers called these "re-organizers." Another group held on to their mid-life roles and stayed active. The researchers said these people were "holding-on." A third group stayed active but narrowed the range of their activities. The researchers called this group "focused." Most recent studies also find that high activity correlates with high life-satisfaction.

Continuity Theory

A third theory of aging says that people feel most satisfied if they continue the roles and activities of their middle years (Atchley 1982). This theory says that old age is a continuation of a person's past (rather than a break with their past or a change in direction from their past) and that people will choose the lifestyle in old age most like the pattern of life they lived in middle age. Mildly active people in their younger years will prefer a mild level of activity in later life and feel satisfied with this lifestyle, but active people will want to keep up their activity — though activity might take new forms in old age.

Some research supports each of these theories. Researchers have found that older people tend to be more passive, more introverted, and less committed to achievement in old age (Riley and Foner 1968; Neugarten 1969). Neugarten, Havighurst, and Tobin (1968, 175) found support for both activity and disengagement theory. They found that many disengaged people report high life-satisfaction and have integrated personalities. These people want to live a "rocking-chair" style of aging. They leave their social roles by choice and live contented lives with few social contacts. Other people, high in life-satisfaction, either stay active in their middle-life roles or replace these with new roles in old age.

Research by MacLean (1982) supports both activity and continuity theory. He found that men who could continue their activities and interests into later life showed the highest life-satisfaction. These findings support the idea that people enjoy old age if they continue the activities and relationships they enjoyed in the past.

These three theories tell part of the truth about life-satisfaction in later life, but all of them give too simple a picture of old age. People can disengage from some roles and still have high life-satisfaction (Maddox 1970; Palmore 1970; Atchley 1971a), but life-satisfaction depends on what kind of activity declines. Lemon, Bengtson, and Peterson (1972) found that a decline in group activities did not lead to lower life-satisfaction, but a decline in social activity with friends did lead to a decrease in life-satisfaction. Kozma and Stones (1978, 248) conclude that activity or disengagement alone do not lead to happiness, but that "people appear to be happy if most of their experiences are pleasant and their perceived needs are met."

Exhibit 6.7

MEN, WOMEN, AND LIFE-SATISFACTION

Many studies have found differences in life-satisfaction and personality when they compared men and women (Lowenthal 1975; Lowenthal, Thurner, and Chiriboga 1975). Connidis (1983b) asked a sample of 400 older Canadians how they felt about aging. She found that most people had a positive view of later life, though they had a realistic view of the problems that come with aging. She also found that men and women differed in how much they liked, disliked, and worried about old age. For example, 71 percent of men compared to 56 percent of women reported no worries about growing older. When the older people in Connidis's sample did complain about old age, men complained more often about physical restrictions while women complained more often about poor health. Men and women also liked different things about aging.

Men more often mentioned good health and freedom from work as things they liked about old age. Women more often mentioned contentment and freedom from family responsibility. These findings probably reflect the different social roles played by this generation of older men and women in their middle years. Most of these women had worked at home raising families, while the men had worked in the labour force. In later life they each feel a different kind of freedom — women feel the freedom from child-rearing, and men feel the freedom from work. These kinds of responses may change in the future as women today spend time on careers as well as child-rearing.

CONCLUSION

Older Canadians, in general, report high life-satisfaction. They know about the problems of old age, such as widowhood, illness, and physical decline, but they also see many good things about old age. Connidis (1983b) found that older people enjoyed their personal freedom and the chance to do the things they want to do. These advantages, she found, outweigh the problems that come with age. Northcott (1982) found similar results in a study of 440 people in Edmonton. "The elderly," he says, "are more likely than the nonelderly to report no area of life as a major source of pressure and the older the respondent the less pressure reported from all areas of life except health. As pressure falls satisfaction tends to rise .... In short, the picture one gets of old age is that it is a period of relatively low pressure and relatively high satisfaction, though not without its problems." Each stage of life has its good and bad points, but "old age," Northcott (1982, 77) concludes, "looks far more attractive than stereotypes suggest."

SUMMARY

1. Theories of personality development state that people go through a series of predictable stages as they age. Erikson described eight stages — five for youth and three for middle and old age. Other theorists have found more stages, showing that people go through many changes in adulthood. Some studies question the universality of these stages.
2. The life-span developmental perspective sees crisis and change as an essential part of life from birth to death. This view states that as people age, they make choices in response to social demands. This perspective allows for many patterns of aging.
3. Life events shape human development. These include non-normative events, history-graded events, and normative age-graded events. Studies of history-graded and normative age-graded events show the effects of social structures on personal development.
4. The way society treats older people can lead to personal problems like loneliness, suicide, and the breakdown of competence. Social psychologists trace these problems to the lack of social supports for older people today.
5. Kuypers and Bengtson (1973) say that if society views older people negatively, then older people can lose confidence in themselves. This can ultimately lead to dependence and psychological distress. They call this process a social breakdown syndrome. They say that new social values (the beliefs members of a society hold about what is right, good, and true) should judge people by more than their productivity. A change in society's value system, they say, can reverse this syndrome. So can adequate social supports.
6. Social psychologists describe at least three models of good aging — disengagement, activity, and continuity. Research shows that each of these patterns can lead to high life-satisfaction.
7. Men and women adapt to aging differently, but most older Canadians of both sexes report high life-satisfaction. They report that they feel less pressure and that they enjoy more personal freedom in old age than in their middle years.

SELECTED READINGS

Erikson, Erik. *Childhood and Society*, 2nd ed. New York: W. W. Norton, 1963.
  A classic. Erikson applies his psychoanalytic insights to other cultures and to the life cycle. For a follow-up try his more recent work, *The Life Cycle Completed* (New York: W.W. Norton, 1982). These two books show the continuities and changes in Erikson's thinking over the past thirty years.
Kuypers, J.A., and V.L. Bengtson. "Social Breakdown and Competence: A Model of Normal Aging." *Human Development* 16 (1973):181–201.
  A thought-provoking paper that presents the social, psychological, and environmental conditions that lead to a good old age.
Novak, Mark. *Successful Aging: The Myths, Realities and Future of Aging in Canada.* Markham, Ontario: Penguin, 1985.

This book takes an upbeat look at aging in Canada in the 1980s. It reviews the health care, income, retirement, and housing systems. It also looks at recreation, education, and what it takes to live a good old age. The book gives examples of programs and case studies of older people across the country.

PART IV

INSTITUTIONAL CHANGE

CHAPTER 7

HEALTH CARE

INTRODUCTION

Mrs. Granovetter, 72, lives by herself in a three-room apartment. Until six years ago, she worked as a supervisor in a nursing home, but poor health forced her to quit. She says she has an aortic aneurism that "looks like a bicycle tire with a bubble in it." She also has arthritis, and her joints get so stiff during the night that, she says, it sometimes takes her until noon to get out of bed. Still, she manages to live on her own. Her daughter, who lives on the other side of town, calls her every day, she talks to or visits with her next-door neighbour daily, and she can still drive. A few times a week she drives to a nearby shopping centre to sit and watch the people go by. She knows just where to park and how far she has to

151

walk to the nearest bench. Last year her children took her on a trip to England. She says they didn't get to walk through the castles, but they toured around in the car and she saw the countryside. With help from family and friends Mrs. Granovetter stays active and enjoys life.

Like Mrs. Granovetter, three-quarters of older people suffer from chronic illnesses, and, like her, most of them cope well with some help from their family and friends (Health and Welfare Canada 1982b). Most people use no formal health care services, and over 90 percent of people aged 65 and over have good enough health to live on their own in the community. The health care needs of this diverse older population range from health maintenance for the well elderly to long-term chronic care for people with terminal illnesses.

This chapter looks at: (1) the structure and function of the health care system today, (2) how the present system fits the needs of older people, and (3) how the system is changing to meet the needs of an aging society.

THREE MODELS OF HEALTH CARE

Social scientists use models to simplify and describe complex social systems. A model does not perfectly represent the system, but it describes the system's basic structures, functions, and values. Three models of health care have shaped the development of the health care system in Canada — the medical model, the social model, and the health promotion model.

The Medical Model

The medical model focuses on the treatment of diseases and injuries. Treatment most often takes place in the doctor's office, in a hospital, or in other health care institutions. The medical model favours surgery, drug therapy, and rehabilitation through physical therapies. Within this model "medical care and treatment are defined primarily as technical problems, and the goals of medicine are viewed in terms of technical criteria, such as validity, diagnosis, precision of disease-related treatment, symptom relief and termination of disease process" (Chappell, Strain, and Blandford 1986, 101). Doctors learn this approach to medicine in medical school and often get little training in other forms of health care such as counselling or long-term community care.

The Social Model

The social model sees medical care as only one part of a complete health care system. This model sees personal and family counselling, home care, and adult day care programs as part of the health care system. Care within the social model often takes place in the community — in a person's home, in a drop-in centre, or in a counsellor's office. The doctor, in this model, works as part of a health care team that includes nurses, physio-therapists, counsellors, social workers, and other professionals.

The Health Promotion Model

The health promotion model focuses on prevention and self-care. It aims to prevent disease through lifestyle change, increased knowledge about healthy behaviour, and environmental improvement. The Canadian health care system has only begun to use this model. Programs such as Parti-cipaction that promote fitness and programs that warn about the dangers of smoking or excessive drinking follow this model. This model also includes actions that most people do not associate directly with health care, such as workplace safety regulations, laws that require people to use seatbelts in cars, and pollution control for factories.

Each of these models plays a part in the Canadian health care system today. The social model has gained acceptance as a possible alternative to institutionalization. The health promotion model may save the health care system money in the long run by keeping people healthier longer. Recent decreases in heart disease, for example, may have come about through health promotion programs that encourage low-fat diets and discourage smoking. Still, the medical model dominates the system today. Canadians spend more money (much of it through taxes and health insurance programs) on physicians and hospital care than on any other kind of health care.

THE COST OF CARE TODAY

In 1976 Canada had more than 1,400 hospitals, 38,000 doctors, and 350,000 other health care workers. Canada had almost one health care worker to serve every fifty people (Bennett and Krasny 1981). In 1982 Canadians spent over $30 billion on health care, four times the amount in constant (1971) dollars spent in 1960 (Health and Welfare Canada 1982c). (The concept of constant dollars allows comparison of costs be-tween years. It compares all years to the target year. This controls for increases in dollar figures due to inflation.) This came to an estimated 8.4 percent of the Gross National Product (GNP) in 1982, up from 5.6 percent in 1965 and more than two and a half times the amount (not counting inflation) spent per person in 1960 (Health and Welfare Canada 1982c).

A government report on the health care system (Lalonde 1974) found that Canada had more physicians per capita than five of the world leaders in health care (Australia, Denmark, Sweden, the U.K., and the United States). It had more nurses per capita than any of these countries except Australia. It ranked fourth in the number of hospital beds per capita, and Canadian medical and hospital insurance matched the most complete coverage in the world, with almost 100 percent of Canadians covered.

These facts show both the strengths and weaknesses of the system today. Canada has created one of the most complete health care systems in the world. Older people, for example, receive free hospital and surgical care as well as free access to a range of programs that include chiropractic and optometric services (Health and Welfare Canada 1982b). But Canada also spends more on health care than other countries with comparable systems. Britain — one of the few countries with broader health care coverage than Canada — spent only $160 per person in 1976 for medical care or 5.4 percent of its GNP, compared to Canada's $600 per person or 7 percent of its GNP.

Canada's commitment to the medical model of care explains part of this high cost. Rising numbers of doctors, rising costs for complex treatments, unionization of hospital workers, and more tests to diagnose disease have led to increases in the cost of health care (Evans 1984). Some critics of the system today question whether this model fits the needs of an aging society. They argue that for the same cost Canadians could buy care that more closely fits their needs (Evans 1984). "As a society," Chappel, Strain, and Blandford (1986, 112) say, "we have not yet dealt with the issue — especially during old age — 'When is health care servicing inappropriate or too much?'"

THE HEALTH CARE SYSTEM AND OLDER PEOPLE'S HEALTH CARE NEEDS

By any standards older people have more health problems than younger people, and they use more health care services. A study by the Alberta Senior Citizens Bureau (1984), for example, reports that people 65 and over make up 7.3 percent of the population, but they accounted for 18.4 percent of hospital discharges in 1981 and used 36.7 percent of patient days. Both measures show an increase from 1976. The study also shows that people aged 75 and over used most of the patient days and accounted for most of the discharges by seniors in 1980/81. The Alberta Department of Social Services and Community Health (Alberta Senior Citizen's Bureau 1984) spent $16.5 million for hearing aids, medical equipment, and surgical supplies for 40,400 older clients in 1982/83, double the $8 million spent in 1980/81 (though the number of clients increased by only about 10 percent).

Barer and his colleagues (1986) studied the reasons why older people use more health care services today than in the past. They asked whether this increase in costs reflects changes in diseases older people have today, or whether it reflects the way the system cares for older patients. If the costs reflect older people's needs for treatment, then population aging could lead to a sharp increase in health care costs. But if changes reflect the way the system operates, then new approaches to treatment could contain costs. Little data exists to test the first possibility (that older people have different diseases or more diseases today than in the past), but a number of studies suggest that the way the system responds to older people's needs leads them to make heavier use of the medical care system today than in the past.

First, doctors, not patients, have the biggest say in how much and what kind of medical care a person uses. Studies show that treatment rates vary by province, by county, and even by physician. For one surgical procedure (transurethral prostactectomy), for example, Saskatchewan had a rate ten times that of Prince Edward Island (Statistics Canada 1980c; Statistics Canada 1981b). A study in Ontario (Stockwell and Vayda 1979, cited in Roos, Shapiro, and Roos 1984) found that surgery rates vary widely even within one county. These findings suggest that how doctors diagnose disease and the type of treatment they choose (if any) plays a major part in determining use patterns by older patients.

Chappell, Strain, and Blandford (1986, 100) report that physicians "control approximately 80 percent of health care costs." Only a quarter of this figure goes directly to physicians; the rest goes to hospital use (half of all health care costs), drugs, tests, and other medical expenses. Doctors control these expenses through the decisions they make about treatment and through their reliance on high technology in hospital settings.

Second, individual need cannot explain the pattern of use of acute hospitals. Data from the Manitoba longitudinal study on aging found that hospital use differs by region (Roos, Shapiro, and Roos 1984). The Manitoba study found that older rural Manitobans used more hospital days and had more admissions than urban Manitobans. This difference showed up even when the researchers looked at people with the same health status. The researchers suggest that the number of hospital beds in the country and the cities explains this difference. Rural settings in Manitoba have 2.3 more hospital beds per 1,000 population than urban settings, and doctors in rural areas, knowing there are beds available, tend to use them.

Government policy created this difference in use patterns. From 1948 into the 1960s the government shared the cost of building more hospital beds with the provinces, and rural areas took this opportunity to increase their medical facilities. Hospitals gave people in rural communities a medical safety net; increased profits to business due to construction, equipment, and drugs; and increased employment (Crichton 1980). Hospitals also allowed small towns to compete for and attract doctors.

These incentives led rural communities to build the most hospital beds, and, once open, these hospitals tended to stay open. Hospitals provide jobs for people in the community and they allow doctors to carry out complex surgical and diagnostic procedures. Shapiro and Roos (1984) see high hospital use by rural older people continuing into the future — because the system benefits from this approach to treatment.

Third, the federal government began to insure hospital care in 1957, ten years before it insured care for visits to doctors' offices. This encouraged doctors to admit patients to hospitals for treatment, since this approach saved patients money. Gross and Schwenger (1981, 129) blame the high cost of the health care system on "a heavy reliance on institutional care." They compared health care costs in Ontario with costs in the U.S.

Exhibit 7.1

THE COSTS OF CARE

A report titled *Health: A Need for Redirection* (Canadian Medical Association 1984) reported the costs of some current health care procedures. The study (1984, 44) says that "when a new technology becomes available, there is pressure to disseminate it widely and quickly. To some extent, technologies are 'overtaking' us. ..." This pressure and the use of expensive new technologies drive up the cost of health care. This report gives some of the costs of modern medical procedures. Some of the figures only approximate the real costs. Still, these figures show why chronic illnesses can cost so much.

Open heart surgery. A pilot study estimates the in-hospital costs for this operation at $9,300 (in 1983 dollars). Doctors performed 6,357 coronary by-pass operations in 1980–81.

Hip and knee joint replacement. Estimated cost is $19,000 per replacement. Doctors carried out 17,847 of these operations in 1980–81.

Heart transplantation. Costs may run from $17,000 for the surgery to $125,000 for the after-care costs. Twenty operations were done between 1981 and 1984 (not counting operations done in Montreal).

The report recognizes the value of these methods, but calls the belief that they will solve all health problems "misplaced." Instead, the report recommends a greater emphasis on "wellness."

and found that, when it came to institutional care, Ontario spent $323 more per year per person aged 65 and over on institutional care. "This amounts to a difference of 31 per cent, some of which can be attributed to inflation and variation in currency. However, the primary reason for Ontario's higher per capita institutional costs is that the province has more of its elderly in institutions" (Gross and Schwenger 1981, 129). Lower the rate of institutionalization, they say, and the costs of health care will come down.

These studies show that Canada's commitment to the medical model accounts for much of the increase in health care costs today. Health and Welfare Canada (1983) reports that from 1970 to 1979 institutions accounted for 50 percent of health care costs. Professional services (doctors and other professionals) accounted for 25 percent of health care costs, 10 percent went to pay for drugs and appliances, and 15 percent went to all other costs. Continued reliance on doctors, hospitals, drugs, and expensive treatments will drive up the costs of medical care in the future.

The current system, Chappell, Strain, and Blandford (1986, 108) say, focuses on "institutional care rather than community care, on acute care

Exhibit 7.2

OLDER PEOPLE AND THE USE OF HEALTH CARE SERVICES

Different groups of older people use different amounts of health care services. Studies that report aggregate data, such as use per 1,000 population or average length of hospital stay, miss these differences within the older population. "The aggregate statistics," Roos and Shapiro (1981, 656) say, "may reinforce the negative attitudes of health professionals and planners toward the elderly and add fuel to growing feelings that a so-called 'crisis' is looming as the population ages." Roos and Shapiro (1981) and a number of other researchers (Mossey et al. 1981) have used data from the Manitoba Longitudinal Study on Aging (MLSA) to shatter the myth that older people as a group are high consumers of health care.

First, the MLSA provides detailed information about individual use of the health care system. The study shows that older people do not form a single group. Some people use larger amounts of health care than others. Residents in senior citizen housing (self-contained apartments built by the government, religious groups, or service clubs for seniors), for example, saw the doctor more often and used more hospital days than people in other kinds of housing. Most older people use a small amount of formal health care service or none at all, and these differences in use patterns stay stable from year to year (Mossey et al. 1981, 557).

Second, the study found that less than one-quarter of Manitoba's older population stays in a hospital in any given year (Roos and Shapiro 1981). And only 5 percent of the older population uses almost three-fifths (59 percent) of the hospital days used by older people in the year (Roos and Shapiro 1981). A small group (2 percent) of older people admitted to hospitals used 20 percent of hospital days in a five-year period. Even among people 85 and over, 4 percent of this age group accounted for 32 percent of acute hospital days used by people 85 and over, and 9 percent of the 85 and over group accounted for 57 percent of the acute and chronic hospital days used by people in this age group (Roos and Shapiro 1981).

The study found that the average length of hospital stay for all older people rose from 1972 to 1976 (it rose 15 percent for people 75 years old and over), but closer analysis showed large differences within the older population. The length of stay for older people who stayed in the hospital fewer than 90 days dropped by one day during the years 1972–76. At the same time, those who stayed for more than 90 days showed an increase from 117 to 218 days in 1976 for the oldest group (75 years of age and older) (Roos, Shapiro, and Roos 1984).

Third, Roos, Shapiro, and Roos (1984) found that older people as a group do not make large numbers of visits to doctors and do not use large numbers of hospital days. The older population makes only 1.7 more visits to doctors per year than the group aged 15–44 and only 0.9

more visits than the group aged 45–64. About 20 percent of all age groups, including older people, do not visit a doctor at all in a year (Roos and Shapiro 1981). They found that the very old (aged 85+) use more home care, nursing homes, and hospitals than younger groups, but make the same number of visits to doctors' offices as people aged 65–69. They also found that older people get referred to medical consultants at a lower rate than the rest of the population (Roos, Shapiro, and Roos 1984). These studies show that most older people do not need or use excessive amounts of institutional or medical care. The health care they do need can often be delivered in the community.

rather than chronic care and on medical care rather than health care broadly defined." An aging population, Myles and Boyd (1982, 274–75) say, "requires a qualitative as well as a quantitative change in the health care system. An aging population requires a fundamental restructuring of health care and a redefinition of what constitutes health care" (see also Bayne 1978). The social model of health care provides a framework for this redefinition.

COMMUNITY CARE

The social model of health care looks for ways to keep people out of institutions. A health care system based on the social model of care would "have at its core a broad definition of health and would make adequate provision for noninstitutionally based chronic care" (Chappell, Strain, and Blandford 1986). Community care programs include hospitals, nursing homes, and doctors' services. Community care also includes community-based services such as visiting nurse services, meals on wheels, and adult day care programs.

The following programs form a continuum of care — from more institutional contact to little or no institutional contact. They show how the Canadian health care system has applied some of the principles of the social model of health care to meet older people's needs. A few notes of caution. As you read about these programs, keep in mind that: (1) Some of the evaluations of programs presented here have been done by the same people who run the programs, and this could bias their reports. (2) Few evaluations use control groups to see what would have happened to a similar group if they had not used this kind of program. A program that claims to save money by keeping people out of institutions should also show that a similar group of people to those in the program had to enter an institution. If the report cannot show this, then the program may have cost more money than if nothing were done. (3) Evaluation studies often report short-term changes. This makes it hard to judge the long-term effects of a program. Even with these shortcomings, however, evaluations and reports often provide the only information about new programs, and they give some idea of what these programs do and how well they work.

Geriatric Day Hospitals

Geriatric day hospitals offer a full range of hospital services to people who live in the community. A day hospital will assess an older person's needs and plan a rehabilitation and care program for them. Services include physical checkups, drug monitoring, dental clinics, diagnosis, treatment, and rehabilitation. Day hospitals can also keep an eye on older patients at risk in the community and ease older acute care patients back into the community when they leave the hospital.

A report on a day hospital at the Seven Oaks Hospital in Winnipeg found that the program detected many patient problems that referral agencies had missed. The study found that 20 percent of the cases had medical needs unidentified by referral agencies, 10 percent had unidentified nursing needs, and 11 percent had unidentified needs concerning how to care for themselves (Kaban and Block 1984). The day hospital assessment allowed staff to meet these needs before they created more problems for the patient. This program cared for about ten patients per day, and most people in the program used the hospital once or twice a week for an average of twelve to thirteen weeks. All of these people stayed in their own homes during treatment.

Flathman and Larsen (1976) studied three day hospital programs in Alberta. They found that, on average, people in the programs improved their physical, mental, and social well-being. Participants also showed more independence in tasks of daily living (like grooming, bathing, and toileting). Flathman and Larsen say that patients, physicians, hospital administrators, and families all felt satisfied with the program. The researchers found that less healthy people in the program showed the most improvement.

Some day hospitals offer counselling and education for patients. The Seven Oaks Day Hospital in Winnipeg, for example, taught many of its patients how to care for themselves. This allowed the program to discharge 44 percent of its patients. A report on the program says that many of the patients went on to attend adult day care programs after they left the day hospital program (Hurwitz 1984).

Adult Day Care

Adult day care programs "provide noninstitutional support for those unable to remain in the community without it" (Chappell, Strain, and Blandford 1986, 121). These programs include hot meals, recreation programs, and a chance for the older person to socialize. The programs also give family caregivers time off to rest, shop, and maintain their own social life. Adult day care offers fewer medical services and more social and recreational services than day hospitals. Some provinces require that people pay for day care services themselves, while other provinces include the service as part of the provincial health program.

As yet research has not been able to show a reduction in the use of other services due to adult day care (or day hospital care) alone, but studies do report an increase in participants' well-being (Chappell 1983b; Flathman and Larsen 1976). A study of the first day care centre for handicapped older people in Victoria, B.C., showed that most clients improved their social skills and their self-esteem, and some improved their physical skills. Families reported better family relationships and better health for the client's spouse (Jackson 1983).

A study by Chappell (1983b) found that people who lived alone or with few relatives and those with muscle or bone problems showed the greatest improvement. Those with the poorest function at the time they started in an adult day care program showed the most improvement over time.

Home Care

Home care is one of the most important parts of a comprehensive health care system. A report by the National Advisory Council on Aging (1986d) defines community support or home care services as "a co-ordinated and integrated range of services designed to help people live as independently as possible in the community." In 1977 the Canadian federal government started the Extended Health Care Services program to support provincial home care programs. Home care programs differ from province to province, but all of the provinces and territories in Canada have some home care and nursing services. Most provinces at least have senior activity centres. Some have extensive programs that include meals on wheels, home repair services, laundry and cleaning help, emergency alert services, friendly visitors, nutrition counselling, and transportation. Manitoba, Saskatchewan, and British Columbia have co-ordinated home care programs (Ross 1983). This means that one office assesses the older person's needs, sets up a program of services tailored to the individual, and monitors the client's need for help.

A large system like Manitoba's Continuing Care program, for example, can tailor a program to a person's or family's unique needs. In one case an unmarried middle-aged daughter lived with and cared for her mother in their home. Because the daughter worked days, the Continuing Care office arranged for a sitter to stay with the elderly mother while the daughter worked. During the football season another sitter came in during the evening so that the daughter could go to Winnipeg Blue Bomber games. This may seem an extravagant use of resources, but the night sitter helped relieve the stress of caregiving enough that the daughter could continue to care for her mother at home.

Some home care programs will arrange for respite care. Respite care places an older person in a nursing home or hospital for a few days a month or for a two-week stay once a year. Respite gives family members

Exhibit 7.3

HOME CARE SERVICES

Sometimes simple low-cost community service programs for seniors work as well as complex costly ones. A Daily Hello Service in Ottawa asks program members to call in to a switchboard each day. If a person does not call in, someone calls them or checks on them. Members in the program said they felt more secure, less lonely, and more self-reliant. Also, of the volunteers over age 65, 25 percent said they began as daily hello receivers (Psychogeriatric Clinic n. d.).

"It makes me feel somewhat independent of my children," one person said of the program.

Another said, "Now that there is no longer a family doctor who comes to see me and who cares about me, at least I know that there is someone else who cares."

"When I wake up in the morning, I usually feel blue; this is the first phone call I make."

a chance to take a vacation or catch up on much-needed sleep (Dunn, MacBeath, and Robertson 1983).

Home care programs best express the philosophy of the social model of health care. They respond to the individual needs of the older person and to the needs of his or her caregiver. They also increase the older person's social network by supplying household help and other services.

Greater use of home care could decrease the number of people who need to enter an institution. Studies report that many older people now live in hospitals and nursing homes because they lack the supports that would allow them to live in their own homes (Health and Welfare Canada 1982b; Shapiro and Tate 1985; Brown 1981). A study by Shapiro and Tate (1985), for example, found that people with the fewest community supports (people who need home care supports most) run the highest risk of institutionalization (see also Chappell 1980a; Cape et al. 1977). Home care could help reduce the institutionalization of these people.

A move to increase home care will require a change in the priorities of the health care system. Until recently the system favoured medical care and institutions. In 1980–81 the federal government gave over $700 million to the provinces, most of it for institutional care. In 1978–79 the provinces spent over $920 million on special care in homes for the elderly. In that same year in Ontario the home care and support services budget came to "less than a quarter of that spent just on extended care" (Community Care Services, Inc. 1978, 10). Some of this emphasis on institutions has begun to change. Ontario, for example, set out "A New Agenda" for health and social services (Van Horne 1986). This plan includes more emphasis on preventive assessments, expanded community programs, and more co-ordination of services.

Community care *may* offer a cost-effective alternative to institutionalization for many older people, and this makes it attractive to governments. But do these programs actually save money? A number of research studies have looked at the potential cost savings from community care.

The Costs of Community Care

Reports on alternative health care programs like day hospitals, adult day care, or home care programs often end with a statement about how much money they save over institutional care. One program in Saskatchewan, for example, estimates that it saves taxpayers more than $450,000 a year in institutional costs. The program offers older people home care services that include a security check system, help with chores and meals, transportation, health education, and health care (Harshman 1982).

The Manitoba Home Care program also claims to save taxpayers money. The Annual Report for the year 1984 (Government of Manitoba 1984, 4) says that "without the availability of Home Care 20% of persons admitted to the program ... would have required Personal Care Home placement; 44% would have been admitted to or remained in hospital and 36% would have been in the community without appropriate care."

But not everyone agrees that community-based health care programs save money. Kane and Kane (1985) conducted a review of community care programs across Canada. They say that increases in community care will increase health care costs in the short run. First, most of these new programs start as "add-ons" to the current system. They would save money *if* the number of hospital or nursing home beds decreased as more people used community care services, but the system has not cut down the number of beds as community care programs have grown (though in some provinces the government has limited the development of new institutional beds). So community care programs add more costs to the system (Denton and Spencer 1983, 161).

Second, community-based programs promise to keep older people out of institutions, but research studies disagree on whether community care decreases institutionalization. Librach, Davidson, and Peretz (1972, 50) say that with home care fewer patients "need placement in long term facilities or else their placement can be postponed." Flathman and Larsen (1976) found opposite results in a study of geriatric day hospitals in Alberta. They did not find clear evidence that the program prevented or retarded institutionalization of patients. Chappell (1983b) and Chappell and Blandford (1983) found contrary results. They did find differences in how much adult day care participants used in-patient hospital services. They studied adult day care users before and after these people entered adult day care. The researchers found that 39 percent of the

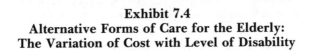

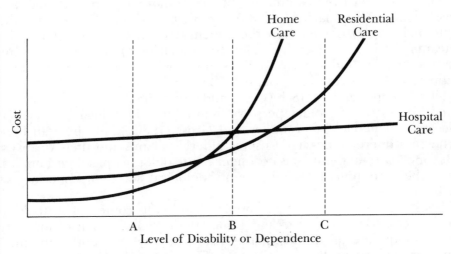

A: Person requires help with bathing, shovelling the walk,
doing housework.
B: Person cannot prepare daily meals or do personal care.
C: Person requires constant medical supervision.

Consider the case of a woman who cannot work for herself
(Level of Disability B). This graph shows that home care will
cost as much as hospital care and more than residential care.
The preferred support method for this woman (from the
point of view of cost savings for the system) will be
residential care. If her health gets worse and she requires
constant medical care (Level of Disability C), hospital care
will cost the least.

Source: A.M. Clarfield, "Home Care: Is It Cost Effective?" *Canadian Medical Association Journal* 129 (1983); 1182. Adapted from M.F. Drummond, *Principles of Economic Appraisal in Health Care* (Oxford: Oxford University Press, 1980): 100. Reprinted with permission.

sample decreased their total number of hospital admissions and 42 percent decreased the total number of days they spent in the hospital. Adult day care does seem to decrease the number of days a person will spend in the hospital, but adult day care may not prevent or delay the use of long-term institutional care (Chappell, Strain, and Blandford 1986, 130). These studies used different methods, studied different types of community care, and used different time frames to complete the research.

These differences could explain the lack of agreement in their findings. At the moment, research leaves open the question of whether community care programs save enough money (assuming they lead to some decrease in institution use) to make up for their cost.

Third, in some cases community care costs more than institutional care (see Exhibit 7.4). Clarfield (1983) says that the cost of care (and the potential saving) depends on the patient's functional level. It may be cheaper to admit a person with a low functional level into a nursing home or hospital. An "older person may be much worse off, even more 'institutionalized' in a certain sense, if bedfast or housebound and with few available home services" (Schwenger and Gross 1980). A long-term illness can also destroy the older person's family life. "The slogan, 'Keep the old folks at home,' " Schwenger and Gross (1980, 256) say, "can be a cruel and onerous message to some elderly persons and their relatives. [Beyond a certain point,] it is no longer fair to older people, their families, or to the community to sustain the psychological, social, or financial cost of home care."

Does this mean that Canada should abandon its commitment to community care? Hardly. Kane and Kane (1985, 253) say that community care cannot cure all the ills of the health care system, but community care may be able to decrease the rate of institutionalization. Studies also show that community care leads to higher life-satisfaction than institutionalization (Chappell and Penning 1979). "The current trend [toward community care]," Chappell and Penning (1979, 380) say, "seems to reflect one situation in which economic efficiency and humanism are not contradictory."

HEALTH PROMOTION

So far, this chapter has focused on illness rather than health, but there is no other way to talk about the health care system. We call it a health care system, but it is actually a sickness treatment system. It serves people who are already sick, and it focuses on curing disease. This approach has its limits. Hospitals, doctors, nursing homes, or home care do not prevent disease, but only treat illness after it occurs. Lalonde (1974) discussed this and other problems with Canada's health care system in a report called *A New Perspective on the Health of Canadians*. There he proposed the concept of the *health field*. The health field includes the usual health services. But within the health field the health care system is *one* way — not the only way, or even the best way — to improve health. In addition to traditional medical services, the health field also includes improvements in human biology (through basic research), improvements in lifestyle, and improvements in the environment as ways to better health.

This model makes sense in Canada today. Studies show that "the majority of the aged remain functionally well until an advanced age" (Health and Welfare Canada 1982b, 43). A study of community-dwelling older people in Ontario, for example, found that only 6 percent of the 65-

year-olds in the sample and 35 percent of the 85-year-olds lacked competence in five activities of daily living (Cape and Henschke 1980). Studies of seniors in both Calgary (Research and Planning Unit 1983) and Saskatchewan (Senior Citizens' Provincial Council 1983) found that 60 percent of seniors report good or excellent health.

A study of rural older people in Alberta found that about three-quarters of the people studied reported few or no health problems and high life-satisfaction. This included older as well as younger seniors, men and women, rural and town-dwelling older people, and people who live alone or with others. The researchers say that older people present "a picture of health not illness" (Thurston et al. 1982, 16).

Some of the newest health programs work to keep older people well. In 1981 Health and Welfare Canada set up a Health Promotion Directorate to "inform and motivate people to adopt and maintain healthy lifestyles" (Hansen and Ledoux 1985). The Health Promotion Directorate runs public education and advertising campaigns, publishes health information, and funds health promotion projects (Hansen and Ledoux 1985). Programs supported by the Directorate include an Alzheimer's Family Resource Centre, an education program for seniors called "Fully Alive," anti-smoking campaigns, and a program to help poorer older people stay healthy.

Health promotion in Canada takes two forms: risk reduction or lifestyle change and social-environmental change.

Most health promotion programs in Canada take the risk reduction approach. Risk reduction programs assume that individual actions lead to illness and that lifestyle change can prevent illness. Risk reduction includes programs that decrease smoking and drug abuse, improve nutrition, and increase exercise and fitness. A number of studies have linked changes in lifestyles and habits to better mental and physical health (Rechnitzer 1982; Hogan 1984; DeVries 1980).

Social-environmental improvement programs work to change the social and physical environment, and so prevent illness (Hansen and Chappell 1985). Loneliness and the lack of a social network, for example, can cause mental distress. Also, the most isolated older people, who would benefit most from recreation or fitness programs, often do not use them (Biette, Matthews, and Schwenger 1983; Caloren 1980).

A program in Vancouver called the "Seniors Well-Being Activation Team and Society (SWAT) took an activist stance toward environmental change and health promotion (Wallace and Thompson 1985). The program organizers went door to door to talk to seniors about forming a health promotion program for older people in the Grandview-Woodlands section of Vancouver. The program included meal service, counselling, and the establishment of links between people in need and service agencies. This kind of program works to overcome the environmental barriers to good health (like lack of transportation, poor housing, or the lack of informal supports).

Social-environmental change can lead to even broader improvements in health care. Reduction of pollutants in food, land, and water could reduce illness. This abuse of the environment may cause as many as 75 percent of cancers (Bennett and Krasny 1981). Improved working conditions could reduce lung diseases, cancer, silicosis, asbestosis, and hearing loss that often show up as illnesses in later life. The 1979 Canada Health Survey (Health and Welfare Canada and Statistics Canada 1981, cited in Stone and Fletcher 1986b) found that among men and women aged 70 and over the lowest socioeconomic group had the highest proportion of people with chronic hypertension (an illness that can lead to stroke and dementia). Stone and Fletcher (1986b, Section 4.9) say that these findings indicate "the importance of environmental factors in physical and mental health."

Environmentally caused illnesses may be the hardest to prevent. They will require changes in the Canadian economy, in social services, and in workplace safety. A change in the public awareness of environmental causes of disease has already begun to take place. Working conditions have improved in most industries, regulations have set higher standards for pollution control, and anti-smoking lobbies in cities across the country have begun to change attitudes and laws about smoking in public. Changes here may come slowly, but they must come if we want better health in old age.

Canada has only begun to value the health promotion model of health care. Research at present cannot show the direct link between most of these programs and decreased health care costs. They may even lead to higher costs because they keep more people alive long enough to get chronic illnesses in later life (Evans 1984). Still, disease prevention and health promotion have caught on in Canada. More older people exercise now than in the past. Also, 30 percent to 40 percent of older men and women reported eating less fats and less fried foods in the past year than in previous years (Stone and Fletcher 1986b). Health promotion will play a growing part in the health care system in the future.

ISSUES FOR THE FUTURE

The health care system of the future will need to respond to older Canadians' changing needs. Three needs show the kinds of changes that the system will have to undergo: the availability of services, access to services, and co-ordination of services (Sturdy and Tindale 1985).

Availability

A program is available if it exists. Some provinces or parts of provinces have a complete continuum of care — from home care to acute hospital care — for older people. Other parts of the country — many rural areas, for example — offer only a few home care options. One rural community care worker described the meals on wheels program in her community.

She arranges with a local restaurant to pick up a half-dozen to a dozen meals each day at lunch time, then delivers them during her lunch hour to people on her case load. She marvels at the good luck of city-based community workers, who can refer their clients to existing meals on wheels programs. Rural parts of Canada will need more community programs in the future (see, for example, Ontario Council of Health 1978).

Accessibility

A program is accessible if an older person can get to it and make use of it. Havens (1980) studied the unmet needs of older people in Manitoba. She found that in each age cohort both men and women reported that the accessibility of services was more of a problem than the availability of services. In other words, even when a range of well-designed services existed, older people still found it hard to make use of services. The older the person, the more problems they had with access. Better access requires better transportation and more home-based care for very old seniors.

Co-ordination

The health care system needs better co-ordination and integration (Health and Welfare Canada 1982b; Ontario Public Health Association, 1983). This need will increase with the growth of community care, because community programs decentralize care. They bring together nurses, social workers, and therapists, who often work for different agencies and have different views of how to care for a client.

Sturdy and Tindale (1985) interviewed thirty health care providers in Ontario and found that only 30 percent of them felt that the system of services for older people was well co-ordinated. Providers saw two problems with the system: first, they said that professionals in different fields try to defend their territories, and, second, that programs in different government ministries overlapped. The government lacked policies to decide who should take responsibility for a certain problem. Services often "appear fragmented and the elderly person and his or her family do not know who to go to for what. ... The elderly person in need of service can fall through the cracks in the system or become frustrated and give up the search" (Sturdy and Tindale 1985, 14).

Co-ordination avoids overlaps between services, and integration brings health and social services into one system. Changes like these will save time and may save money. They will also give older people better health care services.

Canada's health care system will need to improve availability, accessibility, and co-ordination of services. Provinces with services will need to work on access and co-ordination. Provinces with too few services, and rural areas in all provinces, need more availability. The health care system will have to change in different ways in different parts of the country to meet these needs.

CONCLUSION

Will new programs and policies save money or add to the cost of care? Will the rising numbers of older people overload the system? Can Canada afford the rising cost of health care? Denton and Spencer (1983) studied the potential cost of health care in the future. They looked at three future population projections — a baseline rate with little change, a low fertility rate, and a high fertility rate. They found that all three demographic projections led to higher health care costs in the future. "Under a wide range of assumptions concerning future demographic change," they say, "the costs will rise appreciably by the early decades of the next century" (Denton and Spencer 1983, 160). By 2031, when all of the Baby Boom children have passed age 65, Denton and Spencer (1983) say that health care will take from 1.5 percent to 2 percent more of the Canadian gross national product than in the early 1980s.

They also say that this kind of increase will cost Canada, at worst, about the same proportion of GNP that West Germany paid for health care in the 1970s, and only a little more than Sweden and the United States paid in those years (Maxwell 1981; Denton and Spencer 1983). Changes in the system, such as an emphasis on community care and prevention, could lower costs still more.

The changes taking place today suggest that the health care system will look different in the future than it does today. Closer studies of older people's health care needs will allow the system to fine-tune its programs and treatments. A closer study of methods used to treat older people will allow policy makers and medical practitioners to decide what treatments make the most sense for an older person. The critique of the medical model and growing interest in social models of health care may lead to more community-based services. Also, as the population ages, more people will show an interest in disease prevention and health promotion. More comprehensive models of health care, like the social and health promotion models, will lead to better health care for older people as well as better health at all ages.

SUMMARY

1. Health care needs for the elderly range from maintenance programs for the well elderly to long-term institutional care for those who have severe health problems.
2. Three models of health care exist in Canada today: the medical model, the social model, and the health promotion model. The medical model of health care dominates the health care system today. This model is concerned with treatment of illness.
4. Canada has one of the most comprehensive health care systems in the world, but it spends proportionately more of its gross national product on health care than do some countries with more comprehensive systems.

5. Research shows that the commitment to the medical model may account for higher than necessary health care costs. Complex medical procedures, increased salaries for medical personnel, and high institutional costs all lead to increasing health care costs.

6. The social model of health care supports a continuum of services from institutional care to home care. It calls for health care programs that help older people to live in their own homes. These programs include geriatric day hospitals, adult day care programs, and home care.

7. Home care programs tailor services to fit the needs of the older person. They provide families with help to relieve caregiver burden. These programs may or may not save money, but they do achieve one goal: they allow people to stay in their homes as long as they can.

8. The health promotion model of health care supports healthy lifestyles and a better environment. It takes a broad view of health care that recognizes a need for changes in the workplace and improvements in socioeconomic status.

9. Medical costs will probably rise in the future, but economists say that an increase in the number of older people will not cause a crisis in health care costs. The system will need better co-ordination to limit the cost of care.

SELECTED READINGS

Chappell, Neena L., Laurel A. Strain, and Audrey A. Blandford. *Aging and Health Care: A Social Perspective*. Toronto: Holt, Rinehart and Winston, 1986. An excellent study of Canada's health care system. The authors put health care in a social context. They look at informal and formal types of care, community care, and the health status of older people. A readable and informative introduction to health care in Canada.

Evans, Robert G. *Strained Mercy: The Economics of Canadian Health Care*. Toronto: Butterworths, 1984. A careful economic study of health care in Canada. The book presumes some knowledge of microeconomic theory for a full grasp of the discussion.

Lalonde, Marc. *A New Perspective on the Health of Canadians: A Working Document*. Ottawa: Minister of Supply and Services, 1974. This book describes Lalonde's model of the health field, a concept still used to discuss health care policy and aging today.

CHAPTER 8

FINANCES AND ECONOMICS

INTRODUCTION

Jack Bruckner, aged 65, took early retirement two years ago. He gets a pension from his job and an Old Age Security cheque each month. His wife Betty, 59, never worked outside the home, so she gets no pension. They live in a small government-subsidized apartment. Last spring Jack and Betty decided to travel east for a holiday when Betty's brother came to visit from England. Jack knew their old car would never make the

171

trip, so he went to the bank for a car loan. "I never thought they'd give me a loan," he says. "I went in thinking they'd just laugh at the idea. But the bank manager looked at my pension income and approved the loan. I can't believe it — I never thought, with the little we make, that we'd be able to buy a new car."

Like many older people, Jack and Betty do not have much, but they feel satisfied with what they have. Both of them lived through the Depression and through lean times after they first got married. They worry less about money now than in the past, and, Jack says, when Betty gets her pension from the government in a few years their financial worries will be over.

Canada's pension system can take some of the credit for the Bruckners' financial well-being. The National Advisory Council on Aging (1985b, 2) says that "the real [after inflation] income of families headed by seniors rose by 49 percent between 1967 and 1982." As a group, older people had more money for basics and more money to spend on things that improved the quality of their lives.

The retirement income system has also decreased the amount of poverty among older people during the 1980s. In 1980, for example, 61.5 percent of unattached older people lived below the low-income line in Canada. That figure dropped to 46.1 percent in 1985 (Statistics Canada 1986b).

Cheal (1983; 1985a; 1985b) looked at *intergenerational family transfers* — the amount of money that passes from one generation of family members to another — to assess older people's financial well-being. He (1985a) found that older people gave (in net value) more than they got and that they showed a larger difference between what they gave and what they got than any other age group. He concludes that older people have more money to spend than earlier studies suggested.

A number of studies and reports like these show that as a group older people have better incomes than many people imagine. Still, the retirement income system has its flaws, some of them serious. While income has risen in the past few years for older people in general, certain groups still have incomes below the poverty line in old age. Older people from lower-income backgrounds, people who cannot speak English or French, people without much education, and people who live in small towns all have lower than average incomes. Very old people, women, and *unattached* individuals (a term used by Statistics Canada (Health and Welfare Canada 1983, 42) to describe a "person living alone or in a household where he/she is not related to other household members") often live below the poverty line (National Council of Welfare 1985c, 3).

Almost half the unattached population of older people (80 percent of them women) live in poverty. In 1983 "one elderly Canadian in four lived below the low income line"; about 71 percent of these people are women (National Council of Welfare 1985b, 28).

Even middle-class families can face a sharp drop in income when they retire. The National Council of Welfare (1984d) reports that in 1981 the median income of families with heads aged 65–69 came to only 61 percent of the income of families with a head aged 55–64. Unattached people aged 65 to 69 in that year had a median income only three-quarters that of unattached people aged 55–64. A closer look showed that "public programs for the elderly replace little more than half of the single person's pre-retirement disposable income. ... The two-earner couple fares little better; its retirement income is only 56 percent of pre-retirement net income" (National Council of Welfare 1984d, 50). Couples on a *fixed pension* (a pension that is not indexed to the cost of living) get poorer every year because of inflation. Most people, except the very rich and the very poor, will feel a drop in their standard of living when they retire.

The system needs to change. First, all older people should receive enough income to keep them out of poverty. Second, the poorest people today — many of them very old, single women — need special increases in their pensions. Third, the system should ensure that all Canadians have decent pensions in the future. The federal and provincial governments, the National Council of Women, the Royal Canadian Legion, and dozens of other groups have suggested changes in the pension system (Health and Welfare Canada 1982f). Writers call this "The Great Pension Debate," and the results of this debate will decide the retirement incomes of older Canadians now and in the years to come.

This chapter looks at (1) the structure of the Canadian pension system and how it works, (2) the flaws in the system and suggestions for pension reform, and (3) the future of retirement income in Canada.

THE HISTORY OF CANADA'S PENSION SYSTEM

Bryden (1974, 19) says that until the 1920s Canadian pension policy reflected the "market ethos." This ethos said that individuals should take responsibility for themselves in old age and that those who need help should get it from their families (Bryden 1974, 20). Bryden reports that city life and industrialization in Canada made this ethos hard to practise. The *Labour Gazette*, for example, stated in 1924 that "high rents, [and] overcrowding in houses, make it difficult for the poor to provide for their aged parents. It has been the experience of social agencies that many of the old men and women in their districts are suffering from the lack of the necessities of life" (*Labour Gazette* 1924, 665, cited in Bryden 1974, 42).

The government decided to act to relieve the poverty among older people. A Commons committee issued a report in 1925 that called for a $20 pension to people aged 70 or older who passed a residence requirement and a means test (a test of financial need). The committee proposed that the federal government and the provinces should each pay half the cost of pension benefits. The plan did not require pensioners to pay anything into the program. The committee saw the program as a supplement to income more than as a pension. The Old Age Pension Act became law in 1927, and all the provinces and the Northwest Territories agreed to the plan by 1936. This plan, for the first time, defined pensions as a right due to all older Canadians.

In 1951 the federal government passed the Old Age Security Act and the Old Age Assistance Act to replace the Old Age Pension Act. The Old Age Security Act set up a pension plan run solely by the federal government. The new plan paid up to $40 a month at age 70 without a means test. The government increased this pension to $55 a month in 1961. The Old Age Assistance Act set up a means-tested pension for people between 65 and 69 years old who could demonstrate financial need. The provinces and the federal government shared the cost for this program. The plan required no contributions and paid the same pension to all poorer pensioners, including homemakers.

These early programs supplemented the incomes of older people (they offered basic income security), but the government kept payments low, so people would have an incentive to provide for their own old age (National Health and Welfare 1973, cited in Chappell 1980b). In the 1960s the government broadened the pension system by setting up the Guaranteed Income Supplement program to supplement Old Age Security. This program was designed to help the poorest older people. In 1966 the government started the Canada and Quebec Pension Plans. All wage earners in Canada pay a part of their incomes into these plans. By the 1970s Canada had two types of programs in place: *income security* programs (the Old Age Security and the Guaranteed Income Supplement) and *income maintenance* programs (the Canada and Quebec Pension Plans). These programs form the basis of the Canadian pension system today. The government designed the first type of program to help people meet their basic needs in retirement. It designed the second type of program to help people maintain their pre-retirement income and lifestyle.

By the mid-1970s *government transfers* (the Old Age Security and the Guaranteed Income Supplement, paid for from tax revenues) and the Canada Pension Plan accounted for about 60 percent of older Canadians' pension incomes. Private pensions, from former employers, made up only 20 percent of older people's total income, and assets (investments and savings) made up a little more than 20 percent (Myles 1984). Myles reports that government transfers make up increasingly larger portions of individuals' incomes as they age. "As each year passes," he writes, "the number of wage earners declines, savings are spent and inflation erodes the real value of both savings and private pensions" (1984, 22). This means that older people are more dependent on public policy for their well-being than ever before. This makes the study of pensions vital to an understanding of old age today.

THE CANADIAN RETIREMENT INCOME SYSTEM TODAY

Tier One: Government Transfers

Canada has a three-tiered pension system shaped like a pyramid (see Exhibit 8.1). The Old Age Security (OAS), the Guaranteed Income Supplement (GIS), and the Spouse's Allowance (SA) — called government transfer programs — make up the first tier. All Canadians aged 65 or over, rich or poor, get the same OAS pension. The GIS goes to people with no income other than the OAS. The SA goes to spouses between ages 60 and 64 who are married to a GIS pensioner. People do not have to pay into these pensions; rather, the government pays them out of tax revenue. These programs protect older people's incomes — especially those of the very poor — from falling below a specified level.

Not surprisingly, poorer people depend on transfers most. Older people in 1980, with less than a Grade 9 education, for example, had an average income slightly above the low-income cutoff for that year. Transfer payments made up about two-thirds of their income (51 percent for men, 72 percent for women) (Statistics Canada 1984b).

The OAS in January 1985 came to $273.80 a month per person. It went to almost 2.5 million people — over 99 percent of all Canadians aged 65 and over. The government taxes the OAS as income, so pensioners with enough income to pay taxes will pay some or all of their OAS back to the

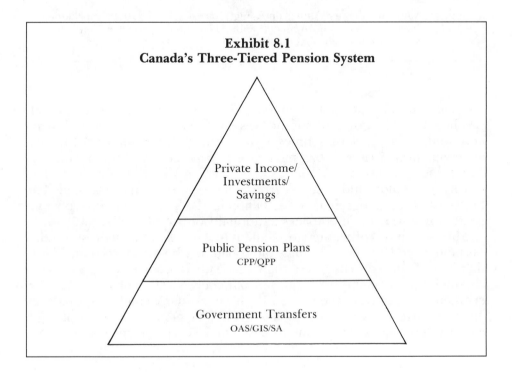

Exhibit 8.1
Canada's Three-Tiered Pension System

Private Income/
Investments/
Savings

Public Pension Plans
CPP/QPP

Government Transfers
OAS/GIS/SA

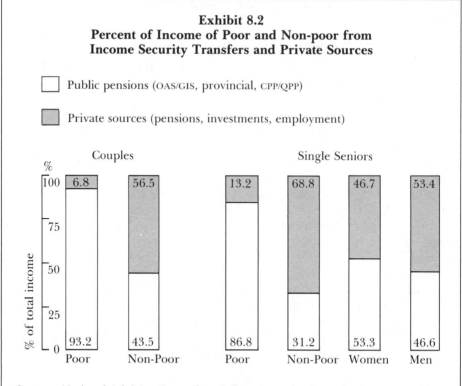

Exhibit 8.2
Percent of Income of Poor and Non-poor from
Income Security Transfers and Private Sources

☐ Public pensions (OAS/GIS, provincial, CPP/QPP)

▨ Private sources (pensions, investments, employment)

Source: National Advisory Council on Aging, *Expression* 3, no. 1. (Ottawa: National
         Advisory Council on Aging, 1985b). "Poor" and "non-poor" refer to in-
         comes below or above the poverty line.

government. The poorest older people, who pay no tax, keep all their
OAS benefits. The government indexes OAS payments to the cost of living
and adjusts the rates four times a year. But in 1983 and 1984 the government capped rises in OAS payments to 6 percent and 5 percent. The
government planned to de-index OAS payments in 1985, but it backed
down after seniors and business groups across the country protested. The
high cost of this program (over $8 billion in 1984–85) makes it an obvious
target for government cutbacks (National Council of Welfare 1984b).

The Guaranteed Income Supplement (GIS) goes to the poorest seniors.
GIS benefits in 1985 went to single older people who made less than $7,800
that year from sources other than the OAS. It went to couples with a
combined (non-OAS) income of approximately $10,000 or less. The gov-
ernment does not tax the GIS, and it indexes GIS payments so that they
go up quarterly as the cost of living rises. A person (or a couple) get
either full or partial GIS payments based on a yearly income test. In 1985,

Exhibit 8.3
The Canada Pension System

Program	Benefits/Month	Requirements
Old Age Security	$294.43 (October 1986) increases quarterly	– 65 years or over – residence requirement – Canadian citizen or legal resident – non-contributory
Guaranteed Income Supplement	$349.91 (single, max., October 1986) $455.78 (couple, max., October 1986)	– low or no income besides OAS – non-contributory
Spouse's Allowance	$522.32 (October 1986)	– equal to the sum of OAS and max. GIS at married rate – spouse married to OAS pensioner who gets GIS – spouse between 60 and 64 – must satisfy other OAS requirements – non-contributory
Widow or Widower's Benefit	$576.66 (October 1986)	– paid to widow or widower (60–64 years old) of OAS recipient
Canada Pension Plan	$486.11 (max. 1986)	– 3.6% of income paid into plan, half by worker, half by employer (minus a basic deduction and up to Year's Maximum Pensionable Earnings (YMPE)
Survivor's Benefits	$291.67 (CPP max., 1986, spouse 65 and over) $273.35 (CPP max., 1986, spouse 55–64)	– 60% of contributor's retirement pension – min. 3 years contributions of deceased
Death Benefit	$2,580 max. lump sum, 1986	– paid to estate of deceased contributor

| Disability Benefits | $455.64 (max., CPP, 1986) | – paid to contributor with severe and prolonged disability |
| Children and Orphan Benefits | $91.06 (CPP, 1986) | – to each orphan of contributor |

Source: Health and Welfare Canada, *Canada Pension Plan, Family Allowance, Old Age Security, Canada Pension Plan, Statement on Current Benefits,* 1986a. Reproduced with permission of the Minister of Supply and Services Canada.

a single person could receive a maximum total of approximately $600 per month in combined OAS and GIS payments, or approximately $7,200 per year. Each person in a married couple could get a maximum of almost $500 apiece or about $1,000 per month for two (almost $12,000 per year for the couple). Widowers or widows could get a maximum of approximately $6,400 per year. Single pensioners, more often than married pensioners, have low enough incomes to need the GIS. Women, many of them widows, make up over three-fifths of all people who get the GIS (Health and Welfare Canada 1985b).

The government added the Spouse's Allowance (SA) program to Tier One of the system in 1975. The SA goes to a low-income pensioner's spouse who is aged 60 to 64 years old. It pays an amount equal to the OAS and the maximum GIS at the married rate. This couple gets the same transfer payments as a poor couple with both spouses aged 65 and over. If the GIS pensioner dies, the spouse continues to get SA payments. When the survivor reaches 65 the government stops SA payments and the person then gets an OAS/GIS pension. About 90 percent of Spouse's Allowances go to women (National Council of Welfare 1984b).

Without GIS and SA benefits more than half of all older Canadians would live below the poverty line. One quarter of all people who receive the GIS are so poor that they get the full amount. This program cost the government almost $300 million in 1984–85 (National Council of Welfare 1984b).

Nova Scotia, Ontario, Manitoba, Saskatchewan, Alberta, British Columbia, Yukon, and the Northwest Territories also have provincial supplement plans to help the poorest seniors. These supplements range from 3–4 percent of the OAS/GIS in Manitoba to 18–21 percent of the OAS/GIS in the Yukon (National Council of Welfare 1984b). In Ontario and British Columbia about half the seniors have incomes low enough to entitle them to provincial supplements.

All provinces reduce taxes for older property owners and give rent rebates to seniors. Ontario, for example, offers seniors an annual $500 property tax rebate and a $50 sales tax rebate (National Council of Welfare 1984b). These programs play an important part in keeping very old people and even people with private pensions at a decent income level.

Tier Two: The Canada Pension Plan and the Quebec Pension Plan

The Canada Pension Plan (CPP) and the Quebec Pension Plan (QPP) form the pension system's second, smaller tier. Workers who earned over $1,600, employers, and self-employed people paid over $3.2 billion into the CPP in 1982. (Note: The CPP allows a province to opt out of the plan. Quebec took this option and decided to set up its own plan. The QPP differs from the CPP in a few details, but in most ways it mirrors the CPP. This text will use the term CPP to refer to both plans.)

The CPP does two things: first, it ensures that workers will have some pension beyond the OAS/GIS/SA when they retire, and, second, it will save the government money in GIS and SA payments in the future. The CPP combines two types of pension plans: a savings plan and a transfer plan. It works like a savings plan because each worker pays a percentage of his or her salary into it each month. In 1986, the law required workers to pay 1.8 percent of their wages into the plan (up to a maximum of $444.60 per year for 1986) (Health and Welfare Canada 1986b). Their employers paid a matching amount. Self-employed people paid 3.6 percent of their incomes into the plan. The CPP plans gradually to increase the contribution for all workers from 3.6 percent (the total that the employee and employer paid in 1986) to 7.6 percent in 2011. The plan needs to increase these rates because more people in the future will be eligible for CPP/QPP pensions. This money goes to the worker's credit, and, when a person retires, the pension they get depends on how much they paid into the plan. The CPP also works like a transfer plan because the money paid in today does not go into a private account for each person. It goes to pay the pensions of retired plan members today. Today's workers will get their CPP pensions from workers' contributions in the future.

The CPP does some things well. First, it protects people from inflation. Personal savings, for example, can decrease in value over time, but the CPP promises that a person will get a pension in the future geared to the cost of living at that time. Second, the CPP covers almost all workers, so most workers will enter retirement with some CPP benefits. Third, the plan moves with workers when they change jobs. This is called "portability." In a fluid job market, where people change jobs often, this can make the difference between having a pension or not. Fourth, the plan locks in both workers' *and* employers' contributions from the start. This is called *vesting*. Workers get credit for their total payments (their own and their employer's contributions) even if they move from one employer to another. Fifth, the CPP promises to pay workers up to 25 percent of their pre-retirement earnings (to a maximum of 25 percent of the year's average industrial wage) for life. Sixth, the plan applies the same rules to men and women. Women pay in at the same rates as men, and the plan entitles them to the same benefits. Some private plans base benefits on different mortality tables for men and women, so women in some plans get smaller payments because on average they live longer than men. Seventh, all CPP members get survivor and disability benefits, a vital point because in Canada women often outlive their husbands and many women have no pensions of their own. Eighth, and not least, the government indexes the CPP to the cost of living. It goes up as the cost of living increases, so people do not fall behind each year as they do with a fixed-income pension.

The CPP now pays benefits to more older people than ever before. In 1967, the CPP paid benefits to less than one-half of one percent of older people, but in June of 1983 the CPP went to half of all people 65 and over (National Council of Welfare 1984b). The number of people who get CPP pensions, the size of their pensions, and the total paid out in CPP pensions will all increase in the years ahead.

Tier Three: Private Pensions, Savings, and Work

Private income makes up the third tier of the Canadian pension system. The OAS/GIS and CPP make up less than 40 percent of a middle-income earner's average pre-retirement income.[1]

For some people it makes up even less of their pre-retirement income. In 1984, for example, OAS/GIS and CPP benefits for an unattached person came to only $1,384 over the poverty line for a person who lives in a city of half a million or more people (National Council of Welfare 1984b). All workers will need private pensions and savings to make up the difference between government pensions and pre-retirement income.

How many workers can count on private pension plans to help them in retirement? The National Council of Welfare (1984b) reports that about 14,000 private pension plans existed in Canada in 1981, but these plans covered less than 40 percent of all workers. Private pension benefits in 1981 made up only 16 percent of unattached men's incomes, 13 percent of older couples' incomes, and 9 percent of unattached women's incomes. Most older people rely on savings to make up for lost pre-retirement income. Private savings and investment income made up about 30 percent of older people's incomes in 1981. These sources ranked second, after transfer payments, as the major source of seniors' income (Health and Welfare Canada 1983).

The government has encouraged more savings through Registered Retirement Savings Plans (RRSPs). Beginning in 1986–87, self-employed individuals, or employees with no private pension plan, can save 20 per-

---

[1]The government defines a middle-income earner as someone in the middle 60 percent of households. In 1982 the middle-income earner earned between $15,000 and $40,000 (Health and Welfare Canada 1982a).

cent of their earned income up to a maximum of $7,500 a year without paying income tax on this money. (Individuals who belong to a private pension plan can contribute $3,500 minus their contribution to their private pension plan or 20 percent of earned income if less than $3,500 a year.) RRSP members pay tax on the money only when they withdraw it in retirement. This defers taxes to a time when the person has a lower income — and so a lower tax rate. The number of RRSPs grew from 248,000 in 1970 to 2 million in 1980 (Amiel 1981; Daly 1981). In 1981 alone, contributors saved over $3.9 billion in RRSPs, half a billion more than in private pension plans (National Council of Welfare 1984b). Proposed higher limits for RRSP contributions could make them even more attractive to middle- and upper-income earners in the future.

Other income in retirement includes earnings, rent subsidies, and tax exemptions. In 1981 older couples earned 15 percent of their income, unattached males earned 9 percent, and unattached females 5 percent (Health and Welfare Canada 1983). In 1976 almost 20 percent of spending units (families or individuals) aged 65 and over reported rent subsidies. The federal government allows special tax exemptions for older people, like the age exemption on income tax above the personal exemption (Health and Welfare Canada 1982b). Also, corporations offer subsidies for goods and services, like reduced theatre ticket prices or reduced air fares for older people. Stone and MacLean (1979) say that these indirect subsidies could add at least 30 percent to older people's average total income, and this does not count other benefits such as subsidized health care costs and home care services.

This complex system of plans and programs, along with earnings from work, should create a decent old age for all Canadians, but it does not. Many older people still suffer a sharp loss in income and a shocking change in lifestyle when they retire. Almost every tier and subsection of the system fails in some way to do its job.

SHORTCOMINGS OF THE SYSTEM

The Canadian retirement income system has two goals. The first is to keep all older people out of poverty, no matter how little they earned before retirement. The government designed the OAS/GIS/SA program to achieve this goal. The second is to protect people from a sharp drop in their income after retirement. The government designed the CPP to achieve this goal. The National Council of Welfare (1984b) calls these the anti-poverty and the income-replacement goals of the system. The Canadian system achieves neither of these goals. A look at each tier of the system will show where the system fails.

Government Transfers

The OAS/GIS/SA program does not keep all older people out of poverty. A couple living in a large Canadian city had an income from these programs that fell $117 below the poverty line in December 1984. A single person's income fell $276 below the poverty line (National Council of Welfare 1984c). The February 1984 budget gave single people and one-pension couples a $50 per month raise in their GIS. This raised a single pensioner's income from 56 percent to 62 percent of that of a married couple and closed the gap in living standard between unattached and married pensioners. Still, many single people lived in poverty. In 1985 a single person got a maximum OAS and GIS payment of $599.21 a month or $7,190.52 a year. But the Statistics Canada low-income estimate for 1985 for a single person in a large city came to $10,238, or almost one-and-a-half times the OAS/GIS payments (National Council of Welfare 1985b).

The Canada and Quebec Pension Plans

The CPP does not help people maintain their pre-retirement income — the second goal of the system. For many older people today — those who retired before 1966 or those who never worked for a wage — the CPP/QPP offers no help at all. Some people who get the CPP find that it does not pay enough. In 1984, for example, the OAS and CPP paid a maximum of only $7,845.36 a year, more than $2,000 below the poverty line for a single person living a large city. Also, people who get the GIS lose $1 of their benefits for each $2 they make through the CPP. These low CPP payments do not replace much of the average person's income. Half of all retirees currently face a 5 percent drop in living standard, a third face a 15 percent drop, and a sixth face a 25 percent drop (Health and Welfare Canada 1982b). People need private pensions or savings to maintain their pre-retirement lifestyles.

Private Pensions

How does the private pension system help most people cope with retirement? Not very well. First, only 44 percent of all Canadian workers in 1980 had private pension plans (National Council of Welfare 1984b). This includes workers in the public sector (government workers and workers for Crown corporations) and workers in the private sector (workers for private corporations). Only 34 percent of private sector workers in Canada in 1980 had private pensions (National Council of Welfare 1984b). People who work part-time, seasonal workers, and those who work for small businesses and at low-paying jobs often have no private pensions. Only one worker in ten either at or below the average industrial wage has a private pension plan. This means the poorest people have the least chance to get a private pension.

Second, outside the civil service, less than one-third of pension plans index payments to make up for inflation, and only one-fifth offer full inflation protection (National Council of Welfare 1984b). In an inflationary economy people on a fixed pension — even a good one — become poorer as they age. At 8 percent inflation (a moderate rate in the early

1980s) a $900 pension will be worth only $566 five years after a person retires — more than a one-third drop in their pension's value (Royal Commission on the Status of Pensions in Ontario 1980, cited in National Council of Welfare 1984b). The National Council of Welfare (1984b) reports that the average annual income from private plans came to $3,930 in 1979. Men averaged $4,516, and women averaged only $2,929. The Council says "it is clear that few are doing well" (1984b, 43).

Third, only 4 percent to 10 percent of people who belong to private pension plans ever collect a full pension (Senate of Canada 1979). Two things account for this. First, few plans have early vesting (vesting refers to a person's right to their own pension contributions and their employer's contributions if they change jobs). Early vesting locks both the employer's and the employee's payments in the plan soon after employment begins. Second, most plans lack *portability* (portability means that workers can transfer their pension money to another plan with a new employer). When workers leave a company today, most of them get either a deferred pension (if their money is vested and locked in) or they get their own (but not their employer's) pension contributions back — sometimes with no interest. The employer's share stays in the fund, so each time a person changes jobs they lose half their fund and have to start again. This means that even if the whole labour force belongs to private pension plans, as long as workers change jobs often (as they do today) only a small number of people will ever collect a full pension.

Private Savings

The government started the Registered Retirement Savings Program (RRSP) to encourage private savings for retirement. This program cost the Canadian government $5 billion dollars in lost tax revenues in 1983. The program helps people in higher income brackets the most. First, people with higher incomes can pay in the most (for a self-employed individual, 20 percent of his or her income to a maximum of $7,500). Poorer people simply do not have this much money to put aside. Also, people in higher tax brackets get more money back through tax deductions through this program. The higher their tax bracket, the more they get back. Exhibit 8.4 shows the proportion of people from each income level who paid into RRSPs and the average amount they contributed.

INEQUALITY IN LATER LIFE

The National Council of Welfare (1985c) reports that the older population has a more unequal income distribution than younger age groups. A small percentage of older people have savings and investments and live on comfortable incomes, but people who live near or below the poverty line in Canada before they retire will stay there in old age. "At present," a 1982 government report on pensions says, "4 percent of the

Exhibit 8.4
RRSP Contributors, by Income Level, 1981

Income Level	Proportion of Tax Filers	Average Contribution
Under $6,000	0.6%	$ 411
$ 6,000 – $ 9,999	3.3	832
$10,000 – $13,999	7.5	1,154
$14,000 – $19,999	14.1	1,395
$20,000 – $24,999	21.0	1,687
$25,000 – $29,999	28.4	1,899
$30,000 – $34,999	34.9	2,127
$35,000 – $39,999	43.0	2,306
$40,000 – $49,999	49.5	2,621
$50,000 – $69,999	52.7	3,469
$70,000 – $99,999	56.9	4,460
$100,000 and over	55.1	5,346
Average	12.9	1,986

"The pattern is clear. In general the higher his or her income group, the more likely the taxfiler is to have an RRSP and the larger his or her average contribution. Very few low-income Canadians can afford an RRSP. The average RRSP contribution for the $100,000-and-over group was thirteen times as large as the average amount for contributors with incomes under $6,000."

Source: National Council of Welfare, *A Pension Primer*, 1984b, 60, Table 24 (using data from Revenue Canada, *Taxation Statistics* (Ottawa: Minister of Supply and Services, 1983), Tables 2 and 3). Reproduced with permission of the Minister of Supply and Services Canada.

elderly have over 40 percent of the investment income" (Government of Canada 1982a, 19–22). The report goes on to say that over half of middle-aged, middle-income couples today will not save enough money for their retirement to replace more than 5 percent of their income, and only about one person or couple in five will be able to replace 15 percent of their earnings from their savings.

Some groups face worse financial dangers than others in old age. Women, for example, show higher rates of poverty than men. This reflects differences in men's and women's work careers, salaries, and pension options.

Women and Pensions

"To be old and female," the Canadian Council on Social Development reports in its *Fact Book on Poverty*, "is the best combination to ensure being poor in Canada" (Canadian Council on Social Development 1975, 22–23, cited in Dulude 1978, 38). In 1983, for example, women over age 65 made up 70.7 percent of all seniors below the low-income line (though they made up only 57.2 percent of all seniors (poor and non-poor) (National Council of Welfare 1985c). In 1984 more than half of unattached women over age 65 lived below the poverty line (National Council of Welfare 1985c). "After a lifetime spent taking care of their spouses and children," the National Council of Welfare (1979, 48) says, "these women who had no opportunity to become financially self-sufficient are now abandoned by the generation that benefited most from their work." A government commission (Senate of Canada 1979, 65) concludes that "the retirement income system has failed and the failure is especially dismal with elderly women."

Why do women have such low incomes in old age? First, the structure of private and public pensions discriminates against women — sometimes in hidden ways. Women often work for smaller non-unionized companies with no private pension plans, and they also tend to work part-time and thus fail to qualify for pension coverage (Government of Canada 1982b).

Second, women in general earn less than men and hold lower-status jobs. Armstrong and Armstrong (1981) report that women work in low-wage jobs that demand little skill and offer little chance for advancement. Women make up the largest percentage of babysitters, typists, and variety-store sales clerks, and many of the small firms they work for have no pension plans. Only 34.6 percent of women in paid labour belong to a private pension plan (compared to 50.6 percent of men), and 60 percent of these women work for government or Crown corporations. In private industry only 19 percent of women have pension plans (National Council of Welfare 1984b).

Armstrong and Armstrong (1984, 42) found that women get lower pay than men for the same job. In 1980, for example, "in only four of the twenty-one leading occupations (elementary and secondary teachers, nurses and nursing aides) do women make on average as much as three-quarters of what men make." Low pay means that these women pay a smaller amount into the CPP than men, and this will mean smaller public pensions when they retire. In 1978 only 18 percent of women 65 and over outside Quebec got the maximum CPP pension, and in 1981 unattached women 65 and over received only 7 percent of their income from the Canada or Quebec Pension Plan (Health and Welfare Canada 1983).

Third, women have a different work pattern than men. Women often leave work after a first job to raise children; they spend three times longer than men between jobs and tend to work at each job for a shorter time than men (National Council of Welfare 1984b). This pattern keeps them from storing up pension credits.

Widows

Widows make up the largest group among women 65 and over, and, of all women, widows benefit least from Canada's pension system. "After fifty years or so of unpaid, faithful service," the National Council of Welfare (1979, 32) says, "a woman's only reward is likely to be poverty."

Why do older widows have such low incomes? First, only 44.3 percent of all workers belong to a private pension plan (National Council of Welfare 1984b), and only 44 percent of these private pension plans pay survivor benefits to widows. Of those that do, 24 percent pay a pension to the survivor for five years or less, and only 10 percent of the married men who have a plan with a survivor-benefit option take up the survivor-benefit option for their wives (Senate of Canada 1979). Instead men often choose higher benefits while they are alive. This means that fewer than one in four widows will get a regular pension from her husband's workplace, and even when a woman does get a benefit, in most cases she gets only 50 percent of his pension (Statistics Canada 1976b, cited in National Council of Welfare 1979). Thirty percent of private sector pension plans "promise not a cent to the surviving spouse — not even a refund of the contributions that might have been made by the husband or wife" (National Council of Welfare 1984b, 55).

The public pension system also lets widows down. The National Council of Welfare (1984b, 38) says that "a woman with no retirement pension of her own will suffer a drastic reduction in her living standard when her husband dies." The Council makes the point with an example. A couple in October 1983 received $521 in Old Age Security, $286 from the Guaranteed Income Supplement, and $234 from the husband's CPP pension (an average amount for a new pension). Their total retirement income each month came to $1,041 or $52 above the poverty line for a large city. The husband died that year, and his widow's income dropped to $261 from the OAS, $191 from the GIS, and only $141 from the CPP. Her total income each month came to $593, 25 percent below the poverty line. "She must get by on 57 percent of the income coming into the household before her husband died, while it is generally accepted that a replacement rate of 60 to 70 percent is necessary" (National Council of Welfare 1984b, 38).

Women coming into old age today will do a little better. More of them work, and some of them will get CPP pensions. But even so, many women will get only small pensions. In September 1983 55.1 percent of women got CPP pensions worth less than $150 per month. Survivor benefits for the CPP averaged only $161.30 per month in January 1984 or only $1,936 for the year (National Council of Welfare 1984b). Homemakers will have no private pensions, they will get no CPP pension of their own, and if their husband's pension plan pays no survivor benefits they will get no pension at all. Younger women will do better in the future because more of them work, but low wages and part-time work will leave most women without private pensions. They too will have small CPP pensions.

The system needs reform. Women and men need better private pension plans, better survivor and homemaker benefits, and more help from the OAS/GIS/SA. The government has proposed some changes to the system. This has sparked what some people call "The Great Pension Debate."

PENSION REFORM

Canada has stewed over pension reform for years. In 1981 the government held a National Pensions Conference, but the participants could not agree on reforms. In 1982 the government produced a report called *Better Pensions for Canadians* (Government of Canada 1982a), but the government decided not to act on the report's recommendations until it reached consensus on changes with interest groups and the public. In 1983 the House of Commons set up a Parliamentary Task Force on Pension Reform to review the 1982 report's proposals and propose a set of legislative reforms (House of Commons Canada 1983). The Task Force (also known as the Frith Commission) made its final report to the House of Commons at the end of 1983. The report proposed sixty-five changes that would solve many of the pension system's worst problems. The sections below give some highlights of those proposals.

Private Pension Reform

First, the Task Force says workers should have portable pensions. They should be able to take their total pension savings with them when they change jobs. The Task Force proposes a new tax-assisted retirement fund — the Registered Pension Account (RPA). The worker and the employer would both pay into the RPA, but an RPA would belong to the worker. The account would go with him or her wherever he or she worked, and all payments would be locked in until retirement.

Second, the Task Force calls for full vesting of private pension funds after only two years. People who change jobs often will be able to keep all their pension savings when they move to a new job.

Third, the Task Force says that private pension plans should index pensions to increase with the cost of living.

Fourth, the Task Force says that pension laws and the Bankruptcy Act should prevent creditors from claiming pension funds if a firm goes bankrupt.

Fifth, the Task Force proposes an end to unfair treatment of women. The report proposes: (1) that employer-sponsored pension plans include all full-time workers after a year of service, (2) that firms phase in pensions for all part-time workers, (3) that in the case of a marriage breakup each spouse should get one-half of the other's pension credits and retirement savings, (4) that all private plans provide a "joint life/last survivor benefit," a benefit that, on the death of the first spouse, pays the surviving spouse 60 percent of the pension, and (5) that the survivor in this kind of plan should continue to receive his or her pension even if he or she remarries (House of Commons Canada 1983).

These proposed changes in private pension plans will benefit people with middle incomes most. They will do little for people in firms that have no private pension plan, and they will do little for people with low incomes. Only reform of the public pension system will lead to better pensions for all (National Council of Welfare 1984c).

Public Pension Reform

The Task Force also proposed changes in the Canada Pension Plan. First, it proposed an increase in the Yearly Maximum Pensionable Earnings (YMPE) to equal the Average Industrial Wage (AIW) (the average amount earned by workers in industry). (The maximum CPP pension now comes to only about 80 percent of the AIW.) With the new scheme, people could pay more into the CPP and get more out when they retired. The Task Force also proposed that the government index increases in CPP maximum benefits to a measure like the Average Industrial Wage.

Second, the Task Force proposed that spouses automatically split CPP benefits when the younger spouse turns 65, when a marriage breaks down, when a spouse dies, or when a non-earner spouse becomes disabled. This means that each spouse has a right to half the pension benefits paid by the plan. *Credit-splitting* spreads retirement benefits over the lives of both spouses. A surviving spouse would get 65 percent of the couple's CPP benefit.

Third, the Task Force recommends a homemaker pension for people who work only in the home. This refers to "the spouse, not attached to the labour force, but whose work is caring for home and children" (National Advisory Council on Aging 1985b). Couples that expect to get a homemaker pension will have to pay more into the CPP. This will cost a husband who earns $30,000 about $312 more per year than it would a husband whose wife works outside the home (House of Commons Canada 1983). The report proposed that the government subsidize the cost of homemaker pension payments for low-income families.

Fourth, the Task Force proposed: (1) that the government increase the GIS by $102 a month for single older people; this will raise the guaranteed income to single seniors to two-thirds the guarantee for couples, (2) that the government extend the Spouse's Allowance program to include widows and widowers aged 60 to 64, and (3) that the government raise the OAS to bring it closer to the Average Industrial Wage (House of Commons Canada 1983).

CHANGES IN THE PUBLIC SYSTEM

The system has begun to change (see Exhibit 8.5), and more changes will take place in the years ahead. In June 1984, for example, all the provinces

Exhibit 8.5

CHANGES TO THE PENSION BENEFITS STANDARDS ACT

In May 1985 the federal government announced changes in the Canada Pension Benefits Standards Act. These changes set minimum standards for 1 million government workers and workers in government industries such as Crown corporations. The government will ask provinces to change their rules to meet these new standards. These changes will affect 3.5 million workers. They include:

1. Locked-in vesting mandatory after two years in a private plan.
2. Improved portability by transfer of vested pensions to locked-in RRSPs.
3. The right of all full-time workers to join a private plan after two years of work; all part-time workers must have the right to join if they have earned at least 35 percent of the Yearly Maximum Pensionable Earnings ($8,190 in 1985).
4. Payment of survivor benefits worth at least 60 percent of the amount the couple would have received had the contributor lived. These benefits will continue if the survivor remarries.
5. Division of pension credits and payments 50–50 if a couple divorces, unless the couple or the courts choose a different option.

These changes serve as a model for the private sector as it considers pension reform.

Source: Adapted from National Council of Welfare, *Giving and Taking: The May 1985 Budget and the Poor* (Ottawa: Minister of Supply and Services, 1985a), 36–37.

agreed to allow a woman or man to deduct the years they spend child-rearing from their pensionable years. (Until 1984 these years counted as zero income and lowered a person's average lifetime salary.) People who take time off to care for their children can now deduct from their work record the years when their children were under 7 years old.

Finance Minister Michael Wilson's May 1983 Budget proposed more reform. The provinces still have to approve these changes before they become law, but proposed reforms include equal pension payments for women and men in the same pension plan, vesting after only two years of service, and credit-splitting for spouses when a marriage breaks down. Part-time workers will also be able to join a pension plan if they earn 35 percent of the Average Industrial Wage in two consecutive years. People who do not belong to a private pension plan where they work will be able to almost triple their tax-assisted RRSP savings by 1990 (Schiele 1985).

These changes will balance some of the inequalities in the system. The poorest older people on the GIS will benefit from these changes, and so will widows and women who work part-time, but the government will still have to tackle some tough issues in the future. These include home-makers' pensions, the rising cost of indexed OAS pensions, and indexation of private pension plans.

THE COST OF REFORM

All the proposed changes in private and public pension plans will mean one thing: pensions will cost more money. CPP rates, for example, will have to rise to about 9 percent of workers' earnings by the year 2030 (from 3.6 percent in 1986) just to keep CPP benefits at 25 percent of the Average Industrial Wage. This will cost workers about $300 a year. Better private plans will cost more — the government estimates a rise in costs to about 11 percent more of a worker's pay, or an average of about $125 a year. Better survivor benefits will cost about 0.7 percent of a worker's pay or about $80 a year. This will total about $500 a year in take-home pay (in 1983 dollars) (Health and Welfare Canada 1982a).

How will people feel about these changes? The state of Canada's economy will partly determine how people feel about pension costs. A strong economy and low inflation will make it easier to pay more for pensions; increased costs and low wages will make it harder.

Myles (1982) offers two reasons why Canadians will support a stronger pension system in the future. First, he says, "the elderly are the *elderly parents* of the younger generation of producers." Without state support, the young would have to help care for their parents themselves, and younger people will prefer to "pool their risks" through a central pension system. Second, he says, middle-aged people, because they will be old soon themselves, have a self-interest in supporting a strong pension and social security system for the elderly.

In the end a strong pension system — given the longer life expectancy today — makes sense for everyone. As long as taxpayers see this they will continue to support improvements in Canada's retirement income system (Myles 1981).

SUMMARY

1. Canada's pension system has a sound structure, but the current system "is out of balance" (National Council of Welfare 1984b, 71). Some people — very old women, people from lower income brackets, people with low levels of education, widows, and homemakers — all run a higher than average risk of poverty in old age.

2. Canada has a three-tiered system: the OAS, GIS, and SA make up Tier One, the CPP/QPP make up Tier Two, and private pensions and savings make up Tier Three. Each tier of the system needs reform.
3. The Canadian retirement system has two goals: (1) to keep all older people out of poverty, and (2) to replace pre-retirement income. At present it meets neither goal for many Canadians.
4. Poorer Canadians, who are the people who need private savings the most in retirement, have the least chance of having any. Private pension plans cover fewer than half of Canadian workers. The CPP at best replaces only 25 percent of a person's income up to the average industrial wage, and the OAS/GIS/SA leave the poorest older people in poverty.
5. The government has proposed reforms in the system. Proposed reforms include better GIS/SA payments, better CPP pensions, rules that encourage RRSP savings, and rules that strengthen private pension plans.
6. Reforms to the CPP and to private plans try to ensure that more Canadians get pension coverage — including homemakers, part-time workers, and parents who take time out of the labour force to raise a family. Better public and private pensions for these people may reduce the costs of government transfers in the future. This will save the government money and give people better income in retirement.
7. People will pay for these reforms because everyone — young and old — gains from a strong pension system.

SELECTED READINGS

Armstrong, Pat, and Hugh Armstrong. *The Double Ghetto: Canadian Women and Their Segregated Work*, rev. ed. Toronto: McClelland and Stewart, 1984.
A revealing look at the inequalities women face at work. The Armstrongs compare women to men across occupations and within occupations. They find that in almost every case men earn more money than women for the same work. A good place to begin a study of women and inequality in Canada.

Bryden, Kenneth. *Old Age Pensions and Policy-Making in Canada*. Montreal: McGill-Queen's University Press, 1974.
One of the few reports on the history of the pension system. Bryden is a political scientist, so he looks behind the historical events to discover trends in public policy.

National Council of Welfare. *A Pension Primer*. Ottawa: Minister of Supply and Services, 1984b.
This report on Canada's pension system presents facts and information in an interesting, readable style. The report also has a glossary of terms used to discuss pensions. Like other National Council of Welfare reports (*Pension Reform* and *Sixty-Five and Older*), this report argues that the pension system needs improvement. The Council sends out these and other reports at no cost.

CHAPTER 9

RETIREMENT AND WORK

INTRODUCTION

Claude Rioux retired six months after his sixty-fifth birthday. He had worked as a warehouseman for an electronic supply company. Claude never thought much about retirement in his middle years, but a year or two before he retired he began to feel he had nothing in common with his fellow workers. Most of his friends had retired, and most of his new co-workers had just left high school. They talked about girls and motorcycles and listened to loud music. He had always liked work, but he began to enjoy it less each day. After he turned 65 his boss came by to ask if he had any retirement plans. One time the boss called him into his office and asked him when he planned to leave. "I said I didn't know," Claude says. "Why give him the satisfaction of thinking he could push me out.

193

Hell, I still do a good job. Better than some of the kids who work here now. Oh, I planned to leave in January, but I wouldn't tell him. I thought, 'I'll leave when I'm good and ready.'"

No one forced Claude to retire, but he did. And he left work just about on schedule. He had little reason to keep working past age 65. He had a small pension from work as well as his CPP and OAS pensions, and he planned to open a small electronics repair shop at home. He stayed on until January only to show that no one could push him around.

Retirement has become a part of Canadian society, a stage of life most people will go through. Some people will spend a quarter or more of their adult life in retirement. Gerontologists view retirement today from two points of view: first as a social institution and second as a process of personal adjustment. This chapter will look at retirement from each of these perspectives. It will look at (1) the origin and role of retirement in modern society, (2) the forces that lead a person to retire, and (3) how people adjust to retirement.

RETIREMENT AS A SOCIAL INSTITUTION

The Origins of Retirement

Myles (1984) traces old age today to two developments. The first is the *retirement principle* — the idea that at a fixed age, regardless of mental or physical ability, a person leaves work. The second is the *retirement wage* — a pension paid by the state to support all older people. Myles (1984, 7) says that a new group of people grew out of these two developments — "a population of elders still fit for production who do not engage in economic activity." Employers and employees both supported the retirement principle in North America. Industry supported it for two reasons: first, retirement allowed companies to retire older, skilled workers and hire younger, less skilled workers at lower wages; and, second, companies, using a philosophy of "scientific management" wanted to speed up production and get more out of their workers. Unions offered to have workers work faster if companies reduced the workday, but a faster pace of work made it hard for older workers to compete with younger workers (Atchley 1985). Retirement gave older workers a graceful way to leave work. The federal government in Canada supported the retirement principle for a number of reasons. Canada's first civil service commissioner, Adam Shortt, said in 1922 that retirement:

relieves the government of the embarrassment and extravagance of retaining the services of officers who have outlived their usefulness; creates a proper flow of promotions; renders the service more mobile; deters efficient workers from leaving the public service for private employment ... [and] in general tends to promote efficiency in every way (quoted in Bolger, 1980, 8, cited in Myles 1984, 13).

Unions in North America supported retirement for their own reasons.

Unions wanted companies to use seniority (first hired, last fired) as a method for deciding layoffs or cutbacks. Seniority gave workers a right to a job, and it gave the oldest workers the most job security. But companies resisted the seniority system because older workers cost them more and seniority rights made it hard for them to fire inefficient older workers. Retirement served both unions and employers. It limited seniority rights to people under the age of retirement and allowed companies to let older workers go. The unions traded the older worker's right to a job for job security in middle age (Haber 1978, cited in Atchley 1985, 54).

Still, few people retired in the past compared to today. First, in Canada many people worked on farms or in small businesses with no retirement age. Second, and most important, a lack of retirement income kept most people working as long as they could. Only with the increase in public pensions and social supports for older people after World War II did retirement spread (Myles 1984).

The U.S. Social Security program led the way for this change. The U.S. designed Social Security as a way to get people to retire (Myles 1984, 16). Until then governments gave social assistance to older people, but this assistance, like Canada's early old age assistance program, gave only the poorest older people a small amount of money to help them survive. The government based the program on the English poor law notion of "less eligibility." This rule held that assistance should relieve poverty, but should come to less than the lowest working wage.

Social Security, and later Canada's public pension system, set a new goal for public pensions. These programs promised to make up for a retiree's lost income. "By 1980," Myles (1984, 21) says, "the institution of retirement had been consolidated and old age had become a period in the life cycle defined and sustained by the welfare state."

Government now plays the major role in guaranteeing pensions to older retirees. Public pensions and transfer payments act as a deferred wage because people pay into the program through taxes and CPP/QPP payments while they work. In Canada, though, the amount a person gets does not depend only on how much they paid in. People today get "a share of the social product over and above any claims they may have possessed in their capacity as wage earners" (Myles 1984, 29). Myles calls this a *citizen's wage*. This wage makes retirement a time of economic security and freedom for many older people.

Schulz (1980) estimates that, without government support, workers would have to save 20 percent of their income each year just to get a pension equal to 60–65 percent of their earnings during the last five years before retirement. Few people could afford to save this much on their own. With government help, retirement has become an option for many more people than ever before. Statistics Canada reports that in January 1972, for example, only 10.2 percent of men and women aged 65 and over worked. This figure dropped to 8.7 percent by January 1979 and to 6.9 percent in August 1986 (Statistics Canada 1972; Statistics Canada 1979b; Statistics Canada 1986c). A study done by Health and Welfare

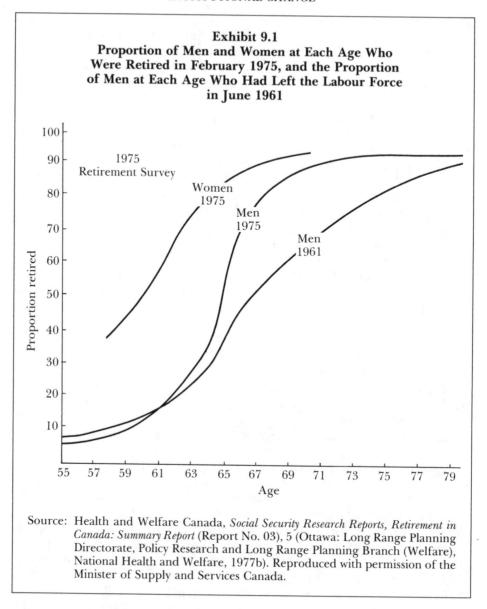

Exhibit 9.1
Proportion of Men and Women at Each Age Who Were Retired in February 1975, and the Proportion of Men at Each Age Who Had Left the Labour Force in June 1961

Source: Health and Welfare Canada, *Social Security Research Reports, Retirement in Canada: Summary Report* (Report No. 03), 5 (Ottawa: Long Range Planning Directorate, Policy Research and Long Range Planning Branch (Welfare), National Health and Welfare, 1977b). Reproduced with permission of the Minister of Supply and Services Canada.

Canada says that by age 60, 13 percent of men and 50 percent of women who worked sometime between age 45 and 60 had retired. By age 65 about 50 percent of men and 75 percent of women had retired, and by age 70 about 90 percent of both groups had retired (Ciffin and Martin 1977).

Exhibit 9.1 shows that at every age after age 61, a higher proportion of men had retired in 1975 than in 1961. Ciffin and Martin (1977, 86) conclude that "there was a major shift towards earlier retirement ages

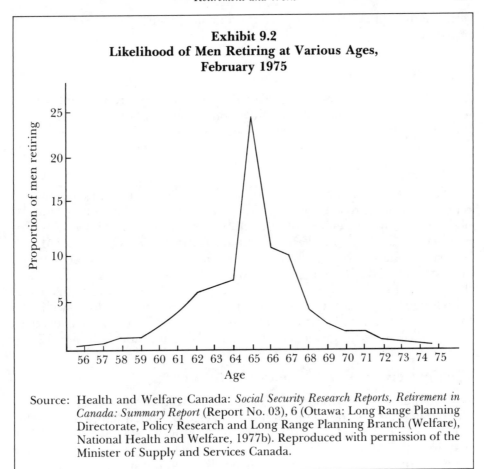

Exhibit 9.2
Likelihood of Men Retiring at Various Ages,
February 1975

Source: Health and Welfare Canada: *Social Security Research Reports, Retirement in Canada: Summary Report* (Report No. 03), 6 (Ottawa: Long Range Planning Directorate, Policy Research and Long Range Planning Branch (Welfare), National Health and Welfare, 1977b). Reproduced with permission of the Minister of Supply and Services Canada.

between 1961 and 1975." Men shifted away from retirement at about age 70 to retirement at about age 65. Ciffin and Martin (1977, 87) predict "a further shift towards earlier retirement ages" in the future, if men have enough income. (A higher proportion of women than men had retired at all ages in 1975.)

Exhibit 9.2 shows that more men retire at age 65 today than ever before. "In 1975," Ciffin and Martin (1977, 85) say, "age 65 clearly was 'institutionalized' with about 25 percent of men retiring at 65 and over 40 percent of the active men expecting to retire at 65. No normal retirement age existed for women." A study by Atchley (1982, 159) supports this difference in patterns of retirement for men and women. He reports that men more often than women planned to retire at a specific age. Also, that women were more likely than men to plan to retire before age 60 or after age 70. Atchley (1982) says that these figures should "caution against relying too heavily on very general statements about women's retirement." They should also caution against using data based on male retirement patterns to draw conclusions about retirement for women.

WHY DO PEOPLE RETIRE?

A number of social forces today lead a person to choose retirement. These forces include: (1) mandatory retirement rules, (2) better pensions that start at age 65, and (3) a more positive attitude toward retirement.

Mandatory Retirement

No law in Canada forces a person to retire at age 65, and no statute requires a worker to leave work at a certain age, but 80 percent of pension plans, covering 72 percent of all members, used 65 as the normal retirement age (Health and Welfare Canada 1979, 119). One government report concluded that "mandatory retirement at 65 is practised by government and educational institutions, and employers in general follow this policy" (Statistics Canada 1979a, Chart 9). "Retirement in most cases is no longer a question of personal choice. It is no longer a luxury chosen by those who could afford it. Compulsory retirement (at 65) has become standard practice in business and industry" (Adams and Lefebvre 1980).

The Controversy over Mandatory Retirement

A Canadian report titled *Retirement Age* (Health and Welfare Canada 1979) states some of the common beliefs that support mandatory retirement.

First, the report (1979, 42) says, "as employees advance in age they may lose the ambition and drive that are necessary to carry out their duties, especially at the more senior levels." Mandatory retirement saves the worker the humiliation of getting demoted or fired.

Second, mandatory retirement supposedly helps older people accept the end of their work career. "The sense of discrimination and the loss of status and prestige felt by some older persons would perhaps be deepened if it were not felt that retirement was an acceptable and indeed inevitable end to a working career" (1979, 43).

Third, mandatory retirement may open jobs for the young (Gunderson and Pesando 1980). This view sees mandatory retirement as a way to control high rates of youth unemployment.

Research on older workers questions all of these claims. Robinson, Coberly, and Paul (1985) reviewed the literature on age and performance at work. They drew five conclusions from the research. First, declines show up in some types of work, but not in others. In some industries, research shows that older workers outperform younger workers. Second, productivity varies within any one age group. Third, physical decline takes place in older workers, but a supportive environment can overcome the effects of these changes. Fourth, age alone does not predict a decline in a worker's ability even up to age 70. Reaction time and speed of work

---

Exhibit 9.3

FUNCTIONAL VS. FORMAL CRITERIA FOR RETIREMENT

Mandatory retirement uses a formal criterion (a specific age) to decide when a person should retire. Critics of this approach say that people should be judged on their functional ability. People who can still do their jobs should not be forced to retire. This raises the question of how to evaluate a worker's performance. Some researchers have developed functional measures of workers' abilities that allow an employer to judge a worker's competence.

Koyl (1974) created a test called the "GULHEMP" scale (General physique, Upper extremities, Lower extremities, Hearing, Eyesight, Mentality [Intelligence], and Personality) that does this. The civil service in Canada uses this measure, and so does the de Havilland Aircraft company in Toronto. This scale has its limits. Stagner (1985) says that the GULHEMP measures of intelligence and personality need to be broken down into more precise measures. Also, the GULHEMP puts too much emphasis on physical ability, given the increase in high-technology, white-collar jobs. Still, employers have used the measure with some success to place older employees in new jobs (Meier and Kerr 1976; Quirk and Skinner 1973). The GULHEMP and other measures of workers' abilities could help employers find and keep the best workers for the job, regardless of the worker's age. These measures can also help older workers find work that best suits their abilities.

---

slows, but older workers show more creativity, lower accident rates, and less turnover than younger workers. "A study of 18,000 workers in manufacturing plants, for example, found that workers beyond age 65 have about one-half the rate of non-disabling injuries as those under 65, and older workers have substantially lower rates of disabling injuries" (Atchley 1980, 157). Fifth, older workers can learn new things and gain as much from retraining as younger workers (Robinson, Coberly, and Paul 1985).

The reviewers note that more research needs to be done on the question of older workers' abilities. They mention that much of the current research sets out to support the value of older workers. Also, measures of ability vary between industries, and different studies use different ages to define "older workers." Some of these studies, for example, define older workers as aged 40 and over, while others define older workers as aged 65 and over. At best, these findings question the assumption that work ability declines with age and that age alone should decide when someone should retire.

Mandatory retirement may allow some workers a graceful exit from

Exhibit 9.4
Proportion of Men and Women by
Status of Old Position

After Retirement the Retiree's Old Position Was	Retired Men	Retired Women
Filled	75%	80%
Unfilled	4%	3%
Eliminated	12%	12%
Other	9%	5%
	100%	100%

This table shows that retirement does not always open jobs for the young. In this study of retirement in Canada, 16 percent of men's jobs and 15 percent of women's jobs either were eliminated or went unfilled after the worker retired. Some companies use retirement as a way to thin the workforce, rather than as a way to promote or hire young workers.

Source: Health and Welfare Canada, *Social Security Research Reports. Retirement in Canada Summary Report* (Report No. 03), 13 (Ottawa: Long Range Planning Directorate, Policy Research and Long Range Planning Branch (Welfare), National Health and Welfare, 1977b). Reproduced with permission of the Minister of Supply and Services Canada.

work, but it discriminates against the older worker who still works as well as ever. It also creates problems for older workers in poor health or with low motivation. Mandatory retirement at age 65 leads some employers to keep older inefficient workers on at work until age 65. This can lead to humiliation or bitterness. A worker aged 60 or 62 may stop getting memos, lose his or her place on important committees, and get put on a shelf for four or five years. This is just as cruel (maybe more so) than giving the person a decent pension and letting them go at age 60. Mandatory retirement can thus create problems for management and workers.

Does mandatory retirement decrease unemployment for the young? This could make a persuasive argument for mandatory retirement in times, such as these, of high youth unemployment. Kettle (1982, 12) says that an increase in the retirement age leads to an increase in unemployment: "in round numbers, every year added to the retirement age adds 0.4 percent points to the unemployment rate." A lower retirement age, he says, would open more jobs (some of them for young people) and decrease unemployment.

But Ross (1979) disagrees. He says that an end to mandatory retirement and an increase of 30 percent in labour force participation by people

Exhibit 9.5

THE FIGHT AGAINST MANDATORY RETIREMENT

Some workers want to keep working after age 65. These people enjoy their work, and most of them do their jobs as well after age 65 as before. They see mandatory retirement as a form of discrimination like racism or sexism. A number of people have challenged mandatory retirement rules in the Canadian courts, but as of December 1986 court appeals of mandatory retirement have had mixed results.

- Mr. Justice Taylor of the Supreme Court of British Columbia ruled in favour of mandatory retirement for university faculty in that province.
- Mr. Justice Gibson Gray of the Ontario Supreme Court upheld mandatory retirement for university faculty in Ontario. The Canadian Association of University Teachers (CAUT) (1986, 22) says that "if Mr. Justice Gray's judgement

stands, it will mean that all employees in Ontario over the age of 65 will be denied protection against discrimination in all matters relating to employment." The CAUT plans to appeal this ruling.
- The Manitoba Human Rights Commission said that the forced retirement of a worker by Flyer Industries, Inc. violated the province's Human Relations code. Also in Manitoba, a Court of Appeal ruled that employers cannot force workers to retire. Dr. Dwight Parkinson, a neurosurgeon, challenged the right of Winnipeg's Health Sciences Centre to force him to retire. The court ruled that the Health Sciences Centre can no longer take away a doctor's operating and admitting privileges after age 65. The hospital will now have to judge doctors on their competence and qualifications (McVeigh 1980).

over age 65 would lead to less than a 0.5 percent increase in unemployment and less than 0.01 percent in the first few years.

James Pesando (1979, 21–22) says that the proposed use of retirement to lower unemployment assumes "the 'lump-of-labour fallacy,' the mistaken notion that there exists a fixed number of jobs that must be allocated among competing workers." He goes on to say that the economy can find jobs for new workers without firing older workers. An attempt to end unemployment should begin with a broad review of government economic policies. "The important point," Pesando (1979, 21–22) says, "is that the postponement of retirement by elderly workers does *not* imply a corresponding reduction in the job opportunities available to [others]."

The Croll Commission Report, *Retirement Without Tears* (Senate of Canada 1979), takes an ethical stand against mandatory retirement. The

Exhibit 9.6
Why Do People Retire?

Individual Reasons	Institutional Forces
Finances	Working conditions and employer policies
Health	Retirement age policies, pension policies, and rules
Attitudes to work and retirement	Societal economic conditions
Social supports or pressures	Historical events and social values

Source: Adapted from Pauline K. Robinson, Sally Coberly, and Carolyn E. Paul, "Work and Retirement," in *Handbook of Aging and the Social Sciences*, 2nd ed., ed. Robert H. Binstock and Ethel Shanas (New York: Van Nostrand Reinhold, 1985), 513.

report says that mandatory retirement violates the older worker's human rights. "Discriminating against people in employment because they are no longer young," the report says, "[is] clearly objectionable on social grounds. [It is] no more justifiable than discrimination because of religion" (Senate of Canada 1979, 128).

The future of mandatory retirement in Canada may ultimately be settled in the courts (see Exhibit 9.5), but research suggests that the abolition of mandatory retirement will affect only a small number of workers. Other social forces, like better pensions, will lead more workers than ever before to choose retirement at or before age 65.

Better Pensions

Studies show again and again that most workers retire as soon as they can afford to (Barfield and Morgan 1969; Bixby 1976). For most Canadians this means age 65. The Senate of Canada (1979) estimates that an end to mandatory retirement would increase the percentage of older workers by only about 2 percent (from 15 percent in 1977 to 17 percent in the mid-1980s).

At least three economic forces lead workers to retirement at age 65 today. First, most private pension plans begin to pay full benefits at age 65. This leads many people to retire at 65 so that they can enjoy retirement while they still have good health. Second, OAS/GIS payments start at 65, as do the Canada and Quebec Pension Plans. A person who works past age 65 will still get these benefits, but will lose a large portion of them through higher taxes. The GIS program also discourages older people from working. The federal government reduces the GIS by $1 for each

Exhibit 9.7
Proportions Retiring for Various Reasons*

Reason for Retirement	Retired Men	Retired Women
Compulsory retirement	29%	11%
Other reasons	29%	39%
Poor health	34%	38%
Laid off	7%	4%
No answer	2%	8%

*Columns do not add to 100% due to rounding to the nearest whole number.

   Poor health ranks first for men and second for women as the main reason for retirement. Few of these people would have kept working past age 65. Compulsory retirement affects the retirement decisions of men more often than women; women more often than men give "other reasons" for retiring. One U.S. study found that women tend to leave work when their spouse retires (Anderson, Clark, and Johnson 1980). Sometimes an older working woman will quit work to care for a sick older parent or spouse.

Source: Health and Welfare Canada, *Social Security Research Reports. Retirement in Canada Summary Report* (Report No. 03), 9. (Ottawa: Long Range Planning Directorate, Policy Research and Long Range Planning Branch (Welfare), National Health and Welfare, 1977b). Reproduced with permission of the Minister of Supply and Services Canada.

$2 a person earns this year. A person who earns a provincial supplement will lose the other $1 from their supplement benefits. This results in a 100 percent "taxback" on the poorest people. They get nothing for work up to the amount equal to their GIS and Provincial Supplement. The taxback takes money from the older person's income *next* year for money earned *this* year. This means that low-income older people who work risk losing next year's income supplements (as well as their salary) if they get sick or cannot find a job. These rules create a strong incentive for retirement (Burbidge and Robb 1980).

   A survey of retirement in Canada (Health and Welfare Canada 1979) found that most of the people who retired due to mandatory retirement felt content with when they retired. Some said they would have left work earlier if they had had the money (Pesando 1979). Only about 13 percent of retired men and 3 percent of retired women who had to retire were not satisfied with the timing of their retirement, and only 4–5 percent of the men would have preferred to keep on working.

   Better pensions and decreased incentives to work have increased the trend toward retirement. This and increased leisure and recreational opportunities have also changed social attitudes toward retirement.

New Attitudes toward Retirement

Atchley (1976, 87) says that "everyone seems to know people ... who carefully planned for retirement only to become sick and die within six months after leaving their jobs." He goes on to say that, no matter what their job, he has "yet to encounter an occupational group for which retirement is related to a decline in self-reported health. It is true that many people expect retirement to adversely affect health, but very few realized their expectations."

A Canadian study by Shapiro and Roos (1982) supports this view. They studied retirees' use of health care services in Manitoba and found that retirees and workers visited the doctor for minor and serious problems at about the same rate. They conclude that "there is no evidence that retirement per se is associated with increased utilization of ambulatory physician services or admission to the hospital" (Shapiro and Roos 1982, 192).

These facts seem to have filtered down to younger workers. Today, Atchley (1974) says, people 45 years old and over have "very positive" views of retirement, regardless of their age and sex. He found that only people who wanted to keep on working felt that it was unjust.

Studies now show that many people prefer to retire before age 65 if they can. A Canadian Council on Social Development study (Laframboise 1975) found that "81 percent of those under age 65 and 62 percent over 65 thought the pensionable age should be lowered to 60 years." An Ontario study (Crawford and Matlow 1972) found that 68 percent of workers opted for retirement earlier than 65 when given the chance. And the Canadian Pension Plan Advisory Commission (1980, 12–13) reports a "growing social pressure for early retirement."

Two types of workers tend to take early retirement: workers in poor health and those who expect a good income in retirement. Also, people who retire early want more leisure time and less work, and they have a positive image of retirement (Orbach 1969). Neugarten (1980) says that only a small percentage of workers (about 8 to 10 percent) fit the stereotype of the faithful worker who is forced out of work. "The evidence shows that as one gets older, the desire to continue working is clearly not as strong as it was once thought to be by many sociologists" (Schulz 1980, 199). A survey of retirement in Canada conducted by the Canadian Pension Plan Advisory Commission (1980) found that 37 percent of men had retired early, by age 64. "Of these," the report says, "58 percent had retired because of ill-health and a further 10 percent because of layoff." None of these people would have stayed at work past age 65 (1980, 17).

Some private pension plans encourage people to choose early retirement. Companies in Canada such as MacMillan Bloedel, Metropolitan Life, and General Motors sponsor early retirement plans. Early retirement allows companies to hire less costly young workers or to leave jobs empty after a retiree leaves. Imperial Oil Ltd. of Toronto says that early retirement saves as much as 30 percent of the cost of keeping an older worker on until age 65. In 1984 68 percent of their 220 retirees retired early; on average people retired at age 58 (Finlayson 1985).

Canada's Public Service Superannuation Act allows retirement as early as age 55 with 30 years' service (Health and Welfare Canada 1979). In addition to a pension, some plans give workers a large lump sum payment to encourage early retirement, and workers tend to take these payments when companies offer them (Pesando and Rea 1977). Other pension plans in Canada allow early retirement on a reduced pension. Ninety-seven percent of pension plans covering 95 percent of their members offer this option (Health and Welfare Canada 1979). Some private plans even include a special rule allowing early retirement on an *unreduced* pension for a certain number of years of service or age plus service. The Canadian Pension Plan Advisory Commission (1980) reports that 12 percent of public sector plans covering well over half of their members and 3 percent of private sector plans covering 28 percent of their members offer this option.

Changes in the Canada Pension Plan (CPP) in 1987 also encourage a more flexible retirement age. The plan now allows payments to begin as early as age 60 or as late as age 70. The person who retires early gets a decrease in their basic pension equal to 0.5 percent for each month between the date the pension begins and the month after the retiree's sixty-fifth birthday. The person cannot earn more than the current maximum annual CPP pension at 65 ($6,240 in 1987). A person who retires after age 70 receives an increase of 0.5 percent on their basic pension for every month between the date the pension begins and the month after the pensioner's sixty-fifth birthday.

Will these changes lead more people to retire early? Or will they lead people to stay at work longer? No one can say yet. One thing seems certain: these changes give workers more choice in timing their retirement than ever before.

Summary

The argument over mandatory retirement makes it seem as if most workers want to work past age 65. But studies show that given poor health or a good income most people will leave work before age 65. People now accept retirement as a reward they have earned for years of work, and they will collect that reward as soon as they can.

ALTERNATIVES TO A FIXED RETIREMENT AGE

Early or delayed retirement are two options workers can choose instead of mandatory retirement at age 65. But a number of other options exist. These include flexible retirement, part-time work, and second careers.

Flexible Retirement

Atchley (1985, 192) predicts that in the future "the small proportion [of people that do] not want to retire can expect to find it increasingly easier to stay on as long as they can still do the job." Some of these workers may choose flexible retirement. This option allows a person to slowly cut back the number of hours they work each week.

A study by Health and Welfare Canada (1979) found that 38 percent of retired men and 41 percent of retired women would have preferred a part-time transition to retirement. Thirty-five percent of working men and 47 percent of working women said they preferred this option. The survey asked respondents to give their first choice for a retirement pattern with no change in pay. Forty-three percent of working men and 44 percent of working women chose a gradual shift into retirement (fewer weeks, fewer days, or fewer hours per day for the same pay). "Most of those failing to retire in the way they wanted," the report says, "were those who preferred a part-time pattern but had to work full-time until retirement" (Health and Welfare Canada 1979, 50).

McConnell and his colleagues (1980) surveyed workers near retirement in two large companies in the U.S. They found that half of these workers would stay on at work if they had alternatives to the normal working day, but the workers said they preferred this option only if they got fringe benefits and could use their pension benefits to make up for lost income. These workers said they preferred to retire or find work with another employer if they had to take a pay reduction. This study and the Canadian study by Health and Welfare Canada (1979) show that older workers need some incentive (like fewer hours for the same pay) to choose flexible retirement.

Today no formal system of flexible retirement exists in Canada, but Sweden has a program that shows some of the costs and benefits of flexible retirement. In Sweden workers aged 60 to 64 can switch to part-time work without loss of pension credits and with 50 percent of their lost wages paid by the government. Workers have to cut their work week to a maximum of 35 hours, but they can work as few as 17 hours a week. They also have to work at least every second month; they cannot work six months and take six months off. Nearly all workers who choose partial pensions go from a 40-hour to a 17- to 21-hour work week. By 1980 about 25 percent of all people who could take partial pensions had taken them. The Swedish system gives workers a chance to ease into retirement, and this gives them a better chance to make a successful shift to full retirement (Health and Welfare Canada 1979; Rix and Fisher 1982).

This program has one drawback that might make it hard to implement in Canada: the program was so expensive that the government had to double employers' payments into the pension system (Rix and Fisher 1982).

Still, some less expensive version of this plan might work in Canada. For example, during an economic slowdown, employers could reduce older workers' hours rather than lay them off. A flexible retirement plan gives employers as well as employees more choice. Rosen and Jerdee (1982) found that when managers had the chance to reassign older workers to other jobs or redesign present jobs a majority chose to keep workers on past 65.

Part-Time Work

Part-time work offers older workers an alternative to full retirement. Research shows that about 5 percent of older people work and another 6 percent of older people would like to work. About 70 percent of the people who want to work prefer to work part-time (Health and Welfare Canada 1979). In 1981 24 percent of employed men aged 65–69 and 32 percent of those aged 70 and over held part-time jobs. Among women, 43 percent of those aged 65–69 and 47 percent of those aged 70 and over worked on a part-time basis (Health and Welfare Canada 1983). Some people (women without pensions, widows) want to work part-time because they need the money. Others like to work because it gives them a chance to meet new people. Sometimes a person who retired because of bad health finds that their health improves enough that they can manage a part-time job. A Canadian study (Health and Welfare Canada 1979), for example, found that 35 percent of men and 63 percent of women who retired due to ill health (about 35 percent of all retirees retire for this reason) said their health had improved. Some of these people may want to work part-time. A report by Health and Welfare Canada says that "opportunities to work part-time are very important to the employment of senior citizens" (1982b, 3).

Older people sometimes have trouble finding work. A study in Quebec, for example, found that only 8 percent of the older people who registered with Canada Employment found work (Canadian Council on Social Development 1976b). Studies in the U.S. (U. S. Congressional Budget Office 1982) report that in a tight employment market, older people may not find work that suits them, so they give up looking and retire. The older the person, a report on retirement in Canada says, the more difficulty they will have finding work (Health and Welfare Canada 1979).

The Canadian government now sponsors Senior Citizens' Job Bureaus to help retired workers find part-time work. They help seniors find work that suits their needs. Seniors who leave Canada for the winter sometimes want seasonal work (like gardening) or short-term jobs (like office help). The Winnipeg Senior Citizens' Job Bureau, in the first eight months of

1986, for example, got requests for almost 16,000 jobs (most of them for casual work). The Bureau filled over 13,000 of these requests (Senior Citizens' Job Bureau 1986).

Second Careers

Some people retire to a "second career." Job bureaus for seniors report that teachers sometimes want to work as cabinet makers, accountants want to work as painters, and homemakers want to work in an office or a retail store. Neugarten (1980, 74) says that "many business executives become engaged in community affairs in the last years of their employment and find it relatively easy to move into those areas after they retire." These people work at second careers for more than the money. A second career allows them to develop skills they could not use when they worked full-time.

Tournier (1972, 129) calls a second career "a free career." A second career, he says, differs from leisure and from the kind of work a person does in middle age. "It has a goal, a mission, and that implies organization, loyalty, and even priority over other more selfish pleasures — not in line of duty, since professional obligations are not involved, but for the love of people. It is, therefore, not an escape, but a presence in the world" (1972, 130). A second career, Tournier says, grows out of interests that lay dormant or undeveloped in middle age. A saleswoman at The Bay, for example, spent her weekends cooking traditional Ukrainian food for her family. When she retired from work she began a career as volunteer kitchen director at her local senior centre. The work gives her a sense of purpose and allows her to use her talents in a new way.

Tournier (1972, 136) also calls a second career a "personal career" because "one has to formulate one's own aim, choose one's own method of work, set one's own daily task and assert one's identity in one's work." A bus driver began a second career as an actor when he joined a seniors' theatre group, and an electrician began a second career as a public figure when a seniors' club elected him president. These people became resources in their communities, and their second careers brought meaning and purpose to their retirement.

Tournier says that before some people can take up a second career they will need more education. They will also have to have "sufficient resources ... for them no longer to have to earn their living" (1972, 134). Guillemard (1977) agrees, arguing that second careers best fit the lifestyles and backgrounds of middle-class workers (executives, technicians, or engineers). These people form a new privileged group in society. They have good pensions, good health, and higher aspirations than working-class retirees. They may also have the verbal or technical skills that volunteer organizations or community groups value and need. Guillemard raises the issue of unequal opportunity in retirement.

INEQUALITY AND RETIREMENT

Social Class and Retirement Options

Discussions about mandatory or early retirement obscure the issue of pension adequacy. Studies show again and again that people will retire if they have a good pension. A study in Quebec (Baillargeon 1982), for example, found that men in both the public and private sectors with indexed pensions had a good attitude to retirement. Baillargeon (1982) and Atchley (1971a; 1971b) report that half of higher-level workers look forward to retirement.

Studies show that a person with a good income and from a middle-class or upper-middle-class occupation stands a good chance of being satisfied with retirement.[1] People with money have more chance to take part in leisure activity, while people with poor pensions and no savings may not be able to retire at all. Middle-class and upper-middle-class workers (white-collar workers, managers, professionals) with orderly work careers (few layoffs or job changes) report high satisfaction in retirement (Simpson, Back, and McKinney 1966).

Studies also show that people with the most education and the highest incomes have the best chance to find or keep work, if they choose to, after age 65. Quinn (1981) studied men 58 to 63 years old. He reports that about a third of the men on salary or wages worked part-time, while 60 percent of self-employed men (many of them professionals) worked part-time. Health and Welfare Canada (1982b) reports that older men with university degrees, for example, have four times the labour force participation rate of older men with less than Grade 5 education. Older women with university degrees have five times the participation rate of older women with less than Grade 5. Professionals such as doctors, lawyers, and professors can work as consultants or work part-time at their careers (Health and Welfare Canada 1982b).

A study of fifty-eight older physicians in Quebec found that 93 percent of them still worked in their practices and 65 percent said they had no plans for retirement, even though they averaged 71.54 years of age (Grauer and Campbell 1983). A report by Statistics Canada (1986c) on husbands and wives in the top percentile of families by income showed that at every age more husbands and wives in these families work compared with all families, and that this gap between the top percentile and other families in the proportion of those working grows with age. In 1980, for example,

---

[1]The term "social class" refers to both the market condition and work situation of a worker. The market condition refers to the pay, security, and opportunity for promotion of a job. The work situation refers to the tasks a person does, the social relations between workers and managers, and the control systems in a workplace. This definition assumes that the market rewards and the working conditions get better as a person moves from a lower to a higher social class (Abercrombie, Hill, and Turner 1984).

in all husband–wife families aged 65 and over, 25 percent of the husbands and 7 percent of the wives worked. In high-income families with both spouses aged 65 and over, 69 percent of the men and 21 percent of the women worked. Statistics Canada (1986c, 104) says that in high-income families people worked "well beyond the normal age of retirement." Even at ages 75 and over almost half of the high-income men and more than 10 percent of the high-income women still work (Statistics Canada 1986c). The fact that they work puts these people in the high-income group, but also the kinds of work they do — they own their own companies or work as independent professionals — allows them to ease out of work at their own pace. In sum, good income predicts that a person can and will retire. But independent professionals, even though they have a good income, often choose to continue working.

Social Structures and Retirement Options

Dowd (1980) says that social structures and economic conditions, more than personal preferences, explain why people retire when they do. Dowd (1980, 77) divides the economy into two sectors: "one sector is highly organized and characterized by high wages and pension systems, and the other is marked by low wages and few, if any fringe benefits." Exhibit 9.8 shows the effect of social structure on the chances of getting a private pension. It shows that workers in the core sector stand a better chance of getting a private pension than workers in the periphery.

In Canada women more often than men work in the peripheral sector — 45.8 percent of all women workers provide services, 17.9 percent work in trade occupations, and 2.9 percent work in agriculture (Labour Canada 1986). These occupations often have no mandatory retirement rules, and they allow for easy entry, flexible hours, and part-time work (Robinson, Coberly, and Paul, 1985). At the same time, these occupations pay less than core occupations, and in general they offer fewer private pensions. This gives women fewer choices than men when it comes time to retire. McDonald and Wanner (1984), for example, found that *single* women have one of the lowest rates of early retirement in Canada. They say this "probably reflects their concentration in occupations with lower incomes and poorer pensions" (1984, 108). They go on to show (1984, 114) that poorer people of either sex tend not to retire early.

Orbach (1981, 126) sums up the research on retirement today. "One would have to conclude," he says, "that most persons today have a generally positive attitude toward retirement as a future status, and are more likely to strongly exhibit this attitude the higher their expected retirement income, the better their health, the greater their educational and occupational level and attainment, and the less they find work to be the major or only source of intrinsic satisfaction in life...." Today, not all Canadians have an income or occupation that produces a satisfactory retirement. Greater equality in retirement opportunity will come only with a decrease in general social inequality based on class and gender.

Exhibit 9.8
Private Pension Plan Coverage of Paid Workers by
Industry and Sex, Canada, December 1984

Industry	Pension Plan Members as % of Paid Workers			Women as % of All Pension Plan Members
	Women	Men	Total	
Core				
Mines, quarries, oil wells	65.4	66.2	66.1	14.0
Construction	13.2	40.4	38.1	3.5
Manufacturing	39.5	59.7	54.1	20.2
Transportation and communications	61.3	73.2	70.3	21.0
Finance, insurance/real estate	50.9	61.3	54.5	60.8
Public administration	71.9	85.1	79.9	36.1
Periphery				
Agriculture	*	*	5.6	*
Trade	17.6	30.0	24.0	35.7
Community, business, and personal service	38.1	45.6	40.8	59.5

*Sample inadequate for reliable estimate.

As a percentage of paid workers, a higher percentage of men compared to women belong to a pension plan (this is true of both sectors). Except for construction, the core industries, compared to the peripheral industries, have higher percentages of the total labour force in pension plans. Women have less chance to get private pensions because more than two-thirds of them work in the peripheral sector. Except in real estate and service occupations, women make up fewer than half of all pension plan members.

Source: Adapted from Labour Canada, *Women in the Labour Force*, 1985–1986, Cat. No. L 38–30/1986 (Ottawa: Minister of Supply and Services, 1986), Table I–6 and Table IV–5. Reproduced by permission of the Minister of Supply and Services Canada.

ADJUSTMENT TO RETIREMENT

Social class and occupational structures determine some of the options a person will have in retirement. But retirement is also a personal choice and a social process. Atchley, for example, describes eight phases of retirement. He cautions that these phases "represent a device for making it easier to view retirement as a process, *not* as an inevitable sequence that everyone must go through" (1985, 196). These stages give some idea of the changes a person goes through when they leave the labour force. They describe the changing relationship between the individual and social structures as well as the methods people use to cope with these changes.

Phase 1: Pre-Retirement

This phase has two stages — a near and a remote stage. The remote stage takes place many years before retirement. A person may start an RRSP in their forties or buy a piece of land in the country for a future retirement home.

In the near stage people get ready to leave their jobs. They check on pension payments, fill out the necessary forms, and train someone to take over their job. They also worry about their future income and their health. Atchley, Kunkel, and Adlon (1978) report that people create detailed fantasies of retirement and that people with unrealistic fantasies about retirement have some of the worst problems when they retire. In one case a man bought some land for his retirement on an island off the coast of British Columbia. He fantasized his retirement as a return to nature and saw himself roaming around the island bird-watching, taking pictures of animals, and collecting mushrooms. His fantasy turned into a nightmare when he told his wife about his plans. "I have no intention of leaving my sister and my bridge club and moving into the woods," she said. "You can go yourself if that's what you want. But count me out." This man spent the first two years of his retirement coping with his anger and disappointment.

Phase 2: The Honeymoon

A euphoric time for most people. They do all the things they never had time for. People with enough money often travel during this phase, taking cruises and long winter vacations.

Phase 3: The Retirement Routine

When they get back from their trip to Hawaii people begin to find a stable routine. This might include an exercise program a few times a week, part-time work, volunteer work, or study. People will keep this routine if they find it satisfying. Some people keep up as busy a schedule as they had before they retired. They often complain about all their appointments and keep saying they plan to slow down. These busy people choose the amount of activity they find satisfying. Other retirees like to take things slower; they disengage from social obligations and schedule more time for socializing and leisure.

Phase 4: Rest and Relaxation

Some people cut back their activity at first, then gradually increase it until they find a schedule that suits them. One man withdrew from all his service clubs and board memberships just after he retired. He and his wife travelled and then settled in a new city. There he started a new part-time job and got involved in community service again.

Phase 5: Disenchantment

A small number of people feel let down by retirement. Atchley (1976) found, in a cross-sectional study, that less than 10 percent of retirees feel this way. A study by Ekerdt, Bossé, and Levkoff (1985) found high life-satisfaction in retirees six months after retirement. But they found a decrease in life-satisfaction in men between thirteen and eighteen months after retirement. This drop in satisfaction passed after the first year and a half.

A crisis in a person's life at the time of retirement, like the death of a spouse or a sudden drop in income, can lead to disenchantment with retirement. In one case a man retired early so he could open a small art gallery in a resort. He found that after he moved to the resort his pension did not allow him to keep up his pre-retirement lifestyle. He was forced to get a part-time job as the manager of a small restaurant. He felt frustrated and sorry that he retired when he did.

Phase 6: Reorientation

People who feel disenchanted need to take stock and pull themselves together. Family and friends can help, and in time most people reorient themselves and adjust to retirement.

Phase 7: Routine

Many people move into this stable, enjoyable phase right after the honeymoon phase. Sociologists say these people take up the *retirement role*. The retirement role specifies the rights and obligations a person has in retirement. A person has the right, for example, to collect a pension, but is also obliged not to work full-time. Atchley (1985, 196) says that people who adjust to this phase "know what is expected of them and they know what they have to work with — what their capabilities and limitations are. They are self-sufficient adults, going their own way, managing their own affairs."

Phase 8: Termination

A person needs independence and good health to play the retirement role. This role ends when a person returns to work or when illness or disability takes away their independence.

A number of studies have tested this stage model to see how well it fits the reality of retirement. At least three studies, one in the U.S., one in Norway, and one in Canada, support the existence of a honeymoon phase and a disenchantment phase in retirement (Haynes, McMichael, and Tyroler 1977; Solem 1976; Adams and Lefebvre 1980). These studies all based their conclusions on mortality rates after retirement. All three studies report a low mortality rate just after retirement and a rise in mortality about three years after retirement (the disenchantment phase). Mortality rates probably reflect only the most extreme cases of enjoyment or disenchantment. More subtle measures are needed to see whether most retirees follow the pattern Atchley describes.

Atchley's model, if it proves accurate, will most likely apply to one type of worker: the middle-class, Anglo male worker who retires at age 65. Roadburg (1985), for example, says that this model does not describe the pattern of someone who retires early. Roadburg found that many early retirees want to go back to work. He also found that, even after age 81, about half his subjects wanted to go back to work. These people missed the social contacts that work provided, and they wanted something to do.

Connidis (1982) found that women follow different career paths than men. Some take up careers after raising a family, others work during their childrearing years, some never enter the labour force, and many single women show unbroken work records (Keating and Jeffrey 1983). This makes it hard to describe a typical pattern of retirement for women. Few studies have looked at how women adjust to retirement or what retirement means to them. The studies that have focused on women show diverse patterns among women subjects and large differences between women and men. Atchley (1982) says that different factors shape male and female attitudes to retirement, and different factors lead to life-satisfaction for each group. He concludes that "women's retirement is indeed a separate issue compared to men's" (1982, 165). In the past, Beeson (1975) says, researchers have treated women's retirement as a non-event. Szinovacz (1982) says that until 1975 the annual Gerontological Society of America meetings contained almost no discussion of women's retirement. This has begun to change as more women have started working outside the home. Researchers have begun to study women's transitions to retirement as a normative event.

Retirement research has also taken some new directions. Bertaux (1981) reports on retirement for dual career couples. Studies have also begun to look at how life changes in other family members (sickness of a spouse or parent, marriage of children, or widowhood) affect women's careers and retirement patterns.

The study of retirement will change as retirement itself changes. As more women enter the labour force, as more single women enter old age, and as better pensions make retirement an established part of adult life, social structures and individual responses to retirement will change. This will lead to new research approaches and new ideas about later life.

PRE-RETIREMENT EDUCATION (PRE)

People often make the transition into retirement without any help, but research shows that pre-retirement education can help people avoid problems and set new goals for themselves (Bond and Bond 1980). PRE programs also give support to people who already have positive attitudes to retirement. These people say they are most interested in, and benefit most from, early knowledge about pensions and income. Workers also report an interest in how to stay healthy and active and how to find part-time work (Atchley, Kunkel, and Adlon 1978; Pitts 1983).

People who want a second career (or even people who want flexible retirement or part-time work) stand the best chance of success if they plan their retirement in advance. A study of retirement in Alberta found that people who planned for retirement had the greatest satisfaction when they retired (Perry 1980). Szinovacz (1982) found that women who planned for retirement, and especially women who carried out their plans, reported high retirement satisfaction.

PRE in Canada began in the 1950s. T. Eaton Co. in Toronto offered the first PRE course in Canada in 1953 (T.Eaton Company Ltd., April 16, 1958, cited in Health and Welfare Canada 1979). Saskatchewan held the first public PRE program in 1961 for two provincial government departments and a Crown corporation. In the late 1960s and early 1970s PRE began to catch on across the country. In the 1970s, the federal Department of Public Works and a number of other departments including Health and Welfare offered PRE to staff.

Today, workers throughout Canada can find PRE programs where they work, through the government, or at local community colleges and social agencies. PRE programs vary in length, content, and format. They range from group training sessions about retirement to special counselling for individuals (Health and Welfare Canada 1979). Some programs offer short, intensive courses on one to three consecutive days. Other programs offer two- or three-hour classes once a week over several weeks. Some programs begin a few weeks or months before retirement; others start in middle age. Most programs include lectures and discussion on retirement issues. Some programs counsel people on topics of specific interest to them.

Though they differ in many ways, most PRE programs share some basic goals. First, they educate workers about early retirement, investment options, and pension benefits. Second, PRE programs help workers and their spouses plan for changes in their relationship after retirement.

Third, PRE programs help people carry out their plans. They can put workers in touch with investment counsellors or help individuals sort out their goals.

Do PRE programs work? A study by Health and Welfare Canada (1979) compared PRE students with those who had not taken a PRE course. The researchers asked each group questions about government retirement benefits, but found no significant difference in knowledge between those who had and those who had not taken a PRE program. Other studies show positive effects from PRE programs. Bond and Bond (1980, 68) studied a Canadian PRE program and found that "attitudes toward retirement consistently improved, both during the program ... and six months following completion of the program ... ." Poser and Engels (1983) studied the results of a fifteen-hour weekend seminar PRE program. A three-month follow-up study found that people who took the program, compared to those who did not, had better self-esteem and better morale in retirement. Other studies show that PRE programs allow workers to explore new roles and activities with other retirees. They also help reduce stress and decrease negative attitudes to retirement (Cox and Bhak 1978–79; Kaplan 1979). One study found that regardless of the program's format (lecture or discussion), or the program's length (long or short), PRE improved workers' sense of satisfaction with retirement (Barfield and Morgan 1974).

Many workers say they would like to take part in a PRE program (Health and Welfare Canada 1979), but people in some provinces have a better chance of finding a program than others: in 1982, for example, more than seventy companies offered programs in the Toronto–Hamilton region, while in other parts of the country these programs did not exist at all. Beck (1984) found that people with the highest incomes and highest status jobs have most access to these programs while people with low educational levels, low incomes, and no pensions have the least chance to attend. Also, workers in large companies, members of active unions, and government workers have the easiest access to PRE. Workers for small non-unionized firms have the least chance of getting PRE (Collins and Brown 1978).

The Croll Commission report in Canada says that "much more should be done to devise and implement effective [PRE] programs in this country," and for good reason (Senate of Canada 1979, 119). "Of all employees now aged 55 and working with an employer with a pension plan, 71 percent will never work past 65 and 50 percent will retire early, either because of early retirement provisions or illness ..." (Gherson 1980). Retirement has become a normal part of adult life.

SUMMARY

1. Most people want to retire. And they retire as early as they can if they have a good pension.
2. Some people want to stay on at work, and they have challenged compulsory retirement rules in court.
3. Canadians now have more choice about when they retire and what pattern of retirement they follow. Some people take full retirement at age 65, others work part-time, and still others start second careers. In the future, older workers may have the option of flexible retirement.
4. A good income gives retirees the most options and the best chance to plan for and enjoy retirement.
5. Some studies of retirement show that retirees adjust to retirement in stages. New theories of retirement and new research approaches to the study of retirement may emerge as more women retire from the labour force.
6. Retirement planning helps workers make the most of their resources in retirement. These programs now exist in all parts of Canada, though some parts of the country have more programs than others. More programs will be needed in the future.

SELECTED READINGS

Myles, John. *Old Age in the Welfare State: The Political Economy of Public Pensions.* Boston: Little, Brown and Co., 1984.
One of the few Canadian studies in the field of aging that takes a political economy perspective. The author presents a sociohistorical view of retirement. He compares retirement in a variety of industrial societies, develops a typology of pension systems, and discusses poverty and social inequality in modern society. A thought-provoking book about how society shapes the experience of aging.

Roadburg, Alan. *Aging: Retirement, Leisure and Work in Canada.* Toronto: Methuen, 1985.
One of the few Canadian books on retirement. The book gives an overview of the Canadian pension system. It then describes the results of a study on retirement conducted by the author. The book presents cases of how people respond to retirement and quotations from them about their experience.

Senate of Canada. *Retirement Without Tears: A Report of the Special Senate Committee on Retirement Age Policies* (Croll Commission). Ottawa: Minister of Supply and Services, 1979.
A classic Canadian statement on retirement. The report presents a humanistic view of retirement and a critique of retirement income policies.

HOUSING AND TRANSPORTATION

INTRODUCTION

Lydia Wosk, 73, lives alone in her own home — a one-and-a-half-storey wood frame house just outside the downtown core. She has only a half-block walk to the bus, and she goes downtown almost every day. Three times a week she rides out to the university for classes. Lydia's husband died seven years ago of a sudden heart attack. The loss left Lydia in shock. One Sunday, about six months after the funeral, her three sons and their wives came over for dinner. "Mom," her oldest son said, "we've been thinking. You don't need a house this big. And you're all alone. Why not move in with us? You could live part of the year with each of us so you wouldn't have to worry about being a burden on anyone."

"I knew what they were planning," Lydia says. "So I was ready. 'This is my house,' I told them, 'I own it. I paid for it. And this is where I'm going to stay.' "

Lydia's house gives her more than just a place to live. It gives meaning to her life. The wall over the TV, for example, holds pictures of her children and grandchildren. The couch and chairs all have hand-crocheted covers she made herself. She says the couch reminds her of the times she and her husband used to watch Saturday night hockey together.

A home also allows older people like Lydia to feel more independent. "I love my home," one woman said simply in a letter to the Ontario Advisory Council on Senior Citizens. "I live alone," another woman said, "but I am never lonely. I like baking, and my door is always open to visitors. I am never too busy to make them a cup of tea with a scone and black currant jelly" (Ontario Advisory Council on Senior Citizens 1978; 1980–81).

Not all older people need or want to live in a single-family house. Some older people live in apartments, some live with their children, some live in sheltered housing (where they get help with meals and cleaning), and others live in rooming houses. The kind of housing that an older person needs depends on their health, marital status, income, and lifestyle. A single-family house, for example, demands good health, knowledge about home repairs, and enough income to pay for heat and taxes. An apartment demands less know-how and less worry about heating costs. An apartment with meals served in a common dining room helps people too frail to prepare their own meals. A nursing home cares for people too ill to care for themselves. People's housing needs change as they age. Havens (1980, 218–19) found that housing ranked as the second highest unmet need for women 65–79, the third-highest unmet need for women 80–84, and the fourth- or fifth-highest unmet need for women aged 85 and over. Housing declines as an unmet need with age in part because more very old people, compared to younger old people, live in institutions. Loss of a spouse, changes in a person's informal supports, and illness may all lead to changes in housing and housing need.

Lawton and Nahemow (1973) created a "transactional model" that describes the relationship between the older person and his or her environment. Their model describes the interrelation of two variables: individual capability and the demands of the environment. Lawton and Nahemow define compatibility as the collection of a person's abilities, including health, psychological adjustment, and intelligence. They define environmental demand as environmental forces that, combined with need, lead a person to make a response (1973, 659). A person feels the most comfort when their capability matches the demands of the environment and they can fulfil their needs. Too great or too little environmental demand leads to a decreased feeling of well-being and a maladaptive response (see Exhibit 10.1). A healthy person in a hospital bed, for example, will feel bored and lethargic because the environment demands too little. A person recovering from a stroke may feel fatigued after a ten-minute conversation because the conversation demands too much from them. The Law-

Exhibit 10.1
Person–Environment Interaction

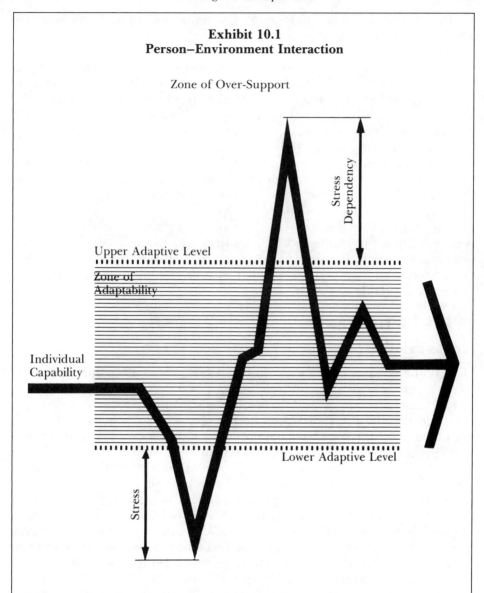

Zone of Over-Support

Stress Dependency

Upper Adaptive Level

Zone of Adaptability

Individual Capability

Lower Adaptive Level

Stress

Zone of Under-Support

People function best when their capacity allows them to meet environmental demands. This chart shows that too much or too little support leads to stress. Not enough support leads to stress due to the failure to meet basic needs. Too much support leads to stress due to dependence and an absence of meaning in life.

Source: Louis E. Gelwicks and Robert J. Newcomer. *Planning Housing Environments for the Elderly*. Washington: National Council on the Aging, 1974, p. 41.

ton–Nahemow model says that people try to find a comfortable fit between what they can do and what they need to do to meet their needs.

This chapter will apply the transactional model to housing and transportation for older people. An ideal housing system would help people match their ability to the environment's demands. It would help people to stay where they are for as long as they want to stay there, and it would allow a smooth movement from one setting to another when a change in a person's ability or needs makes a move necessary.

Canada's housing system today allows older people many choices about where to live. Housing options range from private houses, to apartments, to congregate housing, to homes for the elderly and nursing homes (see Exhibit 10.2). All of these housing options have a place in the housing market.

This chapter will look at (1) the housing options available to older people, (2) the programs and policies that exist in Canada to help older people meet their housing needs, and (3) transportation systems that enable older people to keep in touch with their community and use the resources available to them.

TYPES OF HOUSING

Single-Family Houses

Most home-owners want to stay in their own homes after they retire. In 1982 75 percent of men and 50 percent of women aged 65 and over owned their own homes, and three-quarters of these people owned single detached two- or three-bedroom homes (Fraser 1982). Sixty percent of people aged 65 and over have paid off their mortgages. This figure jumps to 95 percent for people over age 80 (Health and Welfare Canada 1983).

Most older home-owners take good care of their houses. Only 12 percent of home-owners 65 to 79 years old and 10 percent of people aged 80 and over say their houses need major repair. More than three-quarters of people aged 65 and over say their houses need only regular maintenance (Health and Welfare Canada 1983). A study of retirees in Canada found that 71 percent of people who owned their own homes said they were satisfied with their housing (compared to two-thirds of all men and women) (Health and Welfare Canada 1977b).

Older men, more often than older women, tend to live in single-family houses. Rose and Macdonald (1984) found that in southern Ontario 78 percent of men compared to 63.3 percent of women lived in a house (rather than an apartment or collective dwelling). Four-fifths of men who lived in a single-family house, compared to a little more than three-fifths of women, owned their own homes. Connidis and Rempel (1983) say that fewer women own their own homes because a woman often has to move out of a single-family home as she ages. First, when her husband dies she may have less money to spend on housing. Increased heating costs, maintenance, and taxes can all force a woman to sell her home and move

Exhibit 10.2
Continuum of Housing by Degree of Independence

Housing Type	Criteria
Independent Household	
Fully Independent (approx. 87% of Canadians aged 65 and over)	Self-contained and self-sufficient; resident does 90% of housework. Includes house, apartment, townhouse, duplex, condominium.
Supported Independent Living (4% of Canadians aged 65 and over)	Self-contained but some help with chores (e.g., Meals on Wheels, Homemaker Services, etc.). Sheltered or enriched housing. Cooking and household chores may be part of community life (e.g., communal dining room).
Collective Dwellings	
Collective Dwellings (9% of Canadians aged 65 and over)	Dependent Living
Hotels and Rooming Houses (2% of Canadians aged 65 and over)	Serviced dwellings may provide meals and housekeeping services.
Personal care home, Home for the Aged, or Nursing home (7% of Canadians aged 65 and over)	Not self-contained, not self-sufficient. Personal care help in health care, grooming, bathing, and household work.

This chart shows that the need for support increases as people's ability to care for themselves decreases. A good system gives people the support they need, while allowing them to do as much for themselves as they can.

Source: Adapted from Satya Brink, "Housing Elderly People in Canada: Working Towards a Continuum of Housing Choices Appropriate to Their Needs," in *Innovations in Housing and Living Arrangements for Seniors*, ed. Gloria Gutman and Norman Blackie (Burnaby, B.C.: Gerontology Research Centre, Simon Fraser University, 1985), 17. Reproduced with permission of Simon Fraser University Press.

into an apartment. Second, women give up their homes because they know less about how to care for a home. "This is not to say that women are incapable of such tasks but rather that their patterns of socialization have not typically included the knowledge and practice necesary for a comfortable sense of mastery over them" (Connidis and Rempel 1983,

10). This and the cost of hiring people to do work leads many women to sell their homes. A number of programs in Canada work to help men and women stay in their own homes.

Tax and Home Maintenance Programs

Home-owners without mortgages live rent-free and have more financial assets than people who rent (Fraser 1982), so they should have the least trouble paying for housing. But many older people have trouble keeping up their homes. They own large older houses — 85 percent of them are single-family detached — that cost a high proportion of the owner's income to heat and maintain (Statistics Canada 1978a, cited in Health and Welfare Canada 1982b). A study supported by the Canada Mortgage and Housing Corporation (Fraser 1982) found that a third of older home-owners in cities had trouble paying their housing costs, and that half of the money they spent on housing went to pay for utilities. A study in Saskatchewan found that one-third of the home-owners in the province paid over 30 percent of their income for housing costs (Saskatchewan Housing Corporation 1984). The federal government and the provinces help older home-owners with grants, loans, and tax rebates. The federal government Residential Rehabilitation Assistance Program (RRAP) offers loans of up to $10,000 to help people improve run-down housing. The government also grants loans to improve building structures, fire safety, wiring, plumbing, or heating or to make a house accessible for a wheel-chair. By May 1981 loans for house repairs in Canada totalled $118 million. The government forgave close to 90 percent of the loans to those 3,400 older households with low incomes (Health and Welfare Canada 1982b).

Some provinces also sponsor home repair programs that offer low-interest and forgivable loans to low-income older people. Many provinces also offer older people a rebate or tax credit on school property tax. These programs help some older people stay in their own homes.

Reverse Mortgages

A program known but almost ignored in Canada could give some older people enough income to stay in their homes. Experts call this a reverse-annuity mortgage (RAM). Reverse-annuity mortgages allow older people to unfreeze the money tied up in their houses. Statistics Canada reports that between 1969 and 1976 home-owners aged 65 and over had 46 percent of their total wealth invested in their homes (Statistics Canada 1980a, 23). Some home-owners would like to use this money to live on, but as long as they live in their homes they live asset-rich but cash-poor. Someone with $150,000 in equity might not have enough cash income to pay the gas or water bill.

Several types of reverse mortgages exist. The most common plan is called the Reverse Annuity Mortgage (RAM) (Bartel and Daly 1981). In

Exhibit 10.3

CASE STUDY OF REVERSE MORTGAGES

Few companies offer reverse mortgages in Canada, and few people know about them, but they may become more common in the future. A company in Vancouver now offers a RAM program that gives some idea of what reverse mortgages can offer home-owners.

James Rogers, the president of a company in Vancouver that offers one of the few programs in Canada, calls the program a "reverse insurance policy." People collect the policy's payment in instalments while they live and make one lump-sum payment (their house) when they die. Two examples will show how this plan worked in 1986.

A man 65 years old, who owns a $135,000 house, joins the reverse mortgage plan. The plan allows him and his wife to live in the house rent-free, and it also pays him $350 a month for life. If he dies before his wife, she continues to receive payments. The company gets the house after they both die.

What about younger people with less equity in their homes? Take the case of a woman, aged 60, who owns a $100,000 house. She joins the program and is able to live in her home rent-free until she dies. She also gets $260 a month for life. The house goes to the company when she dies. Lower interest rates and rising house prices today make this an attractive plan for mortgage companies (Author's notes based on a Canadian Broadcasting Corporation production, 1986).

this plan an older person uses their house to secure a loan from a bank. They then buy a lifetime annuity from an insurance company with the money from the loan. The insurance company pays the bank loan and pays the older person a set amount to live on for life. The older person can stay in their home as long as they want. The bank takes over the house when the last survivor of a couple dies (Bartel and Daly 1981). This plan has at least one major limitation. The interest payments to the bank will go up if interest rates rise, thus reducing the older person's income. Some firms in the U.S. stopped offering RAMs when interest rates soared in the late 1970s and early 1980s. In a time of low interest rates RAMs could solve the economic and housing problems of many older people.

Reverse mortgages will not catch on in Canada until the government decides to support their use. Revenue Canada has not ruled whether the government will tax RAM income. If RAM income counts as taxable income, many people would lose part of this income to taxes. Also, poorer people,

---

Exhibit 10.4

THE CANADA MORTGAGE AND HOUSING CORPORATION (CMHC)

In the past twenty-five years CMHC programs have built 146,000 housing units and 47,000 hostel beds for older people. Forty thousand more units in Canada, mostly for older people, receive a rent subsidy through CMHC, and in the past ten years 174,000 houses (85 percent owned by seniors) have gotten forgivable loans through the Residential Rehabilitation Assistance Program (RRAP). Gross (1985) says that in the past twenty-five years the CMHC has helped renew, build, or support 16,000 housing units a year for older people. The CMHC also helps older people buy and sell homes through loan insurance programs.

The CMHC supports non-profit groups and co-operatives through Section 56.1 of the National Housing Act. These groups build low-income housing for older people. The CMHC will insure up to 100 percent of a loan to one of these groups and will lower interest costs to as low as 2 percent. People who live in these projects can pay as little as 16 percent to 25 percent of their income for housing (Nicklin 1985). CMHC policies and programs like these create new rental housing for seniors and give them more choice about where they can live.

---

who get the GIS, might lose some of their benefits due to their RAM income. A tax break for reverse mortgage income would attract more people to the program. Bairstow (1985) estimates that if the program catches on at least 400,000 older people who own homes might use reverse mortgage programs.

Reverse mortgages alone will not solve all the financial problems older home-owners face, but along with tax credits and government aid for repairs, reverse mortgages can help some people stay in their own homes. Bartel and Daly say that "faced with the rising costs and consequent financial strain of home ownership, the very act of parting with an interest in their home, through a reverse mortgage, may generate the income to financially enable senior citizens to remain there for the rest of their lives" (cited in Economic Council of Canada 1981).

Apartment Living

Statistics Canada (Health and Welfare Canada 1983) says that 29 percent of people aged 65–69 who live in private households live in apartments.

Exhibit 10.5

LITTLE OLD LADY IN A HARD HAT

Most older people adapt their lifestyles to fit the housing option they can afford, but a small number of older people adapt to environmental demands by transforming their environment. Alice Thompson in Calgary chose this approach to meet her housing needs.

Twice a month for nearly a year, 75-year-old Alice Thompson put on a hard hat and inspected a 60-suite apartment block rising in Downtown Calgary.

She was past president of the Elder Statesmen, a group of old people who organized to design, build and manage housing for the elderly. Alice and the rest of the executive of the Elder Statesmen would attend meetings in a trailer on the construction site. The four women and one man — all retired — would then don their blue hard hats and follow their architect, construction manager and the city inspectors, even climbing ladders to get from floor to floor of their six-storey building.

They knew what they wanted. They would not be deterred by workmen accustomed to doing things their own way. They endured freezing weather, strikes and construction errors, once spotting a concrete patio ceiling that had been incorrectly measured and had to be torn out. Finally, several months behind schedule and $182,000 over the $1,850,000 budget, Bow Claire was opened in June 1978, with Alice Thompson as one of its first tenants.

Bow Claire was more than home to Alice; it was a testament to the bold notion that elderly people can have a role in planning their own destiny. ...

Source: Audrey Grescoe, "Little Old Lady in a Hard Hat," *Today Magazine,* January 17, 1981.

This figure increases to 44 percent of people aged 80 and over. People move into apartments when they can no longer care for a house. A study in British Columbia found that almost one older person in five who moved into a senior high-rise did so because they had "difficulty looking after their residence" (Gutman 1983, Table 12). A study (Hodge 1984a) of seniors in eastern Ontario who wanted assisted housing found that about one in six said they could not stay in their home due to age, and about one in ten said they were not well enough to look after their home.

People with good incomes can choose from a wide range of apartments: a high-rise or a low-rise, a two-bedroom suite with a balcony and a view, an apartment near a bus route and shopping. Other older renters have to settle for less. A study published by the Canada Mortgage and Housing Corporation in 1982 reports that older renters had average assets of only $14,000 and had less than $8,000 in liquid assets that year (Fraser 1982). In that same year the CMHC found that "24 percent of renter households with heads aged 65–69 and 32 percent of the households with heads over 70 experienced 'core need'" (i.e., they spent more than 30 percent of their total income on housing) (Canada Mortgage and Housing Corporation 1982, cited in Brink 1985). These figures show that many older people need rent support to ease the burden of housing costs.

The provincial governments offer two kinds of help to renters: subsidized low-income housing and shelter allowances.

Most provinces have built subsidized apartments for low-income seniors. Alberta spent $62 million in 1979–80 to build or support self-contained apartments for older people. Most of the other provinces, along with the federal government, also offer aid to renters in low-income housing. These programs keep a person's rent payment at or below 25 percent of their income (Health and Welfare Canada 1982b).

Some provinces offer shelter allowances to older people. These allowances subsidize the person, not the housing project (Zamprelli 1985). They allow older people to choose their own apartment in the marketplace. This frees people from having to move into government housing. About 40,000 households now get these allowances in Canada (compared to 350,000–400,000 social/public housing units) (Canada Mortgage and Housing Corporation 1981, cited in Zamprelli 1985). The Manitoba SAFER program (Shelter Allowance for Elderly Renters), for example, pays cash rebates (up to a maximum limit) to older tenants who pay more than 27.5 percent to 30.0 percent of their income for housing. The rebate depends on how much housing costs go beyond the allowed amount. Manitoba spent $5 million in 1979–80 to subsidize rent for people over age 60 with low incomes.

A study of the SAFER program by the Manitoba government found that the program increases older people's choice of housing. The study found that 96 percent of the people who get allowances said they feel satisfied or very satisfied with their current housing, and 86 percent of the people in the program said that the program allowed them to spend more money on food (Minuk and Davidson 1981).

Zamprelli (1985) compared shelter allowances and low-income housing programs in Canada. He concluded that:

1. Shelter allowances offer a simple, easy-to-use system to support older people. They give people more freedom to choose the housing they want.
2. Low-income housing offers more control of housing quality, and government-subsidized housing can offer health and social services where people live. This can help many older people live in an apartment on their own, even if their health declines. Both shelter allowances and

subsidized apartments for seniors give low-income older people more opportunity to choose an apartment that meets their needs.

Preferences in Apartment Living

Lawton (1982) cautions that no single statement about housing fits all older people, but older people do show a preference for some types of apartments and neighbourhoods. Studies have looked at senior preferences for age-segregated vs. age-integrated housing, high-rise vs. low-rise housing, and normal vs. special design.

Age-Segregated vs. Age-Integrated Housing

A survey in Ontario (Hough 1981), for example, found that 66 percent of senior respondents wanted neighbours without children, and that more than 64 percent of senior respondents preferred to live in a building with people their own age.

A study by Lawton (1982) of 150 housing sites in the U.S. found that older people who lived in age-segregated housing showed more feelings of well-being. Hough (1981) reports that seniors accept mixed-age housing if they make up the majority of tenants and if each age group lives in its own building. This allows the seniors to choose when and how often they want to interact with families (see also Canada Mortgage and Housing Corporation 1978).

Kaill (1980) concludes that people prefer building segregation because it gives them more control over their social contacts with other age groups. He adds that "this interpretation does not necessarily imply that older people do not wish to be in contact with younger members of the population, but simply that they wish to retain choice in the matter" (1980, 85).

High-Rise vs. Low-Rise Housing

Studies show that older people prefer single homes and low-rise apartments to high-rise buildings. Lawton (1982, 42), in the U.S., says that "the higher the building, the less satisfied were its tenants with their housing and the less mobile they were in the surrounding community ... ."

Another U.S. study found that people in high-rises compared with people in garden apartments showed more boredom, knew fewer people by sight, and engaged in less activity. The study also found that smaller numbers of units (under 100) led to better quality of life (Cranz and Schumacher 1975).

A study of 219 people 55 years old and over in Winnipeg with middle to low incomes (Epstein 1976) found that people in low-rise buildings and in single homes preferred the kinds of settings they already lived in. (Lawton (1982, 39) calls this the principle of people preferring what they have.) Still, 48 percent of people in single detached houses said they preferred medium-rise or row housing to high-rises, and 40 percent of the sample made high-rises their last choice (Epstein 1976).

Other studies in Canada show that older people can and do adapt to high-rise housing. Gutman (1983) reports in one study that 52.8 percent of people living in a high-rise building preferred this type of building. She says that "where a trade-off is required between a high-rise in a 'good' location (i.e. close to public transportation and to community facilities and services) and a low-rise in a 'poor' location, the high-rise should be the structure of choice" (1983, 193).

Normal Design vs. Special Design

Appropriate design can help a person stay in their apartment even if they lose some abilities. Appropriate design also creates a safer, more secure environment. "Design," a CMHC guide says, "can be a positive factor in stimulating effective employment of leisure time, the development of new roles, and a sense of purpose for those of advancing years" (Canada Mortgage and Housing Corporation 1978, 2). Gutman (1983, 187) says that "greater compliance with such guidelines would do much to improve the quality of units built for seniors while not substantially increasing construction costs." She found, for example, that older residents liked having easy access to public transportation and downtown services.

A study done by the University of Winnipeg Institute of Urban Studies found that people wanted their own kitchen, a separate bedroom, and a caretaker for the housing block (Epstein 1976). The study also found that older people dislike bachelor apartments (apartments without a bedroom). A study by the Canadian Council on Social Development (1976a) reports this same finding.

Older people also need space for meetings, lounges, coffee shops, chapels, greenhouses, beauty parlours, and exercise rooms. Apartment housing in the past often ignored this need, but some new buildings now include extra public space. They also include recreation and entertainment programs that help people use the space.

Studies of housing design show that seniors choose the kind of housing that gives them both security and freedom. Beland (1984, 184) says that "senior housing represents for [the] elderly a place where some protection is available, while enabling them to preserve personal autonomy."

Enriched Housing

Enriched housing (sometimes called sheltered or congregate housing) builds extra protection for the older person into the housing design. This type of housing gives people more social and health care support than they get in a normal apartment building. Minuk and Davidson (1981, 55) describe enriched housing as "a housing facility where supportive services (meals, housekeeping, medical services) are available on-site on a regular basis for a moderate fee." Baker (1987b), in a review of the literature on enriched housing, concludes that all enriched housing includes a resident warden and an alarm system, and that most also include communal facilities like a dining room and laundry rooms (citing Harper 1984). Heumann and Boldy (1982) estimate that in Great Britain between 5 and 10 percent of older people need this kind of housing.

The term "enriched housing" applies to many kinds of settings. Enriched housing in Canada ranges from converted hotels which offer rooms and hot meals for single men, to campus-like settings with high- and low-rise housing and many levels of health care (Byerts 1982). The amount of enrichment differs from setting to setting. Sometimes enrichment means only a lounge with a television set in an apartment building. More elaborate enriched housing includes lounges, shops, and in some cases clinics. Some buildings employ activity workers and program planners who show films and organize exercise programs and field trips for residents. Half the people who got SAFER (Shelter Allowance for Elderly Residents) support in Manitoba said they would move to this kind of building (Minuk and Davidson 1981). A study in Ontario (United Senior Citizens of Ontario 1985) found that 47 percent of respondents chose supportive housing as a preferred future housing option.

Critics of enriched housing say that it can lead to early dependency by giving people too many services and that it attracts sick or less able people (Gutman 1978; Lawton 1985), but studies have found more benefits than drawbacks to this kind of housing. Lawton (1976), for example, found that people in enriched housing reported high morale and high life-satisfaction. He says that proper planning can discourage dependence. In some cases enriched housing can even foster independence, because it allows individuals to live on their own rather than in institutions. Enriched housing offers an important alternative to people who need support, but who do not need the high levels of care given in a nursing home or hospital.

Multi-Level Enriched Housing

Multi-level housing bridges the gap between enriched housing and institutional care. Multi-level enriched housing refers to an enriched housing complex or building with a mix of self-contained suites, board-residence, and personal, intermediate, or extended care settings all in one building or on one site. People who approve of multi-level housing say it decreases stress due to relocation, allows couples to stay near one another if the health of one spouse declines, and lowers costs because developers can build one large complex (Gutman 1978).

Gutman (1978) studied satisfaction with multi-level housing in British Columbia. She compared tenants in multi-level housing with a control group in the community. She found that eighteen months after their move, multi-level housing tenants showed higher morale and increased

---

Exhibit 10.6

JACK'S HOTEL: A UNIQUE ENRICHED HOUSING OPTION

The term "single room occupant (SRO) hotel" implies a "low-cost, central-city" hotel that serves a "clientele likely to consist of socially marginal people" (Lawton 1985, 466; Ehrlich and Ehrlich 1976). These hotels offer privacy and tolerance for deviant lifestyles (Eckert 1980; Sokolovsky and Cohen 1981). Only a small number of older people in Canada (less than 0.7 percent of men and 0.4 percent of women 65 and over) live in these hotels. Still, Lawton (1985, 466) says, they meet the needs of a specific group of older people and "an active effort should be made to preserve this resource."

In Winnipeg Jack's Hotel serves as a model for how a city can maintain this kind of housing. Jack's houses forty-two older men in an enriched setting. The building sits on Winnipeg's Main Street strip in the core of the city. A group of designers, social workers, and architects formed a corporation that arranged to remodel the building. The designers left the foot-thick walls in the building and the old wooden doors on the rooms, but they built a game room, a TV lounge, laundry rooms on each floor and a restaurant and dining room. They also hired a housekeeper as part of the staff. This person works at the front desk, sets up field trips and billiard tournaments, and helps the men with medical needs. She will call in a nurse if someone needs help, or arrange for a man to see an eye doctor.

The men who stay at Jack's say they like it there. Most of them had drifted from hotel to hotel along Main Street before they moved to Jack's. Few of them stayed in one place more than a year. A study by Smith (1979) found that half of Jack's tenants had lived there more than three years, a sign that Jack's meets the needs of these men.

---

interaction with neighbours than the control group. She also found no decrease in satisfaction with friends or decrease in visiting friends. People "got out" and "dressed up" more often after eighteen months in multi-level housing than before their move.

Gutman (1985) went back to study these people again nine years later. She found that the proportion of people who liked living in a high-rise multi-level building went from 75 percent to 85 percent over nine years. She also found even more improvement in lifestyle for the multi-level tenants and found that tenants showed an increase in visiting and entertaining friends, while controls in the community showed a decrease in visiting with friends. All of the data Gutman collected on health, physical function, morale, and interaction with others, she says, "failed to support the hypothesis that residence in a multi-level, multi-service housing environment fosters dependency and disengagement" (1985, 6).

She did, however, find three problems with multi-level housing. First, these settings can lead healthy residents to report decreased satisfaction if the nursing home group goes beyond 25 percent of the population. Second, low-rise structures, where the healthy people see the less healthy people all the time, lead to dissatisfaction. Gutman (1985) says that multi-level housing should be built as high-rises to keep the groups more clearly apart. Third, these settings cannot always allow people to shift from one level of care to another as promoters of multi-level housing often promise. The high cost and demand for personal care beds means that, when a bed comes open, the staff will fill it with someone from outside the building. This means that an open bed might not be available when a resident in the building needs it.

This kind of setting will not appeal to everyone, because older people have diverse needs. But multi-level housing serves people who want or need nearby support if their health declines.

Apartment housing comes in many packages. High-rise, low-rise, public, private, non-profit, age-segregated, age-integrated, without services or enriched with services. Older people need this variety because their needs and abilities differ. They also need tax rebates, shelter allowances, and subsidized housing so that they can freely choose the housing that best suits their needs. This variety suits the relatively healthy older person, but some older people need more care than the most enriched setting can provide. These people will need to live in an institution to meet their combined housing and health care needs.

Collective Dwellings

In 1981 20 percent of women 75 and over, and 13 percent of men, lived in collective dwellings — hospitals, hotels, rooming houses, mental hospitals, and nursing homes (Statistics Canada 1984b). The largest number of older people in collective dwellings live in health care institutions or special care homes (Statistics Canada 1984b). Eighty-two percent of women and 79 percent of men aged 75 and over who live in collective dwellings live in these kinds of settings (Health and Welfare 1983).[1]

---

[1]Special care homes go by different names in different provinces. Manitoba calls them Personal Care Homes; Saskatchewan calls them Special Care Homes. The term "nursing home" used here refers to a non-hospital institution that offers care for chronically ill older people. Each province has its own system for classifying patients. Most provinces define four levels of nursing home care. Saskatchewan defines the levels as follows: Level 1 patients need some guidance and support for about twenty minutes a day. Level 2 patients need help with personal care like bathing and dressing for about forty-five minutes a day. Level 3 patients need about two hours of care a day. Level 4 patients need more than

On any one day in 1981, for example, almost 6 percent of men and 9 percent of women in Canada aged 65 and over lived in health care institutions (nursing homes and hospitals) (Statistics Canada 1984b). Some provinces have even higher rates. In Alberta nearly 10 percent of older people live in some kind of institution, not counting people who live in semi-institutionalized "lodges." Manitoba, Ontario, and Saskatchewan have rates of about 9 percent each. These are some of the highest rates in the world. England in 1971, for example, had only 5 percent of its older people in institutions, and the U.S., from 1973 to 1977, had only 6.3 percent (Schwenger and Gross 1980).

Studies show that these figures underestimate the number of people who will live in an institution at some time in their lives. Shapiro and Tate report that in a longitudinal study of more than 3,000 older Manitobans, 11.7 percent entered a long-term care setting between 1971 and the end of 1977. They also found that people over age 85 had almost a seven times greater chance of using a long term care bed than people 65–74 (1985, 12–13). Gross and Schwenger (1981, 127) say that "the aged individual stands more than a one-in-four chance of spending some time in a long-stay institution before his death." As the population ages the numbers and percent of older people who spend some time in an institution will increase.

This would be an unfortunate development, because a number of studies show that institutionalization can lead to decreased well-being and even death for older residents. Gutman and her colleagues in British Columbia (1986), for example, found a high percentage of deaths among patients within the first six months of admission to a personal care home. They conclude that admission to a long-term care institution in itself causes severe stress to older people (Gutman et al. 1986; Gutman and Herbert 1976; Wershow 1976). Chappell and Penning (1979) studied the well-being of over 4,000 older people and found that, given matching levels of health, people in institutionalized settings showed lower well-being than people in the community.

Most people, including government leaders, doctors, nursing home staff, and older people themselves, agree that we should keep older people out of institutions when we can. Still, sometimes a person needs to live in a nursing home. Canada's long winters, the long distances between older people and hospitals, and the complex equipment or techniques needed to treat some illnesses sometimes make institutional life the only way for a person to get the care they need.

Nursing homes can do some things to decrease the effects of institutionalization. MacLean and Bonar (1983), for example, say that institutions can and should make life in the institution as much like life outside as possible. They call this the "normalization principle."

---

two hours of care a day (Senior Citizens' Provincial Council 1980). British Columbia plans to phase out Level 1 care in institutions, and in many cases Level 4 care takes place in an extended care hospital (Stark et al. 1984).

Exhibit 10.7

HOMELESS OLDER PEOPLE

Some people fall through the cracks of the current housing and social welfare system. They move from place to place, and some of them live on the street or stay in missions or the Salvation Army. Doolin (1986, 229) says that "the older person on the street is a multiply-disadvantaged individual," often someone who suffers from alcoholism, unemployment, and a broken family.

Men in this category can find a bed at the Salvation Army or the Harbour Light Mission, but homeless women — some of whom carry everything they own in a shopping bag — have few places to go. Almost no research exists on these women in Canada.

Schull (1981) reported on one of these women for *Today Magazine*.

Ruby, an 80 year old woman, lived for 15 years in a culvert in a Montreal park. Lucy Stofle of Auberge Transition, a shelter in Montreal, found her one day in 1976. "It started to rain," she says, "and I ran for cover under some concrete steps. I looked down and there was a dugout hole, a depression in the earth where there were some rags. The rags started to move. I just freaked! I thought, 'Oh, my god, what's that?' I saw it was an old woman. She was just wearing a couple of coats and looked like a part of the earth. She sat up, and I said hello, and she said hello, and I felt embarrassed because I was in her home. She told me she would sleep there and then she'd leave and go down to Ogilvy's department store and use their washroom and sit the rest of the day on the benches of Ste-Catherine and Crescent streets."

Source: Christiane Schull, "Bag Ladies," *Today Magazine*, April 15, 1981, 15–16.

First, people should feel the normal rhythm of the day, week, and year. They should get dressed each day, have a weekly routine, and celebrate yearly holidays, birthdays, and anniversaries.

Second, people should get normal respect from others. Sometimes staff forget that patients have a right to decide things for themselves. Buzzell (1981) reports that in one nursing home the staff decided that Edna, a 74-year-old patient, should begin walking again after a hip fracture. Buzzell calls the attempt a "nightmare." First, the staff took her wheelchair away so she would have no choice but to walk. Then the nurses on staff called her "lazy" and threatened her if she moved too slowly. Edna suffered dizzy spells, but an aide tried to force her to walk "non-stop to the end of the corridor, sixty feet." "Edna pleaded for rest," Buzzell (1981) says. But the aide refused to let her rest in her wheelchair and threatened to take her off the active treatment program.

MacLean and Bonar (1983) say that staff should treat the older patient as an adult. They should avoid baby talk, talking down to the person, or making decisions without consulting the patient. Penning and Chappell (1982) found that older residents who felt they had freedom and the ability to make choices showed improved mental health (see also Penning and Chappell 1980).

Third, people should lead as normal a social life as possible. This should include sexual contact — and sexual intimacy if a person has a willing partner. People should also have access to their money, and they should have their own pictures, small pieces of furniture, or pets to make the institution more like their home. MacLennan (1983) says that the institution should also expect patients to socialize and to do as much for themselves as they can.

Sinclair (1984) says that a normalized environment should also include a weekly staff meeting. Meetings allow staff to talk about problem patients and help staff members channel their frustration into methods for helping patients function better. Devine (1980) found that normalizing encourages nursing staff "to become leaders and teachers of the residents" instead of just caretakers. She found that staff stopped stereotyping older people as senile and useless because it worked against the goals of the program.

Nursing homes and other institutions will never take the place of a person's own home or apartment, but the changes suggested here can make a nursing home more comfortable for older people who have to live there.

NEW IDEAS IN HOUSING

Granny Flats

Connidis (1983a, 361) asked 400 older people in an Ontario community a simple question: "If circumstances were to change and you had to choose between living with a child or in a facility for seniors, which would you prefer?" She found an "overwhelming tendency to choose a facility for seniors rather than living with children" (1983a, 363). A study in Regina supports Connidis's findings. The Regina study found that "only 8% of the sample indicated that they would move in with a child if they needed 'someone to keep an eye on them' (no health care) suggesting that the majority of seniors 'draw the line' at placing this type of demand on a younger family member" (Senior Citizens' Provincial Council 1981, 47).

The design of modern houses may have influenced these findings. Most modern houses have only two or three bedrooms and no room for another kitchen, bedroom, or bathroom to house an aging parent. The Australian State of Victoria started a new kind of housing for older people that overcomes the problems of modern house design. They call this alternative a "granny flat." A granny flat consists of a portable modular cottage for a parent. The government arranges to move the cottage onto a son's or daughter's property, then the government connects the flat to the electricity, sewer, water, and telephone services of the house. When the older person dies or moves to a nursing home, or if the family moves, the government takes the cottage away. This allows children to care for their parents as long as they can. The Australian government set up about 1,000 granny flats between 1975 and 1982 (Lazarowich and Haley 1982). Granny flats cost little (compared to a house), and the older person and the relatives can support one another.

Lazarowich (1986) says that almost all moves to a granny flat start out with an invitation from the older person's children. When a family does agree to set up a flat, the family — parents and children — need to talk about what they expect from one another. Most older people do not want to become twenty-four-hour babysitters. Neighbours will also have to accept the granny flat idea, because the flats increase the density of housing in a neighbourhood.

A trial program in Ontario called PLUS (Portable Living Units for Seniors) has adapted the granny flat concept to Canada. The PLUS program will run for three years. It will study how well the units work and how neighbours, the host family, and the older residents feel about them. So far, Corke (1986, 11) says, "the reception which has been given to the demonstration has been so heartwarming that we are confident some good will come of it." The Ontario program found that most neighbourhoods accepted the granny flats (Romanick 1986), and already other provinces have started to plan trial projects, some of them in rural areas where zoning laws and lot size will pose less of a problem.

Corke (1986) reports one problem with the granny flat concept. A flat in Canada costs about $42,000 installed (almost double the cost of early estimates). She describes this finding as a "price shock." But the price could come down if the idea catches on and factories produce more units.

A program in Vancouver uses duplexes and four-plexes like granny flats. This program overcomes some of the zoning and building problems in cities. In the Vancouver system, an older person sells their home and then uses the money to help buy a duplex that houses them and their child's family. The older person and younger family members share the taxes, repair costs, and any mortgage costs for the new property. This system works best for families with a combined income (older person and younger family) of $42,400 or more (Evans and Purdie 1985).

These new housing arrangements will lead to new social interdependencies and new challenges to family relations. What will happen if the older person's child separates from or divorces his or her spouse? Or if the child's family moves to another city? Studies of these options will have to show that they make social as well as financial sense, and trial projects can answer only some of these questions. Only longer-term studies will show whether or not granny flats can work in Canada.

Home Sharing

Blackie (1985) defines home sharing as a situation where two people share the bathroom, kitchen, and living rooms of a house, but each have their own bedrooms. A person with a home may need help with household chores due to poor health. A person in good health may need companionship and a lower rent. They both gain by living in a shared home. Shared homes (unlike boarding homes) make no profit.

Many models exist for home sharing. People in a shared home can hire a housekeeper and someone to cook, or they can do the housework themselves. One person can move into another's home, or two or more people can move into a new house together. People can decide on their own to move in together, or an agency can arrange a match, set up a trial stay, and then offer counselling after the home gets going.

A program in Ontario found that people *shared their home* for three reasons: they wanted to stay in their home, they needed income from a sharer, or they felt lonely. The program found that people want to *move into* a shared home because they want companionship, they need cheaper housing, or they have poor health (Rapelje 1985). Turner and Mangum (1982, cited in Blackie 1985) found that 6 percent of people who own homes and 10 percent of people who rent housing said they had an interest in shared housing, and Rapelje (1985) predicts that as many as 52,000 older people in Ontario might want to share a home. But shared housing has some problems. First, the Ontario program found more people who want to share their homes than those who want to move into a shared home. Second, Rapelje (1985) says that most matches last less than a year (see also Pritchard 1983). Sharers split up for a few reasons: one of the sharers may decide to move into their own apartment, one sharer may want to live closer to their family, or one of the pair may remarry.

Rapelje (1985) says that of sixty people in a home-sharing program only three left the program because of a bad match, and most say they would consider sharing a home again. Still, Rapelje's data show that sharers stay together only a short time, and this raises several questions. First, is home sharing worth the trouble and the cost, given the short time that matches last? Second, does the breakup of a match lead to hardship or distress for some sharers? If it does, is this a housing option worth pursuing? More research may be able to answer these questions. In the meantime, shared housing will probably appeal to some people because it will give them a housing option they can afford, the companionship they need, and an alternative to living in an institution (Blackie 1985).

TRANSPORTATION

A home has to suit an older person's abilities and meet the person's needs, but a house or an apartment becomes a prison if the older person cannot get to services, friends, and recreation (Bernardin-Haldemann 1982).

Public Transportation

Only a few studies have looked at the transport needs and use patterns of older people in Canada. Most of these studies report that current transport systems fail to meet older people's needs. A national study of older people's needs, sponsored by the Canadian Red Cross Society (1983), found that older people need better transport for shopping, making social contacts, and getting medical care. Transportation ranked as one of the top five senior needs in all provinces. Baker and Thompson (1985) conducted a random sample study of people 55 and older in Victoria, B.C. Nearly 20 percent of their respondents reported that transportation was a problem for them. These studies support Havens's earlier research in Manitoba (1980). She found that for older men and women "accessibility of resources" ranked as the highest unmet need for each age cohort in the study (Havens 1980, 218–19). The National Advisory Council on Aging (1985e, 2) says that 11 percent of people aged 55–64 are "transportation handicapped" — either they have no public transport or they have trouble using it. This figure jumps to 34 percent of people 80 years old and over.

Rural and urban seniors have different transportation problems. Cities have services, but older people often cannot use them. A survey by the United Senior Citizens of Ontario (1985) found that 9 percent of older people had problems using public transportation. These seniors placed inconvenience first on their list of transportation problems. Rigid routes and schedules make it hard for older people in the suburbs to travel. In the winter long waits for buses, icy sidewalks, or snow mounds at bus stops keep people housebound.

Rural areas often lack public transportation (Health and Welfare Canada 1982b). Grant and Rice (1983) describe many rural seniors as "transportation disadvantaged." This group includes (1) people who feel lonely, dissatisfied, and without a confidant, (2) physically frail people over age 74 who never socialize outside their homes, and (3) low-income, widowed women without a car or someone to drive them. A study by the Senior Citizens' Provincial Council (1982) reported that 20 percent of rural seniors could not find transportation to shop in their town and 23 percent said that due to a lack of adequate transportation they had trouble getting to a larger centre once a month.

People in rural areas need more options. These might include volunteer-run shuttle buses or car pools for seniors. In the cities most older people do not need special transport services; instead they need the improvement of existing services. Only 9 percent of older people in 1981 either used special transport or said they needed services but could not get them (National Advisory Council on Aging 1985e). Ninety percent of the transportation disadvantaged said they could use services that exist if the services changed slightly. Changes include well-lit subway stations (55 percent of seniors in Montreal say they fear using public transit at night), wider doors, easy-to-read signs, lower steps and rails, and bus stops cleared of snow and ice (National Advisory Council on Aging 1985e). These changes will help people of all ages.

Private Transportation

Discussion about public transport needs ignores the fact that 60 percent of Canadians 65 and over own and drive their own cars (Statistics Canada 1984c). Canada now has over 2.5 million drivers over age 55, and the number of older drivers has increased in the past few years. In 1966 35 percent of older people in Ontario had driver's licences, but by 1982 50 percent had licences (National Advisory Council on Aging 1986c). A nation-wide study in 1982 found that seniors preferred private cars to any other form of transport (National Advisory Council on Aging 1986c).

A study in Saskatchewan by Grant and Rice (1983) found 51 percent of rural older people drive themselves, 17 percent ride with another household member, and 33 percent ride with a relative or friend outside the house. A survey by the Senior Citizens' Forum of Montreal found that 33 percent of seniors said they used a car more than any other form of transport (National Advisory Council on Aging 1985e).

This increase in senior drivers raises some new transportation issues. First, older people who drive will have to include the rising cost of auto insurance in their budgets. Second, people over age 55 have more accidents per kilometre than middle-aged drivers. This has led the Canada Safety Council to set up a program called Alive/Mature Driving. The program helps seniors improve their driving skills and understand how aging affects driving. Some people have suggested special driver's licences for daytime-only drivers and non-highway driving. Some provinces require drivers over age 65 to take a driver's test every year. Third, older people in high-rises and downtown apartments will need parking spaces for their cars. These issues point to the changing transportation needs of a healthier, more affluent older population.

New Transportation Needs and Programs

Transportation needs for older people in the future will go beyond current use patterns. New programs may rely less on technological change and more on "organizational and service-related innovations" (National Advisory Council on Aging 1986c, 3). Older people will run some of these programs themselves. One program in Edmonton, called a "transportation brokerage," matches passengers with services that meet their needs. Another program called a "mobility club" in Moncton and the

---

Exhibit 10.8

A TYPOLOGY OF TRANSPORT LIFESTYLE GROUPS

A Independent, Own Auto — people with money and physical ability to drive own car and live alone; most mobile seniors. Finances and physical ability impose major limits on car use. This group may switch to other means of transport as they age.
B Dependent, Access to Auto — people who live with others (mostly for financial reasons) with own car, less mobile.
C Independent, No Auto — have money and independence but may not be able to afford many transport options like car rental, taxis, buses.
D Dependent, No Access to Auto — live with others, no auto, much less mobile.
E Sheltered or Group Housing — some physical and economic depen-dence, can meet transport needs because of group setting.
F Disabled — all income types, but these people have some physical disability, and they need special transit programs like those used by disabled non-seniors.
G Institutionalized — poor health, others care for needs, these people have the least unmet mobility needs (because the institution meets their needs).

Groups vary in their physical ability, their income, and the support they get. Each lifestyle group has its own transportation needs. More transportation options will give all older people more freedom and independence.

Source: Adapted from Ontario Ministry of Municipal Affairs and Housing, Research and Special Projects Branch, *Towards Community Planning for an Aging Society* (Toronto: Queen's Printer for Ontario, 1983), 7.

Acadian Peninsula helps people in small towns and rural areas. This club formed a non-profit, self-help transport service. People with cars call in to tell a dispatcher about trips they plan to make in the next week or so. People who need rides call in one day before they have to take a trip. A dispatcher matches riders with drivers. Drivers also volunteer for up to one emergency trip per month (Grant and Rice 1983).

In Ottawa senior volunteers help run a bus service that takes 25 to 30 seniors grocery shopping each week. Volunteers help people on and off the bus, help people carry packages, and give people rides to other appointments during the week (National Advisory Council on Aging 1986c). Saskatchewan has set up a Rural Transportation Assistance Program (RTAP). This program helps small rural communities form a local transit service. The provincial government subsidizes the cost of using a car or van to travel twice a week between these towns and a larger centre (Grant 1983). Grant and Rice (1983) say that rural communities may need to combine a number of options to serve their older people.

CONCLUSION

People can cope with environmental demands in several ways as they age. They can improve their abilities (through self-help or rehabilitation) or change their environment (by modifying their homes or getting help through changes in social policy). This chapter has focused on the policies and programs in Canada that help older people live in an environment that suits their abilities. This review shows that with some help older people can live high-quality lives in their own homes and apartments into late old age.

SUMMARY

1. Research on housing and transportation shows that older people enjoy old age most when they feel in control of their environment. People can maintain this control by changing their environment (for example, moving to an apartment from a single-family home or getting help through social policy reform).
2. A good match between a person's ability and environmental demand leads to high life-satisfaction. An ideal housing system offers older people a range of housing choices. These choices serve people with different needs. People should be able to move from one type of housing to another — from a house, to an apartment, to enriched housing — as their needs change. Or they should be able to get support to help them stay where they are.
3. Most older people want to stay in the kind of housing they now occupy. Government policies and programs — like rent subsidies, tax rebates, and repair loans — help older people stay where they are. Other programs — like loan guarantees, new building programs, and shelter allowances — allow older people to move to the kind of housing that suits their needs.
4. Canada offers older people a wide range of housing options to choose from. These include single-family homes, apartments, enriched housing, and multi-level enriched housing. New types of housing — granny flats and share-a-home programs — will increase seniors' housing options in the future.
5. Good transportation links older people to their community — to services, recreation, and friends, but both urban and rural transportation systems need improvement. Most older people in cities could use the transportation that exists if it were modified to suit their needs. Poor lighting in subways, snow at bus routes, and rigid schedules make urban transport unsuitable for older people. Urban transport today

increases environmental demand when it should increase the older person's capability.

6. Rural seniors often have no transportation available to them, but new transportation programs in rural settings are developing. They include bus services shared by a number of small towns, volunteer bus services, and people who pool their resources to help one another get around. Older people in rural settings have begun to work to set up the transportation services they need.

7. Good housing and transportation lead to increased life-satisfaction for older people. An environment that fits the person's abilities helps keep older people satisfied, active, and in touch with their community.

SELECTED READINGS

Canada Mortgage and Housing Corporation. *Housing the Elderly.* Ottawa: Minister of Supply and Services, 1978.
A manual that describes the specifications for high-quality senior housing design. It includes the dimensions of bathrooms, doorways, and hallways to allow easy wheelchair access. A glance through this book will make you look at the environment in a new way. You will begin to see things from the point of view of the older person with special needs.

Grant, Peter R., and Bruce Rice. "Transportation Problems of the Rural Elderly: A Needs Assessment." *Canadian Journal on Aging* 2 (1983):107–24.
The authors focus on a study done in Saskatchewan, but their results could apply to most rural locations in Canada. They find that many rural seniors are "transportation disadvantaged" and need better public transportation. This should include access to long-distance transport (intercity buses) and short-distance transport (local buses) so that people can shop and get to health care resources.

Gutman, Gloria, and Norman Blackie, eds. *Innovations in Housing and Living Arrangements for Seniors.* Burnaby, B.C.: Gerontology Research Centre, Simon Fraser University, 1985.
A collection of papers presented at a 1984 symposium on housing for older people in Canada. The book includes selections by scholars, private consultants, and government policy makers. It presents discussions of some of Canada's most creative housing programs for seniors.

CHAPTER 11

PERSONAL DEVELOPMENT AND COMMUNITY SERVICE

INTRODUCTION

Dan Kreske worked as an insurance agent until he retired six years ago. He had a good income from his investments, savings, and Canada Pension Plan. He heard about free university classes and started to attend. Now he goes to class two or three afternoons a week (depending on the courses offered). He has also renewed his interest in athletics. He played golf all through his working years, and he jogged and swam, but in retirement he found he had more time to develop his ability. In the winter of 1986 he competed at Lake Placid, New York, in the Masters Division of the North American Speed Skating Championships. He made two third- and two fourth-place finishes and won ten points for his team. "I lost to guys twenty-five years younger than I am — it was one of the greatest thrills of my life."

Many older people like Dan Kreske continue to develop established skills and talents in retirement. Other older people discover new interests when they retire, or they discover a talent for poetry, acting, or art. Still other people turn to community service or they may start to do volunteer work in a hospital or senior centre part-time.

Seniors today have more opportunities for self-development and community service than ever before, and many of them have a great desire to develop themselves and give to others as they age. For many older people the years after retirement become a time of search, discovery, and fulfilment. This chapter will review some of the programs and activities that help seniors live a satisfying old age. This chapter will look at: (1) how seniors today spend their time, (2) new personal development programs for seniors (recreation, fitness, and education), and (3) seniors' community involvement.

WHAT DO OLDER PEOPLE DO?

Research shows that older people spend most of their time on solitary activities. Statistics Canada (1977) reports that 40 percent of older people watch more more than fifteen hours of television a week. Older people say they spend more time watching television than doing any other leisure activity (Statistics Canada 1977). The 1981 Canadian Time Use Pilot Study found that men and women aged 56 and over watched more television than any other age group (Statistics Canada 1986a). Women watched TV an average of more than two and a half hours a day; men averaged more than three hours a day.

A study of seniors living in enriched housing in eastern Ontario found that 93 percent of them watched TV every day (Hodge 1984b). Some writers say that people who live alone use TV as a form of social contact (Werner 1976). Other writers (Huang 1974) say that TV keeps people in touch with the world and current events. McPherson (1983) says that TV helps structure time for people who live alone. An older person may watch a morning talk show over breakfast, eat supper with the evening news, and go to sleep after the national news. Some people schedule their days around the afternoon soap operas.

Older people also spend a lot of time reading. The Canadian Radio-television Commission, for example, found that 83 percent of older people read the newspaper an average of one and a quarter hours on weekdays — twice as much time as the average person in the study (Environics Research Group 1974). All studies show the same trend: older people spend most of their time — 56 percent — on passive, "receptive," media-related leisure (Environics Research Group 1974). They spend a lot of this time alone at home or indoors with friends and relatives.

Eight out of ten older people in one study said they had visited friends or relatives in the past week, 40 percent of retired people said they saw friends or relatives more than three times a week, and 20 percent said they saw them daily (Health and Welfare Canada 1983). Chappell (1983a) found that doing something relaxing (like playing cards, walking, or talking) with someone their own age brought older people the greatest pleasure. A study by Romsa and Johnson (1983) found that more participation in activity did not increase life-satisfaction, but seeing friends, talking on the phone, and visiting a community centre did.

Other research supports these findings. Tenants in a seniors' housing co-op, for example, ranked talking on the telephone, visiting friends, and visiting relatives in that order as their three most important activities (Marmel, Sawyer, and Shell 1983). People look forward to these activities in retirement. A study of working men and women asked them what activities they considered led to a good retirement. Almost three-quarters of the men and women in the study rated seeing relatives and family as an important activity, more than half rated seeing friends as important, and more than three-fifths of these men and women said they expected to have more time to see relatives and friends in retirement (Health and Welfare Canada 1977b).

Income and social status make a difference in an older person's activity. People with the lowest income and those with the highest income show the least interest in spectator sports (McPherson and Kozlik 1980). Those with no income and little education and those with high incomes and a university degree show the lowest involvement in popular culture activities (like watching TV, listening to records, going to movies, engaging in crafts, and reading newspapers). People with middle incomes and either a high school diploma or some secondary education show the most involvement in popular culture activities. People with university degrees tend to read more books than other groups. "Even within the same age cohort," McPherson and Kozlik (1980, 115) say, "life chances and life-styles vary because of differences in social status." Other studies in Canada show that higher income and more education lead to more active leisure (Milton 1975; Hobart 1975). Roadburg (1985) found that (middle-income) service workers took part in sports, exercise, and dancing, but (lower-income) clerical and sales workers mostly read.

Studies also find that gender influences activity level. McPherson and Kozlik (1980) found that at all ages men are more active than women in sports, and also that men report more satisfaction with the amount of their activity (Statistics Canada 1976a, cited in McPherson and Kozlik 1980). This low participation in sports by women may reflect the fact that fewer women than men have spouses with whom to share sports activity. Studies show that married people living with their spouses have more active lifestyles (Roadburg 1985). Low participation in sports by women may also reflect the lack of opportunity women have had to participate in sports in the past. In either case the difference in activity level between men and women may disappear in the future. Longer life expectancy means that couples will live together and stay active together longer. Also, fitness programs (more than sports) appeal to both sexes. Already, women show the same amount of participation in exercise programs as men (McPherson and Kozlik 1980).

The research shows that health, education, income, and social status all shape leisure in retirement. McPherson (1985) says that most often people follow the pattern of leisure in retirement that they followed in middle age. People who enjoyed athletic activity, socializing, or travelling will continue to do these things when they retire (unless something like a sharp drop in health prevents them). This means that future cohorts of older people will bring their own interests with them into old age. Some changes in seniors' interests and activities suggest that this has already begun.

NEW ACTIVITIES IN OLD AGE

Outdoor Recreation

Leisure and recreation programs for seniors exist all across the country. In Saskatchewan seniors can get free fishing licences and free access to provincial parks. British Columbia gives seniors free camping privileges and reduced rates on fishing licences. Manitoba, Saskatchewan, and Quebec schedule assisted travel tours. Nova Scotia runs fitness and recreation classes. Alberta has a recreation consulting service and promotes senior involvement in the theatre. Airlines, buses, theatres, restaurants, and travel agencies across the country offer senior citizens' discounts.

Most of Canada's national parks now have wheelchair facilities, special picnic tables, and parking areas. Also, parks across Canada have programs for seniors. Riding Mountain National Park in Manitoba, for example, has "grandparent hikes" for grandparents and their grandchildren. Prince Albert National Park in Saskatchewan has a yearly seniors' golf tournament and La Mauricie National Park in Quebec has three lakes reserved for seniors. Parks in Cape Breton and Nova Scotia have special films for seniors. Riding Mountain National Park also has a program that gives older people a chance to do something for others. It offers special camping privileges to seniors if they agree to give information and help to other visitors (Hayashida 1983). All of these programs and services help older people stay active.

Recreation planners need to keep some seniors' special needs in mind when they plan programs. Sometimes, for example, older people lack the transportation to get to parks, concerts, or recreation sites. Many cultural events take place in the evening, when older people tend to stay at home. Also, poor design of recreation settings sometimes keeps older people out. One woman says she drove with a friend to a historical site. When they got there they noticed that the rest rooms in the souvenir shop had been redesigned for wheelchair use, but to get to that rest room a person in a wheelchair would have had to climb twenty steps up the side of a hill. More awareness of the needs of handicapped people (young and old) will make it easier for handicapped seniors to use facilities and enjoy recreational activities.

Fitness

The Canada Health Survey (Health and Welfare Canada and Statistics Canada 1981) found that activity declines with age, but a closer look at the findings shows that decline after age 65 depends more on health than on age. Comparisons of the healthy people in each age group showed that people stayed active into old age. Of the healthiest 45–64-year-olds, 13 percent ranked as "very active" and 18 percent as "sedentary." Of the healthiest people aged 65 and over, the same proportion — 13 percent — ranked as "very active." Moreover, only 15 percent ranked as "sedentary" — 3 percent *less* than the 45–64-year-olds. Finally, the figures for healthy people 65 and over do not differ that much from the total population (20 percent "very active" and 14 percent "sedentary") (Health and Welfare Canada and Statistics Canada 1981, 79–80). The Canada Health Survey (1981, 72) says that people in good health and with positive emotional well-being at all ages tend to remain very active, and this is particularly true of older people.

A study of seniors in one housing co-op found that even people with health problems try to stay active. The study found that 49 percent of the tenants had fair to poor health, 18 percent had heart or circulation problems, and 45 percent had arthritis and rheumatism. Twenty-eight percent of these people use wheelchairs, walkers, and canes. Still, this study found that 60 percent of these people did full or partial body exercise and that 60 percent of those who exercised did so every day (Marmel, Sawyer, and Shell 1983).

Research shows that, as a group, older people are becoming more active. The Canada Fitness Survey (Fitness and Amateur Sport 1982) found that the two oldest groups (55–64 years and 65+) showed the largest increases in fitness activity from 1976 to 1981. The second-oldest age group (55–64 years) doubled its participation in sports from 1976 to 1981, and the oldest group (65+) reported nearly a three-fold increase in sports activity in those years.

The oldest group showed an even more rapid increase in *exercise* activities. On average, able-bodied people aged 65 and over reported a 13 percent increase in exercise activity between 1976 and 1981, compared to only a 3 percent increase for able-bodied people of all ages. This gave able-bodied older people a higher rate of exercise participation than all of the other groups in the study except the 15–24-year-olds. (This measure excluded people with disabilities. Older people have lower rates of participation than younger groups, if the figures include people with disabilities.)

Exhibit 11.1

FITNESS AND AGING

Percentage of Able-Bodied People in Four Age
Groups Who Participated in Sports* During the
Previous Year (1981)

Percent	1976	1981	
90			15–24 years
70			25–54 years
50			55–64 years
30			65 + years
10			

*Includes individual, dual, team, aquatic, winter sports. Excludes exercise activity.

Source: Adapted from Fitness and Amateur Sport, *Fitness and Aging: Canada Fitness Survey* (Ottawa: Minister of Supply and Services, 1982), 4. Reproduced with permission of the Minister of Supply and Services Canada.

Percentage of Able-Bodied People in Four Age Groups
Who Participated in Exercise Activities* in the Previous
Month (1981)

Percent	1976	1981	
80			
70			15–24 years
60			65 + years / 25–54 years
50			55–64 years
40			

*Walking, running, jogging, cycling, calisthenics, and exercise classes.

Source: Adapted from Fitness and Amateur Sport, *Fitness and Aging: Canada Fitness Survey* (Ottawa: Minister of Supply and Services, 1982), 5. Reproduced with permission of the Minister of Supply and Services Canada.

Fitness and Health

Some decline in physical function is due to true aging (for example, the slowdown in cell metabolism or a decrease in lung elasticity) (DeVries 1975). Research shows, for example, that aerobic capacity declines with age even in trained athletes (Stones and Kozma 1980). Researchers still do not know how much of this decline is due to aging and how much is due to past health problems, past habit and underuse of the body (Stones and Kozma 1982). Studies of fitness training show that exercise can slow and even reverse some of this decline.

DeVries (1975, citing Wessel and Van Huss 1969), one of the first researchers to study the effects of exercise on older people, says that declines in physical function have more to do with decreased activity than with true aging. Kraus and Raab (1961) call this the "hypokinetic disease." They say that the lack of activity can lead to mental and physical problems, while increases in activity can prevent or reverse these problems.

Other studies find clear signs of improvement in physical well-being as a result of exercise. Studies by Fischer (1977) and Clarke (1977) show improvements in arterial and muscle flexibility. Shephard (1978), for example, studied thirty-eight people in Toronto over age 65 who took an exercise program four times a week. In seven weeks these people increased aerobic power by 30 percent. After a year they had increased muscle mass and bone density, and people in the program had lost three-quarters of their excess fat (Edwards 1983). Smith (1982), in a study of older women, found increases in bone mass due to exercise. DeVries (1975, 265) concludes from this literature that "the older organism is definitely trainable. Indeed the percentage of improvement [shown by older people who exercise] is entirely similar to that of the young."

Fitness and Well-Being

Fitness programs can improve the psychological well-being of older people as well as their health. A controlled study by Gutman, Herbert, and Brown (1977) studied two kinds of exercise program: a standard program of walking, bending, and running in place, and a program called "Awareness Through Movement" designed by Dr. Moshe Feldenkrais. The Feldenkrais method, which is used by a number of senior programs across Canada, works to reduce pain and help older people do more for themselves. The program increases people's awareness of how they move and teaches them to make smoother, more integrated movements.

The researchers ran these two programs for six weeks and then asked people how much they liked their program. About 85 percent of the people in each exercise class rated their program as excellent. One hundred percent of the people in both groups said they felt satisfied with their program and said they would tell others to take it. Four-fifths or more of the people in each group said they would take another six-week class.

The people in both programs claimed physical benefits, said they felt stronger and more flexible, and had better health in general.

They also said the programs gave them a "mental lift" and made them feel more relaxed. They reported that the standard program led to "better contact" with new people. Other fitness programs show similar results. Perri and Templer (1984–85) report that older people in an exercise program improved their self-concept and felt more mastery over their environment. Even in institutions, exercise programs can improve participants' sense of well-being. People in an activity program in a nursing home reported that they felt better, slept better, and did more of their own personal care (LaRocque and Campagna 1983). Studies (Stacey, Kozma, and Stones 1985; Myers and Hamilton 1985) also show that exercise leads to improved social life and increased happiness. "This finding alone," Stacey, Kozma, and Stones (1985, 73) say, "provides sufficient justification for enrolling in an exercise program."

The Challenge to Fitness Programs

All fitness programs for older people face two problems: how to get older people involved and how to keep them involved. The Canada Fitness Survey, for example, found that people aged 65 and over, more than any other group, said they did not want to increase their present level of activity. And, more than any other group, they said that nothing would get them to increase their activity (Fitness and Amateur Sport 1982). A report by the Red Cross admits that most seniors today will not join fitness programs. The report says that seniors avoid groups and they avoid fitness classes because they have not done much of this kind of exercise in the past. (Canadian Red Cross Society 1983).

Gutman, Herbert, and Brown (1977) found that half the people in their exercise study had dropped out by the end of the program. Cape (1983) also reported problems with attendance. She ran a fitness program in a nursing home and found that people dropped out, missed classes, or joined in the middle of the program. Stacey, Kozma, and Stones (1985) report that the people who drop out may need the programs the most. They say that older, less happy, and more anxious people tend to drop out of programs.

Programs have to motivate people to get them to join and to keep them in the program. Experts in program design report that:

1. People stay in programs when they have some say in the content of the program. Program leaders should consult with seniors when they start a program, and they should allow older people to help shape the program once they join.
2. People stay in programs when they enjoy them.
3. People stay in programs when they feel welcome.

Exhibit 11.2

NEW ACTIVITY IN OLD AGE

Two years ago, Hugh Clifford, 75, ran a marathon for the first time. He finished the 26-mile race in a slow four hours, 41 minutes and 46 seconds. Last May he competed in the Vancouver International Marathon and won the Canadian masters medal as the fastest marathoner over 70, with a time of 4:04:17. ...

When he retired at 64, he had a mild heart attack, a warning that set him to cycling, swimming and losing 25 pounds. He eventually gave up swimming for jogging, an activity he hated but kept at until he'd done a mile three times. Then he was addicted. Now he's replaced the hiking boots he first ran in with six pairs of good running shoes. He paid $5 for his first pair, and he still owns them;

he calls them his dancing shoes. He runs every second or third day, about 50 kilometres a week, following a route along city streets and blacktopped seaside paths. In between runs, he does stretching exercises, reads magazines about running, lifts weights, keeps a daily diary of his distances in which he works out his minutes-per-kilometre rate. He trains for many annual distance races, attending a weekly marathon clinic at his local YMCA and joining "fun runs," where he gets a kick out of running with people much younger than himself.

He has a sense of physical well-being he never had before: "I am fit. Without a blush, I tell you that I am really fit."

Source: Excerpted from Audrey Grescoe, "Good Old," *Today Magazine*, January 9, 1982, 11–14, 16.

Leaders say that a good program minimizes competition and threat. Also, programs should give people a chance to socialize before and after classes (Stewart 1982). Programs that follow this advice may decrease their dropout rates.

Fitness in the Future

The Canada Fitness Survey found that middle-aged people (25–54 years old) had a better attitude to fitness than older people (55+) today. More of them than the older group said they took part in activity for fun and pleasure, to relax and reduce stress, to learn new things, and to challenge their abilities (Fitness and Amateur Sport 1982). This group will bring these attitudes with them into old age. Canada's recreation system has already begun to change to meet their needs (Delisle 1982; Parks Canada 1973).

In 1980, for example, Alberta sponsored Canada's first Seniors Games for people aged 55 and over. Alberta also has a Senior Citizens Sport & Recreation Association (ASCSRA). The association has branches in eight Alberta Games zones in the province. Christie (1983) says that in 1982 (the second time the province held the Games) 21,000 older people competed in playoffs for the Games. The twenty-six events ranged from trap shooting to tennis to handicrafts and performing arts. Nine hundred seniors, including retired doctors, homemakers, and homesteaders, made the playoffs. The average age of the competitors was 67. The oldest was a 92-year-old man from northern Alberta. The Alberta government has agreed to give $200,000 to support future games every two years.

Christie (1983) reports that people get more from the games than medals. Senior volunteers plan and run the games, serving as scorekeepers, referees, and administrators as well as contestants. The games, she says, inspire seniors to improve their skills. They also lead to new friendships and give seniors a chance to try new activities in a non-threatening way.

Senior Centres

Most cities and towns across Canada also have senior centres. They form the closest thing to a nation-wide recreation system for older people. People drop in to their local centre, meet other seniors, play cards, take classes, and in some cases get medical help. The federal government calls senior centres "the most important source of recreation and cultural activity" for older people in Canada (Health and Welfare Canada 1982b). The Canadian Red Cross Society (1983) found that seniors used seniors' clubs more than any other recreation service.

The number of centres in Canada has grown in the past fifteen years. In Saskatchewan, for example, the number of centres in the province grew from 3 in 1971 to 412 in April of 1983. Today seniors go to most centres to socialize, to take part in recreation, or to get information. In small communities the centres sometimes offer the only opportunity for social contacts. Some centres offer social and health care services as well as recreation. The Regina Native Elders Incorporated runs a centre that offers meals on wheels, crafts, and health checkups. Other Native centres offer help with letter writing, filling out forms, and transportation to activities. Almost all activity centres in Saskatchewan belong to the Saskatchewan Seniors Association Incorporated (SSAI). This group promotes new programs and helps centres share information. The Council says that the SSAI has over 20,000 members. This makes it one of the largest organizations of seniors in the country (Senior Citizens' Provincial Council 1983).

In Winnipeg a non-profit agency called Age and Opportunity, Inc. (A&O), runs a system of full-service centres. These centres meet the strict standards set by the National Institute of Senior Centres in the United States. A & O centres offer programs like bingo, billiards, and folk danc-

Exhibit 11.3

HANGING AROUND THE MALL

Some older people choose not to join a senior centre or other organized group. Researchers Sijpkes, MacLean, and Brown (1983) of McGill University studied older people who spend their days at the Complexe Desjardins mall in Montreal. They found that many older people use the mall as a drop-in centre.

They describe a typical case:

An old man who lives in a twenty dollar a week room on Sherbrooke Street in Montreal leaves his room at eleven in the morning of a cold windy day. The streets are treacherously slippery. He carefully negotiates the two blocks to the Jeanne Mance entrance of the subway system. There he takes the escalator down to begin a long subterranean walk, occasionally enlightened by a glimpse of the outdoors, past the metro station, through the Place des Arts complex; he nips under St. Catherine Street to finally end up in the main space of Complexe Desjardins. By now he is quite warmed up from his cold outside walk, and he sits down on one of the many benches in the space, talks to some of the older people he knows, reads a newspaper which one of them has bequeathed him, and carefully smokes a cigarette.

Around noon he wanders over to the very centre of the space where he stands for a while watching the daily production of a live TV show for a French local channel. He splurges on a coffee which is available from a variety of little shops in the complex. On his way home he talks to some more people he knows and winds his way back through the underground system.

Source: Excerpted from Peter Sijpkes, Michael MacLean, and David Brown, "Hanging Around the Mall," *Recreation Canada*, February 1983, 44–46.

ing, but they also offer members financial and personal counselling and health care. The staff and the members of A & O centres share the work. The staff ensure that the centres have programs like counselling, education, and health clinics. The centre members decide on recreation programs, fund-raising, and centre maintenance (Age and Opportunity, Inc. 1983b). Each centre has a unique program that reflects members' interests and needs. At one centre classes might include English as a second language, at another conversational French. Centres also offer lunch and supper meals. In 1983 A & O served almost 25,000 meals to older people at five centres, the centres responded to almost 12,000 requests for information, and centres' staffs counselled and gave health information on almost 8,000 occasions (Age and Opportunity, Inc. 1983a).

Seniors at A & O centres also give to their communities. Members plan programs and help prepare meals, sing in centre choirs, and visit local schools to perform for the students.

Senior centres serve an important function for seniors as places to meet others and engage in recreational activity. But neighbourhood centres face a challenge today from other recreational programs. Many young-old seniors see senior centres as one recreational option among many. Education programs at universities and colleges now attract many seniors who might once have been satisfied with the programs at a senior centre. Senior centres will need to alter their programs to fit the needs of a changing older population.

Education

Most schools today serve basically the same function they did a century and a half ago, when they first began: they teach children to become adults, and they prepare young people for specific jobs in society. This system offers little to the older person, who is already an adult and retired from a job. Statistics Canada says that in 1981 fewer than 1 percent of men and women aged 65 and over enrolled in credit courses. Of those who went to school, 70 percent went part-time (Health and Welfare Canada 1983).

These figures suggest that the school system, with its emphasis on testing, grading, and credentials, does not appeal to older learners. Adult educators (Kidd 1973) say that older people have different needs than younger learners. Older learners come back to school for personal development and to find meaning in later life. Older learners ask, "Is the knowledge useful? Does it help me make better sense of my life and the world around me? Does it help me live more fully and enjoy my life more? A government report (Devereaux 1985) says that of the people aged 65 and over enrolled in adult education courses, more than three-quarters of men and over 90 percent of women took hobby courses (e.g., woodworking, painting, cooking) or personal development courses (e.g., history, music appreciation).

Schools will have to change their ideas about education and educational settings if they hope to attract older learners. Myles and Boyd (1982, 271) give an example of what an older person faces when he or she walks onto a university campus.

Mrs. Smith arrives ... and finds classes dispersed over a large campus with limited facilities for getting around. The principles of credentialism which lead to the organization of academic activity around exams and the accumulation of credits are of little relevance to her. When she attempts to relax in a recreation area she is subjected to loud music which she

Exhibit 11.4

TEACHING METHODS FOR USE WITH SENIOR STUDENTS

Hultsch and Deutsch (1981) suggest the following methods to help older people learn better in the classroom. Some of these methods should be used no matter what the student's age (taking breaks, giving immediate feedback on tests), while others apply more to seniors than to other age groups (giving visual and aural cues to help memory, speaking slowly and distinctly).

Technique	Description of the Technique
1. Pacing	Remove time pressures. Let people set their own pace.
2. Arousal Anxiety	Decrease anxiety. Decrease competition and testing. Let people get used to new ideas or techniques.
3. Fatigue	Give older students rest breaks or cut down the length of time for each lesson.
4. Difficulty	Build people up by starting with simple and moving on to more complex work. Break the work into segments.
5. Practice	Give people a chance to use what they know in different ways.
6. Feedback	Let people know how they did as soon as possible so they can fix mistakes.
7. Cues	Give older people visual and aural cues to help them with their work. Use clear diagrams, speak clearly, and repeat questions from the class so that everyone follows the discussion.
8. Organization	Group information for students. Use memory aids like pictures, mental images, or verbal cues.
9. Relevance/ Experience	Find out what the older student wants to know. Build on students' past experience. Show them how to apply what they learn.

Source: Adapted from David F. Hultsch and Francine Deutsch, *Adult Development and Aging: A Life-Span Perspective* (New York: McGraw-Hill, 1981), 152, "Educational Interventions for Adults."

finds noxious. ... In effect, what Mrs. Smith is encountering is a social institution designed and organized for the young.

Exhibit 11.5

PROFILE:
"BACK TO SCHOOL AT 68"

Henry Friedman, 74, was about 50 years older than his classmates when he graduated from the University of British Columbia in 1979. It had taken him six years, rather than the usual four, to complete his studies, which he began soon after retiring from his job as the Vancouver agent for a Montreal manufacturer of women's gloves and handbags. After graduating from Montreal High School in the 1920s, he had had no more formal education. He could not afford to go to university. But he loved to read and to talk about what he had read. For years his great pleasure had been the fortnightly meetings of the Northwest Great Books Institute; at university, he reasoned that he could take part in more of these stimulating discussions.

Mr. Friedman says that he's an introvert but university has changed him. He enjoys parties with fellow students and professors, and he likes to spark debate in class. He wants to test and modify his ideas. He's thrilled when he's able to challenge a visiting professor with a thoughtful question.

Source: Excerpted from Audrey Grescoe, "Good Old," *Today Magazine*, January 9, 1982, 11–14.

To meet the needs of older learners like Mrs. Smith, universities will have to give older students more options about class times, subject choices, and testing methods. They will also have to increase the kinds of social supports — like counselling or pre-registration assistance — that they give to older students. Some of these changes have begun, and others will take place as more older people come back to school.

Universities, for example, have begun to adapt their programs to older learners. Many offer free tuition and special classes for seniors. They give library cards to seniors and involve them in the planning and design of senior education programs. Teachers learn that they need to change their teaching style to fit older students' learning styles. They need to take more time to present material, allow time for students to ask questions or state their views, and match their pace of instruction to the students' abilities. Studies on learning and memory, for example, show that older people take more time to learn something new, and that anxiety, fatigue, and a lack of practice at school tasks make it harder for older people to succeed. Also, older people will drop out of a program if they cannot link what they learn to what they already know.

The use of appropriate teaching methods along with more flexible

Exhibit 11.6

ELDERHOSTEL

As more older people continue their education, new educational programs will emerge to meet their needs. The Elderhostel program serves as an example of educational innovation for seniors. Sixty-six universities in Canada (at least one in each province and the Northwest Territories) now sponsor an Elderhostel program on their campus. Elderhostel combines university campus life with the European concept of hosteling (travelling from place to place and staying in inexpensive, safe lodgings). Elderhostel students live on a university campus while they take courses. This gives them a chance to travel, meet new people, and learn things in a variety of settings they might not otherwise see.

The Elderhostel program accepts students over age 60 and their spouses. It does not matter how much education a person has had in the past. Most programs last one week — from Sunday afternoon until the following Saturday morning. A one-week program typically includes three courses. Elderhostel tries to keep the class size small: most programs enrol from thirty-five to forty-five students at a time. In 1987 the typical total fee for the week — including food, rooms, course fees, and fees for extracurricular tours and activities — was $240 in Canada ($215 in the U.S.). The Elderhostel program offers "Hostelships" (scholarships) to assist people who cannot afford the program fee.

Elderhostel began in 1975 and now offers courses in 900 colleges and universities in countries around the world, including Mexico, Bermuda, England, France, the Netherlands, the U.S., and Canada. The University of New Brunswick offered the first course in 1980, and Canadian programs have expanded quickly. From 1980 to 1981 the number of participants in Ontario more than doubled, and in the Maritimes the number of programs grew from one in 1980 to programs in all four provinces by 1981 (Elderhostel 1981). In 1987 Elderhostel sponsored programs at twenty-one sites in the Maritime provinces (Elderhostel 1987).

A few excerpts from the May to October 1987 Canadian Elderhostel Catalogue (Elderhostel 1987) will give you some idea why this program has grown so fast.

- Dalhousie University in Halifax, Nova Scotia, offers three courses in its early July program: Regional Roots (a study of the history and settlement patterns of Nova Scotia); Introduction to Computers (hands-on use of microcomputers and discussions of software applications); Chemistry — A Central Science (this course shows the relationship of chemistry to the other sciences and its applications).
- Queen's University at Kingston, Ontario, offers three courses in early July: Greek Tragedy and the Battle of the Sexes (a study of Euripides' tragedy *Medea* and the conflict between the sexes throughout history); Contemporary Issues of the Modern World: A Geographic View (a look at the transformation of societies from traditional to modern forms

throughout the world); Roots: Searching for Your Family Roots? (methods for constructing family trees, ways to search records and archives in conducting a study of your own family).

- Strathcona Park Lodge and Outdoor Education Centre in the mountains of central Vancouver Island offers three courses at the end of June that deal with the outdoors: Forest Familiarization (students will study, first-hand, the giant red cedars, western hemlock, and Douglas fir rain forests); Trout (the brochure says "try your luck fishing for rainbow and cutthroat trout using trolling and fly-casting methods.... Please bring a fishing rod." The course also offers cooking tips and a visit to a fish hatchery); Provisioning for Backcountry Trips (this course teaches students how to outfit themselves for back country travel, and it teaches wilderness skills like firelighting and shelter building) (Elderhostel 1987, 5).

This selection of programs from across the country gives a glimpse of the options Elderhostelers can choose. Each institution also has its own character and history, and Elderhostel students can choose the courses and the ambiance to suit their interests.

schedules and open enrolment will encourage more older students to take secondary or post-secondary courses. A number of universities have started special programs for seniors. The University of Regina extension division, for example, worked with seniors to open a "Seniors' Education Centre" in 1977. The program began with twenty-four non-credit courses for 466 students, and in 1982–83 it offered forty-three classes to 981 students. The program also offers courses to communities outside Regina and to people in long-term care institutions. The University of Moncton in New Brunswick and the Université de Sherbrooke in Quebec each support a program for francophone seniors called Université du Troisième Age (U3A). Each U3A group arranges to set up its own programs with the help of a university. Programs often include access to normal university classes, study groups, study trips, and fitness programs. Courses most often focus on the arts, social issues, and the humanities (Radcliffe 1982).

In the future more older people will probably return to school, and life-long learning will become a part of Canadian society. Already, more people go to school for more years than ever before. Statistics Canada says that in 1981 24 percent of people aged 65 and over had a high school education or better, but 39 percent of people 45–64 had more than a high school diploma and 64 percent of people 25–44 had at least a high school education (Health and Welfare Canada 1983). Cyr and Schnore (1982) project a 15 percent increase between 1971 and 2011 in young-old men (65–74 years) with post-secondary education and an 8 percent increase in young-old women with post-secondary education. Young-old men and women with secondary education will also increase between

Exhibit 11.7

A PHILOSOPHY FOR CREATIVE RETIREMENT

Farrell Fleming, Executive Director of Creative Retirement Manitoba, one of the largest seniors' learning centres in Canada, describes some educational principles that present a new view of education for older people.

1. Retirement represents a great opportunity both to the individual and for society.
2. People have the ability to learn, to mature, to grow, to change, and to be of use regardless of their age.
3. Individuals can grow and develop in the period between 55 and 85 as much as they did in the first twenty years of life. However, the nature of that growth will be different from that undergone earlier.
4. The maturity, wisdom, and experience that many older people possess are the very values our community needs more of.
5. Retired people, both individually and collectively, are a great resource, still largely untapped by our communities, our province, and our country.
6. Older people have as much right to appropriate forms of education as do younger people.

Source: Farrell Fleming, "Manitoba's Creative Retirement Program," *Creative Retirement Manitoba: Fall Program* (Winnipeg: Creative Retirement Manitoba, 1986), 21–23. By permission of author.

1971 and 2001 by 29 percent for men and 38 percent for women. Almost three-quarters of men and half of women (of all ages) in the labour force take job-related or academic education programs (Devereaux 1985). Studies show that people with more education tend to keep taking classes as they age (Vigoda, Crawford, and Hirdes 1985). This will mean that more older people will take part in education in the future.

Community Service

Volunteer Work

Exercise, recreation, and education lead to increased life-satisfaction for older people. So does community service work — the chance to give to others. Statistics Canada reports that 11 percent of men and 17 percent

Exhibit 11.8

PROFILE

Older people can provide valuable resources to their community when the community finds ways to use seniors' talents. The example below shows one potential use for senior volunteers.

Every Monday and Wednesday after school, 10-year-old Kenny arrives at the apartment of Alexander Gold-ring, 86, for five or six cookies, a glass of milk and an hour's reading aloud followed by a spelling test. His tutor is a retired chartered accountant who speaks with a broad New York accent. ... Kenny says proudly that because of Mr. Goldring's tutoring, his marks in reading have risen from mostly Cs to As and Bs.

A love of books and children and the simple conviction that "if I want to be happy I should make others happy" led Mr. Goldring to join a group of volunteers in Manhattan who worked as tutors. When he moved to Toronto with his wife seven years ago from New York, he discovered that volunteer tutoring in the public schools was virtually non-existent. Fortunately, he found Clinton Street Public School receptive to the idea, and he now holds weekly readings of poetry and stories for three classes and assigns them compositions and spelling tests. "There's always a glass of water and a nice chair waiting for me. The other day, a grade six class gave me a tearful ovation after I read a very sad story about two boys raising money to support their sick sister's stay in hospital."

Source: Excerpted from Penelope Jahn, "Good Old," *Today Magazine*, January 9, 1982, 11–14, 16.

of women 65–69 and 7 percent of men and 10 percent of women aged 70 or over work as volunteers (Health and Welfare Canada 1983). Some research suggests that more older people would work as volunteers if they had the opportunity.

A study of people aged 60 and over in Northumberland and Newcastle, Ontario, for example, found that many older people would like to work as volunteers in schools (Hawkins 1980). Many of the subjects in this study said they would start work right away, if they had the chance. Seventeen percent said they would work in a library, 14 percent said they would listen to a child read, and 14 percent said they would teach students about seniors' hobbies and skills.

Some programs already use older people's talents in the schools. Studio Two, a seniors' drama group, presents plays and skits for students. Creative Retirement Manitoba (a learning centre for seniors) arranges for

Exhibit 11.9

THE NEW HORIZONS PROGRAM

Government programs often confine themselves to helping people meet their basic needs. Most Canadians know about the Canada Pension Plan and the health care system. But government can also help older people meet their higher needs — the needs for esteem, creative expression, and a sense of purpose in life. A little-known federal government–sponsored program called New Horizons began in 1972 to help seniors meet these higher needs.

New Horizons was designed to help groups of seniors start their own recreation and service projects. The program requires that seniors' groups have at least ten members, most of whom must be over 60 years old and retired. New Horizons will not pay a salary for full-time staff except in special cases, and it will not give money to groups or agencies that perform services for seniors. All the money goes as direct contributions to older people to use for projects they design. New Horizons allocates its funds according to the percentage of older people in each electoral district. This spreads the money across the country to urban and rural areas. On average New Horizons supports 2,000 projects a year (1,903 projects in 1985–86). It has assisted a total of 25,000 projects since 1972.

When the program began, most groups started recreation centres. But since 1982 New Horizons has encouraged seniors to start community service and mutual help projects. Through these projects seniors do things for their communities. Proj-

ects range from meals on wheels programs to home repair services to a theatre group that tours nursing homes, schools, and hospitals. A massage class visits two nursing homes once a week to give residents treatments and to teach self-massage.

New Horizons has also funded advocacy and lobby groups across the country. It has helped start regional seniors' councils and provincial seniors' societies. These groups sponsor programs like the Alberta Seniors' Games and education programs. They also lobby the government for better policies. By 1982, a report on New Horizons says, seniors had "formed seventy-eight major regional groups which are affiliated with approximately twenty-five provincial organizations. These in turn are affiliated with one of several national federations" (Health and Welfare Canada 1982d, 8).

The total New Horizons budget in 1985–86 came to almost $17 million. Almost 80 percent ($13.4 million) of this money went directly to support seniors' projects (the rest goes to staff salaries and administrative costs). Each project received an average of $6,214 in 1984–85 and served an average of 120 people (though programs ranged from small writing workshops to large senior centres). The cost to run programs in 1984–85 came to $51.97 for each person in a program. The cost to the government, per capita for all Canadians over age 65, came to a little over $6 for the year.

The New Horizons program costs

very little and serves people in all parts of the country. Each year nearly 12 percent of people aged 65 or over take part in a New Horizons project; the total of all older people who have taken part in projects since 1972 is much higher. New Horizons en-courages self-respect, indepen-dence, and self-sufficiency; it shows that given the opportunity, "older people will continue to be active, cre-ative, and productive members of their communities" (Health and Welfare Canada 1982d, 8).

Source: Adapted from Mark Novak, "The Canadian New Horizons Program," *The Gerontologist* 27 (1987), 353–55.

older people to visit schools and speak about Manitoba history. A similar program started in Montreal to enrich the school curriculum and to bridge the generation gap. In this program, a worker from the *Centre local de services communautaires* arranged for a group of seven older people in the downtown core to work with children in a local school. The seniors, who ranged from 55 to 90 years of age, worked with a class of twenty-seven students for ten weeks. Classes included a visit to the Montreal Symphony, a slide show of Venice by the seniors, and a play put on for the seniors by the students. The classes ended with a bus trip to Canadiana Village and a picnic lunch (Nahmiash 1985).

Volunteer programs can benefit seniors and their communities, but they require co-ordination. A program in Niagara, Ontario, called Senior Volunteers in Service links volunteers with community needs. The program uses the services of volunteers aged 55 or older. In 1986 250 people volunteered for more than 3,000 hours a month as friendly visitors, meals on wheels helpers, and foster grandparents. Some volunteers helped older people with transportation, shopping, or household chores (Rapelje, Goodman, and Swick 1986).

Senior volunteers can have a global as well as a local impact. The federal government sponsors a program called Canadian Executive Service Overseas (CESO). The program recruits senior volunteers and assigns them to work in underdeveloped countries or with Native groups in Canada. The program mostly attracts retired people between the ages of 60 and 70. Volunteers give technical and management advice to businesses, do feasibility studies, and help train workers and managers. The program pays travel and maintenance expenses. From 1969 to 1982 the program sent about 3,000 volunteers to work with Native groups, and it has about 750 volunteers on its active list. From 1967 to 1982 CESO had finished about 3,000 overseas projects, and it has about 2,700 people ready to take on new projects (Health and Welfare Canada 1982b).

Volunteering, whether at a local school or in a foreign country, can give an older person a sense of purpose in life. Bond (1982) studied 323 older volunteers and found that people who volunteer their services have higher life-satisfaction than people who do not. He suggests that counsellors prescribe volunteer work for clients who feel dissatisfied with their lives.

CONCLUSION

A look at older people engaged in recreation, education, and volunteer work gives a rounded picture of aging today. It shows that most older people live active lives; they take part in arts, crafts, sports, education, and travel. It also shows that many older people spend time helping others in their communities. Canada's seniors have just begun to explore the meaning of old age today.

SUMMARY

1. Older people spend a great deal of their time on passive media-related activities like reading the newspaper and watching television. Older people often spend their time alone, but they also enjoy spending time with others.
2. Income, lifestyle, gender, and health influence what people do and how active they remain in old age. Older people in good health show one of the highest rates of increase in sports and exercise activities in the past few years.
3. Older people will join and stay in fitness programs if they have control over program content and feel relaxed and unthreatened by competition. More and more older people now value fitness and exercise.
4. Physical functions do decline with age, but fitness training can reverse some physical decline. Fitness training can also lead to better sleep patterns, a better self-image, more social contacts, and increased happiness.
5. Seniors' centres across the country offer education, counselling, and recreation for older people. They form the closest thing to a network of recreational programs in Canada.
6. People with many years of schooling will keep on learning as they age. Universities often sponsor special programs for seniors. So do programs like Elderhostel, Creative Retirement Manitoba, and the University of the Third Age. These programs are designed to fit the older person's interests and learning styles.
7. Many older people volunteer to help others. More older people might offer their skills and services to the community if they had the opportunity. New programs help older people find ways to use their skills. Studies show that volunteers report an increase in life-satisfaction.
8. The New Horizons Program helps older people fulfill their own aspirations. This program has helped set up thousands of self-help, community aid, and mutual aid programs, all run by seniors. New Horizons also sponsors political action groups that help create better government policies for all seniors.

SELECTED READINGS

Fitness and Amateur Sport. *Fitness and Aging: Canada Fitness Survey.* Ottawa: Minister of Supply and Services, 1982.
A summary, with charts, of seniors' participation in fitness and athletic programs. The report shows the trend toward growing senior interest in exercise and fitness.

McPherson, Barry D., and Carol Kozlik. "Canadian Leisure Patterns: Disengagement, Continuity or Ageism." In *Aging in Canada*, ed. Victor W. Marshall. Toronto: Fitzhenry and Whiteside, 1980a.
A sociological study of differences in leisure patterns by age, occupation, and income. The study shows a continuity of leisure patterns from mid-life to old age.

CHAPTER 12

FAMILY LIFE AND SOCIAL SUPPORTS

INTRODUCTION

Rising divorce rates, the generation gap, and high residential mobility all point to a crisis in the modern family. Add to this the fact that more older people live alone than ever before, and it seems as though families have abandoned their aging members. Shanas (1979) calls this the "hydra-headed myth" of family breakdown. People continue to believe it, even though studies show over and over again that it is not true. Research shows that older people keep in contact with their families, that they rely on family members for help when they need it, and that middle-aged children feel responsible for their aging parents (Campbell and Brody 1985). Studies also show that (not including spouses) children supply most of the help older people need (Morris and Sherwood 1983–84). Brody (1983, 597) concludes, in a study of three generations, that "values about family care of elderly adults have not eroded despite demographic and socioeconomic changes."

Today, most older people, even single older women, prefer to see their children, but not to live with them. Better incomes, government rent supports, and health services allow more people to choose this option than ever before. This chapter will look at three influences on family life and social supports: (1) normative age-graded life events (such as marriage and widowhood), (2) cultural background (ethnicity), and (3) personal methods of adapting to aging (such as taking on new roles).

NORMATIVE AGE-GRADED LIFE EVENTS

Normative age-graded life events are correlated with chronological age. They include high school graduation, retirement, and marriage. Some gerontologists now also define widowhood as a normative life event for older women. Normative age-graded events define a person's status in society, the person's roles, and the person's social support system. When an event takes place it signals a change in a person's social status and often a change in their social network. The following discussion will focus on two normative events: marriage and widowhood.

Marriage

Most Canadians get married. Kalbach and McVey (1979) report that by age 30, 86.6 percent of Canadian males and females have married. The proportion of people married drops (largely due to mortality) from about age 40 onward. For people aged 65 and over, three-quarters of men but only two-fifths of women are married. Past the age of 85, 45.5 percent of men, but only 8.5 percent of women, are married (Statistics Canada 1984b). These figures show that women face a greater chance of widowhood than men and a greater chance of living alone in old age.

Marriage gives people some advantages over their unmarried age mates. First, married couples have more financial resources than unmarried people aged 65 and over. Couples tend to be younger than single older people, and often one or both members of the couple work. Even among people the same age, married couples have more money. This may be because they had a higher lifetime income than single people, more savings, and a family home.

Second, almost three-quarters of married couples aged 65 and over say they are "very satisfied" with their romantic relationship, and these people report higher satisfaction with their romantic relationship than

Exhibit 12.1
Percentages of Population Aged 50 and Over in
Selected Marital Status Groups, by Sex and Age,
Canada, 1981

Marital status groups

▬ ▬ Married males[1]   ▪▪▪▪▪ Never-married males   ——— Widowed males

▪—▪ Married females[1]   ▪▬▬▪ Never-married females   ▬▬ Widowed females

•••• Divorced males   ----- Divorced females

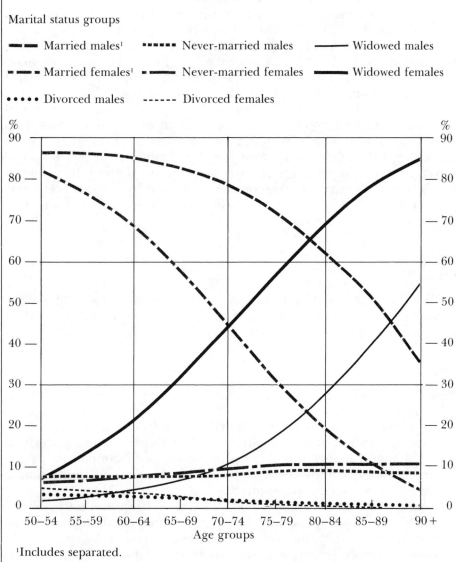

¹Includes separated.

Source: Health and Welfare Canada, *Fact Book on Aging in Canada* (Ottawa: Minister
of Supply and Services, 1983), Figure 9.1.1, p. 67. Reproduced with permission of the Minister of Supply and Services Canada.

any other age group (Statistics Canada 1980b). Hess and Soldo (1985) say that older couples report high life-satisfaction because these people (and their marriages) have survived economic hard times, the stress of raising children, and their partner's odd quirks and habits. Couples with children also enjoy a new freedom in old age. They live adult-centred lives that allow them to travel, visit with friends, share work at home, and do things together (Abu-Laban 1978).

Third, research shows that married people adjust better than non-married people to aging. A good marriage gives the couple intimacy, mutual support, and high life-satisfaction (Strain and Chappell 1982). It also leads to longer life (especially for men) and better health. Married older people, compared to non-marrieds, have fewer acute and chronic illnesses, fewer limits on their activities, and shorter hospital stays (Hess and Soldo, 1985). They also stand the best chance of staying out of an institution if they get sick, because they have someone to care for them. Marriage gives a person a live-in support system. Wister (1986), for example, found that married seniors feel less need for outside social relations. They also report a greater likelihood than non-married seniors of having sexual relations.

Sexuality

Studies show that most older people have an interest in sex throughout life and that, given good health and a partner, older people can (and do) have sexual relations into late old age.

Sexual Activity

Pfeiffer, Verwoerdt, and Wang (1968; also Verwoerdt, Pfeiffer, and Wang 1969) report on a ten-year study of 254 people between the ages of 60 and 94 years old. Cross-sectional analysis showed a drop in sexual interest and activity with age, but longitudinal data showed many patterns of sexual change. About 20 percent of the men, for example, showed an increase in interest and activity with age. The researchers found that on average men stopped having intercourse at age 68, but the age when men stopped ranged from 49 to 90. Masters and Johnson (1970) report that men stop having sex because of boredom, interest in outside activities, fatigue, eating or drinking too much, illness, or fear of failure.

Women stopped having sexual relations earlier than men, on average at age 60. This reflects the higher rates of widowhood for women in old age. Research shows that whether a woman maintains an active sex life or not depends on the presence of an active sexual partner. Widowhood or a husband's choice to stop having sex often put an end to a woman's sexual activity.

The Duke University research found that sexual activity in old age depends most on a person's pattern of sexual activity in the past. Men and women who have a partner and who enjoyed sex in the past will continue to enjoy it as they age (Palmore 1981). The Duke study also found that sexual activity leads to life-satisfaction and health for people between ages 45 and 70. Palmore sums up the Duke findings: "These statistics," he writes, "show that most older married persons are not asexual; on the contrary, substantial proportions remain sexually active until at least their 80s. They also show that impotence and sexual problems in old age are reversible, and that substantial proportions at all ages report increasing sexual activity" (1981, 89).

Adjustments Due to Age

Sexually active older people do have to adjust to changes in their bodies as they age. A man, as he ages, takes longer to get an erection, takes longer to feel ready for intercourse again, and may have shorter, less intense orgasms. A woman, as she ages, may find that her vagina loses elasticity, and opens less fully, and that she may have shorter orgasms. Older couples may need to use vaginal lubrication. Sometimes a couple will need medical help or counselling to stay sexually active (Szasz 1980). Studies show that older people can (and do) adjust to these changes in their bodies as they age.

Changing Attitudes to Sex in Old Age

Mullens (1983) studied the sexual activity of older people in seniors' housing and in nursing homes. He found that people in nursing homes, compared with people in seniors' housing, had less privacy and freedom. Only 28 percent of the homes gave staff training in sexuality and aging. "With a few exceptions," Mullens (1983, 5) says, "sexual relations among residents were either not allowed or not encouraged except for married couples." Mullens found that older people themselves took a restrictive view of sex. He concludes that seniors "adhere to their Victorian upbringing" (1983, 7).

These attitudes of staff and older people toward sexuality will change as new cohorts of people enter old age. First, gerontology courses teach younger people and professionals the facts about sex in old age. This can change the attitudes of those who work with older people (Damrosch 1984). Second, books that give advice to older people now, more than in the past, encourage sexual activity. In the past these books typically spoke to middle-aged children about care for their aging parents, but a recent study of these books found that they now give advice directly to older people (Arluke, Levin, and Suchwalko 1984). Third, cohorts differ in their views on sexual relations. Older cohorts have a more conservative view of sex, and most older people today do not favour sex outside of marriage. When a spouse dies, many women are left without a chance to enjoy sexual relations. Younger cohorts have more open attitudes to sex, and if they bring these attitudes with them into old age, there will be more sexual activity among older people in the future.

Widowhood

Statistics Canada reports that in 1981 only 8.4 percent of men but 37 percent of women aged 65–74 were widowed. By age 85 and over, 45.1 percent of men and 80.9 percent of women were widowed (Health and Welfare Canada 1983). Widows outnumber widowers for three reasons: (1) women live longer than men, (2) women marry older men, and (3) men tend to remarry after widowhood. Statistics Canada reports that in 1981 the remarriage rate for widowers (of all ages, per 1,000) came to 28.5 per year. The remarriage rate for widows in that year came to 6.32 per year (Statistics Canada 1985b).

Today almost 70 percent of widows are over age 65. Statistics Canada says that a widow at age 65 can expect to live almost nineteen more years. A woman widowed at age 80 can expect to live almost nine years after her spouse dies (Statistics Canada 1984d, cited in Matthews 1985). Matthews (1986) calls widowhood an "expectable life event," one that creates a great deal of stress (Holmes and Rahe 1967; Matthews 1982; Matthews et al. 1982). This means that many men and most women will go through the pain of widowhood. Studies of widowhood have focused on two themes: the social supports that buffer widows' and widowers' stress and the differences between widows' and widowers' responses to widowhood.

Widowers

Studies of widowhood often contain too few men to compare with women, but a few studies show how loss of a spouse affects each sex. First, studies of family supports, friendship, and *confidants* (someone the subject confides in) show that women have more social supports than men. Most older men today have spent their lives focused on their careers, while older women today have spent their lives focused on people. This gives older women more close relationships than men in old age. It also makes men more vulnerable to illness and death. "Widowed men," Hess and Soldo (1985, 75) say, "are doubly bereft — they have lost both a helpmate and confidante.... Conversely, the widowed woman is unlikely to be entirely devoid of close friends."

Second, wives link men to wider social networks. Women more often than men say they have close relationships with family and friends besides their husband. They often name these family members and friends as their confidants, and they keep up these relationships when their husband dies. A man whose wife dies loses a wife, a confidant, and a social secretary. This may explain why many men rush into another marriage after they lose a spouse.

Third, men find it harder to make new friends or to join groups for help. Dr. Alan Lyall, who directed a program for widowers at the Clarke Institute of Psychiatry in Toronto, says that "men are not apt to use talking as a source of support. The women come to the Clarke and the men go across the street to the Silver Dollar tavern" (Wylie 1981, 34–38). Studies show that widowers suffer from isolation and loneliness (Pihlblad, Adams, and Rosencranz 1972). Compared to women, they also run a higher risk of suicide (Resnick and Cantor 1970; Rushing 1968; Maris 1969). This literature suggests that men suffer more than women when they lose a spouse because they have fewer social contacts than women.

Most studies of widowers use small non-random samples. They rarely allow for a direct comparison of widowed men and women in the same sample. A recent study by Wister and Strain (1986) did use a large random sample to compare widows and widowers. Unlike previous studies, this study found no difference between the well-being of men and women, even though women had more friends and confidants than men. They say that widowers may need less social support than widows to feel satisfied. Also, men may enjoy comradeship and sharing interests with others rather than the closeness of a confidant relationship.

Wister and Strain (1986) conclude that older men may not want or need the same kinds of social relations as older women. "Overall," they say, "it is clear from the results that there is little support for the view expressed in the literature that older widowers suffer from greater social and psychological disadvantages than widows. It would appear that this myth has developed out of an inherent bias among some researchers to assume similar social-psychological needs across genders" (1986, 18). This study suggests that men and women have different friendship and confidant needs, possibly due to the kinds of relationships men and women learn to form earlier in life. More research on the social lives of widowers will show just how their needs differ (if they do) from those of widows.

Widows

Social supports and family roles buffer the stress of widowhood for women. Norris (1980) found that women stayed socially active in mother and grandmother roles after their husbands died, and that they also held onto their wife role. These women had lost their husbands on average ten years before, but when Norris (1980, 142) asked them if "Being married makes my daily activities more satisfying and easy to deal with," many of these widows agreed. She found that these widows "remained emotionally committed to being wives" even many years after their husbands died.

Studies show that a woman's age predicts how much grief she will feel when her husband dies. Younger widows whose husbands die suddenly feel more intense grief than older widows (Vachon et al. 1976; Vachon 1981). A woman who loses a spouse "on time" (for example, in her late sixties) tends to expect her husband's death. She has made this a part of her life plan (Matthews 1986), and, more often than a widower, she will have widowed friends, as well as siblings to give her support.

Strain and Chappell (1982) asked 400 older people whether they had any confidants — friends or relatives they confide in and talk to about their problems. They found that 77 percent of the people in their sample had at least one confidant and 51 percent had two or more confidants. More women than men had confidants, and men more often than women chose their spouse as their confidant (Keith et al. 1984).

Studies show that confidants lead to good morale. They also buffer people from anxiety and tension. Lowenthal and Haven (1968) studied role loss in old age (not just widowhood). They found that people with no confidant felt more depressed than people with a confidant. This finding held even if the person with no confidant increased their interactions, while the person with a confidant decreased their interactions. Strain and Chappell (1982, 496) say that "the existence of at least one confidant relationship, irrespective of the number of times one might have contact with that confidant — emerges as a significant predictor of life satisfaction. This lends support to the argument ... that it may not be the usually reported frequency of interaction that is important to the quality of life, but rather the quality of that interaction."

Strain and Chappell (1982) found that widows often chose a sister or brother or a friend their age as a confidant. Matthews (1985) found that many widowed women get support from their sisters. She says that more than half the widows in her study saw at least one of their sisters or brothers several times a month and that more than half of them listed a sibling, often a sister, as someone who gives them social support. Harvey (1984, cited in Matthews 1985) found that 25 percent of the widows in her sample had contact with a sibling at least once a week, and 10 percent had contact more than once a week.

The research on widowhood shows that both men and women benefit from social relationships after a spouse dies, but that men may require different types of relationships than women. Men less often have confidant relationships than women. This may be the result of unique male social needs in later life or of life-long patterns of social relations. Women come into old age with more social supports. They tend to keep up and use these supports when their spouse dies. Supports for women include sisters, brothers, and other widows. A woman will find that many of her friends share her widowed status. This can buffer the stress of losing her husband. Men say they feel abandoned when their spouse dies, and this may lead them to remarry soon after they become widowed.

Living Arrangements

The large number of older widows in Canadian society has led to a new trend in living arrangements for women: elderly women now make up

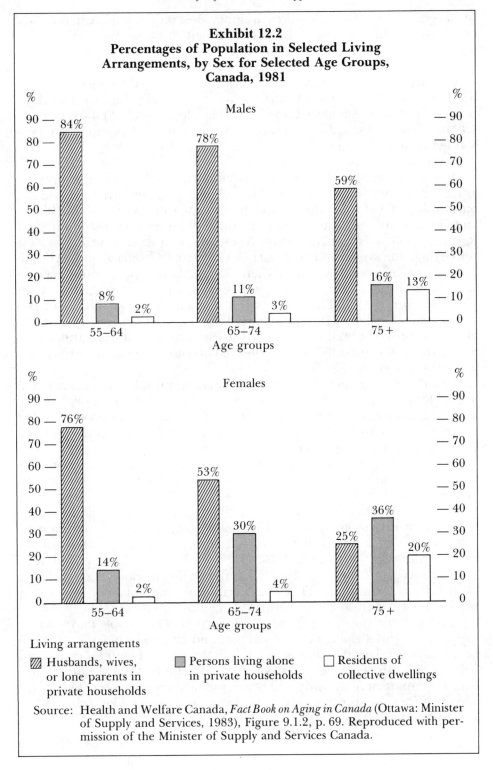

Exhibit 12.2
Percentages of Population in Selected Living
Arrangements, by Sex for Selected Age Groups,
Canada, 1981

Males

Females

Living arrangements

▨ Husbands, wives, or lone parents in private households

■ Persons living alone in private households

□ Residents of collective dwellings

Source: Health and Welfare Canada, *Fact Book on Aging in Canada* (Ottawa: Minister of Supply and Services, 1983), Figure 9.1.2, p. 69. Reproduced with permission of the Minister of Supply and Services Canada.

the largest group of people who live alone. Most older men live in families, either with their wives or with never-married children. In 1981, even at age 75, almost 60 percent of men lived in family settings (with a wife or never-married child) and only 13 percent of men aged 65 and over lived alone. But in 1981 nearly one-third of all women aged 65 and over lived by themselves (up from 24 percent for women 65+ in 1971 and 16 percent in 1961) (Statistics Canada 1985c; Health and Welfare Canada 1983). Wister (1985, 127) calls this an "unprecedented rise in single person living among seniors."

Three things explain this change.

First, demographic changes and social norms make it more likely that a woman, rather than a man, will live alone in old age. In 1981 widows outnumbered widowers three and a half to one (Statistics Canada 1985c), and fewer widowed women remarry than widowed men (Connidis and Rempel 1983; Fletcher and Stone 1980). Social pressure works against remarriage for women. Also, social norms say that a woman should choose a man her own age or older when she remarries (it is more socially acceptable if a man chooses to remarry a younger woman) (Abu-Laban 1978; Veevers 1987). This leaves older women with a small pool of potential mates. Veevers (1987) estimates that in Canada in 1981 there were only thirty-three potential grooms for every one hundred unmarried women aged 60 and only twenty potential grooms for every one hundred unmarried women aged 70.

Second, better government pension plans and subsidized housing make living alone in a private household a more viable option for more women today. Community-based health care supports also make it possible for older women with health problems to stay in their own homes, rather than move to a nursing home.

Third, a change in attitudes and values explains this trend. Connidis (1983a), for example, found that most older people say they would rather not live with their children, and Wister (1985) found that older people prefer the privacy and independence that come with living alone. They prefer what Rosenmayr and Kockeis (1963) call "intimacy at a distance."

Wister (1985) predicts that an increasing proportion of older women will live alone in the future. Priest (1985) projects a 6 percent per year average increase of women aged 75 and over living alone over the next twenty years. Stone and Fletcher (1986a) say that this will lead to an explosion of the number of women living alone past age 75.

This trend has policy implications. Unmarried older people have smaller support networks than married people, and they rely more on formal health care services (like home care) than do married couples (Hess and Soldo 1985). More single older people living alone also increase the demand for apartment housing and better public transportation. This trend may also increase the interest in housing alternatives like granny flats and home-sharing programs.

Exhibit 12.3

INTIMACY AT A DISTANCE

Children and their elderly parents now share what Rosenmayr and Kockeis (1963) call "intimacy at a distance." Young people keep in contact with their parents. Parents and children visit one another, help one another, and keep in touch by phone, but they rarely live with each other.

The National Advisory Council on Aging (1986b) asked seniors living in a seniors' residence why they prefer to live alone. Here are some of their comments:

Albina Tennier: When my doctor advised me that I shouldn't be living alone, my daughter was willing to have me move in with her, but I prefer the independence we have here.

Violet Smith: My son lives in Toronto, and he used to worry about me, but now he knows that someone looks in on me every day. I looked after my mother-in-law for 14 years, and I decided that no one was going to go through that with me.

Hilda Tickell: My son-in-law and grandsons are very supportive, but they respect my independence. They're only a phonecall away if I need them, but I wouldn't want to be waiting around for them to call, nor would I ever want them to feel that they have to call. I have my own life to live.

Velma Would: I lived with my granddaughter and her husband and that would have worked out except that I began to feel isolated because they were away at work all day. We didn't live close to public transportation, and I began to feel I couldn't get out, especially in winter. I decided to move here because I'm the kind of person who likes to have other people around.

These comments raise some important questions. How much of older people's desire for independence comes from their feeling that they do not want to become a burden on their children? And how much of their desire for independence reflects the fact that in modern society older people have no place in their children's busy lives? Intimacy at a distance helps to solve this cultural dilemma. It allows older people to keep in touch with their children, but without intruding on them.

Source: Excerpts from National Advisory Council on Aging, *Expression* 3, no. 1 (Ottawa: Natioinal Advisory Council on Aging, 1986b), 3.

ETHNICITY AND SOCIAL SUPPORTS

Sociologists define an *ethnic group* as a group of people who see themselves as being alike because of their common ancestry and who are seen as being alike by others (Hughes and Hughes 1952, cited in Driedger and

Chappell 1987). Culture and ethnicity form the backdrop for family life in old age. Ethnic culture gives meaning to life events and correlates highly with socioeconomic status (Wanner and McDonald 1986). The size and age composition of an ethnic community also determines the number of social supports a person has available in old age.

Gerontologists in Canada have done only a small amount of research on ethnicity, aging, and social supports (Wong and Reker 1985, Ujimoto 1983; Driedger and Chappell 1987), but studies done so far show that older people from different ethnic groups (including people from British and French backgrounds) experience old age differently. Most of the research so far has explored one of three theories that explain these differences:

1. "Levelling theory" says that age levels ethnic differences. A decline in health or loss of a spouse will lead all older people (regardless of their ethnicity) to depend more on their families and on social services for help. These changes outweigh cultural differences in family structure or differences in cultural values of parent–child relations.
2. "Buffer theory" (Holzberg 1981) says that ethnic identity buffers a person from role loss as they age.
3. "Multiple jeopardy theory" says that aging makes life worse for members of an ethnic group. Minority members have low status to begin with, and they often have low incomes too. Aging only adds to their troubles (Havens and Chappell 1983).

Researchers have found some support for all of these theories.

Levelling Theory

Rosenthal (1983) found support for the levelling theory of aging and ethnicity. She studied Anglo and non-Anglo older people in Ontario (Anglos are people who report British background). Modernization theory predicts that Anglo families will show weaker family ties compared to non-Anglos and that non-Anglos will show more traditional family structures and more support for older people. She did not find support for this theory. Instead, she found that older Anglos and non-Anglos in her study reported similar family structures, similar views of family life, and similar family relations. She did find that slightly more non-Anglos lived with their middle-aged children, but this difference disappeared in older age groups. Rosenthal (1983, 14) says "there is a strong suggestion that age levels these differences [between groups]."

Buffer Theory

A number of studies have found support for the buffer theory of aging and ethnicity. Strain and Chappell (1984; see also Chappell and Strain 1984) compared the social supports of older Native Indians and non-

Natives in Winnipeg. They found that Natives had larger numbers of friends and relatives than non-Natives. Natives reported two and a half times as many relatives outside their household as non-Natives. Natives report six times as many friends as do non-Natives. (Strain and Chappell (1984) say that Natives may have a broader definition of friends than do non-Natives.) Natives also have more weekly contact with their friends and relatives than do non-Natives. A third of the Natives, but only 6.4 percent of the non-Natives, live with their grandchildren. Strain and Chappell trace this difference to Native culture. Native culture says, for example, that the elders should teach the young. "One native person explained that it was the duty of her grandparents to raise her. She lived with them and was taught the native way of life, thereby freeing her own parents for other responsibilities" (1984, 12).

Gold (1980) supports this finding. She describes the start of a small senior recreation program for Natives. She says that the program wanted to serve a dozen or so Native seniors, but the planners found that they also had to include the rest of the Native senior's family. "The culture demanded that the young serve the old," she says, but it also required that the old look after the very young. "So the food was prepared and served to the old, while the old tended youngsters" (Gold 1980, 3). This program for twelve Native older people became a program for fifty to one hundred people of all ages. Native elders have roles to play in their culture even if they lose status in white society. This can buffer some of the stress of aging.

Holzberg (1982) also found support for the buffer theory. She started an ethnic history program for Eastern European Jews at the Baycrest Centre in Toronto. These older people believed that they had to preserve their memories of the past for their children and grandchildren. The members of the project decided to write and publish a book of their memoirs. This gave them a purpose in life and increased their self-worth. Holzberg (1982, 253) says that "it was the value of ethnic history to the group rather than the value of life history to the individual as a reaffirmation of self that was the rallying point of collective effort." Work for a higher cultural purpose can buffer people from the threat of meaninglessness that sometimes comes with old age and death.

Multiple Jeopardy Theory

Wong and Reker (1985) found support for the multiple jeopardy theory. They compared a sample of forty first-generation Chinese immigrants and forty Anglo people in Ontario. Both groups averaged 68 years old. Wong and Reker asked each group about problems they faced and the methods they used to cope with these problems. They found that both groups had about the same number of problems, but the Chinese group viewed their problems as more serious than the Anglo group. The Chinese group also felt that they coped less well than the Anglos, and they had lower well-being scores. Wong and Reker say that these findings support the multiple jeopardy theory. They say that stress due to living in a foreign culture and minority status add to the problems of physical aging.

Havens and Chappell (1983) also found support for the multiple jeopardy theory. They studied the added effects of being old, female, and a member of a minority group. They found that on an objective measure of mental function "old-elderly women of Polish, Russian, and Ukrainian descent are signficantly more disadvantaged ... than any of the other groups" (1983, 129). Havens and Chappell found less support for multiple jeopardy when they used subjective measures of well-being. It seems that older people do not feel (or do not report feeling) worse off than non-ethnic elders.

Statistics Canada also reports multiple jeopardy for ethnic elders. Statistics Canada (1984a) used an objective measure of economic well-being and found that older immigrants have a greater chance than non-immigrants of living in a low-income family (see also Penning 1983). Ten percent of non-immigrants aged 65 and over lived in low-income families, compared to 11 percent of immigrants who came to Canada before 1961, 14 percent of immigrants who arrived between 1961 and 1970, and 22.5 percent of the most recent immigrants. Immigrants also get more of their income from the OAS and CPP than do non-immigrants (Statistics Canada 1984a). Older members of Asian, African, and Latin American ethnic groups show some of the lowest economic well-being on measures of labour force activity, retirement income, and investment income (Wanner and McDonald 1986). These figures show that being old and an immigrant (especially a recent immigrant from a Third World nation) increases the chance that a person will have a low income.

Each of these theories gives some clue about how ethnicity affects aging, but each theory has its limits. Levelling theory, for example, may hold true only for people in late old age. At that point almost everyone turns to government-run services like home care or institutions for help. Buffer theory describes aging in a culture that holds the old in high esteem, but an ethnic group with a different belief system, or a group with few members in Canada, may find that ethnicity does not buffer the effects of aging. Many Estonian men, for example, came to Canada alone and never married. A study of this group in Toronto found that 68 percent of them had no families and that, because they form a small group, they had no community resources to draw on. Membership in this ethnic group will not buffer the effects of declining health or resources. Groups such as this may need more social services than other groups (Kneem 1963, cited in Department of Social and Family Services 1969).

Research on multiple jeopardy theory shows that ethnic elders rate less well on objective measures than non-ethnic older people. But ethnic elders may feel as positive about life in old age as non-ethnic seniors. Ethnicity alone does not predict a decrease in well-being in old age.

What can we conclude about the effects of ethnicity on aging from these conflicting theories and research reports? We can conclude that the effects of ethnicity on aging depend on many things other than membership in an ethnic group. The age distribution of the ethnic group's population (the ratio of younger to older people in the group), the geographic closeness of the group (how easily members can pool their resources), the degree of assimilation of the group into Canadian society (how well members can use available resources) and the time of immigration (recent immigrants have less access to public pension funds) all influence the experience of aging for ethnic elders. These conditions differ for each ethnic group, so that "ethnicity" or membership in an ethnic group can mean many things. Membership in some groups will buffer aging, while membership in other groups will lead to multiple jeopardy. How similar the experience of aging will be for members of different groups will depend in part on the social structure (the size, age structure, economic status, and values) of the groups. As Rosenthal (1986) points out, many studies of ethnicity fail to take into account the differences between ethnic groups. Eastern and Southern European ethnic groups can differ as much from one another as they do from the British ethnic group. Studies of ethnicity need to specify the social and economic conditions of the groups under study.

Ethnicity and Social Service Use

Some groups need more help from non-family sources than others. Older people of British origin, for example, tend to live on their own; older Italians tend to live with their children. Older Hungarians seldom live with their children; older Polish people usually do (Gerber 1983). Different groups also use institutions at different rates. This may have to do with family values about caring for the elderly, but it also has to do with the average age of the group's members. The Chinese population in Canada, for example, includes a high proportion of people over 85 years old: they have the highest rate of institutional use (Gerber 1983).

Older people from third language groups pose special challenges to the social service system now and in the future.

The first challenge to planners comes from the structure of Canadian society itself. Canada supports two ideals that conflict with one another. The first is the ideal of individual achievement, the second is the ideal of multiculturalism. The concept of achievement says that individuals can and should achieve a higher social status than their parents, while the concept of multiculturalism says that people can and should maintain their ethnic identity. But "structural assimilation [an increase in social status from one generation to the next] is incompatible with continued ethnic pluralism" (Porter 1965, 72).

This conflict between ethnic pluralism and personal achievement often shows up as conflict in immigrant families. As young people move up in social class, they often leave behind the values of their culture. This creates a gap between what parents expect and what their children feel they can give. Sugiman and Nishio (1983) studied family relations among Japanese Canadians. The study focused on second-generation Japanese Canadians (the *Nisei*). These people grew up with the value of respect for their elders, and many of them expected to care for their parents in their own homes. The children of the Nisei (the *Sansei*) express less of the traditional values — deference to elders, nurturance, and belongingness to the group. Instead they hold more North American values of dominance, achievement, and success (Sugiman and Nishio 1983). The Sansei want to live apart from their aging parents. The Nisei know this, and they expect less respect and support from their children than they gave their parents. One woman told Sugiman and Nishio (1983, 28) that "even if I wanted to live with them [her children], I'm not sure I could. I think there would be a lot of conflict — a lot of hidden resentments which wouldn't be good. In such a case, I'd rather be left to die in an old age home." This last comment shows how this woman feels about the Western treatment of older people, but it also shows that she plans to fall back on Canadian services if she has to. Japanese older people and older people from other ethnic groups will make more use of Canada's social and health care services in the future.

A second challenge to planners comes from the diversity within Canada's ethnic groups. These groups each have different religious, language, and age subgroups. Native people in Canada, for example, come from at least four different language groups, and even within one language group (e.g., the Algonquian languages) at least two languages (Cree and Ojibway) exist (Statistics Canada 1985a). The Chinese community also has more than one language group. Chinese immigrants come from different regions of China and from Hong Kong. Some of these people speak Mandarin, others speak Cantonese, and others a local dialect. The Chinese community also has many religious and cultural organizations within it. A study of the Chinese in Ontario, for instance, found that most Chinese belong to the Presbyterian or United Church. But 31 percent claimed no religion (Gerber 1983). Many of these people and the groups they belong to have little contact with one another (Gold 1980, 4).

Gold (1980) says that because of this diversity, programmers and planners need to consult an ethnic group before planning a program. "The fact that people of different cultural backgrounds put their social worlds together differently means that their needs and resources as well as the ways in which they use the services available to them will vary" (Woehrer 1978, 335). Planners should not assume they know what a group wants or needs. She says that in one case a group of older Jewish people needed a senior centre worker. A young Israeli man applied for the job. He belonged to the same ethnic group, he shared their religious and cultural background, but he spoke Hebrew, while the seniors spoke Yiddish. In another case, this time a project to build a high-rise with the Chinese community, Gold (1980) says it took months to learn that women were allowed to play only a low-key role in the project and were excluded from making public decisions. When the developers learned this they had to change their approach to the group.

A third challenge to planners comes from the cultural differences of

Canadian immigrants. Holzberg (1981) says that health care services need to adjust to ethnic differences among their clients. Zay (1978), for example, says that Native people (Inuit and Indians) like to have their own people provide social and health care services. Other groups need advice on how to use the Canadian health care system. Auger (1980) reports that Punjabi older people go to herbalists, card readers, or astrologers when they get sick. Punjabi herbalists give only enough medicine for one day, so a Punjabi elder who gets a prescription for a two-week supply of pills may sometimes take all the pills at once. Doctors and other health care workers need to understand the ethnic older person's culture (Lam 1985). Other groups also have unique needs. Most Jews in nursing homes today want to celebrate Jewish holidays and eat kosher-style food. Italians may want a Catholic mass. Lam offers some suggestions for improving the present system: that a cultural advisor or consultant plan nursing homes and advise on health care, that students in the health sciences learn more about minority group needs, and that nursing home design and food standards take into account the cultural needs of the residents.

Reports on ethnicity and aging show that members of different groups use different social, economic, and health care services. They also have different expectations about old age and different attitudes toward the aging process. Policy planners need to take these differences among ethnic cultures into account when they design programs for seniors (Driedger and Chappell 1987). Future research will need to study the availability and use of formal and informal supports by elders in different ethnic groups.

INFORMAL SUPPORTS FOR OLDER PEOPLE

Normative events and sociocultural conditions influence the quality of life in old age, but they do not determine it. Older people can and do respond to the changes that aging brings. Their response depends on their personality, past experience, and social resources. This section will look at the methods older people use to cope with aging.

The term *formal support* refers to professional caregivers such as doctors, nurses, and social workers. People pay for formal supports either from their own resources or through their taxes. The term *informal support* refers to unpaid help from friends, neighbours, and family. These supports include everyday help like rides to the doctor or to a shopping centre, help with yard work, or just a visit from a neighbour. Informal supporters can also help an older person cope with a personal crisis, adjust to a change in health, or locate a formal service (Snider 1981). Older people who need help with daily chores or health care sometimes use both the formal and informal support systems, but studies show that people usually turn to the formal system only after the informal system breaks down (Chappell and Havens 1985; Brody 1981; O'Brien and Wagner 1980).

Most people get informal support from their families — a married person will most likely get help from their spouse, and a widow or widower will get help from a child (most often a daughter). Rosenthal (in an interview cited in National Advisory Council on Aging 1986b, 4) estimates that 70 percent to 80 percent of health care that allows a person to stay in their home comes from informal supports — a spouse or child. Chappell and Havens (1985) studied 800 older people in Winnipeg. Four hundred of these people used formal home care services; the other 400 came from a random sample of the population not using these services. They found that more than half of their total sample (58 percent) received help of some kind. Ninety-four percent of those who received help got it from informal sources. Also, of the 15 percent who got formal care, 80 percent also got informal care. Chappell and Havens also found that people who got help with everyday activities — dressing, shopping, telephoning — were more likely to get help from informal than formal supports. The researchers conclude that "most elderly persons cope well within the community without an inordinate amount of assistance. Further, ... [these findings] also support the claims that informal care to aging members is alive and well. This is true even when the elderly individuals are recipients of formal care such as that provided by" home care programs (Chappell and Havens 1985, 227).

Friends as a Source of Informal Support

Blau (1973) says that people enjoy friends most in youth and in old age. Synge and Luxton (1984) found that 20 percent of women aged 74 and over received visits from non-relatives every day or two. Almost 30 percent said they received visits once or twice a week. Studies also show that older people get more enjoyment out of visits with friends than with family. Researchers say that people may relate to one another routinely in a family or because they feel obliged to see one another. But when older people see their friends they do so out of choice. Older people also have more in common with their friends than with younger family members, and this leads to greater warmth and good feeling (Chappell 1980a).

Most older people choose friends from their own age group. Chappell (1983a) studied 400 non-institutionalized older people living in Winnipeg. Eighty-three percent of the people in this sample said that their close friends were also older people. On average these older people had less than one friend under the age of sixty. These people reported more contact with friends than with relatives (who lived outside their home) or with neighbours, and they felt more satisfied with their friendships than with other relationships outside the home.

Rempel (1985) found that childless older people create a network of supportive friends and that they report as much life-satisfaction as older people who have children. She found that compared to people with children, childless older people feel more satisfied with their health, housing, and income. Rempel concludes that "family is not necessarily the crucial element in determining high life quality in old age." (1985, 347).

Researchers say that friendships can help older people overcome problems caused by lost work roles and the lost spouse role in old age. Norris and her colleagues (1983) say that older people use friends and family their own age as role models and for emotional support. "Since friendship rests on mutual choice and mutual need and involves a voluntary exchange of sociability between equals, it sustains a person's sense of usefulness and self-esteem more effectively than filial relationships" (Chappell 1980a, 173). Friends who are the same age share the same physical limits, the same interests, and the same historical background. Studies of family supports (by family who live outside the older person's home) and friendships show that older people often rely on friends their own age for social and emotional support. This research suggests that different people in the older person's social network (children, neighbours, friends) serve different functions in the older person's support system.

Informal Support and Caregiver Burden

Research shows that older people often use informal supports (Chappell and Havens 1985) and that these supports succeed in keeping people out of institutions (Hess and Soldo 1985). Married people, for example, have a built-in caregiving system. Hess and Soldo (1985, 78) report that "75% more married than unmarried elderly with functional health limitations rely *exclusively* on care services produced within their own households." Even in late old age, when people have serious functional disabilties, married people have half the institutionalization rate of unmarried older people (Hess and Soldo 1985).

But families sometimes pay an emotional and psychological price when they take on informal caregiving. When policy makers talk about shifting care to "the community" this usually means shifting the job to a daughter or wife (Chappell 1982a; Treas 1977). Caregivers often feel isolated, fatigued, and overwhelmed by the strain of care (Zarit, Reever, and Bach-Peterson 1980). Some research (Horowitz and Shindelman 1981) suggests that spouses suffer more burden from caregiving than do adult children. They may feel the strain more as they see their partner decline (especially if the person shows mental as well as physical decline). Spouses may have health problems themselves that make caregiving difficult. Spouses may have fewer resources (financial and social) to call on than would a middle-aged child.

In the case of single (widowed or divorced) older people with children, middle-aged daughters most often take on the job of caregiving. Aronson (1985) says that the term "informal supports" or "community supports" hides the fact that care for older people falls mostly on their middle-aged female children.

Horowitz (1985) found that sons take on the job of caregiver only when the parents have no daughter to help. She found that sons called and visited parents less often than daughters and that they less often prepared meals, cleaned house, or gave personal care to their parents (1985, 615). Brody (1981) says that women often get caught in the middle — sand-wiched between care for their children and care for their parents. "Such women are in middle age, in the middle from a generational standpoint, and in the middle in that the demands of their various roles compete for their time and energy" (1981, 471). Studies show that females report more strain from caregiving than males (Marcus and Jaeger, 1984). These women suffer physical strain, lower morale, and greater psychological burden than men (Marcus and Jaeger 1984; Zarit, Reever, and Bach-Peterson 1980).

Caregiving can also cost women money, a career, and pension benefits in the future. Brody and Schoonover (1986) say that 28 percent of non-working middle-aged caregiving daughters in their study quit their jobs to take care of their mothers. Other women said they reduced their work hours, and some had thought about quitting. Brody and Schoonover found that the mothers of working women got the same number of hours of care (formal and informal) as the mothers of non-working women, but the working women often had to pay for personal care and meal services. These paid services filled in for them while they worked.

Society expects women to work as caregivers, but Aronson (1985) ar-gues women get little credit or reward for this work. She says that the government should pay for care given by family members. She also says that Canadian society should allow caregivers to leave out the years they spend caregiving when they total up their pensionable years of work. Aronson admits that these reforms will cost the government more money and that the government will probably not want to fund them. Unless some reform takes place, women will continue to absorb the cost of care-giving in the community.

The Future of Informal Support

Changes in demography may decrease the amount of informal support older people will get in the future. First, Abu-Laban (1980a) says about 10 percent of people aged 65 and over also have a child over age 65. The number of elderly children caring for their parents will increase in the future as more people live longer. Some of these children will be unable to care for their parents, and some may need health care help themselves.

Second, as people live longer, their support groups suffer from what Stone (1987) calls *cohort attrition.* Peers die off over time, leaving members of some support networks without help. This makes children a vital source of support for most older people as they age (Marshall, Rosenthal, and Synge 1981). Synge (no date), in a study of social supports, found that the older the woman the more often she turned to a child for emotional support. Thirty-one percent of women aged 40–54 said they turned first to a child, compared to 63 percent of women aged 70 or over. Because women outlive men, more often than men they have to turn to children for support.

Very old people will even lose their children. Shanas and her colleagues (1968, cited in Abu-Laban 1980b) found that in Britain, Denmark, and the U.S. between 20 percent and 25 percent of all older people have no children. Similar trends will show up in Canada in the years ahead. Very old people (many of them women) will need more formal supports as they age.

Third, the Baby Boom children have fewer children of their own than older people today. In the second or third decade of the next century, the middle-aged children of Baby Boom parents may find themselves swamped by their parents' care needs. These trends predict a crisis in informal supports in the future, but other trends might lead to stronger informal supports. First, longer life expectancy means that spouses will live together longer than ever before. This will give married couples more informal support as they age.

Second, current trends in health promotion (better diet and exercise and decreases in smoking) may lead to better health in old age (Stone and Fletcher 1986b). If these trends continue, older people in the future may need less long-term health care support.

Third, new types of groups based on the mutual needs of older people may develop. Some of these groups have already started. Novak and Stone (1985) call these *semi-formal structures* because they fall between the informal (voluntary) support structures of the family and the formal (professionalized) structures of the health and social service systems. Semi-formal structures include car pools, groups of people in the same building who shop together, friendly visitors, or "daily hello" phone callers. These groups and relationships do not rely on informal kinship or friendship bonds or on the fee-for-service bond of formal supports. They rely on a bond of reciprocity and on the fact that they bring mutual benefit to users. More of these groups in the future could make up for losses in older people's networks.

Both trends — the decrease in informal supports and the increase in alternative forms of support (including home care and semi-formal structures) — could get stronger in the future. The well-being of older people in the future will depend on how well alternatives to traditional supports meet their needs.

OLDER PEOPLE AS SUPPORTERS

Most of the writing on older people in families focuses on their needs and what other people do for them, but older people also give help to their families. Shanas (1967) says that "far from being the passive recipients of their adult children's bounty, reciprocal help is given in the form of home services, monetary assistance, assistance in time of illness and

Exhibit 12.4

ELDER ABUSE:
HOW COMMON A PROBLEM?

Every so often the press publishes a story of a battered or abused older person. The typical abuser often turns out to be a family member (spouse or child) who is responsible for the care of the victim (Podnieks 1985). The topic of elder abuse draws a sympathetic response from the public, but how common is it? And what can be done about abuse when it occurs?

Shell (1982) conducted one of the largest elder abuse studies in Canada. She interviewed 105 social service and health care workers in Manitoba about elder abuse cases they have encountered. Based on her data Shell estimated that 0.3 percent of the total population in Manitoba aged 65 and over suffers from abuse (about 3,000 people). She estimated that this increases to 2.2 percent of people 65 and over who get formal or informal care. Most of these cases, she found, involve passive, verbal, emotional, and financial abuse rather than violence or neglect. This fits with the findings of studies in the U. S. (Hickey and Douglass 1981).

What can be done about abuse in its varying forms? Both the abused and the abuser need help. Education programs and changes in the law could decrease abuse.

1. Educational programs can teach caregivers how to deal with stress before it leads to abuse and can teach them better ways to care for their carereceiver. Support groups can also help caregivers

deal with the burden of care (Hess 1982).

2. Legal change could lead to more reporting of abuse. In most provinces in Canada the abused person has to give permission before a professional can look into suspected abuse. Professionals fear that they will get sued by abusers for libel or slander. A requirement that professionals report abuse could protect them from lawsuits by abusers.

3. More public and professional awareness of abuse could lead to early reports. More public knowledge would also lead to more services and help for both victims and abusers. Professional social service and health care workers, as well as the police, need to learn more about abuse. A study in the U.S. looked at the effect of training police officers to detect abuse (Thorman 1980, cited in Shell 1982). The study found that police officers who took a month-long training program made referrals to social service and health care agencies in 55 percent of all cases of family violence. Police who did not take the training program made no referrals.

4. Changes in family law would make it possible to remove the abuser (not the victim) from the home. Crisis shelters for abused older people would protect them from danger and would allow health care workers to find supports for them in the community. Shell

> (1982) also suggests an advocacy program. Volunteers would act on behalf of abuse victims. They would work for legal reform and public education and help victims get the services they need.

other crisis situations and, in addition, older parents often provide child care services."

Older people give at least three kinds of support: First, they help their spouses and children with health care and daily chores, second, they give their children financial support, and third, they give emotional support and serve as role models for younger family members.

Daily Help by Older People

Neysmith (1982) says that society does not see the daily help older people give to their families, because it goes on in private. She studied 200 older men and women in Ontario and found that over 80 percent of these people said they helped their family and friends. Chappell (1983a) found that spouses and peers (many of them over age 65) provide most of the social and health care supports needed by their family and friends. Chappell and Havens (1985) found that, in a sample of elderly home care support users and non-users, 55 percent of users and non-users provided support to others. Most of them gave support through an informal network.

Financial Support

Older people give younger members of their families financial support. The amount of support and the kind of support given differs by social class and ethnic group, but studies show that even middle-aged people think of their parents as givers (Baruch and Barnet 1983). Other studies show that the elderly give more money to their children than they get from them (Schorr 1980; Cheal 1983; 1985b; 1986).

Emotional Supporters and Role Models

Research shows that adult children rely on their parents as role models throughout their lives and turn first to their parents for support and help if they lose a spouse (Bankoff 1983; Schwartz 1979). Older family members derive great satisfaction from the help they give to their children and to other younger family members. Neysmith (1982) asked 200 older people in Ontario about the roles they play in their families. About half the people in her study reported the role of keeping their families to-gether — they told family members about one another and organized family events. All of the people in this study saw this as an important job. Neysmith found that people who played this role had higher morale than people who did not. Rosenthal, Marshall, and Synge (1980) found that older people play many roles in their families. These include the "kinkeeper" (the person who keeps people in touch with one another), the "occupational sponsor" (the person who helps others find jobs or get started in business), the "comforter" (the person people to turn to for personal advice and support), the "ambassador" (the person who represents the family at ceremonies), and the "head of the family" (the person who makes choices that others go along with). Black (1985) found that older people had the best emotional well-being when they gave as well as received support. Reciprocity made older people feel useful, independent, and worthwhile. Black says that professionals should help older people find ways to give to their supporters, since this will create more fulfilling relationships between parents and their children.

GRANDPARENTING

The grandparent role offers older people one of the most satisfying and enjoyable ways to give to other family members.

A study of grandmothers (Robertson 1977) found that 80 percent felt proud and happy about grandmotherhood. The younger grandmothers in the study felt they should be role models for grandchildren and teach grandchildren to work hard and be good. These younger grandmothers often had husbands and jobs and had less time for grandchildren than the older grandmothers. Older grandmothers — most of them widows and women without jobs — took a personal view of grandparenting. They enjoyed their role because it increased their life-satisfaction. These women spent the most time with their grandchildren, and the grandparent role meant more to them than to younger grandmothers.

Research shows that grandchildren value their grandparents. Younger grandchildren say they like grandparents for the presents they bring them, and older children like what they do with their grandparents (Kahana and Kahana 1970). Studies show that children's feelings about their grandparents depend on the relationship between the grandparents and the parents. Robertson (1977) found that only when parents approve do grandmothers get involved in activities with grandchildren.

What a grandparent makes of the grandparent role depends on the older person's gender, age, marital status, and relationship with his or her adult children. Neugarten and Weinstein (1964) studied styles of grandparenting. They describe five styles: a formal style, a fun-seeker style, a surrogate-parent style, a reservoir of family wisdom style, and a distant figure style. Only a few of the grandparents (most of them grandfathers) showed a reservoir of family wisdom style; this type of person had special skills or resources to give. Only a few of the people in this study (all of them grandmothers) showed a surrogate-parent style; this type of person looked after grandchildren while parents worked. About one-third of the grandfathers and one-fifth of the grandmothers showed

---

Exhibit 12.5

SURROGATE FAMILIES: AN ANSWER TO THE LOSS OF FAMILY WITH AGE

In a surrogate family, an older person and a younger family adopt one another. Over time they may build up the kind of feeling for one another that natural families share.

At 51, Marion is a volunteer grandmother.

...

Besides liking small children, Marion says she became a "granny," because her own children were taking her for granted.

"They have their own lives. I was active in the sorority for two years, but now I need to fill the void."

For Brenda Wylie [the mother of Marion's surrogate grandchildren]... Winnipeg's Grandparenting Program has lessened the isolation of being in a city 2,218 km from her own parents.

"They (her parents) are in Ottawa. They're wonderful grandparents, that's why we wanted someone here. We knew what we were missing."

...

Brenda adds that although she was thinking of the children when she asked for a grandparent, Marion has become a friend to the entire family.

"It's nice to have someone else to spend time with. We often chat on the phone."

Marion says she is pleased with how things have turned out since being matched four months ago.

"I think I've got the best family. We fit together so beautifully. It's hard to believe we're not a natural family."

Source: "Volunteer Granny Becomes 'Friend' to All of the Family," *Winnipeg Sun*, December 22, 1985, 53. Reprinted with permission.

---

a distant figure style; this type of person had friendly feelings for their grandchildren, but they did not see them very often. About a quarter of the grandfathers and a third of the grandmothers showed a fun-seeker style; this type of person spent leisure time with their grandchildren and had fun with them. About a third of both grandmothers and grandfathers showed a formal style; this type of person left parenting to the parents and did not offer advice on childrearing. The researchers found that older grandparents (aged 65 or over) more often took on a formal style, while younger grandparents tended to take on a fun-seeker style. This research shows that the grandparent role allows room for personal expression and that older people can use it as a source of emotional satisfaction.

FUTURE RESEARCH

Research on the family and social supports in later life focuses on what Abu-Laban (1980b, 196) calls the "the 'normal' (or at least the research worthy) aged ... [the] gray-haired, Anglo-Celtic, heterosexual, life-long marrieds, who have produced children and grand-children." Studies report how this ideal family copes with the normal crises of growing older. These studies then turn to "the support ties of the white-haired, Anglo-Celtic, widowed, mother and grandmother" (Abu-Laban 1980b, 196).

Abu-Laban (1980b) and others (Hess and Soldo 1985) criticize this narrow view of family life. First, the literature idealizes marriage and the caregiving spouse, but it says little about the dysfunctions that marriage and the use of informal supports can create. Hess and Soldo (1985, 83) say that "under some circumstances, for some couples, there are clear drawbacks to having a spouse." Married couples, for example, make less use of formal services. The caregiver spouse may see the use of formal supports as an admission of defeat. The failure to use available supports can make life harder for both spouses. Also, when spouses rely on one another for support, they can lose contact with friends and relatives. This can lead to feelings of burden, isolation, and depression for both spouses. More research on marriage in later life should focus on both the benefits and the problems that marriage can bring.

Second, research on older people's family life has almost ignored the lives of certain types of people. Little research has been done on single older people (8.5 percent of men and 9.5 percent of women 65+ have never married), divorced older people (1.8 percent of men and 1.5 percent of women 65+), and married older people without children (Statistics Canada 1984b; Abu-Laban 1978). Few studies compare the family life of older people from different ethnic backgrounds. More research on ethnicity in old age should look at family relations, informal supports, and the use of social services by different ethnic groups (Driedger and Chappell 1987).

Third, research during the 1970s and 1980s focused mostly on older women, making up for the absence of research on women in other parts of the social science literature. But few studies have looked at gay people as they age, and few have looked at male friendships, widowers, grandfathering, or male remarriage. Studies that have described men show that they face special challenges in old age.

Fourth, current high divorce rates and remarriages in middle age will lead to new patterns of family life for older people. These trends may produce more single older people, both men and women. They may also lead to more older people with children from several marriages. The study of these unusual family structures in the future will give a more complete picture of family life in old age.

CONCLUSION

Older people live rich social lives. They interact with family members, friends, and neighbours as well as their spouses. Most older people rely on these networks of family and friends for social, emotional, and health care support. Older people also give to their families and serve as role models for the young. Old age is a time of change — the death of a spouse, for example, creates one of life's greatest stresses. But research shows that most older people cope with the challenges of aging and manage to live satisfying social lives.

SUMMARY

1. The myth persists that middle-aged children abandon their elderly parents, but studies show again and again that children maintain contact with their parents, provide help to them, and get help from them when they need it.
2. A good marriage provides support for both partners as they age. Married older people use less formal care, rely less on children and friends for support, and have a lower institutionalization rate than non-married older people. Older women run a higher risk than older men of losing this support due to widowhood.
3. Widowhood has become an expectable life event for women in Canada, though it still creates stress in a woman's life. Researchers disagree about the impact of widowhood on men. Some studies show that men have fewer social supports and that they suffer from isolation, loneliness, and a high risk of suicide. More recent studies suggest that men may need less social support than women and that they adapt in different ways to widowhood.
4. More older women than ever before choose to live alone, rather than with their children. Better pensions, subsidized housing, and enriched housing will make this an option for more older women in the future.
5. An ethnic group's culture and structure both shape the experience of aging. The group's culture, values, beliefs, and degree of assimilation in part determine how young people treat older members. The group's structure, the size of a group, its geographic closeness, and its age structure also determine how it will treat older members. Each ethnic group differs in its attitudes and treatment of older people. Policy makers need to keep this in mind when they plan programs for older people.
6. Most older people keep up social contacts with relatives and friends as they age. Through visits or by using the telephone, older people (mostly women) give one another emotional support. Confidants help older people cope with anxiety and tension.
7. Older people often depend on informal support networks for emotional and health care support, but informal support can place a burden on family members (most often a wife or daughter). These

burdened caregivers may lose their income from work, their pensions, and even their health due to caregiving demands. Government financial support for caregivers would make caregiving a less burdensome option for many people and would recognize their valuable service to the community.

8. Some trends, such as cohort attrition for very old people and smaller families for Baby Boomers, suggest that informal supports will decline in the future. Other trends, like longer life expectancy for spouses and the development of semi-formal structures, suggest that older people will still rely on informal supports in the years ahead. These two trends may counterbalance each other, and older people in the future may develop new types of social supports.

9. Elder abuse takes place, but the media makes this seem like a more common problem than it is. Education for caregivers and changes in the law could help control abuse and give better support to the abused older person.

10. Older people give support as well as receive it. They help their children socially, financially, and emotionally. They help their peers by acting as confidants. Older people, like younger people, get esteem and a sense of purpose from helping others.

11. Grandparenting offers older people one of the most enjoyable roles in old age. Grandparenting has few responsibilities attached to it, so older people can shape the role to suit their personality, lifestyle, and interests.

12. Many gaps still exist in the literature on family life in old age. Research on atypical groups of older people — for example, gay older people, never-married people, and widowers — will increase our understanding of family and intimate relations in later life.

SELECTED READINGS

Driedger, Leo, and Neena L. Chappell. *Aging and Ethnicity: Toward an Interface.* Toronto: Butterworths, 1987.

The only book-length study of ethnicity and aging in Canada. The book provides a theoretical framework for understanding Canada's many ethnic groups. It also shows that ethnicity affects the older person's experience of aging and their use of informal and formal supports. The book concludes with suggestions for future research.

Matthews, Anne Martin. "Widowhood as an Expectable Life Event." In *Aging in Canada*, 2nd ed., ed. Victor W. Marshall. Toronto: Fitzhenry and Whiteside, 1986.

An up-to-date review of the widowhood literature in Canada. Matthews draws on a wide range of sources, including Canadian doctoral dissertations and research papers. She also compares Canadian data with studies done in the U. S.

Statistics Canada. *Women in Canada: A Statistical Report.* Cat. No. 89–503E. Ottawa: Minister of Supply and Services, 1985c.

A good compendium of data on women. Includes data on work, childrearing, and marital status.

CHAPTER 13

DEATH AND DYING

INTRODUCTION

Draw a line across a piece of paper. Put the word "birth" at the left-hand start of the line. Put the word "death" at the right-hand end of the line. Now put a dot for today's date. Put dates under the "birth" dot and today's dot. Now put a date under the dot that says "death."

How did you feel about fixing a date for your death? How did you come up with a date? Do people at different ages think the same way about death? Do you look forward to your next birthday? Or do you think about how few years you have left to do the things you want to do? How do older people think and feel about death?

This chapter will look at death in old age. It will focus on (1) attitudes toward death and on where death takes place, (2) ethical questions about death and dying, and (3) mourning and grief.

Exhibit 13.1

HOW LONG WILL YOU LIVE?

This is a rough guide for calculating your personal longevity. The basic life expectancy for males is age 67 and for females it is age 75. Write down your basic life expectancy. If you are in your 50s or 60s, you should add ten years to the basic figure because you have already proven yourself to be quite durable. If you are over age 60 and active, add another two years.

Basic Life Expectancy   _____

Decide how each item below applies to you and add or subtract the appropriate number of years from your basic life expectancy.

1. **Family history**

   Add 5 years if 2 or more of your grandparents lived to 80 or beyond.   _____

   Subtract 4 years if any parent, grandparent, sister, or brother died of heart attack or stroke before 50. Subtract 2 years if anyone died from these diseases before 60.   _____

   Subtract 3 years for each case of diabetes, thyroid disorders, breast cancer, cancer of the digestive system, asthma, or chronic bronchitis among parents or grandparents.   _____

2. **Marital status**

   If you are married, add 4 years.   _____

   If you are over 25 and not married, subtract 1 year for every unwedded decade.   _____

3. **Economic status**

   Subtract 2 years if your family income is over $40,000 per year.   _____

   Subtract 3 years if you have been poor for greater part of life.   _____

4. **Physique**

   Subtract one year for every 10 pounds you are overweight.   _____

   For each inch your girth measurement exceeds your chest measurement deduct two years.   _____

   Add 3 years if you are over 40 and not overweight.   _____

5. **Exercise**

   Regular and moderate (jogging 3 times a week), add 3 years.   _____

   Regular and vigorous (long distance running 3 times a week), add 5 years.   _____

Subtract 3 years if your job is sedentary. _____

Add 3 years if it is active. _____

6. Alcohol

Add 2 years if you are a light drinker (1–3 drinks a day). _____

Subtract 5 to 10 years if you are a heavy drinker (more than 4 drinks per day). _____

Subtract 1 year if you are a teetotaler. _____

7. Smoking

Two or more packs of cigarettes per day, subtract 8 years. _____

One to two packs per day, subtract 4 years. _____

Less than one pack, subtract 2 years. _____

Subtract 2 years if you regularly smoke a pipe or cigars. _____

8. Disposition

Add 2 years if you are a reasoned, practical person. _____

Subtract 2 years if you are aggressive, intense, and competitive. _____

Add 1–5 years if you are basically happy and content with life. _____

Subtract 1–5 years if you are often unhappy, worried, and often feel guilty. _____

9. Education

Less than high school, subtract 2 years. _____

Four years of school beyond high school, add 1 year. _____

Five or more years beyond high school, add 3 years. _____

10. Environment

If you have lived most of your life in a rural environment, add 4 years. _____

Subtract 2 years if you have lived most of your life in an urban environment. _____

11. Sleep

More than 9 hours a day, subtract 5 years. _____

12. Temperature

Add 2 years if your home's thermostat is set at no more than 68°F. _____

13. Health care

Regular medical checkups and regular dental care, add 3 years. _____

Frequently ill, subtract 2 years. _____

Source: From *The Psychology of Death, Dying and Bereavement* by Richard Schulz. Copyright © 1978 by Newbery Award Records. Reprinted by permission of Random House, Inc. pp. 97–98.

DEATH IN OLD AGE

In the past, high infant mortality rates, childhood diseases, and high female death rates during childbearing years made death among all age groups a common event. Gee (1985, 2) says that "of 1,000 females born in Canada in 1831, approximately two-thirds would survive to age 20, less than one-half to age 45, and substantially less than one-third to age 65." Today, she says, "the vast majority of women survive to ages 20 and 45 and a large percentage (approximately 86 percent) are alive at age 65" (1985, 3). Longer life expectancy today means that death often takes place in old age. Today people aged 65 or over make up 80 percent of all dying patients (Fisher, Nadon, and Shedletsky 1983).

Only a small number of studies have looked at how older people feel about death. Marshall (1975) says that the major theories of aging avoid the subject. According to activity theory, for example, people want to stay active throughout their lives. They substitute new roles and activities for ones that they lose as they age. When people retire, for example, activity theory says that they will have the highest life-satisfaction if they find new things to do. This theory says nothing about death (Marshall 1980b).

Disengagement theory says that people want to disengage from social roles as they age. This theory says that retirement and withdrawal from social responsibilities leads to high life-satisfaction. According to this theory an awareness of impending death starts the process of disengagement. People know that they will die soon, so they ease their way out of social life. Disengagement produces a smooth transition of power from one generation to the next. Death has a less disruptive effect on society if older people disengage from social roles as they age. This theory focuses on the social effects of dying, but it says little about death as a personal experience or about how older people feel about death.

Erikson's (1963) theory of ego development says that the last stage of life leads to a life review. A person looks over his or her life, ties up loose ends, and prepares for death. Erikson describes this as ego integrity. "It is the acceptance of one's one and only life cycle as something that had to be and that, by necessity, permitted of no substitutions ..." (1963, 268). The integrated person accepts his or her biography and culture. And with this acceptance "death loses its sting" (1963, 268). Robert Peck ([1955] 1968) says that in the last part of this last stage a person can achieve ego transcendence. People in this stage feel a deep concern for others and for the culture they will leave when they die.

These theories say that older people respond to death in more than one way — some people deny it, some accept it, and some embrace it. The few studies that have tested these theories have found complex combinations of acceptance and rejection of death.

Marshall (1974) found an ambivalence toward death among older people in a retirement community and in a nursing home. All of his subjects had disengaged from the middle-aged roles of work and parenthood,

savers

Attn: Online Sales
4101K Industry Drive East
Fife, WA 98424
United States
onlinesales@savers.com
March 23, 2004

Order Number: **AMZ234639**

Ship Method: **standard**

Customer Name: Kathleen F. Slevin

Order Date: 3/23/2004 7:57:38 AM

Seller Order: 058-3874776-0498714

Items

Qty	Description	Condition	Location
1	Mark Novak / Aging and Society a Canadian Perspective	Very Good	B60 / 227

most of them said they accepted death, and some of them said they desired it. But Marshall found that these people also wanted to keep on living. Many of these people said they wanted to live because their lives had meaning for others. Some of them worked for their retirement community; others said that someone depended on them and they wanted to live to care for this person.

Chappell (1975) found that relationships with others give older people a more positive view of the future. She asked forty elderly people in a hospital how long they had to live and how they thought about their time left. She found that all of these people knew that they would die soon and they all said they felt ready to die. But only half the people in this study said they saw their future as a time of waiting for death. The other half saw the future as a time to keep on living. Chappell found that people looked forward to activities if they had social contacts outside the hospital. These contacts gave people continuity with the past and allowed them to extend their lives into the future.

Studies that compare older and younger people find that older people think about death more but feel less afraid of death than the young. A Canadian study by Gesser, Wong, and Reker (1986) studied the fear of death and three kinds of death acceptance among old and young people. They found that older people showed less fear of death and more acceptance of death than younger people. They also found that as fear of death decreased, hopelessness decreased and happiness increased. They say that people who get over the fear of death feel satisfied with life. These people find meaning and purpose in the time they have left, and they feel in control of their lives.

People with different religious backgrounds differ in their attitudes to death. Gesser, Wong, and Reker (1986) found that older people more than younger people accepted life after death. "It may be," they say, "that belief in the afterlife helps the elderly to find meaning and purpose in life, as well as in death. ... Fear of Death is successfully overcome because, in effect, life (after) goes on" (1986, 20). Most religions teach that people get the kind of afterlife they deserve. Studies show that people with mild or uncertain religious belief fear death most, while those with strong religious beliefs or no belief at all deal with death best (Gorer 1967; Kalish 1963). People with a mild belief may accept enough of religion to believe in an afterlife, but not enough to feel they will have a good one.

INSTITUTIONAL DEATH

Religious belief and a sense of purpose can help buffer the fear of death, but how and where a person expects to die also affects how they feel about death. In the past most people died at home, surrounded by family, friends, and neighbours. Some cultures still ensure this kind of death (see Exhibit 13.2). But in Canada almost 70 percent of all deaths (for people of all ages) take place in hospitals (Statistics Canada 1978e).

Exhibit 13.2

DEATH AND DYING AMONG THE HUTTERITES

Professor Joseph W. Eaton reports the following letter from a Hutterite farmer to his sister. The letter describes the death of the man's younger brother.

Dear sister, our dear brother came home on September 8, on a Wednesday morning about 5 o'clock. He said that he had a fairly nice trip. He cried a great deal because of pains. He stated that distress teaches one to pray. I went immediately the following day to visit with him. I could hardly look at him, it was so painful to me; he looked so terrible that it made my heart almost break. However, I remained with him until he died, and until the funeral was over.

Two evenings before his death, his home was full of people, approximately 24 were there. He expressed a heavenly pleasure when he saw them all and said he could not express his pleasure in seeing them. It struck me almost as a miracle when I saw this starved and weak body lying there, telling us such a strong story. We listened to him, warned him not to talk so much because it may do him harm. However, he stated, "While I am still alive, I can speak. When I will be dead, then, of course, I won't be able to tell you what I have to say." ...

He stated that dying does not cause him any difficulty; he said that he had a clear conscience and is in peace with God and all people. He asked many people in my presence whether they had something against him. However, everybody replied in the

negative. They said to him that they themselves were in peace with him. ...

[Just before his death] his children stood around him with a sad heart, and all realized that his departure will be soon. He called his oldest son, gave him his hand and pressed a kiss on his forehead, and advised him how he should behave in the future. Among other words he told him he should obey his preacher, the boss and the field boss, and if the community entrusted a position to him, he should execute same as well as he could, and not only superficially. ...

[He then calls to his side his daughter, the colony business manager, his wife and his brother]. He said, "I am at peace with God and with all people. I have a clear and good conscience. I am ready to depart, but now everything goes so slow. I have only one desire and that is to go to my Lord." He said quite frequently how good it is to have a clear and peaceful conscience. He advised us also that we should prepare ourselves, because the pleasure was inexpressible.

So I have described to you the events and experiences which I have seen with my own eyes, and it is my request and my wish that we all should prepare ourselves. Blessed by God.

Source: Joseph W. Eaton, "The Art of Aging and Dying," *The Gerontologist* 4 (1964):94–112, 95. Reprinted with permission of *The Gerontologist*.

A study of the Baycrest Centre for Geriatric Care in Toronto compared the death rate in the Centre's hospital, nursing home, and apartment complex. The study found that the hospital had a death rate more than 20 times greater than the nursing home and more than 130 times greater than the apartment complex. Shapiro (1983) studied hospital use in a group of more than 3,000 patients aged 68 and over and found that about two-thirds of the sample entered the hospital in the year they died.

Hospitals will take in more and more dying patients as the population ages, but studies show that many doctors and nurses in hospitals feel uncomfortable with dying patients. A study in the U.S. found that 76 percent of doctors in hospitals felt uncomfortable dealing with their dying patients. Sixty percent said they needed some kind of educational counselling (Zorza and Zorza 1979). A study of U. S. medical schools (Dickinson 1976) found that only 7 out of 107 had a full course on how to relate to dying patients and their families. Dickinson and Pearson (1980–81) found that physicians who had taken these courses related more easily to dying patients.

A study at Royal Victoria Hospital in Montreal found that patients wanted to know their diagnoses and their chance of recovery, but doctors did not want to speak openly about death, and doctors had little interest in patients' emotions. Social workers also tended to play down patients' problems (Mount, Jones, and Patterson 1974). Shedletsky and Fisher (1986) replicated this study twelve years later. They found that almost all staff (97 percent) felt that patients should be told about their terminal illness, but only 80 percent said that patients on their units were told, and 70 percent of staff members said that discussions of death and dying never or infrequently took place. Nearly all staff members (97.6 percent) felt that hospitals should meet patients' emotional needs. But 41 percent of staff felt that these needs are never or infrequently met. Skelton (1982) reports that medical staff sometimes feel guilty or angry about dying patients. Because they have spent all of their professional lives learning to keep people alive, they think of death as a failure and avoid dying patients or respond less quickly to their needs. Health and Welfare Canada (1982e, 4) says that the dying patient does not fit the model of health care of the acute hospital. "Skills of investigating, diagnosing, curing and prolonging life [the goals of an acute care hospital where people have short-term, curable illnesses] are not relevant to the care of the dying."

CHANGES IN THE TREATMENT OF THE DYING

The health care system has begun to change its approach to dying patients of all ages. Two doctors more than any others — Elisabeth Kubler-Ross in the United States and Dame Cicely Saunders in England — started this reform.

Kubler-Ross wrote a series of books that described death and dying from the patient's point of view. A study of death and dying courses in

Canada found that 55 percent of the courses used her books and that over 20 percent of the departments that taught these courses cited her work as one of the most important reasons for the growth of interest in death and dying (Klug and Waugh 1982).

Saunders created a new institution for caring for the dying — the hospice. Her work has led to a world-wide hospice movement and the growth of treatment centres for the dying across Canada.

Stages of Death and Dying

Kubler-Ross (1969) described five stages that some patients go through before they die. These stages give an ideal picture of death and dying, based on Kubler-Ross's interviews with dying patients.

First, she says, people *deny* that they are dying. They say, "Not me." They may believe that the doctor has the wrong X-rays or someone else's tests. They may go from specialist to specialist looking for a new diagnosis. They may not even hear the doctor tell them they have a fatal illness.

Second, she says, people feel *angry*. They begin to believe that they will die. "Why me?" they ask. At this point the person blames the doctor or a spouse or God for their illness.

Third, they begin to *bargain*. The person says, "Yes, me, but ... ." A person may bargain with the hospital staff. They may promise to be a good patient and to follow doctor's orders, if only they will get better. They may bargain with God, promise to go to church or to live a more pious life. They may bargain for one more summer at the cottage, or for enough time to see a son married, a grandchild born, or their next birthday.

Fourth, the person feels *depressed*. Their illness gets worse and they know they will die. The person says, "Yes, me," and they feel a great sadness. Kubler-Ross says that depression has two stages. In the first stage the person mourns present losses — the loss of family, career, and the things they love, like a home, car, or cottage. In the second stage the person mourns future losses — the loss of good times to come, the chance to see children or grandchildren grow up, and other future events. The person begins to say goodbye in this stage.

Fifth, the person *accepts* death. A person says, "My time is close now ... it's OK." The person accepts that they will die, and they say goodbye to family and friends and die in peace.

Kubler-Ross says that at every stage a patient holds on to *hope*. At first a person may hope the doctor made a mistake, later they may hope for a remission if they have cancer, and later still they may hope for a painless death.

Some writers question the number of Kubler-Ross's stages or their order. Metzger (1979–80) studied two patient–spouse couples where the woman had a terminal illness. She interviewed each couple three times. She found that in both cases patients described "hope" as their main

Exhibit 13.3

CAN PEOPLE BARGAIN FOR MORE TIME AND WIN?

Some research suggests that people can put off death for some time if they have a reason to live. Phillips and Feldman (1973) first reported the hypothesis that the death rate for certain groups of people drops before important events. Likewise, the rate increases after the event passes. They based this hypothesis on several bits of evidence. First, they looked at historical data. They studied the month of death of 1,300 famous people. They found that, statistically, more people died during their birth month and in the following three months than would be expected by chance. Fewer people than expected died before their birth month. They also found fewer deaths than expected in the U.S. before presidential elections from 1904 to 1968. Second, they studied the death rate of Jews in New York City before Yom Kippur (the day that Jews atone for their sins and receive forgiveness). They found that for 90 percent of the years they sampled, New York City (with a larger percentage of Jews than any other U.S. city) showed a greater drop in death rate before Yom Kippur than did the rest of the U.S. "It seems," Kalish (1981, 233) says, "as though some people exert their will to live until a certain important event takes place, then they permit themselves to die."

A number of researchers have attempted to replicate the Phillips and Feldman findings. Some of these studies support the Phillips and Feldman findings; others do not. A study by Kunz and Summers (1980) found that a higher proportion of deaths occur after a person's birthday than just before. This study supports Phillips and Feldman. Kunz and Summers say that birthdays lead to close relations between family and friends, and this may lead to a delay of death.

Most other studies of whether people tend to live past their birthday (rather than die before their birthday) have not supported the Phillips and Feldman results (Baltes 1977–78; Labovitz 1974; Harrison and Moore 1982–83). A more recent study by Harrison and Kroll (1985–86) does support the Phillips and Feldman study. These researchers found a "death dip" before Christmas and a "death surge" just after Christmas. They suggest that holidays improve people's moods and that a happy mood tends to delay death. Phillips and Feldman (1973) concluded that their research needs further support before the death dip can be considered a real phenomenon. Research over the past decade still leaves the question open. But at least some of the research so far suggests that cultural events can have an impact on the will to live and on the biological fact of death.

experience along with some anger. She did not find that these subjects went through a series of stages. Shneidman (1984, 199) rejects Kubler-Ross's stage theory — "the notion that human beings, as they die, are somehow marched in lock step through a series of stages of the dying process" — on clinical grounds. He reports a wide range of emotions, needs, and coping methods that dying people use. "A few of these in some people, dozens in others — experienced in an impressive variety of ways" (1984, 199). Feigenberg (1980) criticizes Kubler-Ross's impressionistic methods and the unscientific presentation of her results. Butler (1968) says that people have as much right to anger or denial as they do to acceptance and that they have a right to these feelings when they have them, not when a stage theory allows them. Feigenberg points out the danger of accepting these stages as a pattern that everyone must follow. "The stages of Kubler-Ross have come to be regarded as a check-list for the process of dying. ... And if a patient clearly deviates from this pattern, one is now liable to hear from the hospital staff that his dying is 'wrong' " (Feigenberg 1980, cited in Shneidman 1984, 199).

Kubler-Ross (1969) herself says that patients can skip stages, stages can overlap, and people can go back over the same stage many times. Some responses, like anger, come up again and again. Also, different illnesses create different *trajectories* of death or different patterns of response. Kubler-Ross based her model on cancer patients in a hospital, but cancer patients who have remissions may go through these stages more than once. People with other illnesses show other trajectories. Sometimes, a person can have long plateaus between times of decline. Someone who dies shortly after an auto accident may not go through any of these stages.

Shneidman (1984, 200) says that people respond to dying in the same way they respond to other major stresses in their lives: "One dies as one has lived in the terrible moments of one's life." However, he presents little research to support this view. He may exaggerate the individual differences among dying patients in the same way that Kubler-Ross exaggerates the commonality. All sides of this debate have one thing in common: they have brought discussion and thinking about death into public life. People who have to cope with death and dying — patients, their families, and medical staff — now have a number of ways to think about and talk about death (Novak and Axelrod 1979). This has freed many people from the fear and silence that surrounded death and dying only a few years ago.

The Hospice Movement

The idea of a hospice dates back to at least the Middle Ages in Europe. Hospices at that time took in travellers who needed food, shelter, and care. Hospices today meet the special needs of dying patients. Dame Cicely Saunders opened the first modern hospice, St. Christopher's, in London in 1967.

St. Christopher's has sixty-two beds. It has in-patient and out-patient services, a home visiting program, a day care centre for children of staff, and private rooms for older people. The hospice welcomes visitors, even children, and allows families to cook for their dying relatives if they want to. The hospice also has rooms for relatives who want to stay overnight. St. Christopher's does not use methods to extend life, but it tries to relieve symptoms and to help the patients enjoy their last days.

Hospice Goals

First, a hospice controls pain. People fear death for many reasons, but people fear the pain that may accompany death more than death itself. Pain relief ensures that the person will die in comfort, and this relieves much of the patient's fear and anxiety. St. Christopher's pioneered pain relief techniques now used by hospices around the world.

St. Christopher's created the Brompton mix — a mixture of heroin or morphine, cocaine, Stemetil syrup, and chloroform water — to relieve chronic pain. Medical staff base pain control on two techniques: first, they adjust drug dosage until it relieves a patient's pain. "The aim," Saunders (1984, 268) says, "is to titrate the level of analgesia against the patient's pain, gradually increasing the dose until the patient is pain-free." Second, the nurses give the next dose before the previous one has worn off. Hospitals often wait until a person shows signs of pain before they give the next dose of pain reliever. By giving the analgesic "before the patient may think it necessary [usually every four hours] ... It is possible to erase the memory and fear of pain" (Saunders 1984, 268). Patients cared for by this method need lower dosages to maintain a pain-free state because the drug does not have to overcome the pain that has begun. Lower dosages mean that patients stay more alert. Skelton (1982), at the University of Alberta, says that 90 percent of people can get complete pain relief in a hospice setting and all but 1–2 percent can get some help.

Second, a hospice allows a person to die a simple death. The hospice does not use respirators or resuscitators to keep someone alive. Staff make dying a part of life in the hospice. They leave the curtains open around a dying person's bed so that patients can see that their roommates have died. Patients also know they have a say in their treatment. They can ask for medication when they feel they need it and they can ask to die at home. Saunders (1984) reports that people who die at home often feel more pain than people who die in the hospice. Also, caregivers often feel burdened by the demands of care. St. Christopher's (and other hospices) agree to readmit patients whenever they want to come back.

Third, a hospice gives people love and care. In a hospice, staff members focus on the comfort of the patient. They take the time to touch patients and hold them. The hospice will serve special foods that patients like or give patients soothing scented baths. The hospice also helps patients do as much for themselves as they can. This increases patients' well-being by giving them a sense of control over their treatment. The family members of dying patients also receive care. A Family Service Project at St. Christopher's offers help to families who find it hard to cope with their grief. Saunders (1984, 269) says that "staff and volunteers visit to assess the need and to offer support, and if more specialized help is indicated, this can be arranged."

Hospices spread to North America during the 1970s and early 1980s. More than 1,000 hospices opened in the U.S between 1974 and 1984. In Canada hospice organizations exist in Quebec, Ontario, British Columbia, and Manitoba (Manitoba Health Organizations n. d.). Most provinces also have palliative (terminal) care units, palliative care teams, or a palliative care expert on staff in a hospital (Health and Welfare Canada 1982e). Palliative care programs do the same work as hospices, but they exist within an acute care hospital. The Palliative Care Foundation (Southall 1982) found 116 palliative care programs operating in Canada in 1983 (up from 2 in 1975). These programs had 266 beds available. Ninety-five percent of the people who used these programs had terminal cancer. The Palliative Care Foundation estimates that 200 community-based palliative care programs (programs to help people stay in their homes) existed in Canada by the end of 1984 (Ley 1985).

Palliative Care

The Royal Victoria Hospital

The Royal Victoria Hospital in Montreal opened a twelve-bed in-patient palliative care unit in 1975 and expanded the unit to eighteen beds by 1982. The unit offers music therapy, counselling, and physiotherapy as well as care by doctors and nurses. The unit's staff works as a team and practices "whole person medicine" (Doutre, Stillwell, and Ajemian 1979). This means that they care for the spiritual, emotional, and psychological needs, as well as the physical needs, of the patient. The program also offers a seven-day-a-week, twenty-four-hour home care service. The unit's staff keeps patients pain-free in their homes through drug therapy and gives family members advice and support in caring for the dying person. The unit ensures that a patient can come back to the hospital at any time. This allows dying patients to leave the hospital and in some cases to die at home. The unit also has a bereavement follow-up team that visits and supports families after the patient dies.

The Royal Victoria unit admits people of all ages. A five-year study of the unit from January 1975 to April 1980 found that about a third of the people admitted had lung, breast, or bowel cancer. Patients stayed on the unit an average of twenty-four days, about half stayed a week or less, and 78 percent stayed less than four weeks. The large majority of patients (86 percent) admitted to the unit died there. About 13 percent of patients in the home care program died at home; the rest came back to the hospital to die (Ajemian and Mount 1981).

One study at the Royal Victoria Hospital compared the palliative care unit with a surgical ward. Buckingham (Buckingham et al. 1976) had himself admitted as a cancer patient to both types of units. He dieted for six months and lost twenty-two pounds, exposed his skin to ultraviolet rays to make it look as if he had received radiation treatment, stuck himself with needles, and had a doctor do minor surgery to make it look as if he had had intravenous injections and a biopsy. He learned how cancer of the pancreas patients behaved, and he imitated their behaviour. He also grew a stubbly beard and failed to bathe for several days.

Buckingham reports that he got more personal attention and kinder treatment on the palliative care ward. On the surgical ward, he found, doctors spent less than ten minutes per day with him and less than five minutes per visit. Also, doctors travelled in groups, and this discouraged patients from talking to their doctors about their feelings. Buckingham reports that staff avoided eye contact with patients, called patients by their disease, not their name, dwelt on the worst things about a patient's illness, and showed little good feeling toward dying patients. His staff contacts lasted on average less than six minutes per visit.

The palliative care unit showed more interest in him as a person. The nurses looked him in the eye when they talked to him and asked him personal, friendly questions, such as what food he enjoyed eating. Buckingham reports that when families wanted to talk to their doctor the staff got the doctor on the phone as soon as possible. Families also spent a lot of time helping to care for patients: they fed patients, brought urinals, and fixed patients' pillows. The staff supported family members as they helped care for their dying relatives. Buckingham's staff contacts averaged nineteen minutes on the palliative care unit. Compared with the surgical ward, on the palliative care unit he spent almost 400 percent more time talking to staff, patients, and their families. A study by Thompson (1985–86) supports Buckingham's findings. Thompson compared palliative care, surgical, and pediatric nurses' attitudes to death. He found that palliative care nurses "approach their work with the dying with greater ease, may enter into more personal relationship with dying patients ... and come away from their work with the feelings that the work itself is rewarding and that they have been useful" (1985–86, 240). Thompson concludes that the values of the palliative care setting (more than nurses' past experiences) explain this positive attitude to dying patients and their needs.

Buckingham also reports that patients supported and comforted one another on the palliative care unit. "The palliative care unit facilitated this powerful support system by allowing more patient-family freedom and mobility, with open visiting and encouragement of family participation in the care of the patient" (Buckingham et al. 1976, 1214). A study by Kane and others (1984) found that, compared to conventional care, palliative care created more family and patient satisfaction and less family anxiety. Buckingham concluded that palliative care units meet the dying person's special need for emotional and social support as well as physical care (see also Mount and Scott 1983).

The Cost of Palliative Care

Health and Welfare Canada (1982e) says that palliative care units create real savings — they do not just create an "add-on" service. A report on the Royal Victoria program says its home care program has saved more than $3.6 million in hospital costs in five years. This comes to a saving of more than $7,000 per patient. From July 1979 to March 1980, for example, the program saved 3,209 hospital days (a hospital day equals the cost of keeping a patient in a hospital for one day). At $276 a day (in 1980) this came to a saving of $885,684. During this time the program cost $248,900 to run, saving the health care system $636,784 (Health and Welfare Canada 1982e).

A study in Ontario also reported savings from a palliative care unit. The study (Salmon and McGee 1980) found that the cost of care for patients in the palliative care unit was only about one-third the cost of active treatment in a hospital ($107 compared to $304 per day). This unit will save about $1.5 million per year when it reaches its full twenty-two-bed size. The report says that if Canada had the same ratio of palliative care beds as the U.K., it could save at least $41 million a year in hospital costs (in 1980 dollars). Health and Welfare Canada (1982e) goes on to say that a national home care program for the terminally ill linked to a system of palliative care units could save over $700 million per year.

Most of the research on costs has been done by people who run these programs. Their results could reflect a tendency to make the programs look more cost-effective than they are. An independent study by Greer and others (Greer et al. 1984) in the U.S. supports the findings that palliative care saves money. Hospice care reduced in-patient days and reduced the cost of expensive services. More controlled independent research on Canadian programs needs to be done to establish the cost-effectiveness of palliative care.

Palliative Care for the Elderly

Palliative care units take in patients of all ages. Patients at Royal Victoria Hospital, for example, ranged from 20 years old to over 90. Studies show that palliative care can help most older people as well as younger people, but some older patients have unique needs. Shedletsky, Fisher, and Nadon (1982) studied the records of forty older patients (average age 80.6 years) who died in the extended care wing of a hospital. Extended care hospital settings take in many older people with long-term illnesses who need constant medical care. These units often have a palliative care or a hospice treatment philosophy. The researchers found that older extended care patients differed from younger palliative care patients. First, they averaged almost three diagnoses each. Second, only about 38 percent of the patients had cancer; most of them suffered from circulatory diseases (63 percent) and respiratory diseases (48 percent) (Shedletsky, Fisher, and Nadon 1982). Third, respiratory failure caused about 50 percent of all deaths.

Shedletsky, Fisher, and Nadon (1982) found that drug treatment helped about 80 percent of the people with pain and skin problems. The staff reported that just before death 75 percent of the patients felt no pain or distress and 75 percent were conscious or semi-conscious. The staff found, however, that patients with respiratory problems got the least benefit from drug treatment, and this group made up the largest proportion of people with discomfort before death. The researchers conclude that some groups of older extended care patients may have special palliative care needs. Fisher and Shedletsky (1979) say that more research needs to focus on the special needs of these dying patients.

Palliative care and other approaches to the treatment of dying patients raise a variety of ethical questions. Is it ethical, for example, to stop actively treating a person's illness? Does the decision not to put someone on a respirator or not to use a heroic life-saving measure contribute to the person's death? Philosophers, physicians, and legal experts have looked at these and other issues related to dying today.

ETHICAL ISSUES

Two ethical questions come up again and again in writing on death and dying. First, should patients be told that they have a terminal illness? Second, when should a doctor allow a person to die?

To Tell or Not to Tell

Glaser and Strauss (1977) describe two "awareness contexts" for dying: an open awareness context and a closed awareness context. In a *closed awareness context* everyone (including the patient) knows the patient is dying, but no one speaks about it. Glaser and Strauss say this leads to a "ritual drama of mutual pretense" (1977, 271). Family members will talk to a patient about next summer at the cottage or Christmas in Hawaii, even though they all know the patient has only a few days to live. Glaser and Strauss say that this approach has some advantages over more open approaches. It protects the staff, family, and patient from exposing their feelings, and some patients may prefer to die this way. Glaser and Strauss go on to say that a closed awareness context can also cause problems: it can lead to loneliness and isolation for the patient.

Most dying patients today prefer an *open awareness context*, where the staff, the patient, and the family all know and share the knowledge that the patient is dying. This allows the patient to speak openly about death and to share his or her feelings about dying. An open awareness context also gives the dying person a chance to make last-minute financial decisions, to settle family affairs, and to arrange the religious support he or she prefers. Some people will not want an open awareness context, and health workers should respect this right. David Skelton (1982, 557), chairman of the Division of Geriatric Medicine at the University of Alberta, says "we should tell everyone as much as they wish to know."

A study at Royal Victoria Hospital in Montreal found that most patients want open and honest answers from their doctors (Mount, Jones, and Patterson 1974). The study also found that whether doctors felt they should tell their patients depended on whether they themselves would want to be told. Eighty-four percent of doctors who would have wanted to know their own *prognosis* (or forecast of the future of their illness), also felt their patients wanted to know. But only 45 percent of doctors who would not have wanted to know their own condition felt their patients wanted to know. Some doctors may be protecting themselves from their discomfort with death when they withhold diagnosis from a patient. These findings suggest that doctors need more education about patients' feelings and needs. They may also need a chance to talk about and reflect on their own feelings about death and dying.

Euthanasia

Doctors sometimes face ethical conflicts when they treat dying patients. Medical ethics says that a doctor should heal and cure patients, but the Hippocratic oath says that a doctor should first "do no harm." What should a doctor do when machines, surgery, or drugs that extend a person's life also prolong their suffering? What should a doctor do when a patient asks to die? And what does the law in Canada say about euthanasia (helping someone achieve a painless death)?

First, when is a person dead? When they stop breathing? When their heart stops beating? Or when their brain waves stop? Harvard Medical School (1968) gives four criteria for death: a person (1) no longer makes a response, (2) no longer breathes or moves, (3) has no reflexes, and (4) has no sign of brain activity on two EEGs taken twenty-four hours apart. But what about when a machine keeps someone breathing? Or when a heart pump keeps someone's heart beating? Is this person alive or dead? When does a family or a doctor have a right to take someone off these machines?

The Law Reform Commission of Canada (1982) reviewed the question of mercy killing in a study called *Euthanasia, Aiding Suicide and Cessation of Treatment*. The Commission found that the Canadian courts have never convicted a doctor in Canada for giving a patient large doses of pain-killing drugs, for stopping useless treatment, or for deciding not to treat a secondary illness (like pneumonia in a terminal cancer patient). The courts, however, *could* try doctors on these grounds. This means that every doctor who decides to stop treatment risks becoming a test case in the courts. The Commission feels that the *Criminal Code of Canada* should give doctors clearer guidance.

Exhibit 13.4

A LIVING WILL

The "living will" below appears in the California Natural Death Act. The Canadian Law Reform Commission does not support the use of living wills in Canada. The "Directive" below gives an idea of what a living will contains. Read it over and consider the pros and cons of living wills. Would you fill one out? Would you witness a friend's? Do you think Canada should allow the use of living wills?

Directive to Physician

Directive made this _____ day of _____ (month, year).
I _____ , being of sound mind, willfully, and voluntarily make known my desire that my life shall not be artificially prolonged under the circumstances set forth below, do hereby declare:

1   If at any time I should have an incurable injury, disease, or illness certified to be a terminal condition by two physicians, and where the application of life-sustaining procedures would serve only to artificially prolong the moment of my death and where my physician determines that my death is imminent whether or not life-sustaining procedures are utilized, I direct that such procedures be withheld or withdrawn and that I be permitted to die naturally.

2   In the absence of my ability to give directions regarding the use of such life-sustaining procedures, it is my intention that this directive shall be honored by my family and physician(s) as the final expression of my legal right to refuse medical or surgical treatment and accept the consequences from such refusal.

3   If I have been diagnosed as pregnant and that diagnosis is known to my physician, this directive shall have no force or effect during the course of my pregnancy.

4   I have been diagnosed and notified at least 14 days ago as having a terminal condition by _____ , M.D. whose address is _____ , and whose telephone number is _____ . I understand that if I have not filled in the physician's name and address, it shall be presumed that I did not have a terminal condition when I made out this directive.

5   This directive shall have no force or effect five years from the date filled in above.

6   I understand the full import of this directive and I am emotionally and mentally competent to make this directive.

Signed _____

City, County and State of Residence _____

The declarant has been personally known to me and I believe him or her to be of sound mind.

Witness _____

Source: Sandra G. Wilcox and Marilyn Sutton, "Directive to Physician," *Understanding Death and Dying*, 3rd ed. (Palo Alto, California: Mayfield, 1985), 417. Reprinted with permission of the publisher.

The Commission reviewed some ways to relieve doctors of criminal liability. California in 1976, for example, passed Bill 3060, called the Natural Death Act. This bill allows a person to write a *living will* that authorizes relatives or doctors to withdraw or withhold artificial methods of life support in the case of a terminal illness. It also attempts to relieve doctors of responsibility for stopping treatment.

Living wills raise raise ethical and practical questions. First, in some cases people will change their minds as they near death, but they will not get a chance to change their living will. Second, why should people have to write living wills to protect themselves from suffering and indignity? The Law Reform Commission of Canada (1982, 10) says, "a terminally ill patient has a right, not a secondary or subordinate right but a primary right, to die with dignity and not to fall victim to heroic measures." The Commission says that in Canada today doctors should not feel compelled to take heroic measures to keep someone alive and that patients should not have to write living wills to protect themselves from a doctor's fear of prosecution.

The Law Reform Commission of Canada (1982) says that the law and medical ethics distinguish between killing someone and allowing someone to die. Walton and Fleming (1980, 58) say that a doctor who sets out to kill a patient — for example, by giving the patient a drug overdose — "has committed himself more firmly. He is therefore more directly accountable for the outcome." A doctor who allows death to happen — for example, by not putting a person on a respirator or by taking someone off a respirator — may or may not cause a person's death. The person may live even without the treatment. Walton and Fleming (1980, 60) say that ethical treatment should offer the most options for the patient. "A passive course of action," they say, "... provides a sensible alternative to aggressive treatment and, at the same time, allows for unexplainable and unforeseen events which may be of great benefit to the patient."

Both the law and medical ethics reject active euthanasia — killing someone because they ask for death or to relieve their suffering. The Law Reform Commission of Canada (1982) says that a law to support active euthanasia would create more risks than benefits. Also, new methods of

Exhibit 13.5

CESSATION OF TREATMENT IN CANADA

Section 198 of the *Criminal Code of Canada* says that a person who gives medical or surgical treatment should act with reasonable skill and care. Section 199 says that a person has to continue an act once they begin, if by stopping the act they endanger someone's life. These sections seem to make a doctor criminally liable for stopping useless treatment. The Law Reform Commission of Canada says that these sections do not apply to a doctor who stops treatment after careful review of a case. The Commission gives an example to show why:

A doctor turns off a respirator, knowing, as he does so, that the patient will no longer be ventilated and thus will probably die. Let us suppose, in one instance, that before doing so he has assured himself, using standard medical procedures and tests, that the patient is already in a state of irreversible coma. Here the act of turning off the respirator, while technically constituting a positive act of cessation of treatment within the meaning of section 199, could not serve as a valid basis for criminal liability, and for two reasons. Firstly, the continuation of treatment is not reasonable in this case given the condition of the patient and, secondly, the cessation of treatment does not reflect wanton or reckless disregard for life on the part of the physician. But on the other hand, let us assume that this same doctor performs the same act without first assuring himself of the patient's condition. There would probably then be grounds for applying these provisions, since by ceasing treatment without taking the precaution of assuring himself that such cessation will not endanger the patient, he would be showing wanton or reckless disregard for the patient's life or safety.

Source: Law Reform Commission of Canada, *Euthanasia, Aiding Suicide and Cessation of Treatment*, Working Paper 28 (Ottawa: Minister of Supply and Services, 1982), 17–18. Reproduced with permission of the Minister of Supply and Services Canada.

palliative care in most cases can relieve the pain that might justify euthanasia. Skelton (1982), a pioneer in palliative care in Canada, states the experts' case simply. He says that requests for active euthanasia often hide a request for better care. "I believe most sincerely," he says, "that if adequate care is given to dying patients the question of responding to requests for active euthanasia is eliminated" (1982, 558).

Henteleff (1978) puts the ethical question in the context of professional responsibility. The patient, he says, has two needs: biological and moral.

Exhibit 13.6

PROPOSED CHANGES IN CANADIAN LAW

The Law Reform Commission proposes that the *Criminal Code of Canada* should include the following statements.

1. Nothing in sections 14, 45, 198, 199 of the *Criminal Code* shall be interpreted as requiring a physician
   (a) to continue to administer or to undertake medical treatment against the clearly expressed wishes of the person for whom such treatment is intended;
   (b) to continue to administer or to undertake medical treatment, when such treatment is medically useless and is not in the best interests of the person for whom it is intended, except in accordance with the clearly expressed wishes of this person.

2. Nothing in sections 14, 45, 198, 199 of the *Criminal Code* shall be interpreted as preventing a physician from undertaking or ceasing to administer palliative care and measures intended to eliminate or to relieve the suffering of a person for the sole reason that such care or measures are likely to shorten the life expectancy of this person.

Source: Law Reform Commission of Canada, *Euthanasia, Aiding Suicide and Cessation of Treatment*, Working Paper 28 (Ottawa: Minister of Supply and Services, 1982), 70–71. Reproduced with permission of the Minister of Supply and Services Canada.

The doctor can help dying patients meet both these needs. The doctor can relieve a person's physical distress and should avoid treatment that will keep a person from finding meaning in their last days. Weisman (1972) says that medicine can and should help people die in the way they want to die. He calls this an "appropriate death."

MOURNING AND GRIEF

When an older person dies they often leave behind children and sometimes a spouse. These survivors need to adjust to the loss, and society can help with this adjustment. Funeral practices and rituals structure the grieving process. They prescribe what mourners should say, what they should wear, and in some cultures how they should sit. Mourners in Christian cultures wear black; Chinese mourners wear white. North American society values silent unemotional grieving; Chinese families hire professional mourners to make loud wailing noises at the funeral. Jewish tradition requires that the family "sit Shiva" for seven days after a funeral. Mourners tear their clothes, sit on low chairs to deny themselves physical comfort, cover the mirrors in their home, and light a candle that burns throughout the week. The mourning family accepts visitors throughout the week, and ten men gather at the house each day for prayer. Mourning continues in less intense stages for a year until the unveiling of a commorative stone on the grave of the deceased (Goldberg 1981–82).

Each culture has its own rules about funeral and mourning practices, but these rules and rituals have a common purpose. They help the bereaved family cope with grief and they reestablish community bonds after the loss of a community member.

Regardless of the culture a person belongs to or the type of funeral they attend, each bereaved person has to work through personal feelings of grief. Some research in North America shows that mourners go through stages of grief. Lindemann (1944) describes three stages of grief: an initial response phase, an intermediate phase, and a recovery phase.

First, the bereaved person feels shock and disbelief. They may report feeling cold and numb, and some people say they feel dazed, empty, and confused. These feelings protect a person from feelings of sorrow. People in this phase often fear that they will break down in public. This phase can last for several weeks.

Second, the person will begin to review what has happened. This takes three forms: (a) The bereaved person obsessively reviews one or two scenes related to the death, or they may berate themselves for something they should have said or done. (b) The bereaved person searches for a meaning for the death. Religious people may find solace in knowing that God willed this death. (c) The bereaved person searches for the deceased. A widow may go to places where she expects to see her spouse. She may detect the presence of her spouse while watching TV or eating dinner or lying in bed. Some people even call out to their spouses and expect an answer. This phase lasts about a year.

Third, the bereaved person begins to recover. Survivors look for social contacts; they may join a club or go on a cruise. They feel that they have come through an ordeal and say they feel stronger and more competent than before. This stage begins around the second year after the death.

Gorer (1965) says that successful grief work includes: (1) breaking bonds to the deceased, (2) readjustment to the environment without the deceased, and (3) forming new relationships. Not everyone makes a smooth trip through these stages. Sometimes a person can show a delayed emotional response to a parent's or spouse's death. The person seems to cope well, displaying lots of zest and energy, but they may have internalized their grief. This can lead to emotional upset and physical illness later. One case will show the cost of morbid grieving.

Joanna's husband died twelve years ago of brain cancer. She visited him in the hospital every day. At the same time she carried on a career in real estate and worked on a Master's degree. For two years she ran herself into the ground. She went to the hospital at noon and at supper time to feed her husband his meals, then she would jump in her car and show another house or run home to work on a paper for her M.A. At the end of the day she fell into bed exhausted.

When her husband died, she was determined that nothing was going to stop her. "I didn't allow myself time to grieve," she says. "After his death, I travelled. At Christmas I went to Spain, Hawaii, or wherever. At Easter I went somewhere. I went to Europe. There was never a day — I didn't allow myself any time at all. Do you get the picture? No time to breathe."

To keep going she used pills and alcohol. Then she started collecting pills and drinking more. "That was my way of coping, my way of standing the pain," she says. "I needed some kind of anaesthetic." At the end of this downward spiral Joanna drove her car through a restaurant window. She got out of her car, walked through the window, sat down at a booth in the restaurant, and waited for the police to take her away (Novak 1985).

Only about 25 percent of bereaved people go through morbid grieving (and few people show Joanna's extreme denial) (Schulz 1978). But older people tend to show a delayed and more extreme grief reaction than younger people. Sanders (1980–81) compared the scores on a Grief Experience Inventory of 45 bereaved spouses in two age groups (people over age 65 and people under age 63). She found that older spouses showed less grief than younger spouses at the time of a first interview (shortly after their spouse's death). At the second interview older spouses showed higher scores than younger spouses on scales of Denial and Physical Symptoms and increases in ten other scales compared to younger spouses. These results suggest that older spouses may need help many months after their spouse's death. Barrett and Schneweis (1980–81, 102) report that life after a spouse's death "persists in being stressful for years." These results suggest that the stage model of bereavement may not fit older widows. Moss and Moss (1984–85) found that the marital tie persists after loss of a spouse. They consider this a normal response to widowhood in old age and "a nourishing link to the past" (1984–85, 204). More research on bereavement in old age will show how this experience differs from bereavement in younger people.

CONCLUSION

This chapter has touched on some of the complex issues related to death and dying. Each religion has its own views on issues like euthanasia, funeral practices, and mourning. Each culture shapes members' beliefs about the meaning of death, about life after death, and about care for the sick and dying. Each person will respond in a unique way to their own death and to the deaths of people they know and love. The study of death and dying can at best help people to think about and understand these issues for themselves.

SUMMARY

1. Attitudes to death vary by age, religion, and culture. Older people generally accept death more than younger people. Like younger people, older people say they want to continue living, if they feel their life has a meaning.
2. People with either no religious belief or very strong religious belief seem to cope with death best.
3. Death occurs more often in old age today than in the past, and it also more often occurs in an institution. These trends will increase as the population ages.
4. Elisabeth Kubler-Ross reports five stages of dying. Not everyone goes through all of these stages or follows the pattern Kubler-Ross describes, but her writings have encouraged a more open discussion of death and dying.
5. Cicely Saunders opened the first modern hospice in England in 1967. St. Christopher's Hospice offers an alternative to hospital care for the dying. Hospices offer pain control and a home-like setting for death.
6. Palliative care units in hospitals offer the same comfort and care as a hospice. These units, like hospices, will help patients die in their own homes. They also assure patients who want to die at home that they can return to the hospital at any time.
7. Most experts and patients prefer an open awareness context for dying. A closed awareness context can lead to isolation and loneliness for the patient (though some people may prefer not to speak openly about death). Doctors today need to understand their own feelings about death and dying, so they can give their patients the kind of care that the patients prefer.
8. The law in Canada today does not require doctors to take heroic measures to keep a terminally ill patient alive. Canada needs clearer guidelines to help doctors decide about stopping treatment for people in comas. Canadian law does prohibit active euthanasia. Doctors say that proper pain control would end the fear that leads people to ask for euthanasia.
9. Death leads to grief and mourning for survivors. Culture and religion help people cope with feelings of grief. Funerals, for example, bring the community together and give mourners support. Still, each person has to work through feelings of grief in his or her own way. Writers say that mourners go through stages of grief and that if all goes well a person will emerge from grieving to carry on their life.

SELECTED READINGS

Kubler-Ross, Elisabeth. *On Death and Dying.* New York: Macmillan, 1969.

A classic in the field. Whether she is right or wrong in promoting a stage theory of dying, Kubler-Ross started the current interest in death. The book gives a humane picture of dying and presents some informative case studies.

Law Reform Commission of Canada. *Euthanasia, Aiding Suicide and Cessation of Treatment.* Working Paper 28. Ottawa: Minister of Supply and Services, 1982. A good, readable summary of the legal and ethical issues dealing with euthanasia, suicide, and cessation of treatment. The Commission puts these issues in a Canadian context — something that few other studies do.

Marshall, Victor W. *Last Chapters: A Sociology of Aging and Dying.* Monterey, California: Brooks/Cole, 1980b. A good source of other writings on death, dying, and aging. Marshall's study contains more material on death and old age than most other books on death and dying.

Shneidman, Edwin S., ed. *Death: Current Perspectives*, 3rd ed. Palo Alto, California: Mayfield, 1984. A collection of philosophical writings and scholarly studies on death and dying. Well-balanced selections on varied topics including historical views of dying, the dying process, and grief.

PART V

SOCIETAL CHANGE

CHAPTER 14

POLITICS AND POLICY

INTRODUCTION

Studies of aging and politics in Canada have only just begun. Pratt (1984) says that before 1980 political scientists saw little reason to study aging. First, in the 1950s and 1960s scholars concerned themselves mostly with voting behaviour and political opinions. They found that the largest changes in opinion took place as people moved from adolescence to adulthood. Opinion change among adult voters stayed stable, for most people, from middle age on. As a result, political scientists tended to ignore the study of older age groups.

Second, the focus on voting behaviour led to a lack of interest in policy issues. Political scientists showed little concern for health care, housing, or pension issues (one exception is Bryden's (1974) study of pension policy).

Third, until the 1980s gerontology sat near the bottom of the disciplinary hierarchy in Canada. Pratt (1984) says that researchers in all disciplines found it hard to get funds for aging research. Under these conditions, political scientists saw little reason to study aging.

The start of a Strategic Grants program for Population Aging in 1979 increased interest in the study of aging and politics. But this interest has grown slowly. Pratt (1984) reported fewer than ten gerontological studies by Canadian political scientists. These studies, at best, give a hint of the issues that concern gerontologists when they study politics.

Pratt's (1984) review shows that gerontologists study aging and politics from at least three points of view. First, they study political participation. This includes studies of seniors' voting patterns and political attitudes and the number of seniors who hold public office. Second, they study senior activism and group conflict. This includes the study of senior pressure groups and public protests. Third, they look at the context of political action — the policies and structures of the government.

This chapter will look at each of these topics. It will (1) describe the range of senior political activity in Canada, (2) describe the government agencies that translate seniors' needs into policy, and (3) consider senior political participation in the future.

POLITICAL PARTICIPATION

Sociologists define *political participation* as behaviour that leads to the selection of leaders and the choice of public policy. Seniors take part in politics in a number of ways. They read about political issues and listen to public affairs radio and TV shows. They also vote, hold political office, and sometimes protest government decisions.

Voting

Studies done on voting patterns during the 1960s in the U.S. (Milbrath 1965) and in other countries supported the disengagement theory of aging. They found that young adults had lower voter turnout than middle-aged people, middle-aged people (in their forties and fifties) showed the highest voter turnout, and older people showed less voter turnout than middle-aged people, though more than young adults. Regenstreif (1965, 88) concluded from Canadian data that "there is strong evidence that people past the age of 65 suffer a diminution of interest in politics for a variety of reasons. Turn-out and general participation follow these patterns."

Later Canadian studies questioned these findings. Van Loon (1970), in a study of 1965 Canadian election figures, found only a slight peak in middle age. Laskin and Baird (1970) studied Saskatchewan local, provincial, and federal voting records in a small town and found no drop-off in voter turnout with age.

More recent studies in the U. S. and Canada also question the conclusion that political participation drops off as a person ages. These studies control for socioeconomic status, health, and physical mobility. They show that given the same background, health, and mobility, people stay politically active in old age (Glenn and Grimes 1968; Glenn 1969; Verba and Nie 1972). Yelaja (1981, 14), for example, reports that in a study of eighty-two Canadians aged 50 and over, "in terms of political attention, ... political participation and activity, the older, retired persons tended to exhibit a higher level of participation and activity than the younger and employed respondents." Kernaghan (1982) found that in the 1974 Canadian federal election voter turnout declined only after age 85.

Curtis and Lambert (1976) found similar results for the 1965 and 1968 Canadian federal elections. In one report they reviewed the voting and political interest patterns for a sample of 2,767 Canadians aged 21 years and older during the 1968 federal election. When they looked at their total sample, they found a drop in voting and election interest among older people. This supported the findings of earlier studies that showed a decrease in voting behaviour and political interest with age. Curtis and Lambert then looked at groups of people with the same income, education, occupation, region, community size, marital status, sex, and language group. When they did this they found that older people with different backgrounds voted at different rates. They found that English Canadian males, for example, have a greater tendency to vote in later life than English Canadian women, but English Canadian men and women show about the same interest in election issues. They found that French Canadian males and females show little difference in voting patterns with age, but French Canadian males show a greater political interest than French Canadian females. They also found differences between the two language groups. They found that older (over age 50) English Canadian males and females are more likely to vote than their French Canadian counterparts.

When they looked at people within each group (French Canadian male, French Canadian female, English Canadian female, English Canadian male) they found no drop in voting or political interest with age for most groups. They say that "there is little or no evidence suggesting a decline in either voting or electoral interest as a function of age" (Curtis and Lambert 1976, 302). They found, instead, that voting and affiliation with political groups showed a modest increase even past the age of 70. When older people did not vote, they gave frailty or illness as a reason, not lack of interest. The researchers say they were "struck with [their] failure to detect any clear evidence for a reduction in reported organizational involvement or affiliation with age once controls are made. ... So far as voting and political interest are concerned, there is either no drop-off with age or even some modest increases" (1976, 305–6).

This active concern for politics among seniors, combined with their growing numbers, may give older people more political power in the future. Gifford (1982) says that the median age for voters has increased in Canada from 30 years in 1881 to 42 years in 1981. He projects that the median age will increase to 48 years by 2031. At that time, he says, voters aged 65 and over will make up 26 percent of the voting public, compared to only 13.3 percent in 1981 (Gifford 1983). The large numbers of seniors in the future and their high rate of voter participation could lead seniors to form a voting bloc. This bloc could then sway government policy through the electoral process.

Will seniors use their voting strength to shape Canadian policy and achieve specific goals? They have on one or two occasions in the past.

Exhibit 14.1
Age Distribution of Canada's Population:
% of Population 65 Years and Over, Median Age
of Voters, and Percent of Voters 65 and Over,
1881–2031

Year	65 + as % of Pop.	Median Age of Voters	65 + as % of Voters
1881	4.1	30	8.5
1931	5.6	40	9.9
1961	7.6	41	12.9
1981	9.7	42	13.3
2001	12.3	45	16.2
2021	16.6	47	20.9
2031	20.9	48	26.0

Source: Adapted from C.G. Gifford, "Senior Politics," *Policy Options*, September 1983, 14.

Gifford (1982) points to "the Diefenbaker 'pension increase' landslide of 1958" as one occasion. Kernaghan (1982) points to the National Pensioners and Senior Citizens Federation campaign to create the Canada Pension Plan between 1963 and 1965 as another (citing Bryden 1974, 194–97). But most experts do *not* think that seniors will form a permanent voting bloc.

First, studies in Canada show that many people keep the same political stance throughout their lives. Conservatives tend to stay that way, and so do Liberals and New Democrats. Regenstreif (1965) found, in an analysis of the 1962 Canadian federal election, that the New Democratic Party got the strongest support from voters who at that time were 40–49 years old. These voters voted for the first time during the 1940s, when the CCF (forerunner of the NDP) led the Liberals in popular support. This historical period shaped their voting patterns, so that "the political atmosphere of the early and middle 1940s continues to cast its spell on political life" (1965, 87). Likewise, people who came of age during the Depression of the 1930s or who served in World War II will have their own view of Canadian political life and their own party affiliations.

Second, older people come from different social classes, different ethnic backgrounds, and different parts of the country. These groups have different needs and define issues differently. Wealthy seniors, for example, may have little interest in the continued indexation of the Guaranteed Income Supplement, while a poor older widow may listen carefully to what a politician says about public pension policy. Voters in the Maritimes tend to favour the Liberal and Progressive Conservative parties, while Ontario and the Prairie provinces show the greatest support for the NDP (Clarke et al. 1980). These and other differences lead older people to vote for different parties and different policies. Clarke and his colleagues reviewed voting patterns by age for three federal elections (1965, 1968, 1974). They did find (for all three elections) a larger proportion of voters who favoured the Progressive Conservative party in older age groups (26 percent of those 21–29 voted PC, compared to 35 percent of respondents aged 60 and over). But they conclude that this relatively small difference provides "no evidence of pronounced differences in voting behaviour of different age groups in Canadian federal elections" (1980, 87).

Third, seniors take into account other needs than their own when they vote. Most older people, for example, have children and grandchildren. A senior may vote for a politician because that person's party promises to provide jobs for the young or day care for mothers. Senior voters will vote as a bloc if a policy or party threatens to cut pensions or increase the costs of services, but most of the time senior issues play only a small part in determining seniors' voting behaviours.

Even if they do not form a voting bloc, seniors can use other methods to shape government policy. Verba, Nie, and Kim (1971, 10) say that elections set the pattern of government policy, but "the most important set of political activities may be the myriad attempts to influence governmental decisions ... between elections." A study by Kernaghan and Kuper (1983) shows that almost all provincial and federal government agencies make policies that affect seniors. Some agencies, like federal and provincial departments of health, play a central role in policy making for seniors, while others, like transportation or consumer affairs, play a smaller role. Pross (1975) says that seniors will have an impact on policy only if federal and provincial public servants recognize their right to participate in policy making.

Seniors can take an active part in Canadian policy making in at least three ways:

1. Governments have set up seniors' councils, advisory groups, and committees to shape policies for seniors. Seniors can work with these councils to create change from within the system.
2. Seniors can form advocacy groups that lobby the government for policy change. These groups pass resolutions, write reports, and meet with government officials on senior issues. These groups may have the greatest impact on policies for seniors. If they achieve legitimacy, advocacy groups can play an ongoing part in policy formation.
3. Seniors can form protest groups. Ongoing advocacy groups (like provincial senior societies) can protest government policies, and so can special groups that emerge to protest a specific issue. The Senate of Canada's Report (Senate of Canada 1979) on retirement age policies

supports this approach. It says that "the retired elderly should organize, protest and show militancy in order to improve their chances of achieving dignity, obtaining higher incomes as well as medical and other services and finding useful work" (Senate of Canada 1979, 115).

Seniors have started to work in all of these directions in the past few years. The following sections review some recent senior political activities.

Senior Advocacy Groups

Sociologists define political *power* as the ability of one group to achieve its interests over others. A group can gain power by having its members elected to office, by violently overthrowing the government, or by putting pressure on government officials. Advocacy groups take this last approach. One of the first advocacy groups for seniors in any country, the Old Age Pensioners' Organization, began in British Columbia in 1932. The group formed to protest the rigid use of a means test for pensioners. Later, in the 1940s and 1950s, provincial senior organizations began on the prairies and in Ontario. These provincial groups then joined to form the National Pensioners and Senior Citizens Federation in 1954. Senior organizations formed in the Maritime provinces during the 1960s and 1970s. These provincial organizations and national federations meet each year to pass resolutions on seniors' issues, like the cost of insurance, the quality of nursing home care, and the price of drugs. They then send these resolutions to the appropriate provincial or federal agencies. These groups also lobby government leaders between yearly meetings (Bryden 1974, 195).

Gifford (1982) says that between 600,000 and 800,000 older people, or one older person in three, belongs to some seniors' group. Most of these people belong to one or more of the 3,700 social clubs or senior centres in Canada. Few of these local clubs do direct advocacy work, but often a club belongs to a provincial or national federation.

Seven provinces have over forty special advocacy groups. These groups respond to specific issues by presenting briefs to government committees or ministers. They include Canadian Pensioners Concerned (twenty local branches in Ontario, Nova Scotia, and Alberta), Seniors Action Now (branches in Saskatchewan and B.C.) and L'Association Québécoise pour la Défense des Droits des Retraités et Preretraités (L'AQDR) (fifteen branches in Quebec) (Gifford 1982).

Hundreds of special needs groups also exist throughout the country. These include teachers' groups, government employee groups, and groups related to a single corporation. These groups work to protect pension plans and benefits for former employees. Other organizations like the Royal Canadian Legion have many older members and a well-developed program to help seniors.

For all of this activity, Canada has no national group as influential as the American Association of Retired Persons (AARP) in the U.S., which

Exhibit 14.2

A PROFILE OF SOME SENIOR GROUPS AND WHAT THEY DO

Quebec

The Fédération de l'Age d'Or du Québec (FADOQ) started in 1973. It is the most highly organized and financially secure of the provincial federations. The FADOQ has twenty-six people on its full-time paid staff and maintains active contact with over a dozen departments in the Quebec government. The federation lobbies for change, publishes a newspaper, and writes briefs to the government on seniors' issues. The federation had about 165,000 members in 1982, and it has considerable influence on policy within the province of Quebec.

Ontario

The United Senior Citizens of Ontario (USCO) now has over 1,000 affiliated clubs and over 260,000 members. Members also automatically belong to the National Federation of Pensioners and Senior Citizens. The USCO works for pension increases, tax relief, and medicare benefits; it also presents briefs to the provincial government on health care, housing, and recreation issues and publishes a monthly newsletter. The USCO takes credit for better government pensions, increases in seniors' housing, and provincial tax credits for seniors.

Alberta

The Alberta Council on Aging represents 40,000 seniors in Alberta. It has two goals: to identify seniors' needs and to get senior (65+) leaders to take action. In 1979 the Council conducted a study of consumer concerns, in 1980 it studied the participation of older people in the performing arts, and in 1982 it set up a community improvement program called Project Involvement. The Council publishes *Foresight*, a magazine for retirement planning that forty-five companies now use in their pre-retirement education programs. The Council writes briefs and letters to tell the provincial government about seniors' needs. In 1983 the Council wrote a letter opposing user fees for health care services, filed a report to the Task Force on Older Women, and expressed concern over crime and the elderly.

These groups keep the channels of communication with government open. Both seniors and the government gain from this relationship. Seniors can use these channels to stimulate policies that meet their needs, and government can learn about seniors' responses to ongoing policies and programs.

has around 10 million members. The AARP has a permanent headquarters in Washington, D.C., and it employs full-time researchers and lobbyists to lobby the government on senior issues. The AARP also publishes a

national magazine titled *Modern Maturity* and offers services like life insurance, wholesale drugs, and travel discounts. The U.S. has a number
of other large groups that speak out on senior issues. These include the
National Association of Retired Federal Employees (NARFE), with more
than 180,000 members; the National Council of Senior Citizens (NCSC),
with about 3 million members; and the National Council on the Aging
(NCA), a federation of more than 1,000 agencies that work for and with
older people (Atchley 1985; Hendricks and Hendricks 1986). These groups
have large budgets and bureaucratic structures that give them legitimacy
in the eyes of government officials.

The U.S. also has a multi-age activist group called the Gray Panthers.
The Gray Panthers began as a coalition of older people and students in
the late 1960s. The group maintains a commitment to multi-age membership, but most new members are older people. This group has a
charismatic leader, Maggie Kuhn, who has appeared on national talk
shows and in the press. The Gray Panthers attracts media attention because it portrays older people as militant activists who will use street
theatre or sit-ins to draw attention to their needs. The Gray Panthers
have organized tenants (of all ages) in Washington, D.C., set up a multi-
age living project in Boston, and helped fight for better food in school
cafeterias in San Diego, California (Jacobs and Hess 1980). Jacobs and
Hess say that the Panthers will probably never attract large numbers of
seniors, but the group does serve a purpose. It casts older people in a
new and dramatic role as social critics and activists who fight to improve
life for young and old.

Canadian seniors' groups lack the national impact of either the AARP
or the Gray Panthers for at least three reasons:

First, in Canada, the provinces set policies for health care, housing,
and social services. This gives lobbying a provincial focus and makes the
provincial federations as important as the national federations as advocates of seniors' needs.

Second, pressure group activity in Canada is "more limited, more se-
cretive and more focused on the bureaucracy than in the United States"
(Kernaghan and Kuper 1983, 30). The policy system in Canada "tends
to be characterized by superficial public deliberations and by the assign-
ment of major responsibility for policy development to the political executive, the administrative arena, and *recognized* pressure groups" (Pross
1975). This makes it harder in Canada than in the U.S. for seniors to
influence policy makers.

Third, Lewis (1986) found that seniors' groups in Canada lack the
experience and style to lobby the government successfully. She studied
reports submitted to federal pension committees from 1950 to 1978 and
found only six organizations that represented seniors in 1950, only four
in 1964, and only five in 1978. These groups had loose memberships
and little knowledge about how the government works. Before seniors
gain power, Lewis says, they will need groups that speak with one voice
for the mass of older people.

Exhibit 14.3

PROFILES

One way that older people can stay active in politics without holding office or lobbying the government is to advise others about how the government works and how to get things done. Two case studies make this point.

Charles-Eugene Dionne

[Charles-Eugene Dionne, 72, from St. Pascal, Quebec] represented the federal riding of Kamouraska for 17 years until his defeat in the May 1979 election. He first went to Ottawa in 1962 as one of 26 Creditiste MPs from Quebec. And he continues to represent the people of Kamouraska County, but now he does it for free. Mainly he gives advice and assistance to a steady stream of people plagued by the intricacies of the Unemployment Insurance Act, but he also deals with income tax hassles and pension worries.

Dionne's first paying job was as a lumberjack, when he was 17. After 22 years in the woods, he became a union organizer and eventually president of a local, organizing forest workers. Now 72, Dionne sits in his rocking chair smoking a pipe in his home in St. Pascal, Quebec — until the phone rings. Then he springs into action, bringing friendship and practical advice to the people of his neighbourhood.

Justice Emmett Hall

Justice Emmett Hall was born November 29, 1898, and began his law career in 1922 in Saskatchewan. He served as vice-president of the Canadian Bar Association, president of the Law Society of Saskatchewan, and member of the Supreme Court of Canada. Hall wrote a report for the federal government in 1964 that structured Canada's medical care system, and he completed a report on education for the Ontario government titled *Living and Learning*. That report led to a decade of reform and experiment in Canada's schools. Elaine Dewar (1981) wrote about Hall's retirement for *Today Magazine*.

In 1973 he retired. But he had no sooner returned to Saskatoon when his phone rang with requests for service. In 1973 he arbitrated a nasty national railway strike. Then it was a commission on Saskatchewan universities, then another on the province's justice system. In 1976 it was another railway dispute. For two years, as chief commissioner of the Grain Handling and Transportation Commission, he sifted out the intricacies of transport. ... He has just started a three-year stint as chancellor of the University of Saskatchewan. And on the day the federal government invoked closure over the constitution, Hall sat in his living room, calling a spade a spade, hinting about taking on a brief in the fight over the ruling principles of Canadian life.

Sources: *Today Magazine*, "Heroes of 1980: Charles-Eugene Dionne," December 27, 1980, 9; Elaine Dewar, "Doctoring Medicare," *Today Magazine*, February 7, 1981, 6–8.

Senior Activism

A social movement forms when a group (1) coalesces around a set of issues, (2) creates an image of itself in the media as concerned and important, (3) exerts pressure on government agencies, public policies, and people who make decisions, and (4) has expertise and can raise money or votes on behalf of the issues it represents (Hendricks and Hendricks 1986). Binstock (1972) says that age alone cannot form the basis of a cohesive social movement because seniors' groups lack the financial stability, the organizational rigour, and the large numbers of supporters needed to form a movement. Pratt (1983) disagrees. He sees a growing class consciousness among seniors in North America today, and he predicts that this will form the basis for a social movement.

Seniors in Canada on occasion have joined together into a national social movement. This has happened three times in the recent past, each time seniors felt threatened by cutbacks in government programs (Gifford 1983). Seniors acted as a movement in 1972 during the federal election campaign, when they protested low Old Age Security payments. Protests included mass meetings in Vancouver and a demonstration at City Hall in Toronto (Gifford 1983). They acted as a movement again in 1980, in British Columbia, when the Social Credit government threatened to postpone a denticare program and to raise automobile insurance rates. Again, in 1985 seniors protested government policy, this time the Conservative government's plan to limit indexation of the Old Age Security and Guaranteed Income Supplement programs. This last case shows that seniors can wield power on specific occasions when they organize.

De-Indexing the Old Age Security Program: A Case Study of Senior Protest and Government Response

In the winter of 1985 the Conservative government, led by Prime Minister Brian Mulroney, faced a dilemma. On the one hand, the business community demanded that the government cut spending and reduce the national debt. On the other hand, the government was obliged, in 1985, to pay out over $11 billion in OAS and GIS pensions. This amount increases each year because the government indexes the OAS and GIS programs to the Consumer Price Index (CPI) (a measure of the cost of living). The government wanted to cut these payments to appease the business community, but the Prime Minister had committed the government to retain these universal programs.

On May 23, 1985, Finance Minister Michael Wilson tried to resolve the dilemma by introducing a federal budget that would only increase government pensions if the CPI rose more than 3 percent. The government would then only increase pensions to cover the difference between the first 3 percent rise and the actual CPI increase. (If the CPI rose 5 percent, pensioners would get only a 2 percent raise. If it rose 2.5 percent, pensioners would get no increase in their pensions.) The government projected that this change would save $1.6 billion by 1990–91. Wilson scheduled the change for January 1, 1986.

The plan brought a howl of protest from older people, interest groups, and politicians across the country. First, the plan cut the income of all older people, rich and poor. The poorest people, many of whom were living below the poverty line already, would fall deeper into poverty. Second, many older people had voted Conservative and expected Mulroney to honour his promise to leave the government pension program alone. This budget reversed his promise to treat universal programs as a "sacred trust," and many older people felt betrayed.

Seniors across the country joined together for the largest senior protest in Canadian history. They signed petitions, held news conferences, and sent letters to Parliament. Seniors also confronted politicians face to face. On June 18, 1985, seniors in Halifax confronted Finance Minister Wilson in a closed meeting and argued against de-indexation (*Globe and Mail* 1985). In the third week of June, seniors marched on Parliament Hill.

Other groups joined seniors in their protests. NDP and Liberal MPs attacked the Conservatives in Parliament daily, and some Tory MPs said that they, too, supported fully indexed pensions. The Council of Maritime Premiers united in opposition to de-indexing. Business groups and business leaders also supported the seniors. The Canadian Chamber of Commerce, the Business Council on National Issues, and the Canadian Organization of Small Business stated that the government should fully protect old age pensions and should find other ways to reduce the deficit.

Interest groups like the Advisory Council on the Status of Women and the Canadian Council of Social Development (CCSD) also protested the proposed budget changes. The CCSD predicted that the government's plan would force as many as 200,000 more older people into poverty by 1990 (Cernetig 1985).

The de-indexation protest made front-page news across the country. By mid-June, after reading a post-budget poll indicating a lack of confidence in the government, the Prime Minister promised to reevaluate the de-indexation plan. On June 27, after five weeks of pressure, the government gave in and agreed to continue indexing pensions to the rate of inflation. Finance Minister Wilson said the government rescinded the plan because the government " 'recognized the anxieties' of senior citizens" (Montgomery 1985).

This nation-wide protest teaches some lessons about senior politics in Canada. First, seniors can act as a group to change federal policy, but only if they speak with a single voice. Second, seniors can use opinion polls, the media, and direct confrontation to pressure the government. Third, seniors need to ally themselves with other power blocs in society — political parties, business, and service groups.

Studies show that senior interest groups cannot succeed by themselves, because they lack the power (Trela 1976). But they can make an issue visible and get other groups to support their cause. Middle-aged people, for example, will often support health care and income policies for older

Exhibit 14.4

EDUCATION FOR ACTION

The National Advisory Council on Aging (NACA), a federal office that gathers and disseminates information about aging, realized that older people needed to learn about political power before they could exercise it. In 1984 the NACA sponsored a program to teach older people about decision making. The Council called the program "Listen to Me!" (1985c). This program "provides an opportunity [for seniors] to study decision-making — who makes the decisions, how the process works, and how seniors might get involved" (National Advisory Council on Aging 1985d, 1). The program also exposes decision makers (civil servants, doctors, politicians) to older people's needs.

The NACA ran "Listen to Me!" workshops in five cities — Saskatoon, Fredericton, Montreal, Toronto, and Vancouver. The workshops met in three sessions. First, the seniors in the workshop chose two or three issues to study, like housing, income, or health care. They then discussed whether decision makers consulted older people about these issues. Second, the sen-

iors met with a decision maker to discuss each issue. They asked decision makers how much older people have to say about decisions on the issue. Third, seniors met again by themselves to talk about the second workshop. They decided on things they could or should do to get more involved, and they summed up their findings on senior involvement in decision making.

A follow-up study (National Advisory Council on Aging 1985c) found that 89 percent of the seniors in the workshops said they understood more about decision making after the meetings. And 94 percent said that the meetings helped prepare them for future involvement in decision making. About a third of the seniors said they began to plan for increased senior involvement in decision making. Eighty-seven percent of the seniors said they now knew more about senior needs.

Programs like "Listen to Me!" meetings play a unique role in senior politics. They give older people more information about the political system, increase their confidence, and encourage them to act.

people because middle-aged people are aware that they will be old someday themselves. Also, middle-aged children prefer to pay for services to their elderly parents through their taxes, rather than support their parents directly. Anti-poverty and women's groups will also support seniors' needs. If seniors can link their concerns with those of other groups, they will increase their political power.

GOVERNMENT AND AGING POLICY

Political participation and power both shape public policy. But political action takes place in a social and historical context. Myles (1984) says that gerontologists need to understand the history and structure of the welfare state to understand old age. "This is simply because the contemporary welfare state in the capitalist democracies is largely a *welfare state for the elderly*" (1984, 2). Programs for older people now make up the biggest part of the welfare state's budget, and attempts to cut this share, like the move to de-index OAS payments, will meet with protests from all parts of society. "The majority of the elderly," Myles 1984, 6) says, "now depend on such benefits for most of their income. The widespread reaction against benefit cuts by both young and old reflected this fact."

Myles (1984) and others (Neugarten and Havighurst 1979) predict that the state will play an even more important role in older people's lives in the future. First, the state budget will increase as the population ages. An aging population, for example, will require a redistribution of resources from younger to older people. The state will manage this transfer through taxation and government programs. The national health care system already does this, and so does the Old Age Security and Guaranteed Income Supplement program. Second, the redistribution of wealth from young people to older people will require more government planning. The government has already had to raise Canada Pension Plan payments to meet the needs of older people today, and it also has to plan for rate increases in the future to meet the needs of a growing older population.

The state has set up a range of agencies to govern the transfer of resources to older people and to plan for the future. These agencies have an ongoing effect on government policies and programs.

- The federal Office on Aging exists within the Department of Health and Welfare. It gathers facts and information about aging in Canada and advises the government on policy issues. The Office also helped produce the *Fact Book on Aging in Canada* (Health and Welfare Canada 1983) and *The Seniors Boom* (Stone and Fletcher 1986b)— two summaries of data on older people in Canada.
- The National Advisory Council on Aging (sponsor of "Listen to Me!") started in May 1980 and has eighteen members. The Council meets twice a year to counsel the Minister of Health and Welfare on issues related to seniors' quality of life. It also promotes a positive image of older people and encourages seniors to take political action. Members of the Council include researchers, members of national and provincial organizations, medical experts, seniors, and the general public. It publishes an annual report and makes recommendations to the government. The Council also publishes a quarterly newsletter called *Expression*. Each issue presents a readable review of the latest facts on aging, comments from seniors, and reports on research.

Exhibit 14.5
Provincial/Territorial Governmental Programs and Systems, 1982

	British Columbia	Alberta	Saskatchewan	Manitoba	Ontario	Quebec
			Advisory and Consultative Mechanisms			
Councils and Commissions		Provincial Senior Citizens Advisory Council(3)	Sask. Senior Citizens' Provincial Council(3)	Man. Council on Aging(1)	Ont. Advisory Council on Senior Citizens(4)	
Departmental Offices and Consultants	Consultants in Gerontology & Geriatrics(3)	Senior Citizens Bureau(3)	Provincial Gerontologist(3)	Provincial Gerontologist(3) Services to Seniors, Dept. of Health(3)		
Interdepartmental Co-ordination		Interdepartmental Co-ordinating Committee on Senior Citizens(3) Planning Committee on Programs/ Services for Older Persons*(3)	Interdepartmental Task Force(3)	Council Liaison Officers(3)	Ont. Seniors Secretariat(4)	Policy Services to Adults and Senior Citizens, Dept. of Social Affairs(1,3)

• Provincial Advisory Councils present seniors' views to provincial governments. They also assess policies and work to co-ordinate provincial programs and services for seniors. Between 1970 and 1980 five provinces set up advisory councils — Alberta, Saskatchewan, Manitoba, Ontario, and Nova Scotia. Councils write newsletters and produce information packages and directories of services for seniors (Long and Shelton 1982). Provincial governments also learn about seniors' needs from departments set up to co-ordinate seniors' programs and from senior citizens' secretariats. These agencies sometimes act as advocates for seniors in their provinces.

THE ROLE OF GOVERNMENT IN IMPROVING LIFE FOR OLDER PEOPLE

A large government deficit and a slow economy will put limits on what older people can achieve through protest and pressure groups. A policy that cuts the federal deficit, for example, will probably also cut social support programs for seniors (Neysmith 1986).

Exhibit 14.5 (Continued)
Provincial/Territorial Governmental Programs and Systems, 1982

	New Brunswick	Nova Scotia	Prince Edward Island	Newfound-land	Yukon Territory	Northwest Territories
			Advisory and Consultative Mechanisms			
Councils and Commissions		N.S. Senior Citizens' Commiss-ion(3)				
Departmental Offices and Consultants	Community Based Services for Seniors, Dept. of Social Services(3)			Division of Services to the Aging, Dept. of Social Services(4)	Division of Services to Senior Citizens, Dept. of Social Services(4)	
Interdepart-mental Co-ordination		N.S. Senior Citizens' Secre-tariat(3)				

1 — Total general population.
3 — Aged 65 and over.
4 — Aged 60 and over.

*Department of Hospitals and Medical Care and Department of Social Services and Community Health,
Numerical Key (Age Group Served by Programs or Systems).

Source: Health and Welfare Canada, *Canadian Governmental Report on Aging* (Ottawa: Minister of Supply and Services, 1982b), 161. Reproduced with permission of the Minister of Supply and Services Canada.

What can seniors do to improve programs and services under these conditions? They can make some gains by lobbying for programs that meet their needs and also save the government money. For example, seniors can support the co-ordination of government departments (Kernaghan 1982). They can support housing programs that build in recreation and health care services to keep older people out of institutions. Chappell and Penning (1979) say that programs like home care could save money and at the same time provide more humane treatment for older people. "The current trend [away from institutionalization]," they say, "seems to reflect one situation in which economic efficiency and humanism are not contradictory" (1979, 380). Seniors can look for and promote other programs and policies like health promotion and education programs that will improve seniors' quality of life.

Seniors who take an active part in lobbying, or who write briefs and letters to the government, do two things: they help create better policies for the future, and they get the government used to consulting with seniors on seniors' issues. The trend today points to more senior activism in the future. Agencies within the government, like the National Advisory Council on Aging, support and promote this new activist stance. Also, the trends in some countries toward proportional representation (a system that gives minority groups more influence in government) and referenda (votes on specific political issues) could give more power to older people, if these trends catch on in Canada. Gifford (1987) says that in "the four European countries in which pensioners have sought to form pensioners' political parties all have proportional representation systems."

Gifford (1987) also reports two other trends that may increase in the future. First, seniors may set up their own sections (similar to youth sections that already exist) within the national political parties. Seniors in the Nova Scotia New Democratic Party have already done this. Second, seniors may spend more time working as advocates for social causes. Seniors in Canada have set up groups like Veterans Against Nuclear Arms and Pensions for Peace. They also work for groups like Amnesty International, Oxfam, and environmental groups. Curtis and Lambert (1976) say that higher levels of education, better health, organizations that support activism, more free time, and the larger number of older people in the future will all lead to more senior political activism.

The study of aging and politics in Canada has just begun, and, as Pratt (1979, 186) says, "there would appear to be challenge enough here for several scholars." Current trends toward senior activism, for example, raise new questions for political scientists and gerontologists. Will new generations of seniors show the same consistency in voting patterns? Or will they shift their votes depending on the issues? Only longitudinal studies of voting can answer these questions. Will seniors become more vocal, organized, and effective in their lobbying efforts? Will they form a social movement? To answer these questions gerontologists need to know more about the structure and decision-making processes in senior political groups. Will more and more seniors turn their attention to larger social issues like environmental protection, peace, and anti-poverty campaigns? Researchers will need to study the values and commitments of new generations of seniors.

The study of politics and aging in Canada has already moved beyond the study of voting patterns. In the future, political scientists will find many new questions to ask about the political behaviour of Canada's growing and changing senior population.

SUMMARY

1. Recent studies of political activity by seniors show that people stay politically active as long as they have good health and mobility.
2. The increase in the median age of voters will likely continue in the near future and may give older voters more political power.
3. Long-standing commitments to political parties, as well as regional, cultural, and social class differences, will keep seniors from forming a single voting bloc.
4. Advocacy or pressure groups can have more effect than voting on government policy-making, but older people will have to organize to have more effect in the future.
5. Seniors' clubs throughout the country are affiliated with provincial and national associations. These groups act as advocates for older people.
6. Because the provinces take most of the responsibility for housing, health, and social service policies, senior advocacy has a provincial focus. This partly explains why seniors in Canada have never formed a powerful national lobby and why they have directed their lobbying efforts at provincial governments.
7. Seniors have joined together to protest government policy at least three times in the recent past. The most recent protest led the federal government to reverse its decision to de-index pensions. A united front, media coverage, plus the support of other influential groups helped seniors confront the government and win.
8. Seniors can influence government policies through the offices of provincial gerontologists, seniors' councils, and the National Advisory Council on Aging. They can also advocate programs that meet seniors' needs and save the government money.
9. Seniors will probably stay politically active in the future. They will also work for social causes that help all age groups.

SELECTED READINGS

Bryden, Kenneth. *Old Age Pensions and Policy-Making in Canada.* Montreal: McGill-Queen's University Press, 1974.
A case study of the politics of pension programs in Canada. The book gives the history of pension legislation, the ideologies that supported or opposed public pensions, and the reasons why Canada's pension programs look the way they do. One of the few book-length studies of public policy and aging.
Curtis, James E., and Ronald D. Lambert. "Voting, Election Interest, and Age: National Findings for English and French Canadians." *Canadian Journal of Political Science* 9 (1976):293–307.
A comparison of French Canadian and English Canadian voting patterns. One of the few recent studies that compares the two groups. The article looks at how age affects voting in each culture. The study concludes that political affiliation and organizational involvement do not decline with age.

Kernaghan, Kenneth. "Politics, Public Administration and Canada's Aging Population." *Canadian Public Policy* 8 (1982):69–79.

This article makes the point that students of aging and politics should look beyond voting patterns. Political scientists should also study the administration of public policies for older people. The article makes a case for more co-ordination between government departments that serve older people.

Kernaghan, Kenneth, and Olivia Kuper. *Coordination in Canadian Governments: A Case Study of Aging Policy.* Toronto: Institute of Public Administration of Canada, 1983.

A monograph that describes the federal and provincial government agencies involved in policy making for seniors. The monograph describes the links between agencies; the degrees of power that agencies, bureaucrats, and politicians have in the policy-making process; and the senior organizations that influence government. The authors call for co-ordination among agencies to ensure that programs for older people meet seniors' needs.

THE FUTURE OF AGING IN CANADA

INTRODUCTION

Each chapter of this book looked at aging from one point of view — demography, biology, psychology, etc. But how do these many perspectives fit together? How will changes in individual and population aging affect each of us in the future? And what new career and research issues will emerge from the study of aging? This chapter (1) reviews the changes that have taken place in aging in the past few years, (2) looks at the future of aging in Canada, and (3) looks at research issues and career options in the field of gerontology.

REVIEW

Part I: Gerontology Today

Chapter 1 of this book looked at the field of gerontology. It described gerontology as a multidisciplinary field that replaces myth with fact, fear with knowledge, and negative stereotypes with a more accurate view of old age. A review of the history of gerontology showed that the field has three dimensions: it includes biomedical research, psychosocial research, and socioeconomic research.

This book has focused on societal and individual aging in Canada. Until 1980 Canada had only a handful of gerontologists, but in the past few years researchers from many disciplines — psychology, sociology, demography, and literature (to name a few) — have all begun to study aging. Researchers bring to gerontology the theories and methods of their disciplines, but gerontologists have also learned to work together on common problems. Some gerontologists have even bridged the gap between academic research and the applied use of knowledge. They have found ways to answer the questions asked by social service and health care professionals, and still to advance theoretical understanding of aging. Gerontology today is an exciting and growing discipline.

Part II: Historical Change

The second part of this book described the history of aging in Canada and Canada's population structure today. Like most industrial societies, Canada has a falling birth rate and a falling death rate. This has had two effects on Canada's population: (1) the falling death rate means that more people than ever before are living to old age, and (2) the falling birth rate means that older people now make up a higher proportion of the population than ever before. Demographers project that these trends will continue in the future and that older people will make up 17 percent or more of Canada's total population by the middle of the next century.

Chapter 2 showed that the treatment of older people has differed from time to time, from place to place, and from one social class to another. Some societies respected their elderly; others did not. In hunting and gathering societies, for example, the demands of the environment allowed people little time or energy to care for the frail elderly. These societies sometimes abandoned or killed their older members. In agricultural societies, ownership of land ensured respect for older people, but this sometimes created psychological tension between the young and the old. The industrial revolution, urbanization, and the demographic transition all changed the meaning of aging. Older people lost the favoured place they held in agricultural society, but this change also had its positive side. Older people have more freedom today than ever before. In the developed nations, like Canada, they have more choice about how they want to live, who they want to live with, and what they want to do. At the same time that Canadian seniors work to achieve more opportunities for themselves, older people in the developing nations of Asia, Africa, and Latin America face a different set of problems. In some nations, young people have migrated from rural villages to the city. This leaves large numbers of rural older people without support from their middle-aged children. Also, in some nations workers return to their home countries in old age without pensions or savings. These problems demand new creative solutions.

Chapter 3 looked at population aging (the increased proportion of older people in the population) in Canada. Demographers study three forces that shape population aging: the rate of in-migration and out-migration, the death rate, and the birth rate. Of these three forces, the declining birth rate since the end of the Baby Boom in the early 1960s accounts for population aging: fewer births leads to a higher proportion of older people in society. If low birth rates continue, then Canadian society will age rapidly over the next fifty years.

A close look at the older population in Canada revealed many subgroups, including the old-old and the young-old, men and women, members of different ethnic groups, and people from different regions of the country. Older people in each of these subgroups have different experiences, opportunities, and needs. The old-old group, for example, needs more health care support, while the young-old group needs more recreation and employment opportunities. The growth in the number and proportion of older people in Canada explains the sudden interest in aging today. Policy makers and researchers both want to know how the increase in older people will affect the distribution of wealth, services, and jobs in society. Some research shows that older people, as a group, use more health care services than younger people. Also, an older population will draw more money from public pension funds (assuming pension rules stay the same as they are today). An older population will have fewer young people to pay the costs for these programs and services. Increases in informal supports could buffer some of these costs (for example, more family care of frail older people could help control hospital and nursing home costs). But some demographic projections show a decrease in potential availability of informal supports for future groups of older people (see Exhibit 15.1). This could lead to increased costs for formal social services, with few young people to pay the bill.

Some gerontologists and writers in the popular press predict a crisis due to population aging. They say that a small younger population will go broke trying to care for a large population of older people. Other researchers disagree. They say that Canada can adapt to changes in its population and that talk of an economic crisis due to population aging exaggerates what will take place. Canada will age gradually over the next fifty years. It will have time to prepare for an aging society, though it will have to start preparing now.

Exhibit 15.1
Index of Potential Availability of Family Support,
Canada, 1951 to 2021

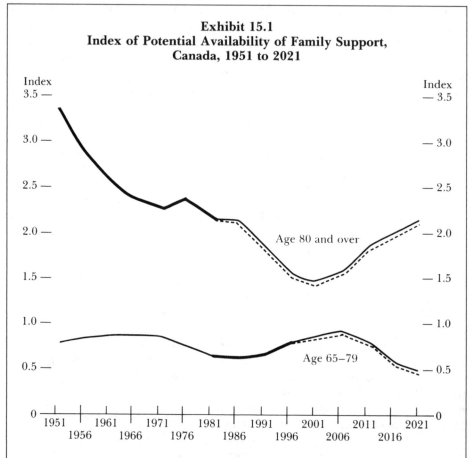

Source: Health and Welfare Canada, *Fact Book on Aging in Canada* (Ottawa: Minister
of Supply and Services, 1983), 77, Fig. 9.2. Reproduced with permission
of the Minister of Supply and Services Canada.

This table shows two measures of potential availability of support. The first is an
index for persons aged 65–79. It "is the ratio of the number of persons aged 45–
49 divided by the number aged 65–79." The second is an index for persons aged
80 and over. This "is the ratio of the number of persons aged 60–64 divided by
the number aged 80 and over (Health and Welfare Canada 1983, 77).

A decreasing birth rate could lead to a decrease in informal supports up to 2021
for people aged 65–79. At the same time the availability of familial supports will
increase for people aged 80 and over. These figures show that the oldest Canadians
will have children available to help them at a time when they need support most.
But no one can guarantee that the children of the oldest older people will give
their parents the support they need. Some children will live too far away to help
their parents, middle-aged women in the work force will have less time to give care
to their parents, and the family may not be able to provide the kinds of care needed
by the old-old. Even with family supports an aging population will probably require
more formal health care supports than does a younger population. This will mean
a need for increased formal supports in Canada in the future.

Part III: Maturational Change

Individuals, as well as societies, age. But what is aging? Is it hardening of the arteries, arthritis, Alzheimer's disease? Is it a normal process or a disease? Chapter 4 looked at the biology of aging. Biologists try to divide normal aging from accident and disease in old age, and they have found some differences between disease and normal aging. Normal changes due to aging take place over many years. For example, the shape of the eye changes, the lungs lose their elasticity, and cells take longer to rid themselves of waste. These changes show up in everyday life as slower reaction time, a decreased ability to resist stress, and an increase in chronic diseases. Gerontologists call this *senescence* — the body's decreased ability to cope with demands from the environment. Researchers say that the body declines by about 1 percent per year on average, though different systems of the body age at different rates and some people show more of the signs of aging than others. Research into the biochemistry of the cell may hold the key to defining old age and to reversing its effects in the future. For now, most people will have to adapt to the changes in physiology and health that come with age. People can change their life-styles, their environment, and their use of technology to adapt to aging.

Chapter 5 looked at psychological studies of aging. Like biologists, psychologists try to define normal aging. After many years of research, researchers still disagree about whether memory, intelligence, and crea-tivity decline with age. Some researchers argue that methods of studying psychological functioning (cross-sectional methods), test biases (questions that favour younger subjects) and speeded tests (that favour younger subjects) all produce the impression that psychological functioning de-clines with age. They say that little, if any, real psychological decline takes place with age. Other researchers disagree. They argue that cross-sec-tional and longitudinal studies both show declines on fluid intelligence measures and that studies of creativity also show declines with age. Most researchers agree that measures of intelligence, memory, or creativity say little about a person's ability to function in everyday life. First, people of the same age show varied scores on psychological tests. Age alone cannot predict a person's mental ability. Second, competence at work or in other responsible positions relies on more than memory and an IQ Score. A top manager, for example, will also need patience, experience, and wis-dom. These may all increase with age. Third, some older people show great creativity for the first time in later life (Grandma Moses), while other people continue to live creative lives into late old age (Picasso, Casals, Rubenstein). Some studies show that older people have more mental potential than they use. Sometimes they lack a sense of challenge and the chance to use their abilities. People need to use their minds in order to stay keen and alert.

Disease and discomfort cause most of the sudden and severe declines in mental ability in old age. Organic disorders include Parkinson's disease, multi-infarct dementia, and Alzheimer's disease. Functional disorders include anxiety, depression, and neuroses. Some drugs can decrease the symptoms of Parkinsonism, and some drugs and behavioural therapies can decrease the symptoms of functional disorders.

Chapter 6 looked at the development of the self in later life. Erikson (1963), Peck ([1955] 1968), Levinson (1978), and Gould (1978) all describe adult development as the passage through a series of stages. These theories emphasize the achievement of stability at each new stage. Erikson (1963), for example, describes old age as a time to accept one's self and look back on life.

The life-span developmental theory emphasizes the role of crisis and change (rather than stability) in later life. It views life as a constant process of negotiation with the environment. According to this theory, growth can take place at every stage in life, even in late old age. Growth occurs as the individual responds to the challenges of the social environment.

Kuypers and Bengtson (1973) created a model that describes the influence of society today on the individual. They call their model the "social breakdown syndrome." This model describes the way that society can undermine the psychological well-being of the older person. The model says that older people decline because others expect them to. This can lead to a breakdown in the older person's self-image and a withdrawal from social contact. When people withdraw from social life, they lose their social skills. This undermines their self-image and creates further decline. Changes in their social setting and improvement in their self-image can restore older people to competence again.

Studies of personality development show many patterns of successful aging. Some older people keep up the same activities as in their middle years, others disengage from middle-aged roles, and still others find new ways to express themselves in later life.

The research on the biology, psychology, and social psychology of aging shows that some people face new problems in old age. Illness or frailty, for example, can lead to a decrease in life-satisfaction. But the research also shows that aging (living a certain number of years) does not cause most problems in old age. Social psychologists find that negative attitudes toward older people, the loss of social roles, and the loss of social supports cause many of the problems older people face. Society cannot stop senescence, but it can stop ageism, or prejudice against older people. Society can also provide social services and health care supports for older people in need.

Part IV: Institutional Change

The fourth part of this book looked at changes in Canada's social institutions — health, income, retirement, and housing. Myles and Boyd (1982) say that social institutions like the schools, the health care system, and the pension system will all have to change to meet the needs of an older society. Some of this change has already begun.

Chapter 7 looked at the health care system. It described three models of health care: (1) the medical model, (2) the social model, and (3) the health promotion model. The medical model — based on physicians and institutions — dominates the health care system today. This system costs more to maintain each year and does not always suit the needs of older patients. An aging society will need new solutions to health care problems — solutions that may save money, but also solutions that give people the kind of care they prefer. The social model — based on community care and non-institutional treatment — can more effectively meet the chronic care needs of an older population.

Some hospitals now have day hospital programs and respite care. These programs help keep people at home and out of institutions. The shift away from institutions to community care makes sense for two reasons. First, it can save money. Community care costs less than care in a hospital. If the system can improve home care *and* cap the growth of hospital care, then home care will save money. Second, older people want to stay out of hospitals and nursing homes. Home care programs can tailor care to a person's needs.

Canada has also begun to value the health promotion model, which is based on prevention of illness. This model supports environmental improvement and lifestyle changes to improve health and decrease illness. In the future the health care system will need to increase the availability, accessibility, and co-ordination of health care.

Chapter 8 looked at Canada's pension system. The public pension system today does more for older people than pension programs in the past. Transfer payments (OAS/GIS/SA) and the CPP/QPP increase with the cost of living. This helps older people cope with inflation. The government also encourages private savings for retirement by giving younger people tax exemptions for RRSP savings. The provinces give pension supplements to the poorest older people.

Still, the system fails to meet some people's needs. Many older people — especially very old, single women — live in poverty. Widows who worked as homemakers often get little or no private pension from their husband's workplace, and they have no CPP benefits of their own. Women also earn less than men and have shorter work careers; this leads to smaller pensions for women. Poorer people, in general, have less chance to earn a decent private pension because of their low salaries and poor pension coverage.

Proposed reforms include better private pension plans, homemaker pensions and increases in the OAS/GIS/SA. These reforms will cost more money. Will Canadians pay for better pensions? Or will the system go bankrupt, as some writers predict? Gerontologists doubt that the pension system will go bankrupt in the future. First, the government pays the OAS and GIS out of general revenues. These programs cannot go bankrupt unless the country does, and if that happens, people will have more than their pensions to worry about. As long as Canadians want to support older people they can and will — though the cost will grow as the population ages.

Second, people will pay more into the Canada Pension Plan (and the Quebec Pension Plan) in the years ahead to keep up with the growing number of older pensioners. This could lead to a revolt against the CPP/QPP and its dissolution. But this seems unlikely. Middle-aged and younger people will both benefit from a national pension plan in the future when they retire. For this reason alone, younger people will probably decide to pay for public pensions even if costs go up.

Chapter 9 looked at retirement in Canada today. It showed that the majority of people retire at age 65. Most retirees leave work because of retirement rules or because of illness. Better pensions also encourage older people to leave work.

A small number of people, most of them professionals, want to stay on their jobs past age 65. Some of these people have charged that mandatory retirement rules violate their human rights, and they have challenged mandatory retirement in the courts. Some courts have agreed that mandatory retirement is illegal, while other courts have supported it. Future court cases will decide whether the Canadian Charter of Rights makes mandatory retirement illegal.

While a few people fight for the right to work, more and more people want to retire as soon as they can. Studies show that given a decent pension people will often leave work at age 60 or even 55. Studies also show that most people enjoy retirement. Many retirees start second careers, take up new hobbies and sports, or work part-time at something they enjoy. Pre-retirement education can help people plan for a satisfying retirement.

Guillemard (1977) cautions that only people with good pensions have these choices. Poorer people with broken job records, no private pensions, or low-paying jobs will not have money to travel, play golf, or buy hobby equipment. Poorer people may have to keep on working past age 65 in order to live a comfortable life. Guillemard sees a growing gap between people who retire with money and people like single older women who often live below the poverty line on government pensions. The rise in labour force participation for older women (and the decrease for men) points to this difference between people who have good pensions and those who do not. Only better pensions will give men and women an equal chance to choose the retirement they want.

Chapter 10 looked at Canada's housing system. Lawton and Nahemow (1973) described a theory of person–environment fit. This theory says that when people's environment fits their abilities they report maximum life-satisfaction. Too little environmental challenge, or too much, leads to either apathy or frustration.

An ideal housing system would offer older people housing options that fit their abilities, and it would also help older people find and live in the kind of housing that best suits their needs. The Canadian housing system today offers older people many choices about where they can live. The provinces and the federal government, for example, offer grants to help people buy a new home or repair or remodel the one they have. Provincial governments also provide seniors' housing and subsidized rents for poorer older people. Since the 1950s the provincial and federal governments have built or helped build thousands of safe, clean housing units for seniors throughout the country. Some apartment buildings now include health clinics, senior centres, dining rooms, guest suites for visitors, and greenhouses. At their best, these buildings also provide recreation and health promotion programs. These improve the quality of older people's lives. New housing programs include reverse mortgages, granny flats, and share-a-home services. The provincial and federal governments have studied and in some cases supported these programs.

The government has also studied and set up transportation systems for older people. These range from shuttle buses and volunteer taxi services in rural areas to transport brokerages and mobility clubs run by volunteers. Older people value their independence, and programs like these increase their ability to do things for themselves. However, older people still need more solutions to transportation problems, both in cities and in rural areas.

Chapter 11 looked at older people's leisure and recreation activities. Studies show that gender, marital status, health, education, and social class all determine the kinds of activities people choose to do. Older people, as a group, spend most of their time on solitary leisure activities such as reading the newspaper and watching TV. But some people engage in more strenuous activities as well. They take part in fitness programs, Seniors' Games, and outdoor recreation programs. These programs will grow in size and number in the years ahead. Also, in the future, people will come into old age with more education and will want to keep on learning. University courses for seniors have sprung up in the past few years. So has a new program called Elderhostel. These and other programs will offer people new options for personal growth in old age.

Some older people find fulfilment in volunteer work. They work in local hospitals or senior centres or travel overseas to assist developing nations. The New Horizons program has helped thousands of older people across the country find new ways to contribute to their communities. This program shows that, given the opportunity, older people can become valuable resources for others.

Chapter 12 looked at family life for older people. Research shows two trends that will continue into the future: First, married couples will live together longer than ever before due to longer life expectancies for men and women. Second, most married older women can expect to live as widows at some time in old age because women tend to marry older men and because women have a longer life expectancy than men.

The increasing number of older widows has led to another trend: more older women live alone now than ever before, and experts on the family in later life say that this trend will grow stronger in the years ahead. This trend could raise new policy issues. Women who live alone may need more formal supports as they age, and they will also rely on their children for support. Researchers have begun to study the effects of informal caregiving on the caregivers. They find that many caregivers feel burdened by their role. Caregiver support groups and respite programs may help caregivers cope with the demands of care. But in the future more caregivers of very old parents will themselves be past the age of 65, and they may also need care. Some research shows that abuse can take place when a caregiver feels overwhelmed by the demands of care. Canada needs better legislation to protect older people from abuse, support groups to help caregivers cope with stress, and education so that professionals and police know the signs of abuse.

The amount of informal and formal care people need and use depends in part on their ethnicity. The values, the size, and the age composition of a group will all determine how much support the group gives its older members. Social service agencies and professionals who work with older people need to know the ethnic backgrounds of the people they serve. They will then be able to give treatment and advice in a form that their clients can use.

Grandparenting offers one of the most satisfying roles an older person can play. Grandparenting means different things to different people. Age, health, and marital status determine how a person sees this role. Gerontologists have just begun to describe the meaning of grandparenthood.

Chapter 13 looked at death and dying today. Studies show that older people accept death more easily than younger people, but older people who have a purpose in life say they want to keep on living. Death today most often takes place in an institution. Elisabeth Kubler-Ross (1969) saw that workers in institutions often ignored dying patients. She found that doctors and nurses saw dying patients as signs of their own failure. Kubler-Ross described the stages dying patients go through. Her work led to an explosion of research and writing on, and reform in, the treatment of the dying.

Cicely Saunders (1984) also changed our way of treating dying patients. She developed a new kind of institution to care for the dying: the hospice. Hospices now exist in Canada, along with palliative care units in hospitals. These institutions only accept dying patients. They aim to make life as comfortable and enjoyable as possible for dying patients and their families. They do not use heroic measures to keep dying patients alive.

The ability to keep people alive by artificial methods has led to new ethical, legal, and social problems. Experts in medicine, philosophy, law, and the social sciences describe a new goal for science and medicine: a good death. Medicine can achieve this goal by putting limits on extreme treatment and by taking people off machines that only keep a patient alive. The medical profession has also begun respecting the patient's right to refuse further treatment. The latest thinking on death and dying respects the right of the patient to a good death. It also recognizes the needs of family members: their need to mourn and grieve for the dead. Research has led to more understanding of grieving and to new therapies for bereaved family members.

Part V: Societal Change

The sixth part of the book looked at how older people can change society. The major theories of aging today describe how people adapt to society's demands in old age. They retire when society says to retire, they disengage when society says to disengage, and they fit into the roleless role of old age or learn crafts when society tells them to. More recent models of aging question this passive view of older people.

Chapter 14 looked at politics and old age. The chapter described three measures of political participation: (1) voting behaviour, (2) advocacy, and (3) activism. Older people today engage in all three forms of political action.

1. Studies show that older people continue to vote in national elections and that they maintain an interest in public affairs. Seniors will probably never form a voting bloc that will shape government policy, but they can influence government in other ways.
2. Advocacy groups across the country lobby for lower bus fares, better tax rates, and more recognition from government. Groups include national federations and provincial councils. These groups write briefs and make presentations to federal and provincial governments.
3. Seniors in the past have taken an activist stance on several occasions. In 1985 seniors protested the de-indexation of public pensions and won.

Seniors can and do play other roles in political life. They participate in provincial seniors' councils, advise the government on policy issues, and work for global causes like world peace and environmental safety. More seniors with more education in the future will lead to more senior political activity in Canada.

THE FUTURE OF AGING IN CANADA

What do all of the findings in the previous chapters have in common? What message can a person draw from this mass of research? All of it shows that individual and population aging brings change. Individual aging leads to changes in all of the body's systems and in memory, intelligence, and social relations. Population aging leads to changes in all major social institutions. An aging society will lead to more changes in the future. It will even lead to changes in our concept of old age and changes in how individuals and society can respond to aging.

In 1981 the National Advisory Council on Aging published *Priorities for Action*. This book lists "the most urgent of the problems facing elderly people in Canada today" (National Advisory Council on Aging 1981, 5). *Priorities for Action* has three parts: (1) public education and learning opportunities, (2) health and social services for older people, and (3) retirement and income. *Priorities for Action* makes forty-eight recommendations for change. The list below presents a selection of the Council's recommendations.

Section One: Public Education and Learning Opportunities

The Council recommends that Canada:

1. Start a public information program to replace myths about old age with facts and to present a positive view of older people.
2. Start an education program for seniors that teaches daily living skills, skills to help people use their leisure, crisis management skills, and intellectual challenges.
3. Start new programs that open new roles and vocations for older people. The Council says that older people should help plan and set up these programs.

Section Two: Health and Social Services

The Council recommends that:

1. Health care and social work students should learn the facts about aging and how to care for older people's unique needs.
2. Non-professionals who work with older people should learn about aging and about how to communicate with older people.
3. The government should conduct inventories of the numbers of people working in jobs related to aging and projections of future job openings. The inventories should also include job profiles.
4. Communities should set up support services like counselling, homemaker, and visiting nurse programs to help families care for older people.
5. Communities should help seniors learn about programs they can use. Large-print phone books, seniors' handbooks, and cable TV announcements could all help older people learn about resources in their community.
6. Physicians should stop extra-billing, and the medical association should work with medicare agencies to set up more acceptable fee schedules for physicians.
7. A group, independent of government and social agencies, should promote the well-being of older people and investigate grievances on their behalf.

Section Three: Retirement Issues and Income as They Affect the Elderly

The Council recommends that:

1. The government should increase benefits to raise all older people above the poverty line.
2. The government should continue to index the OAS and GIS and should review the CPP/QPP to see that benefits keep up with inflation.
3. Employers should work to set up good pre-retirement programs and more flexible retirement programs so that workers can ease into retirement.

Gerontological research can help bring about these reforms. Research can show what older people need and how best to meet those needs. Still, some gaps exist in knowledge about aging in Canada.

FUNDING FOR RESEARCH

This book began by saying that gerontology has two goals: to learn about aging and to use that knowledge to improve life for older people. Both goals depend on research. Today Canada has more gerontologists doing more research on aging than ever before. The Strategic Grants program in Population Aging, sponsored by the Social Sciences and Humanities Research Council of Canada (SSHRCC), deserves most of the credit for this growth of gerontological research in Canada. This program sponsored aging research from 1980 until 1987. The program sponsored one of the first political science studies of aging in Canada, the first study of senior political groups, and the first social-psychological study of successful aging in Canada. These funds drew new researchers into gerontology, developed Canadian expertise in fields as varied as economics, psychology, and political science, established Canadian data banks, and built up respect for aging research in the academic community.

SSHRCC also granted seed money to five centres on aging — two in Ontario and one each in New Brunswick, Manitoba, and British Columbia. These centres (and others with other funding at Mount Saint Vincent University, the University of Victoria, and other schools) promote research on aging and co-ordinate multidisciplinary studies. Centres offer seminars, workshops, and yearly conferences that bring together researchers and direct service workers. These centres and the SSHRCC research programs need ongoing funds. SSHRCC granted start-up funds to centres on aging, but each centre then had to find its own support, either from its university or from outside sources. Hancock (1984) says that without funds from outside the university these centres on aging will close. Some centres have already started to look for new sources of support.

Changes in SSHRCC research grant policies could slow research in some fields within gerontology. A new SSHRCC policy, for example, asks universities and researchers to find funds in business and industry to match research grants. This policy will shape the kinds of research people do. Business may see little reason to fund studies of informal supports to widows, studies of social-psychological stages of aging, or studies of new education programs for seniors. Researchers might turn away from these and other worthwhile studies in the future due to lack of funds.

The federal Office on Aging and the National Advisory Council on Aging both need ongoing funding. Cuts to both groups have reduced their activities. I recently wrote to the Office on Aging to get an updated list of organizations that serve seniors in Canada. The Office said that it no longer had the resources to maintain a list of organizations. I then wrote to the National Advisory Council on Aging (NACA). The NACA said that it would try to compile a list, but that cutbacks in other agencies might make the job impossible. In the end the NACA did send me a list, but this gives an example of how cutbacks could interfere with research.

NEW DIRECTIONS IN RESEARCH

The Gerontology Research Council of Ontario (1985–86) outlined a number of high-priority research themes. These included the study of community health care, the confused elderly, and retirement planning. The National Advisory Council on Aging (1981) called for social research on family and social networks, housing and health care needs for people from different ethnic groups, and the effects of regional differences on social supports. Canada needs more research on ethnicity, mental retardation, and gender differences in old age. Only a few Canadian studies exist on politics, elder abuse, and transportation, and in some cases only government studies or agency reports exist on a topic (for example, reports on geriatric assessment units or other alternative health care programs often come from the people who design and run them). These studies need replication by independent researchers. Researchers also need to replicate past studies with different groups, under different conditions, and in different places.

Most Canadian research shows the same social-psychological bias as American research: studies focus on individual needs, life-satisfaction, and how people adapt to aging. Some Canadian researchers draw on the European tradition of political economy (Myles 1984) and historical studies of social policy (Bryden 1974). These studies open up new ways to think about aging. Canada also needs more aging research in history, literature, and the humanities. These disciplines will broaden the range of methods gerontologists use, and they also open new questions for research.

GERONTOLOGICAL EDUCATION

The Carnegie Foundation in the United States lists three educational philosophies for gerontology courses: scientific, professional, and liberal.

Exhibit 15.2

A PARTIAL LIST OF CERTIFICATE (OR DIPLOMA) GERONTOLOGY PROGRAMS IN CANADA

Connelly (1981) reports that in 1981 eight universities offered certificates in gerontology and two offered diplomas. (The terms "certificate" and "diploma" signify the same types or levels of programs.)

- Mount Saint Vincent University — Program on Gerontology. Certificate program for practitioners.
- Simon Fraser University — Diploma program in Gerontology.
- University of Calgary — Certificate in Gerontology.
- University of Quebec, Hull — Certificate in Gerontology.
- Université Laval — Gerontology Certificate Program.
- University of Manitoba — Advanced Certificate in Gerontology Program through the Continuing Education Division.
- University of Toronto — Woodsworth College diploma in Gerontology.
- Waterloo University — Certificate in Gerontology.

Hancock (1984) says that most certificate programs have a core program of courses including an overview course, psychological and sociological perspectives courses, and courses on death and dying. They all offer a multidisciplinary program and focus on normal aging and healthy older people. In most cases a centre on aging or the university division of continuing education sponsors the program.

The scientific approach focuses on research and data collection using the scientific method. The professional approach focuses on improving services to older people and solving social problems. The liberal approach focuses on teaching everyone about the process of aging and about normal human development. Some courses combine one or more of these approaches. A gerontology course for nurses, for example, might teach students about human development and also involve them in a research project. A course for undergraduates might include a discussion of sociological methods and a study of normal aging. Canadians will need all three kinds of education in the years ahead.

Gutman (1977) found that each province had at least one university that taught some courses related to gerontology. Most universities have undergraduate courses in the psychology of aging, the sociology of aging, or human development. These courses cover factual and theoretical knowledge about aging and social issues. Most courses include a study of attitudes toward older people, retirement, family life, and demography. Marcus (1980; 1978) asked thirty-seven gerontology teachers in Canada about the courses they teach. Twenty-two of her thirty respondents came from departments of social work, psychology, or sociology. She says that this "is probably a correct indication of academic interest in gerontology. Only one instructor classified himself as a gerontologist" (1980, 8).

People who work in institutions need ongoing training. Many workers — registered nurses, licensed practical nurses, and nurse's aides — got little or no special training in gerontology in the past. They need retraining that updates their knowledge of older people. Universities and community colleges offer some of this training. Large institutions like hospitals offer practical training in aging — these programs range from lectures to in-service seminars to on-site training courses.

Certificate and diploma programs also exist in universities and community colleges to upgrade workers' knowledge. Some employers subsidize employees' tuition for these programs, while other employers offer pay raises to employees who complete certificate or diploma programs. The Department of Veterans Affairs, for example, asked its para-professional counselling staff if they wanted more training in gerontology. More than 89 percent of those who answered said they did, and the same proportion wanted a diploma program. The Department then arranged with local certificate and diploma programs across the country to offer their programs at times convenient to Veterans Affairs staff (Boyce and Morgan 1982). The Department offered the program for three weeks in 1981–82 and the program led the Department to plan more training programs for middle management, senior management, and health care workers.

Medical doctors also need more gerontology education. Family doctors and internists see many older people now. Robertson (1981) projects that in the future older people will make up more than half the patients these doctors see. A 1977 Canadian report says that medical students should study gerontology and geriatric medicine each year in school. The report suggested 100 hours of instruction over four years (Health and Welfare Canada 1977a). Robertson (1981, 371) found that in 1979 only fourteen of Canada's sixteen medical schools "offered at least two hours of didactic teaching in gerontology, geriatric medicine or geriatric psychiatry" and that few schools offered teaching in clinical geriatric medicine. Robertson found that only one university required that medical students do clinical work in geriatric medicine in their third and fourth years.

Canada needs to train more researchers, academics, and health care workers in gerontology. Right now, most gerontology education takes place on the job or in post-graduate certificate and diploma programs. Rarely does gerontology education lead to more pay or a raise in job status. Most people take these programs out of personal interest and often at their own expense. People who work as nurse's aides, orderlies,

Exhibit 15.3

AN ADVANCED CERTIFICATE IN GERONTOLOGY PROGRAM

The University of Manitoba offers an Advanced Certificate in Gerontology. It accepts students with a Bachelor's degree (or an equivalent post-secondary degree) and at least one year of experience working with older people. The program does not train people in direct service delivery. It teaches gerontological concepts and focuses on the literature and research in the field. The program enrols about thirty students each year. Students complete the program in two to four years of part-time work.

Most students in the program work as nurses in nursing homes and hospitals. A smaller proportion of students have backgrounds in social work, dentistry, recreation, or teaching. Classes allow people from many professions to learn together and to share their knowledge. The structure of this program gives some idea of what certificate programs offer and what they expect from students.

Core Courses

Gerontology I: The Aging Individual (40 hours of classroom instruction). This course includes four modules: demographics and current issues; geriatrics; health; and psychology of aging.

Gerontology II: Aging and Society (40 hours). This course includes four modules: methodological issues; sociology of aging; social systems and aging; and social policies.

Theories and Skills of Helping (40 hours). This course gives students basic human relations skills. It applies these skills to issues students face in health and social service settings.

Research Methods for the Consumer (20 hours). This course shows practitioners how to read the gerontology literature critically.

Electives

Four electives (20 hours each; total 80 hours). Electives change from year to year. They include: Women and Aging; Geriatric Psychiatry; Drugs and the Elderly; Death and Dying; Legal Issues; and The Family in Later Life.

Independent Research Project (50 hours of supervised research). A research project completed under the guidance of a faculty advisor.

Most graduates from this program report increased awareness of aging, improved relations with their clients (or patients), and a better understanding of aging in their own lives. Some graduates report increases in pay, promotions, and new career opportunities as a result of taking this program.

Source: Continuing Education Division, *Advanced Certificate in Gerontology Program Calendar* (Winnipeg: University of Manitoba, 1987).

and paid homemakers receive low salaries and have the least formal gerontological education. These workers need encouragement and in some cases financial support before they will attend gerontology programs. Employers and the government should support gerontology education so that workers in the field get the knowledge they need.

OCCUPATIONS AND CAREERS IN GERONTOLOGY

Direct service, administrative, and para-professional positions in gerontology will all increase in the future. Health and Welfare Canada (1985a) reports that the number of registered nurses and orderlies in Canada increased by 50 percent from 1974 to 1984, the number of occupational therapists and physiotherapists increased by over 70 percent, and the number of physicians increased by 33 percent in that same time. Not all of these health care workers work only with older people, but many of them do, and more of them will work with older people in the future. Canada will need to train more social workers, nurses, nurse's aides, physiotherapists, physicians, and counsellors in the years ahead.

Students with a Bachelor of Arts degree and a course or two in aging will have a difficult time finding work in gerontology. Students with graduate training in an established discipline like psychology, sociology, or social work will find more opportunities. Social work and the health care professions (nursing, physiotherapy) offer the easiest access to work with older people. A master's degree in social work or a bachelor's degree in nursing open many jobs. A graduate degree in public health or administrative studies can lead to government work designing or administering programs for older people. Some graduates with entrepreneurial drive may start businesses that serve older people. A student with a graduate degree, for example, could consult with major corporations on retirement education or staff training.

THE FUTURE OF GERONTOLOGY

Gerontologists in the future will learn more about aging, and their research will shape social policy. Their research will also help with "the most difficult challenge of all: re-connecting with 'aging' and re-inserting seniors in all dimensions of community life" (Begin 1985, 196). Gerontology can change people's attitudes to aging and give people more knowledge about their families, their friends, and themselves. An incident in my own life made this clear to me.

After my father's funeral, my mother, my sister, my father's brothers, and I got into a rented limousine and drove to the cemetery. The funeral director stopped the cars in the funeral procession at the cemetery gate. We saw the hearse pull ahead and stop a hundred yards away. I turned around to talk to one of my uncles in our car. A few minutes later the director waved all the cars on. We stopped behind the hearse and got out. It was empty. The director led us to the graveside. We stood close to the grave, but we could not see the coffin or any dirt. A blanket of fake grass covered the dirt that had come from the grave. Another blanket covered the coffin. Relatives and friends gathered to the side and behind us. The director said some prayers and a few kind words. My mother, my sister, and I stood and stared at the fake grass. I think we were supposed to leave. But I motioned to the director to pull the grass back. He looked surprised. I told him to pull the grass back. He did. We saw the corner of the coffin and the corner of the grave, and we started to cry.

I tell this story because my knowledge of aging and death and dying gave me the confidence to act. I felt I should do something, and I knew what I had to do. I find that I use my knowledge of aging in dozens of ways each day. I use it to understand my family and friends better and to understand the kinds of changes we go through as we age. Knowledge about aging allows me to plan for my own future without fear and denial. The study of aging can make old age a better time of life for each of us and for the people we love.

SUMMARY

1. Gerontology is a multidisciplinary field that works to replace myth with fact, fear with knowledge, and confusion with understanding. This will create a better old age for everyone.
2. The increased number and greater proportion of older people in the Canadian population will increase demands on social and health care services. Careful planning now will prevent crises and problems in the future.
3. Biological decline takes place with age, and some psychological abilities may also decline, but older people cope with most of these changes and report high life-satisfaction.
4. The health care system will need to change to meet the needs of an aging society. Some of this change has already begun. The health care system now offers older people more community care programs. These programs benefit older people who want to stay in their own homes. Health promotion programs aim to keep people well throughout their lives. Community care and health promotion will create a more efficient and effective health care system in the future.
5. As the population ages, demands on the Canada Pension Plan and on public pension programs will increase. Younger people will probably support these costs, because they will eventually benefit from a strong pension system. Better pensions will allow people more choice about when to retire and what they will do in retirement. Poorer people, including many single older women, have small pensions and fewer options in retirement. The system needs reform to bring these people up to a decent standard of living.

6. Varied housing options allow people to find an environment that suits their ability. New housing options like granny flats and home-sharing give people even more choice. Better transportation allows people to stay in contact with friends and neighbours and to make use of community resources.

7. Recreation and education programs allow people to give their own meaning to later life. The government has supported the development of new programs for seniors, and seniors themselves run these programs. Seniors today have begun to define old age as a time of personal growth and community service.

8. Longer life expectancy is changing family life. Couples will live together longer. Also, widowhood has become an expectable life event for older women. Older people have more independence from their children today, but they still rely on their children and help their children in times of need. More older people than ever before will become grandparents. People will define this role in a way that fits their age, lifestyle, and personality.

9. Modern technology raises ethical and social problems about when, how, and where people will die. New programs like palliative care units and hospices allow people to die without indignity and fear of pain. These programs also help family members cope with the loss of a parent or spouse.

10. Many older people have begun to take a more active part in political and social reform. They belong to advocacy groups, serve on provincial councils, and protest unpopular policies. Better-educated, politically active older people will continue to redefine old age in the future.

11. Researchers study a wide range of gerontological topics, but many questions about aging still remain. Centres on aging throughout the country serve as nuclei for future research on aging. These centres and researchers will need more research funds to carry out their work.

12. Most universities in Canada offer one or more courses related to gerontology. Some schools offer post-graduate certificate or diploma programs. Professionals who work with older people also need on-going training. Gerontology programs and training programs should give professionals a broad interdisciplinary view of later life.

13. Medical doctors and medical students need more knowledge of gerontology and geriatric medicine, because they will see more older patients in the coming years. Health care workers, like nurses and activity workers, also need more training, because they have the most contact with older patients. They often have no incentive, other than personal interest, to get extra training in gerontology. Pay raises linked to continuing education and tuition support for continuing education programs would encourage professionals to learn more about aging.

14. In the future, Canada will need more personnel to work with older

people. People in the health care and social service professions will have the best chance to work with seniors.

15. Knowledge of aging will help you, your friends, and your family to live a good old age.

SELECTED READINGS

Begin, Monique. "The New Society: On Aging and Seniors as an Enrichment to Civilization." In *Canadian Gerontological Collection V*, ed. Ellen M. Gee and Gloria M. Gutman. Winnipeg: Canadian Association on Gerontology, 1985.

APPENDIX

SOURCES OF INFORMATION ON AGING IN CANADA

Seniors' organizations, provincial government departments, and federal government agencies exist to serve seniors throughout the country. Below you will find a small sample of these groups. They fit into five categories: (1) federal government, (2) provincial government, (3) national non-government, (4) provincial non-government, and (5) univerisities. Contact one of these groups if you need more information about a topic.

GOVERNMENT AGENCIES FOR THE ELDERLY

These addresses for federal and provincial government departments were taken from the October/November/December 1986 edition of the *Corpus Administrative Index*, which is published quarterly and is available at main city libraries.

Because government departments frequently change, the listings here should be used as a guideline for what is available, and any required addresses should be checked in the most recent *Index*.

Federal

Canada Mortgage and Housing Corporation, 682 Montreal Road, OTTAWA, Ontario K1A OP7

Canada Pension Plan — Info, P.O. Box 5400, Postal Station D, SCARBOROUGH, Ontario M1R 5E8

Canadian Pension Commission, Daniel J. MacDonald Building, P.O. Box 9900, CHARLOTTETOWN, Prince Edward Island C1A 8V6

Consumer and Corporate Affairs Canada, Consumer Bureau, Phase I, 17th Floor, Zone 5, 50 Victoria Street, HULL, Quebec K1A 0C9

Fitness Development Division, Fitness Canada, Office of the Minister of State for Fitness and Amateur Sport, Room 274, House of Commons, OTTAWA, Ontario K1A 0A6

Health and Welfare Canada, Room 1132, Brooke Claxton Building, Tunney's Pasture, OTTAWA, Ontario K1A OK9

Labour Canada, Policy and Strategic Analysis, 165 Hotel de Ville, 7th Floor, Phase II, Place du Portage, OTTAWA, Ontario K1A 0J2

National Advisory Council on Aging, Health and Welfare Canada, Brooke Claxton Building, OTTAWA, Ontario K1A OK9

National Council of Welfare, Health and Welfare Canada, Room 566, Brooke Claxton Building, OTTAWA, Ontario K1A OK9

New Horizons, Social Service Programs Branch, Health and Welfare Canada, Brooke Claxton Building, OTTAWA, Ontario K1A 0K9

Office on Aging, Policy, Planning and Information Branch, Health and Welfare Canada, Tunney's Pasture, OTTAWA, Ontario K1A OK9

Participaction, P.O. Box 64, 40 Dundas Street West, Suite 220, TORONTO, Ontario M5G 2C2

Statistics Canada, Population Studies Division, 8-D1, Jean-Talon Building, Tunney's Pasture, OTTAWA, Ontario K1A 0T6

Veterans Affairs Canada, East Memorial Building, Lyon and Wellington Streets, OTTAWA, Ontario K1A 0P4

Provincial

Newfoundland

Community Recreation, Sport and Fitness Division, Department of Culture, Recreation and Youth, Confederation Complex Extension, Prince Philip Drive, ST. JOHN'S, Newfoundland A1C 5T7

Department of Health, Confederation Building, ST. JOHN'S, Newfoundland A1C 5T7

Department of Social Services, P.O. Box 4750, ST. JOHN'S, Newfoundland A1C 5T7

Prince Edward Island

Department of Health and Social Services, Sullivan Building, 16 Fitzroy Street, P.O. Box 2000, CHARLOTTETOWN, Prince Edward Island C1A 7N8

Program and Services Branch, Department of Education, Shaw Building, 95 Rochford Street, P.O. Box 2000, CHARLOTTETOWN, Prince Edward Island C1A 7N8

Nova Scotia

Department of Culture, Recreation and Fitness, Terminal Building, 8th Floor, P.O. Box 864, HALIFAX, Nova Scotia B3J 2V2

Department of Health, Joseph Howe Building, P.O. Box 488, HALIFAX, Nova Scotia B3J 2R8

Department of Housing, P.O. Box 185, DARTMOUTH, Nova Scotia B2Y 3Z3

Department of Social Services, Family Benefits Division, Senior Citizens Financial Aid Programs, Johnston Building, Prince Street, P.O. Box 696, HALIFAX, Nova Scotia B3J 2T7

Health Services and Insurance Commission, P.O. Box 760, HALIFAX, Nova Scotia B3J 2V2

Nova Scotia Senior Citizens Commission, Department of Social Services, P.O. Box 696, HALIFAX, Nova Scotia B3J 2T7

Pensions Division, Department of Finance, P.O. Box 187, Provincial Building, Hollis Street, HALIFAX, Nova Scotia B3J 2N3

Senior Citizens Secretariat, 1740 Granville Street, HALIFAX, Nova Scotia B3J 1X3

New Brunswick

Department of Health and Community Services, Community Health Services Division, Carleton Place, P.O. Box 6000, FREDERICTON, New Brunswick E3B 5H1

Department of Social Services, P.O. Box 6000, FREDERICTON, New Brunswick E3B 5H1

New Brunswick Housing Corporation, P.O. Box 611, FREDERICTON, New Brunswick E3B 5B2

Quebec

Ministère de la Santé et des Services Sociaux, Politiques de services sociaux, 1075 Chem Ste. Foy, QUÉBEC, Québec G1S 2M1

Developpement des Secteurs de Loisir et Programmes à la Jeunesse, Ministère du Loisir, de la Chasse et de la Pêche, 150 boul. St. Cyrille est, QUÉBEC, Québec G1R 4Y3

Ontario

Community Health, Health Promotion Branch, Ministry of Health, 8th Floor, 56 Wellesley Street West, TORONTO, Ontario M7A 2B7

Community Health Programs Branch, Ministry of Health, 15 Overlea Boulevard, 6th Floor, TORONTO, Ontario M4H 1A9

Ministry of Community and Social Services, Hepburn Block, 80 Grosvenor Street, TORONTO, Ontario M7A 1E9

Ontario Advisory Council on Senior Citizens, 700 Bay Street, 2nd Floor, TORONTO, Ontario M5G 1Z6

Ontario Ministry of Housing, 777 Bay Street, 2nd Floor, TORONTO, Ontario M5G 2E5

Senior Citizens Affairs, Ferguson Block, 12th Floor, 77 Wellesley Street West, TORONTO, Ontario M7A 1N3

Seniors Secretariat, 700 Bay Street, TORONTO, Ontario M5G 1Z6

Sports and Fitness Branch, Ministry of Tourism and Recreation, 77 Bloor Street West, TORONTO, Ontario M7A 2R9

Manitoba

Administrative Services Division, Department of Health, Medical Supplies and Home Care Equipment, 1500 Regent Avenue, WINNIPEG, Manitoba R3G 0N6

Fitness Development Section, Community Health Services Division, Department of Health, 175 Hargrave Street, 7th Floor, WINNIPEG, Manitoba R3C 0V8

Manitoba Council on Aging, Department of Health, 175 Hargrave Street, 7th Floor, WINNIPEG, Manitoba R3C 0V8

Manitoba Culture, Heritage and Recreation, 177 Lombard Avenue, 2nd Floor, WINNIPEG, Manitoba R3B 0W5

Manitoba Department of Health, 7—175 Hargrave Street, WINNIPEG, Manitoba R3C 0V8

Manitoba Health Services Commission, 599 Empress Street, WINNIPEG, Manitoba R3T 2T6

Manitoba Housing and Renewal Corporation, Department of Housing, 287 Broadway Avenue, WINNIPEG, Manitoba R3C 0R9

Office of Continuing Care, Government of Manitoba, Department of Health, 831 Portage Avenue, WINNIPEG, Manitoba R3G 0N6

Provincial Gerontologist, Department of Health, 175 Hargrave Street, 7th Floor, WINNIPEG, Manitoba R3C 0V8

Service to Seniors Section, Community Health Services Division, Department of Health, 831 Portage Avenue, WINNIPEG, Manitoba R3G 0N6

Saskatchewan

Community Health Services Branch, Department of Health, T.C. Douglas Building, 3475 Albert Street, REGINA, Saskatchewan S4S 6X6

Continuing Care, Home Care and Support Services, Saskatchewan Social Services, 1920 Broad Street, REGINA, Saskatchewan S4P 3V6

Saskatchewan Department of Health, 3475 Albert Street, REGINA, Saskatchewan S4S 6X6

Saskatchewan Housing Corporation, 800 Chestermere Plaza, 2500 Victoria Avenue, REGINA, Saskatchewan S4P 3V6

Saskatchewan Social Services, 1920 Broad Street, REGINA, Saskatchewan S4P 3V6

Senior Citizens Home Repair Program, Housing Programs, 2500 Victoria Street, 8th Floor, REGINA, Saskatchewan S4P 3V7

Senior Citizens Provincial Council, Humford House, 6th Floor, 1855 Victoria Avenue, REGINA, Saskatchewan S4P 3V8

Seniors Bureau, 1920 Broad Street, 14th Floor, REGINA, Saskatchewan S4P 3V6

Alberta

Alberta Hospitals and Medical Care, Hys Centre, 7th Floor, 11010—101 Street, P.O. Box 2222, EDMONTON, Alberta T5H 2T1

Department of Consumer and Corporate Affairs, 12—22nd Floor, 10025 Jasper Avenue, EDMONTON, Alberta T5J 3Z5

Department of Recreation and Parks, Standard Life Centre, 10405 Jasper Avenue, EDMONTON, Alberta T5J 3N4

Department of Social Services, Seventh Street Plaza, 2nd Floor, 10030—107 Street, EDMONTON, Alberta T5J 3E4

Family and Community Support, Community and Occupational Health, 10030—107 Street, EDMONTON, Alberta T5J 3E4

Health Care Insurance Division, Department of Hospitals and Medical Care, 118 Avenue and Groat Road, P.O. Box 1360, EDMONTON, Alberta T5J 2N3

Home Improvement Branch, Dept. of Municipal Affairs and Housing, Devonian Building, Main Floor, 11156 Jasper Avenue, EDMONTON, Alberta T5K 0L1

Income Security Program, Income, Rehabilitation and Day Programs, Policy and Program Development, Department of Social Services, Seventh Street Plaza, 10030—107 Street, EDMONTON, Alberta T5J 3E4

Northwest Territories

Northwest Territories Department of Social Services, Aged and Handicapped Services, P.O. Box 1320, YELLOWKNIFE, Northwest Territories X1A 2L9

North West Territories Housing Corp., Board of Directors, P.O. Box 2100, YELLOWKNIFE, Northwest Territories X1A 2P6

Program Policy Officer, Programs and Standards Division, Department of Health, Government of the Northwest Territories, P.O. Box 1320, YELLOWKNIFE, Northwest Territories X1A 2L9

Sport and Recreational Division, Department of Municipal and Community Affairs, P.O. Box 1320, YELLOWKNIFE, Northwest Territories X1A 2L9

NON-GOVERNMENT GROUPS AND ORGANIZATIONS

National

Alzheimer Society of Canada, 491 Lawrence Avenue West, TORONTO, Ontario M5M 1C6

Arthritis Society, Administration Office, 250 Bloor Street East, TORONTO, Ontario M4W 3P2

Association of Canadian Pension Management, 2 Bloor Street West, TORONTO, Ontario M4W 3E2

Canada Fitness Survey, 506—294 Albert Street, OTTAWA, Ontario K1P 6A9

Canadian Association for Adult Education, 29 Prince Arthur Avenue, TORONTO, Ontario M5R 1B2

Canadian Association of Retired Persons, 27 Queen Street East, TORONTO, Ontario M5C 1R5

Canadian Association on Gerontology, 1080—167 Lombard Avenue, WINNIPEG, Manitoba R3B 0T6

Canadian Geriatrics Research Society, 351 Christie Street, TORONTO, Ontario M6G 3C3

Canadian Institute of Religion and Gerontology, 40 St. Clair Avenue East, TORONTO, Ontario M4T 1M9

Canadian Long Term Care Association, 204—134 York Street, OTTAWA, Ontario K1N 5T4

Canadian Pension Conference, 121 Bloor Street East, TORONTO, Ontario M4W 1B8

Canadian Pensioners Concerned, Inc., 7001 Mumford Road, HALIFAX, Nova Scotia B3L 4P1

The Canadian Stroke Recovery Association, National Office, 170 The Donway, Suite 122A, DON MILLS, Ontario M3C 2G3

Elderhostel, Corbett House, 29 Prince Arthur Street, TORONTO, Ontario M5R 1B2

National Pensioners and Senior Citizens Federation, 3033 Lake Shore Boulevard West, TORONTO, Ontario M8V 1K5

Victorian Order of Nurses for Canada, National Office, 5 Blackburn Avenue, OTTAWA, Ontario K1N 8A2

Provincial

Nova Scotia

Associated Homes for Special Care (Nova Scotia), 1526 Dresden Row, HALIFAX, Nova Scotia B3J 2K2

Canadian Pensioners Concerned Inc., Nova Scotia Division, Tower 1, Suite 103, Halifax Shopping Centre, 7001 Mumford Road, HALIFAX, Nova Scotia B3L 2H9

Nova Scotia Association of Health Organizations, 5614 Fenwick Street, HALIFAX, Nova Scotia B3H 1P9

Senior Citizens Information Line, 2156 Brunswick Street, HALIFAX, Nova Scotia B3K 2Y4

Seniors Educational Health Program, 13 Windmill Road, DARTMOUTH, Nova Scotia B3A 1C6

New Brunswick

New Brunswick Association of Nursing Homes, Inc., 132 Rue Principale, FREDERICTON, New Brunswick E3A 1C7

New Brunswick Housing Corp., Head Office, Bird Building, Industrial Park, FREDERICTON, New Brunswick

New Brunswick Senior Citizens Federation, 95 Foundry, MONCTON, New Brunswick E1C 5H7

Quebec

Association Québecoise pour la Défense des Droits des Retraités et Pre-Retraités, 1850 rue Bercy, MONTRÉAL, Québec H2K 2T9

Fédération de l'Age d'Or du Québec, 4545 Pierre-de-Coubertin Avenue, MONTRÉAL, Québec H1V 3N7

Regie de l'Assurance-Maladie du Québec, 1125 Ch. St.-Louis Sillery, QUÉBEC, Québec G1S 1H4

Ontario

Baycrest Centre for Geriatric Care, 3560 Bathurst Street, TORONTO, Ontario M6A 2E1

Canadian Labour Congress, 15 Gervais Drive, TORONTO, Ontario M3G 1Y8

Canadian Pensioners Concerned Inc., Ontario Division, 51 Bond Street, TORONTO, Ontario M5B 1X1

Gerontology Research Council of Ontario, 88 Maplewood Avenue, HAMILTON, Ontario L8M 1W9

Help the Aged, 287 Eglinton Avenue East, TORONTO, Ontario M4P 1L3

J.W. Crane Library of Geriatrics and Gerontology, 351 Christie Street, 2nd Floor, TORONTO, Ontario M6G 3C3

Ontario Senior Citizens League, 600 Bay Street, TORONTO, Ontario M5G 1M6

Ontario Social Development Council, Committee on Aging, 60 Bloor Street West, TORONTO, Ontario M4W 3B8

Palliative Care Foundation, 33 Prince Arthur Avenue, TORONTO, Ontario M5R 1B2

RAISE, Home Support Service for the Elderly, 115 Water St. North KITCHENER, Ontario M2H 5B1

Senior Citizen Council of Ottawa-Carleton, Information and Referral, 509—294 Albert Street, OTTAWA, Ontario K1P 6E6

Seniors Employment Bureau, 307—63 Sparks Street, OTTAWA, Ontario K1P 5A6

Seniors Outreach Services Glebe Centre, Inc., 950 Bank Street, OTTAWA, Ontario K1S 3W7

United Senior Citizens of Ontario Inc., 3033 Lake Shore Blvd. West, TORONTO, Ontario M8V 1K5

Manitoba

Age and Opportunity Centre Inc. (also Senior Citizens Information Service), 304—323 Portage Avenue, WINNIPEG, Manitoba R3B 2C1

Alzheimer Family Resource Centre, B—170 Hargrave Street, WINNIPEG, Manitoba R3C 3H4

Commission on Aging, Jewish Community Council, 370 Hargrave Street, 2nd Floor, WINNIPEG, Manitoba R3B 2K1

Creative Retirement Manitoba, 185 Smith Street, 21st Floor, WINNIPEG, Manitoba R3C 3G4

Manitoba Association of Gerontology, 320 Sherbrook Street, WINNIPEG, Manitoba R3B 2W6

Manitoba Health Organizations Inc., 360 Broadway, WINNIPEG, Manitoba R3C 0S9

Manitoba Society of Seniors, 1102 Childs Building, 211 Portage Avenue, WINNIPEG, Manitoba R3B 2A2

Senior Citizens Job Bureau, 300—323 Portage Avenue, WINNIPEG, Manitoba R3B 2C1

Saskatchewan

Saskatchewan Association of Special Care Homes, 2—150 Albert Street, REGINA, Saskatchewan S4P 2S4

Saskatchewan Co-Ordinating Council on Social Planning, 314—220 Third Avenue South, SASKATOON, Saskatchewan S7K 1M1

Saskatchewan Health Care Association, 1445 Park Street, REGINA, Saskatchewan S4N 4C5

Senior Citizens "Action Now" Association, 808A—20th Street West, SASKATOON, Saskatchewan S7M 0Y2

Senior Citizens Provincial Council, 1855 Victoria Avenue, REGINA, Saskatchewan S4P 0R2

Senior Citizens Service, 1517—11th Avenue, REGINA, Saskatchewan S4P 0H3

Alberta

Alberta Association on Gerontology, 810 General Services Building, University of Alberta, EDMONTON, Alberta T6G 2H1

Alberta Council on Aging, 390—10665 Jasper Avenue, EDMONTON, Alberta T5J 3S9

Alberta Senior Citizens Sports and Recreation Centre, 890—1520 4th Street S.W., CALGARY, Alberta T2R 0Y3

Senior Citizens Advice and Information, Kirby Centre, 1133—7 Avenue S.W., CALGARY, Alberta T2P 1B2

British Columbia

British Columbia Health Association, 1985 West Broadway, VANCOUVER, British Columbia V6J 4Y3

British Columbia Long Term Care Association, 205—4255 Arbutus Street, Arbutus Village Square, VANCOUVER, British Columbia V6J 4R1

Health Services Research and Development, 400—2194 Health Sciences Mall, VANCOUVER, British Columbia V6T 1Z6

Old Age Information, Information Services of B.C., 3102 Main Street, VANCOUVER, British Columbia V5T 3G6

Seniors Alcoholism and Drug Rehabilitation Society, 411 Dunsmuir Street, VANCOUVER, British Columbia V6B 1X4

Social Planning Research Council of British Columbia, 106—2182 West 12th Avenue, VANCOUVER, British Columbia V6K 2N4

Vancouver Homesharers' Society, 105—2182 West 12th Street, VANCOUVER, British Columbia V6J 2G3

Victoria Institute of Gerontology, 841 Fairfield Road, VICTORIA, British Columbia V8V 3B6

UNIVERSITIES

This is a partial listing of the programs and courses concerning the elderly which are offered in Canadian universities. Check with your local university for more information.

Newfoundland

Gerontology Centre, Memorial University, ST. JOHN'S, Newfoundland A1B 3X9

Newfoundland & Labrador Association for the Aging, Memorial University of Newfoundland, ST. JOHN'S, Newfoundland A1C 5S7

Nova Scotia

Gerontology Association of Nova Scotia, c/o Mount Saint Vincent University, Bedford Highway, HALIFAX, Nova Scotia B3M 2J6

Programme in Gerontology, Mount Saint Vincent University, 166 Bedford Highway, HALIFAX, Nova Scotia B3M 2J6

New Brunswick

Centre d'études du vieillissement, Université de Moncton, MONCTON, New Brunswick E1A 3E9

Quebec

Certificat de Gerontologie, Université de Montréal, Chemin Queen Mary, C.P. 6128 Succursale A, MONTRÉAL, Québec H3C 3J7

Comité d'action gerontologique, Association des anciens de l'Université Laval, Pavillon Lacerte, Université Lavel, STE. FOY, Québec G1K 7P4

Groupe Multidisciplinaire de Récherche en Gerontologie, Université de Sherbrooke, SHERBROOKE, Québec J1K 2R1

Laboratoire de Gerontologie de l'Université Laval, Pavillon Roninck, Chambre 2467, Cité Universitaire, QUÉBEC, Québec G1K 7P4

Ontario

Centre for Gerontological Studies, Divinity College, McMaster University, 1280 Main Street West, Room 221, HAMILTON, Ontario L8S 4M2

Gerontology Research Centre, University of Guelph, GUELPH, Ontario N1G 2W1

Humber College Gerontology Program, Continuing Education, Health Sciences Division, Humber College, REXDALE, Ontario M9W 5L7

Office on Aging, Togo Salmon Hall, McMaster University, 1280 Main Street West, Room 308, HAMILTON, Ontario L8S 4M2

Ontario Gerontology Association, c/o. Dept. of Statistics, University of Waterloo, WATERLOO, Ontario N2L 3G1

Program in Gerontology, University of Waterloo, WATERLOO, Ontario N2L 3G1

Programme in Gerontology, University of Toronto, 455 Spadina Avenue, Room 407, TORONTO, Ontario M5S 1A1

R. Samuel McLaughlin Centre for Gerontological Health Research, Faculty of Health Sciences, McMaster University, 1200 Main Street West, Room 2C10, HAMILTON, Ontario L8N 3Z5

Ryerson Polytechnical Institute, Seniors Studies, Continuing Education, 50 Gould Street, TORONTO, Ontario M5B 1E8

Third Age Learning Associates (TALA), Glendon College, Bayview Avenue, TORONTO, Ontario M4N 3M6

Manitoba

Centre on Aging, University of Manitoba, 338 Isbister Building, WINNIPEG, Manitoba R3T 2N2

University of Manitoba, Advanced Certificate Gerontology Program, Continuing Education Division, WINNIPEG, Manitoba R3T 2N2

Alberta

University of Calgary, Gerontology Certificate Program, 2500 University Drive N.W., CALGARY, Alberta T2N 1N4

British Columbia

Committee on Gerontology, University of British Columbia, VANCOUVER, British Columbia V6T 1W5

Gerontology Research Centre, Simon Fraser University, Program in Gerontology, BURNABY, British Columbia V5A 1S6

REFERENCES

*1, 9 Abercrombie, Nicholas, Stephen Hill, and Bryan S. Turner
1984 *The Penguin Dictionary of Sociology*. Harmondsworth, England: Penguin.

6 Abrahams, R.
1972 "Mutual Help for the Widowed." *Social Work* 19:54–61.

12 Abu-Laban, Sharon McIrvin
1978 "The Family Life of Older Canadians." *Canadian Home Economics Journal* 28:16–25.

12 Abu-Laban, Sharon McIrvin
1980a "The Family Life of Older Canadians." In *Aging in Canada*, ed. Victor W. Marshall. Toronto: Fitzhenry and Whiteside.

12 Abu-Laban, Sharon McIrvin
1980b "Social Supports in Older Age: The Need for New Research Directions." *Essence* 4:195–209.

2 Achenbaum, A., and P.N. Stearns
1978 "Old Age and Modernization." *The Gerontologist* 18:307–12.

9 Adams, O.B., and L.A. Lefebvre
1980 *Retirement and Mortality: An Examination of Mortality in a Group of Retired Canadians*. Cat. No. 83–521E. Ottawa: Minister of Supply and Services.

11 Age and Opportunity, Inc.
1983a *Annual Report*. Winnipeg: Age and Opportunity, Inc.

11 Age and Opportunity, Inc.
1983b *Working Arrangements Between Staff and Senior Centre Membership Organizations*. Winnipeg: Age and Opportunity, Inc.

13 Ajemian, Ina, and Balfour M. Mount, eds.
1981 *The R.V.H. Manual on Palliative/Hospice Care*. New York: Arno Press.

5 Alberta Senior Citizens Bureau
1982 *Older Persons in Alberta: Their Use of Programs and Services*. Edmonton: Alberta Social Services and Community Health.

---

*Numbers indicate the chapter(s) where this source is cited.

7   Alberta Senior Citizen's Bureau
     1984 *Older Persons in Alberta: Their Use of Programs and Services 1984*. Edmonton: Alberta Social Services and Community Health.

5   Alpaugh, Patricia K., and J.E. Birren
     1977 "Variables Affecting Creative Contributions Across the Adult Life Span." *Human Development* 20:240–48.

8   Amiel, Barbara
     1981 "Trouble in Tomorrowland: Ottawa Wants Action on Pension Reform, But Business Wants to Know Who Pays." *Maclean's* 94 (April 13):44–46.

2   Amoss, P.T., and S. Harrell
     1981 "Introduction: An Anthropological Perspective on Aging. In *Other Ways of Growing Old: Anthropological Perspectives*, ed. P.T. Amoss and S. Harrell. Stanford, California: Stanford University Press.

9   Anderson, Kathryn, Robert L. Clark, and Thomas Johnson
     1980 "Retirement in Dual-Career Families." In *Retirement Policy in an Aging Society*, ed. Robert L. Clark. Durham, N.C.: Duke University Press.

5   Arenberg, D.
     1977 "Memory and Learning Do Decline Late in Life." Paper presented at Conference on Aging and Social Policy, Vichy, France.

5   Arenberg, D., and E.A. Robertson-Tchabo
     1977 "Learning and Aging." In *Handbook of the Psychology of Aging*, ed. J.E. Birren and K.W. Schaie. New York: Van Nostrand Reinhold.

1   Aries, Phillipe
     1962 *Centuries of Childhood: A Social History of Family Life*. Trans. Robert Baldick. New York: Alfred A. Knopf.

12   Arluke, Arnold, Jack Levin, and John Suchwalko
     1984 "Sexuality and Romance in Advice Books for the Elderly." *The Gerontologist* 24:415–19.

8   Armstrong, Pat, and Hugh Armstrong
     1981 *Women and Jobs: The Canadian Case*. Ottawa: Canadian Centre for Policy Alternatives.

8   Armstrong, Pat, and Hugh Armstrong
     1984 *The Double Ghetto: Canadian Women and Their Segregated Work*, rev. ed. Toronto: McClelland and Stewart.

12   Aronson, Jane
     1985 "Family Care of the Elderly: Underlying Assumptions and Their Consequences." *Canadian Journal on Aging* 4:115–25.

3   Artibise, A.
             1977 *Winnipeg: An Illustrated History*. Toronto: Lorimer.

6, 9   Atchley, Robert C.
             1971a "Disengagement Among Professors." *Journal of
             Gerontology* 26:476–80.

9   Atchley, Robert C.
             1971b "Retirement and Work Orientation." *The Gerontologist*
             11:29–32.

9   Atchley, Robert C.
             1974 "The Meaning of Retirement." *Journal of
             Communications* 24:97–101.

1, 9   Atchley, Robert C.
             1976 *The Sociology of Retirement*. Cambridge, Massachusetts:
             Schenkman.

2, 9   Atchley, Robert C.
             1980 *The Social Forces in Later Life*, 3rd ed. Belmont,
             California: Wadsworth.

6, 9   Atchley, Robert C.
             1982 "The Process of Retirement: Comparing Women and
             Men." In *Women's Retirement*, ed. Maximiliane Szinovacz.
             Beverly Hills, California: Sage.

1, 9, 14   Atchley, Robert C.
             1985 *Social Forces and Aging*, 4th ed. Belmont, California:
             Wadsworth.

9   Atchley, Robert C., Suzanne R. Kunkel, and Carl Adlon
             1978 *An Evaluation of Preretirement Programs: Results from an
             Experimental Study*. Oxford, Ohio: Scripps Foundation
             Gerontology Center.

3   Auerbach, Lewis, and A. Gerber
             1976 *Perceptions 2: Implications of the Changing Age Structure of
             the Canadian Population*. Ottawa: Supply and Services Canada
             for the Science Council of Canada.

12   Auger, Jeanette
             1980 "Cross Cultural Issues in the Aging Experience." Paper
             presented at the Canadian Association on Gerontology 9th
             Annual Scientific and Educational Meeting, Saskatoon,
             Saskatchewan.

9   Baillargeon, Richard
             1982 "Determinants of Early Retirement." *Canada's Mental
             Health* 30:20–22.

10   Bairstow, Dale
             1985 "Shared Appreciation and Home Equity Conversion:
             Ideas Whose Time Have Come for Canadians." In

Innovations in Housing and Living Arrangements for Seniors, ed. Gloria Gutman and Norman Blackie. Burnaby, B.C.: The Gerontology Research Centre, Simon Fraser University.

2   Baker, Paul M.
1983a "Ageism, Sex, and Age: A Factorial Survey Approach." *Canadian Journal on Aging* 2:177–84.

1   Baker, Paul M.
1983b "Old Before My Time." Personal communication.

2   Baker, Paul M.
1987a "The Dega and the Nacirema: Then and Now." Personal communication.

10   Baker, Paul M.
1987b "A Proposal for Research on Sheltered Housing." Personal communication.

10   Baker, Paul M., and Victor Thompson
1985 "Victoria Seniors Survey 1: Needs and Utilization of Services." Paper presented at the Canadian Association on Gerontology 14th Annual Scientific and Educational Meeting, Hamilton, Ontario.

13   Baltes, M.M.
1977–78 "On the Relationship of Significant Yearly Events and Time of Death: Random or Systematic Distribution." *Omega* 8:165–72.

6   Baltes, Paul B., Steven W. Cornelius, and John R. Nesselroade
1979 "Cohort Effects in Developmental Psychology." In *Longitudinal Research in the Study of Behavior and Development*, ed. John R. Nesselroade and P.B. Baltes. New York: Academic Press.

6   Baltes, P.B., and L.R. Goulet
1970 "Status and Issues of a Life-span Developmental Psychology." In *Life-span Developmental Psychology: Research and Theory*, ed. L.R. Goulet and Paul B. Baltes. New York: Academic Press.

1   Baltes, P.B., H.W. Reese, and J.R. Nesselroade
1977 *Life-span Developmental Psychology: Introduction to Research Methods*. Monterey, California: Brooks/Cole.

1, 5   Baltes, P.B., and K.W. Schaie
1982 "The Myth of the Twilight Years." In *Readings in Aging and Death: Contemporary Perspectives*, 2nd ed., ed. Steven H. Zarit. New York: Harper and Row.

5   Baltes, P.B., and S.L. Willis
1981 "Enhancement (Plasticity) of Intellectual Functioning: Penn State's Adult Development and Enrichment Project (ADEPT)." In *Aging and Cognitive Processes*, ed. F.I.M. Craik and S.E. Trehub. New York: Plenum.

5   Baltes, P.B., and S.L. Willis
         1982 "Toward Psychological Theories of Aging and
         Development." In *Handbook of the Psychology of Aging*, ed. J.E.
         Birren and K.W. Schaie. New York: Van Nostrand Reinhold.

12   Bankoff, Elizabeth A.
         1983 "Aged Parents and their Widowed Daughters: A
         Support Relationship." *Journal of Gerontology* 38:226–30.

7   Barer, Morris L., Robert B. Evans, Clyde Hertzman, and
         Jonathan Lomas
         1986 "Toward Efficient Aging: Rhetoric and Evidence."
         Paper prepared for presentation at Third Canadian
         Conference on Health Economics, Winnipeg, Manitoba.

9   Barfield, Richard E., and James N. Morgan
         1969 *Early Retirement: The Decision and the Experience.* Ann
         Arbor, Michigan: University of Michigan, Institute for Social
         Research.

9   Barfield, R., and J. Morgan
         1974 *Early Retirement: The Decision and the Experience and a
         Second Look.* Ann Arbor, Michigan: Institute for Social
         Research.

13   Barrett, Carol J., and Karen M. Schneweis
         1980–81 "An Empirical Search for Stages of Widowhood."
         Omega 11:97–104.

4   Barrett, J.H.
         1972 *Gerontological Psychology.* Springfield, Illinois: Charles C.
         Thomas.

5   Barrett, J.R., and M. Wright
         1981 "Age-Related Facilitation in Recall Following Semantic
         Processing." *Journal of Gerontology* 2:194–99.

10   Bartel, Henry, and Michael J. Daly
         1981 *Reverse Mortgages: A New Class of Financial Instruments for
         the Elderly.* Discussion Paper No.188. Ottawa: Economic
         Council of Canada.

12   Baruch, G., and R.C. Barnet
         1983 "Adult Daughters' Relationships with their Mothers."
         Journal of Marriage and the Family 45:601–6.

1   Bassili, John N., and Jane E. Reil
         1981 "On the Dominance of the Old-Age Stereotype."
         Journal of Gerontology 36:682–88.

7   Bayne, J.R.D.
         1978 "Health and Care Needs of an Aging Population."
         Paper prepared for the National Symposium on Aging,
         Ottawa.

3   Beaujot, R., and K. McQuillan
      1982 *Growth and Dualism: The Demographic Development of Canadian Society.* Toronto: Gage.

9   Beck, Scott H.
      1984 "Retirement Preparation Programs: Differentials in Opportunity and Use." *Journal of Gerontology* 39:596–602.

9   Beeson, D.
      1975 "Women in Studies of Aging: A Critique and Suggestion." *Social Problems* 23:52–59.

15   Begin, Monique
      1985 "The New Society: On Aging and Seniors as an Enrichment to Civilization." In *Canadian Gerontological Collection V*, ed. Ellen M. Gee and Gloria M. Gutman. Winnipeg: Canadian Association on Gerontology.

10   Beland, François
      1984 "The Decision of Elderly Persons to Leave Their Homes." *The Gerontologist* 24:179–85.

4   Benet, S.
      1976 *How to Live to be 100.* New York: Dial.

2   Bengtson, V.L., J.J. Dowd, D.H. Smith, and A. Inkeles
      1975 "Modernization, Modernity and Perceptions of Aging: A Cross-cultural Study." *Journal of Gerontology* 30: 688–95.

7   Bennett, James, and T. Krasny
      1981 "Health Care in Canada." In *Health and Canadian Society: Sociological Perspectives*, ed. D. Coburn, D. D'Arcy, P. New and G. Torrance. Toronto: Fitzhenry and Whiteside.

4   Bennett, Neil G., and Lea Keil Garson
      1986 "Extraordinary Longevity in the Soviet Union: Fact or Artifact?" *The Gerontologist* 26:358–61.

2   Berkner, Lutz
      1972 "The Stem Family and the Development Cycle of the Peasant Household: An Eighteenth-Century Austrian Example." *American Historical Review* 77:398–418.

1   Berman, L., and I. Sobkowska-Ashcroft
      1985 "Views of Sex in Old Age in the Great Literature of the Western World." Paper presented at the Canadian Association on Gerontology 14th Annual Scientific and Educational Meeting, Hamilton, Ontario.

10   Bernardin-Haldemann, Verena
      1982 "Housing Satisfaction — Life Satisfaction." Paper presented at the Canadian Association on Gerontology 11th Annual Scientific and Educational Meeting, Winnipeg, Manitoba.

9   Bertaux, D., ed.
1981 *Biography and Society: The Life History Approach in the Social Sciences*. Beverly Hills, California: Sage.

2   Biesele, M., and N. Howell
1981 " 'The Old Give You Life': Aging Among Kung Huntergatherers." In *Other Ways of Growing Old: Anthropological Perspectives*, ed. P.T. Amoss and S. Harrell. Stanford, California: Stanford University Press.

7   Biette, M. Gayle, Vince L. Matthews, and Cope W. Schwenger
1983 "Public Health, Prevention and the Aged." *Canadian Journal of Public Health* 74:106–9.

14   Binstock, Robert H.
1972 "Interest-Group Liberalism and the Politics of Aging." *The Gerontologist* 12:265–80.

4   Birren, James E.
1964 *The Psychology of Aging*. Englewood Cliffs, N.J.: Prentice-Hall.

1   Birren, James E.
1968 "Principles of Research on Aging." In *Middle Age and Aging*, ed. Bernice L. Neugarten. Chicago: University of Chicago Press.

1   Birren, James E., and V. Clayton
1975 "History of Gerontology." In *Aging: Scientific Perspectives and Social Issues*, ed. D.S. Woodruff and J.E. Birren. New York: D. Van Nostrand.

5   Birren, J.E., and D.F. Morrison
1961 "Analysis of the WAIS Subtests in Relation to Age and Education." *Journal of Gerontology* 166:363–69.

9   Bixby, Lenore E.
1976 "Retirement Patterns in the United States: Research and Policy Interaction." *Social Security Bulletin* 39:3–19.

4   Bjorksten, J.
1974 "Crosslinkage and the Aging Process." In *Theoretical Aspects of Aging*, ed. M. Rockstein, M.L. Sussman, and J. Chesky. New York: Academic Press.

12   Black, M.
1985 "Health and Social Support of Older Adults in the Community." *Canadian Journal on Aging* 4:213–26.

10   Blackie, Norman
1985 "Shared Housing: Principles and Practices." In *Innovations in Housing and Living Arrangements for Seniors*, ed. Gloria Gutman and Norman Blackie. Burnaby, B.C.: Gerontology Research Centre, Simon Fraser University.

1   Blackie, Norman
         1986 Interview with Dr. Norman Blackie, President of the
         Canadian Association of Gerontology. Winnipeg, Manitoba.

6, 12   Blau, Zena Smith
         1973 *Old Age in a Changing Society.* New York: New
         Viewpoints.

9   Bolger, Joe
         1980 *Bill C–12 and the Debate Over Public Service Pension
         Indexing.* Unpublished master's essay. Ottawa: Carleton
         University.

11   Bond, John B., Jr.
         1982 "Volunteerism and Life Satisfaction Among Older
         Adults." *Canadian Counsellor* 16:168–72.

9   Bond, Sheryl L., and John B. Bond, Jr.
         1980 "The Impact of a Preretirement Program." *Canadian
         Counsellor* 14:68–71.

4   Botwinick, J.
         1970 "Age Differences in Self-rating of Confidence."
         Psychological Reports 27:856–66.

1, 4, 5   Botwinick, J.
         1984 *Aging and Behavior,* 3rd ed. New York: Springer.

4   Botwinick, J., J.F. Brinley, and J.S. Robbin
         1958 "The Interaction Effects of Perceptual Difficulty and
         Stimulus Exposure Time on Age Differences in Speed and
         Accuracy of Response." *Gerontologia* 2:1–10.

4   Botwinick, J., J.R. Brinley, and J.S. Robbin
         1959 "Maintaining Set in Relation to Motivation and Age."
         American Journal of Psychology 72:585–88.

5   Botwinick, J., and I.C. Siegler
         1980 "Intellectual Ability Among the Elderly: Simultaneous
         Cross-Sectional and Longitudinal Comparisons."
         Developmental Psychology 16:49–53.

5   Botwinick, J., and M. Storandt
         1980 "Recall and Recognition of Old Information in Relation
         to Age and Sex." *Journal of Gerontology* 35:70–76.

4   Botwinick, J., and L.W. Thompson
         1968 "A Research Note on Individual Differences in
         Reaction Time in Relation to Age." *Journal of Genetic
         Psychology* 112:73–75.

5   Bowles, N.L., and L.W. Poon
         1982 "An Analysis of the Effect of Aging on Memory."
         Journal of Gerontology 37:212–19.

15   Boyce, M., and D. Morgan
     1982 "Educating a Government Bureaucracy in Gerontology:
     The Department of Veterans Affairs Experience." Paper
     presented at the Canadian Association on Gerontology 11th
     Annual Scientific and Educational Meeting, Winnipeg,
     Manitoba.

6   Boyd, R., and R.N. Koskela
     1970 "A Test of Erikson's Theory of Ego-Stage Development
     by Means of a Self-Report Instrument." *Journal of
     Experimental Education* 38:1–14.

2   Bradbury, Bettina
     1983 "The Family Economy and Work in an Industrializing
     City: Montreal in the 1970's." In *The Social Development of
     Canada: Readings,* compiled by W.P. Ward. Richmond, B.C.:
     Open Learning Institute.

4   Branch, L.G., and A.M. Jette
     1981 "Elders' Use of Informal Long-Term Care Assistance."
     Paper presented at the Annual Meeting of the Gerontological
     Society of America, Toronto, Ontario.

2   Braudel, Fernand
     1981 *The Structure of Everyday Life: Civilization and Capitalism
     15th–18th Century, Vol. I.* Trans. Sian Reynolds. New York:
     Harper and Row.

6   Braun, Peter, and Robert Sweet
     1983–84 "Passages: Fact or Fiction?" *International Journal of
     Aging and Human Development* 18:161–76.

10   Brink, Satya
     1985 "Housing Elderly People in Canada: Working Towards
     a Continuum of Housing Choices Appropriate to Their
     Needs." In *Innovations in Housing and Living Arrangements for
     Seniors,* ed. Gloria Gutman and Norman Blackie. Burnaby,
     B.C.: Gerontology Research Centre, Simon Fraser University.

12   Brody, Elaine M.
     1981 " 'Women in the Middle' and Family Help to Older
     People." *The Gerontologist* 18:471–80.

12   Brody, Elaine M.
     1983 "Women's Changing Roles and Help to Elderly Parents:
     Attitudes of Three Generations of Women." *Journal of
     Gerontology* 38:597–607.

12   Brody, Elaine M., and Claire B. Schoonover
     1986 "Patterns of Parent-Care When Adult Daughters Work
     and When They Do Not." *The Gerontologist* 26:372–81.

5   Bromley, D.B.
     1956 "Some Experimental Tests of the Effect of Age on
     Creative Intellectual Output." *Journal of Gerontology* 11:74–82.

2   Bronowski, Jacob
             1976 *The Ascent of Man.* London: BBC Publishing.

7   Brown, Mabel C.
             1981 "Giving Seniors a Choice of Services and Facilities."
             Ontario Medical Review 48:45–48.

8, 14, 15   Bryden, Kenneth
             1974 *Old Age Pensions and Policy-Making in Canada.* Montreal:
             McGill-Queen's University Press.

13   Buckingham, R.W. III, S.A. Lack, G.M. Mount, L.D. MacLean,
             and J.T. Collins
             1976 "Living with the Dying." *Canadian Medical Association
             Journal* 115:1211–15.

6   Buhler, C.
             1951 "Maturation and Motivation." *Personality* 1:184–211.

9   Burbidge, John B., and A. Leslie Robb
             1980 "Pensions and Retirement Behaviour." *Canadian Journal
             of Economics* 13:421–37.

13   Butler, R.N.
             1968 "The Life Review: An Interpretation of Reminiscence
             in the Aged." In *Middle Age and Aging*, ed. Bernice L.
             Neugarten. Chicago: University of Chicago Press.

1   Butler, R.N.
             1969 "Age-ism: Another Form of Bigotry." *The Gerontologist*
             9:243–46.

5   Butler, R.N.
             1974 "The Creative Life and Old Age." In *Successful Aging*,
             ed. E. Pfeiffer. Durham, N.C.: Center for the Study of Aging
             and Human Development, Duke University.

5, 6   Butler, R.N.
             1975 *Why Survive? Being Old in America.* New York: Harper
             and Row.

5   Butler, R.N., and Marian Emr
             1982 "SDAT Research: Current Trends." *Generations*, Fall:
             14–18.

10   Buzzell, Mary
             1981 "So Very Vulnerable." *Journal of Gerontological Nursing*
             7:286–87.

10   Byerts, Thomas O.
             1982 "The Congregate-Housing Model: Integrating Facilities
             and Services." In *Congregate Housing for Older People: A
             Solution for the 1980s*, ed. Robert D. Chellis, James F. Seagle,
             Jr., and Barbara Mackey Eagle. Lexington, Massachusetts:
             Lexington Books.

6   Cain, L.D., Jr.
        1964 "Life Course and Social Structure." In *Handbook of Modern Sociology*, ed. Robert E.L. Faris. Chicago: Rand McNally.

7   Caloren, Heather
        1980 "Problems of the Independent Elderly in Using the Telephone to Seek Health Care." In *Canadian Gerontological Collection III: Selected Papers 1980: The Family of Later Life*, ed. John Crawford. Winnipeg: Canadian Association on Gerontology.

5   Cameron, D.E.
        1943 "Impairment at the Retention Phase of Remembering." *Psychiatric Quarterly* 19:395–404.

12   Campbell, Ruth, and Elaine Brody
        1985 "Women's Changing Roles and Help to the Elderly: Attitudes of Women in the United States and Japan." *The Gerontologist* 25:584–92.

10   Canada Mortgage and Housing Corporation
        1978 *Housing the Elderly*. Ottawa: Minister of Supply and Services.

10   Canada Mortgage and Housing Corporation
        1981 *Background Document on Social Housing*. Paper prepared for the All Sector National Housing Conference. Ottawa: Canada Mortgage and Housing Corporation.

10   Canada Mortgage and Housing Corporation
        1982 HIFE *Microdata File and Projections*. Ottawa: Canada Mortgage and Housing Corporation.

9   Canadian Association of University Teachers
        1986 "CAUT to Appeal Court Judgement Allowing Faculty Retirement at 65." *CAUT Bulletin* 33:22.

1   Canadian Association on Gerontology
        1977–85 *Canadian Gerontological Collection, Vols. I-V*. Winnipeg: Canadian Association on Gerontology.

10   Canadian Broadcasting Corporation
        1986 "Report on Aging." *Midday*, December 4.

1   Canadian Council on Social Development
        1973 *Beyond Shelter*. Ottawa: Canadian Council on Social Development.

8   Canadian Council on Social Development
        1975 *Fact Book on Poverty*. Ottawa: Canadian Council on Social Development.

10   Canadian Council on Social Development
        1976a *Housing the Elderly*. Ottawa: Canadian Council on Social Development.

9   Canadian Council on Social Development
     1976b *Statement on Retirement Policies.* Ottawa: Canadian
     Council on Social Development.

7   Canadian Medical Association
     1984 *Health: A Need for Redirection, Task Force on the Allocation
     of Health Care Resources.* Ottawa: Canadian Medical
     Association.

9   Canadian Pension Plan Advisory Commission
     1980 *Retirement Ages.* Ottawa: Minister of Supply and
     Services.

10, 11   Canadian Red Cross Society
         1983 *Red Cross National Seniors' Services Needs Assessment.*
         Toronto: Canadian Red Cross Society.

5   Canestrari, R.E.
     1963 "Paced and Self-Paced Learning in Young and Elderly
     Adults." *Journal of Gerontology* 18:165–68.

11   Cape, Elizabeth
     1983 "Activity and Independence: Issues in the
     Implementation of Activity Programs for Institutionalized
     Elders." *Canadian Journal on Aging* 2:185–95.

4, 7   Cape, Ronald D.T., and Philip J. Henschke
       1980 "Perspectives of Health in Old Age." *Journal of the
       American Geriatrics Society* 28:295–99.

7   Cape, Ronald D.T., C. Shorrock, R. Tree, R. Pablo, A.J.
     Campbell, and D.G. Seymour
     1977 "Square Pegs in Round Holes: A Study of Residents in
     Long-Term Institutions in London, Ontario." *Canadian
     Medical Association Journal* 117:1284–87.

5   Cattell, R.B.
     1963 "Theory of Fluid and Crystallized Intelligence: An
     Initial Experiment." *Journal of Educational Psychology*
     54:105–11.

5   Cavanaugh, J.C.
     1983 "Comprehension and Retention of Television Programs
     by 20- and 60-year-olds." *Journal of Gerontology* 38:190–96.

5   Cavanaugh, J.C., J.A. Grady, and M. Perlmutter
     1983 "Forgetting and Use of Memory Aids in 20 to 70 Year-
     Olds' Everyday Life." *International Journal of Aging and
     Human Development* 17:113–22.

4   Cerami, Anthony, Helen Vlassara, and Michael Brownlee
     1987 "Glucose and Aging." *Scientific American* 256:90–96.

4   Cerella, J., L.W. Poon, and J.L. Fozard
     1981 "Mental Rotation and Age Reconsidered." *Journal of
     Gerontology* 36:620–24.

4 Cerella, J., L.W. Poon, and D.H. Williams
1980 "Age and Complexity Hypothesis." In *Aging in the 80's*, ed. L.W. Poon. Washington, D.C.: American Psychological Association.

14 Cernetig, Miro
1985 "Plans to De-Index Old Age Pensions Mean Poverty Jump, Council Says." *Globe and Mail*, June 11.

13 Chappell, Neena L.
1975 "Awareness of Death in Disengagement Theory: A Conceptualization and an Empirical Investigation." *Omega* 6:325–43.

7, 12 Chappell, Neena L.
1980a "Re-examining Conceptual Boundaries: Peer and Intergenerational Relationships." *Essence* 4:169–78.

8 Chappell, Neena L.
1980b "Social Policy and the Elderly." In *Aging in Canada*, ed. Victor W. Marshall. Toronto: Fitzhenry and Whiteside.

12 Chappell, Neena L.
1982a "The Future Impact of the Changing Status of Women." In *Canada's Changing Age Structure: Selected Papers*, ed. Gloria Gutman. Burnaby, B.C.: Simon Fraser University Publications.

1 Chappell, Neena L.
1982b "The Value of Research to Practitioners in Work with the Elderly." *Canadian Journal on Aging* 1:62–65.

11, 12 Chappell, Neena L.
1983a "Informal Support Networks Among the Elderly." *Research on Aging* 5:77–99.

7 Chappell, Neena L.
1983b "Who Benefits from Adult Day Care? Changes in Functional Ability and Mental Functioning During Attendance." *Canadian Journal on Aging* 2:9–26.

5 Chappell, Neena L., and G.E. Barnes
1982 "The Practicing Pharmacist and the Elderly Client." *Contemporary Pharmacy Practice* 5:170–75.

7 Chappell, Neena L., and Audrey A. Blandford
1983 *Adult Day Care: Its Impact on the Utilization of Other Health Care Services and on Quality of Life*. Final report. Ottawa: NHRDP, Health and Welfare Canada.

4 Chappell, Neena L., and Betty Havens
1980 "Old and Female: Testing the Double Jeopardy Hypothesis." *Sociological Quarterly* 21:157–71.

12 Chappell, Neena L., and Betty Havens
1985 "Who Helps the Elderly Person: A Discussion of Informal and Formal Care." In *Social Bonds in Later Life:*

Aging and Interdependence, ed. Warren A. Peterson and Jill Quadagno. Beverly Hills, California: Sage.

7, 10, 14   Chappell, Neena L., and Margaret Penning
1979 "The Trend Away from Institutionalization: Humanism or Economic Efficiency?" *Research on Aging* 1:361–87.

12   Chappell, Neena L., and Laurel A. Strain
1984 *Needs Assessment of Natives 50+ Living in Winnipeg*. Winnipeg: University of Manitoba Centre on Aging.

4, 7   Chappell, Neena L., Laurel A. Strain, and Audrey A. Blandford
1986 *Aging and Health Care: A Social Perspective*. Toronto: Holt, Rinehart and Winston of Canada.

5   Charness, Neil
1982 "Problem Solving and Aging: Evidence from Semantically Rich Domains." *Canadian Journal on Aging* 1:21–28.

8, 12   Cheal, David
1983 "Intergenerational Family Transfers." *Journal of Marriage and the Family* 45:805–13.

8   Cheal, David
1985a *Moral Economy: Gift Giving in an Urban Society. Winnipeg Area Study Report No.5*. Winnipeg: Institute for Social and Economic Research, University of Manitoba.

8, 12   Cheal, David
1985b "The System of Transfers to and from Households in Canada." *Western Economic Review* 4:35–39.

12   Cheal, David
1986 "The Social Dimensions of Gift Behaviour." *Journal of Social and Personal Relationships* 3:423–39.

6   Chiriboga, David A.
1984 "Social Stressors as Antecedents of Change." *Journal of Gerontology* 39:468–77.

11   Christie, J. Lee
1983 "Seniors Play Games Too." *Recreation Canada*, February: 6–9.

6   Ciaccio, N.V.
1971 "A Test of Erikson's Theory of Ego Epigenesis." *Developmental Psychology* 4:306–11.

9   Ciffin, S., and J. Martin
1977 *Retirement in Canada: Volume I, When and Why People Retire*. Health and Welfare Canada, Policy Research and Long Range Planning (Welfare). Ottawa: Minister of Supply and Services.

7
    Clarfield, A.M.
    1983 "Home Care: Is it Cost Effective?" *Canadian Medical Association Journal* 129:1181–83.

14
    Clarke, Harold D., L. LeDuc, J. Jenson, and J. Pammett
    1980 *Political Choice in Canada*, abridged ed. Toronto: McGraw-Hill Ryerson.

11
    Clarke, H.H.
    1977 "Joint and Body Range of Motion." *Physical Fitness Research Digest* 7.

2
    Cohn, R.
    1982 "Economic Development and Status Change of the Aged." *American Journal of Sociology* 87:1150–61.

9
    Collins, K., and J. Brown
    1978 "Canada's Retirement Policies." *Aging and Work* 1:101–8.

2
    Colson, E., and T. Scudder
    1981 "Old Age in Gwembe District, Zambia." In *Other Ways of Growing Old: Anthropological Perspectives*, ed. P.T. Amoss and S. Harrell. Stanford, California: Stanford University Press.

7
    Community Care Services, Inc.
    1978 *A Brief to the Ontario Cabinet*. Toronto: Community Care Services Inc. (Metro Toronto).

15
    Connelly, J. Richard
    1981 "Education and the Future." In *Canada's Changing Age Structure: Implications for the Future*, ed. Gloria Gutman. Burnaby, B.C.: Simon Fraser University.

9
    Connidis, Ingrid
    1982 "Women and Retirement: The Effect of Multiple Careers on Retirement Adjustment." *Canadian Journal on Aging* 1:17–27.

10, 12
    Connidis, Ingrid
    1983a "Living Arrangement Choices of Older Residents: Assessing Quantitative Results with Qualitative Data." *Canadian Journal of Sociology* 8:359–75.

6
    Connidis, Ingrid
    1983b "The Pros, Cons and Worries of Aging." Paper presented at the Canadian Association on Gerontology 12th Annual Scientific and Educational Meeting, Moncton, New Brunswick.

10, 12
    Connidis, Ingrid, and Judith Rempel
    1983 "The Living Arrangements of Older Residents: The Role of Gender, Marital Status, Age, and Family Size." *Canadian Journal on Aging* 2:91–105.

6   Constantinople, A.
1969 "An Eriksonian Measure of Personality Development in College Students." *Developmental Psychology* 1:357–72.

11, 15   Continuing Education Division
1987 *Advanced Certificate in Gerontology Program Calendar.* Winnipeg: University of Manitoba.

3   Corelli, Rae
1986 "A Matter of Care." *Maclean's*, October 6.

10   Corke, Susan
1986 "Granny Flats as an Intensification Option for Housing the Elderly." In *Granny Flats: A Housing Option for the Elderly*, Report No. 13, ed. Susan Corke, Gregory S. Romanick, Michael Lazarowich, and Joan Simon. Winnipeg: Institute of Urban Studies.

2   Cowgill, Donald O.
1974 "Aging and Modernization: A Revision of the Theory." In *Late Life*, ed. Jaber F. Gubrium. Springfield, Illinois: Charles C. Thomas.

2, 3   Cowgill, Donald O.
1986 *Aging Around the World.* Belmont, California: Wadsworth.

2   Cowgill, Donald O., and Lowell D. Holmes, eds.
1972 *Aging and Modernization.* New York: Appleton-Century-Crofts.

9   Cox, Harold, and Albert Bhak
1978–79 "Symbolic Interaction and Retirement Adjustment: An Empirical Assessment." *International Journal of Aging and Human Development* 9:279–86.

5   Craik, F.I.M.
1977 "Age Differences in Human Memory." In *Handbook of the Psychology of Aging*, ed. James E. Birren and K. Warner Schaie. New York: Van Nostrand Reinhold.

5   Craik, F.I.M., and R.S. Lockhart
1972 "Levels of Processing: A Framework for Memory Research." *Journal of Verbal Learning and Verbal Behavior* 11:671–84.

10   Cranz, Galen, and Thomas L. Schumacher
1975 *The Impact of High-Rise Housing on Older Residents. Working Paper 18.* Princeton, N.J.: Research Center for Urban and Environmental Planning, School of Architecture and Urban Planning.

9   Crawford, L., and Jean Matlow
1972 "Some Attitudes Toward Retirement Among Middle-aged Employees in a Longitudinal Study, 1959–1978." *Industrial Relations Quarterly Review* 27:616–31.

7   Crichton, A.
     1980 "Equality: A Concept in Canadian Health Care: From
     Intention to Reality of Provision." *Social Science and Medicine*
     14C:243–57.

2, 3 Cross, D. Suzanne
     1983 "The Neglected Majority: The Changing Role of
     Women in Nineteenth-Century Montreal." In *The Social
     Development of Canada: Readings*, compiled by P.W. Ward.
     Richmond, B.C.: Open Learning Institute.

5   Crosson, C.W., and E.A. Robertson-Tchabo
     1983 "Age and Preference for Complexity Among Manifestly
     Creative Women." *Human Development* 26:149–55.

6   Cumming, E., and W.E. Henry
     1961 *Growing Old: The Process of Disengagement*. New York:
     Basic Books.

14   Curtis, James E., and Ronald D. Lambert
     1976 "Voting, Election Interest, and Age: National Findings
     for English and French Canadians." *Canadian Journal of
     Political Science* 9:293–307.

2   Cutler, N.E., and R.A. Harootyan
     1975 "Demography of the Aged." In *Aging: Scientific
     Perspectives and Social Issues*, ed. D.S. Woodruff and J.E.
     Birren. New York: Van Nostrand.

11   Cyr, J., and M.M. Schnore
     1982 "Level of Education of the Future Elderly:
     Demographic Characteristics and Clinical Implications."
     Essence 5:153–67.

8   Daly, Michael J.
     1981 "Reforming Canada's Retirement Income System: The
     Potential Role of RRSPs." *Canadian Public Policy* 7:550–58.

12   Damrosch, Shirley Petchel
     1984 "Graduate Nursing Students' Attitudes Toward
     Sexually Active Older Persons." *The Gerontologist* 24:299–302.

1   de Beauvoir, Simone
     1978 *Old Age*. Harmondsworth, England: Penguin.

11   Delisle, Marc-André
     1982 "Elderly People's Management of Time and Leisure."
     Canada's Mental Health 30:32.

5   Demming, J.A., and S.L. Pressey
     1957 "Tests 'Indigenous' to the Adult and Older Years."
     Journal of Counselling Psychology 4:144–48.

5   Denney, N.W., and A.M. Palmer
     1981 "Adult Age Differences on Traditional and Practical
     Problem-Solving Measures." *Journal of Gerontology* 4:144–48.

5   Dennis, Wayne
        1968 "Creative Productivity Between the Ages of 20 and 80
        Years." In *Middle Age and Aging*, ed. Bernice L. Neugarten.
        Chicago: University of Chicago Press.

3   Denton, Frank T., and Byron G. Spencer
        1980 "Canada's Population and Labour Force: Past, Present
        and Future." In *Aging in Canada*, ed. Victor W. Marshall.
        Toronto: Fitzhenry and Whiteside.

7   Denton, Frank T., and Byron G. Spencer
        1983 "Population Aging and Future Health Costs in
        Canada." *Canadian Public Policy* 9:155–63.

12   Department of Social and Family Services
        1969 *Cultural Differences Among the Aged in Ontario*. Toronto:
        Department of Social and Family Services.

5   de Santana, Hubert
        1980 "Portrait of the Artist as an Old Man." *Today Magazine*,
        November 29: 12–14.

11   Devereaux, M.S.
        1985 *One in Every Five: A Survey of Adult Education in Canada*.
        Statistics Canada Cat. No. SZ–139/1984E. Ottawa: Minister of
        Supply and Services.

10   Devine, Barbara A.
        1980 "Old Age Stereotyping: A Comparison of Nursing Staff
        Attitudes Toward the Elderly." *Journal of Gerontological
        Nursing* 6:25–32.

11   DeVries, Herbert A.
        1975 "Physiology of Exercise and Aging." In *Aging: Scientific
        Perspectives and Social Issues*, ed. Diana S. Woodruff and
        James E. Birren. New York: Van Nostrand.

7   DeVries, Herbert A.
        1980 "Physiology of Exercise and Aging." In *Health Care of
        the Elderly*, ed. Gari Lesnoff-Caravaglia. New York: Human
        Sciences Press.

14   Dewar, Elaine
        1981 "Doctoring Medicare." *Today Magazine*, February 7:
        6–8.

13   Dickinson, G.E.
        1976 "Death Education in U.S. Medical Schools." *Journal of
        Medical Education* 51:134–36.

13   Dickinson, G.E., and A.A. Pearson
        1980–81 "Death Education and Physicians' Attitudes
        Towards Dying Patients." *Omega* 11:167–74.

5   Dixon, R.A., and D.F. Hultsch
        1983 "Structure and Development of Metamemory in
        Adulthood." *Journal of Gerontology* 38:682–88.

3   Dominion Bureau of Statistics
1964 *Census of Canada* (1961 Census). Bulletin 7:1–4. Ottawa: Queen's Printer.

3   Dominion Bureau of Statistics
1968 *Census of Canada. Volume 1 (1–11).* (1966 Census). Ottawa, Queen's Printer.

10   Doolin, Joseph
1986 "Planning for the Special Needs of the Homeless Elderly." *The Gerontologist* 26:229–31.

13   Doutre, D., D.M. Stillwell, and I. Ajemian
1979 "Physiotherapy in Palliative Care." *Essence* 3:69–77.

9   Dowd, J.J.
1980 *Stratification Among the Aged.* Monterey, California: Brooks/Cole.

3, 12   Driedger, Leo, and Neena L. Chappell
1987 *Aging and Ethnicity: Toward an Interface.* Toronto: Butterworths.

7   Drummond, M.F.
1980 *Principles of Economic Appraisal in Health Care.* Oxford: Oxford University Press.

8   Dulude, Louise
1978 *Women and Aging: A Report on the Rest of Our Lives.* Ottawa: Advisory Council on the Status of Women.

7   Dunn, R.B., L. MacBeath, and D. Robertson
1983 "Respite Admission and the Disabled Elderly." *Journal of the American Geriatric Society* 31:613–16.

13   Eaton, Joseph W.
1964 "The Art of Aging and Dying." *The Gerontologist* 4:94–112.

10   Eckert, J.K.
1980 *The Unseen Elderly.* San Diego, California: The Companile Press.

10   Economic Council of Canada
1981 "Reverse Mortgages: A New Way to Help Pensioners." *Au Courant* 2:21.

11   Edwards, Peggy
1983 "New Frontier in Geriatric Science: Fitness in the 'Third Age.'" *Canadian Journal of Public Health* 74:96–99.

10   Ehrlich, I., and P. Ehrlich
1976 *The Invisible Elderly.* Washington, D.C.: National Council on the Aging.

5   Eisdorfer, Carl
1972 "Mental Health in Later Life." In *Handbook of*

Community Mental Health, ed. S.E. Golann and C. Eisdorfer. New York: Appleton-Century-Crofts.

2   Eisdorfer, Carl
         1981 "Foreword." In *Other Ways of Growing Old: Anthropological Perspectives*, ed. P.T. Amoss and S. Harrell. Stanford, California: Stanford University Press.

9   Ekerdt, David J., Raymond Bossé, and Sue Levkoff
         1985 "An Empirical Test for Phases of Retirement: Findings from the Normative Aging Study." *Journal of Gerontology* 40:95–101.

11   Elderhostel
         1981 *Annual Report*. Boston: Elderhostel.

11   Elderhostel Canada
         1987 *Welcome to Elderhostel Canada*. May to October Issue. Toronto: Elderhostel Canada.

5   Elo, A.E.
         1965 "Age Changes in Master Chess Performance." *Journal of Gerontology* 20:289–99.

11   Environics Research Group
         1974 *Reaching the Retired: A Survey of the Media Habits, Preferences and Needs of Senior Citizens in Metro Toronto*. Montreal: Information Canada.

10   Epstein, Don
         1976 *Retirement Housing in Urban Neighbourhoods: Some Inner City Options*. Winnipeg: Institute of Urban Studies.

5   Erber, J.T., and J. Botwinick
         1983 "Reward in the Learning of Older Adults." *Experimental Aging Research* 9:43–44.

6   Erikson, Erik H.
         1950 "Growth and Crises of the Healthy Personality." In *Symposium on the Healthy Personality*, Supplement II: Problems of Infancy and Childhood. Transaction of Fourth Conference, March 1950, ed. M.J. Senn. New York: Josiah Macy, Jr. Foundation.

6   Erikson, Erik H.
         1959 "Identity and the Life Cycle: Selected Issues." *Psychological Issues* 1:50–100, Appendix.

6, 13, 15   Erikson, Erik H.
             1963 *Childhood and Society*, 2nd ed. New York: W.W. Norton.

6   Erikson, Erik H.
         1976 "Reflections on Dr. Borg's Life Cycle." In *Adulthood*, ed. Erik Erikson. New York: W.W. Norton.

6   Erikson, Erik H.
         1982 *The Life Cycle Completed*. New York: W.W. Norton.

10   Evans, Aeron T., and G.J.M. Purdie
       1985 "Private Sector Financing for Elderly Housing." In
       Innovations in Housing and Living Arrangements for Seniors, ed.
       Gloria Gutman and Norman Blackie. Burnaby, B.C.:
       Gerontology Research Centre, Simon Fraser University.

7   Evans, Robert G.
       1984 *Strained Mercy: The Economics of Canadian Health Care.*
       Toronto: Butterworths.

13   Feigenberg, Loma
       1980 *Terminal Care: Friendship Contracts with Dying Cancer
       Patients.* New York: Brunner/Mazel.

9   Finlayson, Ann
       1985 "The Lure of Early Retirement." *Maclean's*, February 4.

11   Fischer, Andrew A.
       1977 "The Effect of Aging and Physical Activity on the
       Stabile Component of Arterial Distensibility." In *Guide to
       Fitness After Fifty*, ed. R.H. Harris and L.J. Frankel. New
       York: Plenum Press.

1, 2   Fischer, David Hackett
       1978 *Growing Old in America*, expanded ed. New York:
       Oxford University Press.

13   Fisher, Rory H., Grant W. Nadon, and Ralph Shedletsky
       1983 "Management of the Dying Elderly Patient." *Journal of
       the American Geriatric Society* 31:563–64.

13   Fisher, Rory H., and Ralph Shedletsky
       1979 "A Retrospective Study of Terminal Care of
       Hospitalized Elderly." *Essence* 3:91–100.

11   Fitness and Amateur Sport
       1982 *Fitness and Aging: Canada Fitness Survey.* Ottawa:
       Minister of Supply and Services.

7   Flathman, D.P., and D.E. Larsen
       1976 "Evaluation of Three Geriatric Day Hospitals in
       Alberta." Unpublished report, Division of Community Health
       Services, Faculty of Medicine. Calgary, Alberta: University of
       Calgary.

11   Fleming, Farrell
       1986 "Manitoba's Creative Retirement Program." *Creative
       Retirement Manitoba: Fall Program.* Winnipeg: Creative
       Retirement Manitoba.

12   Fletcher, Susan, and Leroy O. Stone
       1980 "The Living Arrangements of Canada's Older Women."
       Essence 4:115–33.

1   Foundations Project
         1980 "Foundations for Gerontological Education." *The
         Gerontologist* 20, Pt.II.

5   Fozard, J.L.
         1980 "The Time for Remembering." In *New Directions in
         Memory and Aging: Proceedings of the George A. Talland
         Memorial Conference*, ed. L.W. Poon, J.L. Fozard, L.S.
         Cermak, D. Arenberg, and L.W. Thompson. Hillsdale, N.J.:
         Lawrence Erlbaum Association.

10   Fraser, D.
         1982 *Defining the Parameters of a Housing Policy for the Elderly.*
         Ottawa: Canada Mortgage and Housing Corporation.

1   Freeman, J.T.
         1979 *Aging: Its History and Literature.* New York: Human
         Sciences Press.

3   Gagan, D.
         1983a "Geographical and Social Mobility in Nineteenth
         Century Ontario: A Microstudy." In *The Social Development of
         Canada: Readings*, compiled by P.W. Ward. Richmond, B.C.:
         Open Learning Institute.

2, 3   Gagan, D.
         1983b "Land, Population, and Social Change: The 'Critical
         Years' in Rural Canada West." In *The Social Development of
         Canada: Readings*, compiled by P.W. Ward. Richmond, B.C.:
         Open Learning Institute.

1   Gallie, Karen A., and John F. Kozak
         1985 "Investigation Into a Possible Relationship Between
         Knowledge of Aging and Attitudes Toward Old People."
         Paper presented at the Canadian Association on Gerontology
         14th Annual Scientific and Educational Meeting, Hamilton,
         Ontario.

13   Gee, Ellen M.
         1985 "Historical Change in the Life Course of Canadian
         Women." Paper presented at the Canadian Association on
         Gerontology 14th Annual Scientific and Educational Meeting,
         Hamilton, Ontario. Forthcoming in *Social Indicators Research.*

10   Gelwicks, Louis E., and Robert J. Newcomer
         1974 *Planning Housing Environments for the Elderly.*
         Washington: National Council on the Aging.

3   George, M.V., and J. Perreault.
         1985 *Population Projections for Canada, Provinces and Territories
         1984–2006.* Statistics Canada Cat. No. 91–520. Ottawa:
         Minister of Supply and Services.

3, 12   Gerber, Linda M.
         1983 "Ethnicity Still Matters: Socio-Demographic Profiles of

the Ethnic Elderly in Ontario." *Canadian Ethnic Studies* 15:60–80.

15   Gerontology Research Council of Ontario
1985–86 *Annual Report*. Hamilton, Ontario: Gerontology Research Council of Ontario.

13   Gesser, Gina, Paul T.P. Wong, and Gary T. Reker
1986 "Death Attitudes Across the Life-Span: The Development and Validation of the Death Attitude Profile (DAP)." Private communication. Forthcoming in *Omega*.

1   Gfellner, Barbara M.
1982 "Case Study Analysis: A Field Placement Program in the Study of Aging." Paper presented at the Canadian Association on Gerontology 11th Annual Scientific and Educational Meeting, Winnipeg, Manitoba.

9   Gherson, Giles
1980 "Retirement 'A Moral, Not an Economic Issue.'" *Financial Post*, March 8.

5   Gibson, R.W.
1970 "Medicare and the Psychiatric Patient." *Psychiatric Opinion* 7:17–22.

14   Gifford, C.G.
1982 "Senior Power in Canada." Poster presentation presented at the Canadian Association on Gerontology 11th Annual Scientific and Educational Meeting, Winnipeg, Manitoba.

14   Gifford, C.G.
1983 "Senior Politics." *Policy Options*, September: 12–15.

14   Gifford, C.G.
1987 Personal communication.

2   Gillin, C.T.
1986 "Aging in the Developing World." Paper presented at the Canadian Sociology and Anthropology Association 21st Annual Meeting, Winnipeg, Manitoba.

2   Glascock, A.P., and S.L. Feinman
1981 "Social Asset or Social Burden: Treatment of the Aged in Non-industrial Societies." In *Dimensions: Aging, Culture, and Health*, ed. C.L. Fry and contributors. New York: Praeger.

13   Glaser, Barney G., and Anselm L. Strauss
1977 "The Ritual Drama of Mutual Pretense." In *Readings in Aging and Death: Contemporary Perspectives*, ed. Steven H. Zarit. New York: Harper and Row.

14   Glenn, Norval D.
1969 "Aging, Disengagement and Opinionation." *Public Opinion Quarterly* 33:17–33.

14   Glenn, Norval D., and Michael Grimes
        1968 "Aging, Voting and Political Interest." *American Sociological Review* 33:563–75.

2   *Globe and Mail*
        1983 "Latin Americans Seek Refuge in Debtors' Club."
        July 11: B8.

14   *Globe and Mail*
        1985 "Seniors Urge Wilson to Drop De-Indexing Plan."
        June 18: 5.

12   Gold, Yhetta
        1980 "Ethnic and Cultural Aspects of Aging." Paper presented at the Canadian Association on Gerontology 9th Annual Scientific and Educational Meeting, Saskatoon, Saskatchewan.

13   Goldberg, Helene S.
        1981–82 "Funeral and Bereavement Rituals of Kota Indians and Orthodox Jews." *Omega* 12:117–28.

4   Goldstein, S.
        1984 "The Cellular Basis of Aging." *Canadian Family Physician* 30:585–89.

4   Gordon, Paul, Bruce Ronsen, and Eric R. Brown
        1974 "Anti-Herpesvirus Action of Isoprinosine." *Antimicrobial Agents and Chemotherapy* 5:153–60.

6   Gordon, S.
        1976 *Lonely in America.* New York: Simon and Schuster.

13   Gorer, Geoffrey
        1965 *Death, Grief and Mourning in Contemporary Britain.* London: Cresset.

13   Gorer, Geoffrey
        1967 *Death, Grief and Mourning.* New York: Anchor.

6, 15   Gould, R.L.
        1978 *Transformations: Growth and Change in Adult Life.* New York: Simon and Schuster.

8   Government of Canada
        1982a *Better Pensions for Canadians* (Green Paper). Ottawa: Minister of Supply and Services.

8   Government of Canada
        1982b *Better Pensions for Canadians: Focus on Women.* Ottawa: Minister of Supply and Services.

1   Government of Manitoba
        1973 *Aging in Manitoba* (10 vols.). Winnipeg: Department of Health and Social Development.

7   Government of Manitoba
1984 *Annual Report of the Provincial Office of Continuing Care.*
Winnipeg: Government of Manitoba.

10   Grant, Peter R.
1983 "Creating a Feasible Transportation System for Rural
Areas: Reflections on a Symposium." *Canadian Journal on
Aging* 2:30–35.

10   Grant, Peter R., and Bruce Rice
1983 "Transportation Problems of the Rural Elderly: A
Needs Assessment." *Canadian Journal on Aging* 2:107–24.

9   Grauer, H., and N.M. Campbell
1983 "The Aging Physician and Retirement." *Canadian
Journal of Psychiatry* 28:552–54.

5   Green, R.F.
1969 "Age–Intelligence Relationship Between Ages Sixteen
and Sixty-four: A Rising Trend." *Developmental Psychology*
1:618–27.

2   Greene, J.P., ed.
1965 *Diary of Colonel Landon Carter of Sabine Hall, 1752–1778*
(2 vols.). Charlottesville, Virginia.

13   Greer, D.S., V. Mor, H. Birnbaum, D. Kidder, S. Sherwood,
and T.N. Morris
1984 *Final Report of the National Hospice Study* (Draft).
Providence, R.I.: Brown University.

10   Grescoe, Audrey
1981 "Little Old Lady in a Hard Hat." *Today Magazine,*
January 17.

11   Grescoe, Audrey
1982 "Good Old." *Today Magazine,* January 9: 11–14,16.

7, 10   Gross, John, and Cope Schwenger
1981 "Health Care Costs for the Elderly in Ontario:
1976–2026." Occasional Paper 11. Toronto: Ontario
Economic Council.

10   Gross, L.P.
1985 "Federal Housing Programs." In *Innovations in Housing
and Living Arrangements for Seniors,* ed. Gloria Gutman and
Norman Blackie. Burnaby, B.C.: The Gerontology Research
Centre, Simon Fraser University.

2   Guemple, L.
1977 "The Dilemma of the Aging Eskimo." In *Sociology
Canada: Readings,* 2nd ed., ed. Christopher Beattie and
Stewart Chrysdale. Toronto: Butterworths.

2   Guemple, L.
1980 "Growing Old in Inuit Society." In *Aging in Canada,* ed.
Victor W. Marshall. Toronto: Fitzhenry and Whiteside.

9, 15   Guillemard, A.M.
             1977 "The Call to Activity Amongst the Old Rehabilitation or
             Regimentation." In *Canadian Gerontological Collection I*, ed.
             Blossom T. Wigdor. Winnipeg: Canadian Association on
             Gerontology.

9   Gunderson, Morley, and James E. Pesando
             1980 "Eliminating Mandatory Retirement: Economics and
             Human Rights." *Canadian Public Policy* 6:352–60.

5   Gurland, B.J., and J.A. Toner
             1983 "Depression in the Elderly: A Review of Recently
             Published Studies." *Annual Review of Gerontology and Geriatrics*
             3:228–65.

15   Gutman, Gloria
             1977 "Survey of Educational Programs in Gerontology and
             Geriatrics Offered at Canadian Universities." Mimeo.
             Vancouver, B.C.: President's Committee on Gerontology,
             University of British Columbia.

10   Gutman, Gloria
             1978 "Issues and Findings Relating to Multi-level
             Accommodation for Seniors." *Journal of Gerontology*
             33:592–600.

10   Gutman, Gloria
             1983 *The Long Term Impact of Multi-Level, Multi-Service
             Accommodation for Seniors*. Senior Citizen Housing Study
             Report No. 3. Ottawa: Canada Mortgage and Housing
             Corporation.

10   Gutman, Gloria
             1985 "The Long-Term Impact of Multi-Level, Multi-Service
             Accommodation for Seniors." Paper presented at the
             Symposium on Alternative Housing and Living
             Arrangements for Independent Living — Design
             Implications, Policy Development and Research, held at the
             13th International Congress of Gerontology, New York.

10   Gutman, Gloria, and Norman Blackie, eds.
             1985 *Innovations in Housing and Living Arrangements for
             Seniors*. Burnaby, B.C.: Gerontology Research Centre, Simon
             Fraser University.

10   Gutman, Gloria, and Carol P. Herbert
             1976 "Mortality Rates Among Relocated Extended Care
             Patients." *Journal of Gerontology* 31:352–57.

11   Gutman, Gloria M., Carol P. Herbert, and Stanley R. Brown
             1977 "Feldenkrais Versus Conventional Exercises for the
             Elderly." *Journal of Gerontology* 32:562–72.

10   Gutman, Gloria, C. Jackson, A.J. Stark, and B. McCashin
            1986 "Mortality Rates Five Years after Admission to a Long
            Term Care Program." *Canadian Journal on Aging* 5:9–17.

2, 9   Haber, Carole
            1978 "Mandatory Retirement in Nineteenth-Century
            America: The Conceptual Basis for a New York Cycle."
            Journal of Social History 12:77–96.

4   Haber, Paul A.L.
            1986 "Technology in Aging." *The Gerontologist* 26:350–57.

1, 15   Hancock, Gordon
            1984 *A Study of Gerontology Activities and of Centres of
            Gerontology on University Campuses in the United States and
            Canada.* Winnipeg: University of Manitoba, Centre on Aging.

7   Hansen, Signy, and Neena L. Chappell
            1985 "Perspectives on Normal Aging and Health Promotion
            in Canada: A Strategic Analysis for Policy Development."
            Paper presented at the Meeting of the International
            Association of Gerontology, New York, N.Y.

7   Hansen, Signy, and Gary Ledoux
            1985 "Developing a Health Promotion Resource for Older
            Adults." Paper presented at the Meeting of the International
            Association of Gerontology, New York, N.Y.

1   Harding, Michele, and Sheila Neysmith
            1984 "Ageism and Health Costs: Reality and Implications."
            Paper presented at the Canadian Association on Gerontology
            13th Annual Scientific and Educational Meeting, Vancouver,
            B.C.

10   Harper, I.
            1984 "Housing Options for the Elderly in the Capital
            Region: Sheltered Housing and Other Alternatives." Victoria,
            B.C.: Capital Regional Hospital District, Hospital and Health
            Planning Commission.

13   Harrison, Albert A., and Neal E.A. Kroll
            1985–86 "Variations in Death Rates in the Proximity of
            Christmas: An Opponent Process Interpretation." *Omega*
            16:181–92.

13   Harrison, A.A., and M. Moore
            1982–83 "Birth Dates and Death Dates: A Closer Look."
            Omega 13:117–25.

7   Harshman, Frederick C.
            1982 "Home Support for Elderly Persons: A Futuristic
            Example." *Canada's Mental Health* 3:4–6.

5   Hartley, J.T., J.O. Harker, and D.A. Walsh
            1980 "Contemporary Issues and New Directions in Adult

Development of Learning and Memory." In *Aging in the 1980s*, ed. Leonard W. Poon. Washington, D.C.: American Psychological Association.

13   Harvard Medical School
1968 "A Definition of Irreversible Coma: Report of the Ad Hoc Committee of the Harvard Medical School to Examine the Definition of Brain Death." *Journal of the American Medical Association* 205:337–40.

12   Harvey, Carol H.
1984 "Decision-Making by Middle-Aged Widows in Winnipeg." Paper presented at the Beatrice Paolucci Symposium, Michigan State University, East Lansing, Michigan.

1, 7, 10   Havens, Betty
1980 "Differentiation of Unmet Needs Using Analysis by Age/Sex Cohorts." In *Aging in Canada*, ed. Victor W. Marshall. Toronto: Fitzhenry and Whiteside.

12   Havens, Betty, and N.L. Chappell
1983 "Triple Jeopardy: Age, Sex and Ethnicity." *Canadian Ethnic Studies* 15:119–32.

11   Hawkins, Terry
1980 *Never Too Old: A Report to the Northumberland Newcastle Board of Education on the Educational Needs of Senior Adults Living in the Area Served by Its Schools*. Newcastle, Ontario: Northumberland Newcastle Board of Education.

11   Hayashida, David
1983 "Take A Closer Look at the National Parks." *Recreation Canada*, February:16–18.

4   Hayflick, L.
1970 "Aging Under Glass." *Experimental Gerontology* 5:291–303.

4   Hayflick, L.
1974 "The Strategy of Senescence." *The Gerontologist* 14:37–45.

4   Hayflick, L.
1985 "Theories of Biological Aging." In *Principles of Genetic Medicine*, ed. R. Andres, E.L. Bierman, and W.R. Hazzard. New York: McGraw-Hill.

4   Hayflick, L., and P.S. Moorhead
1961 "The Serial Cultivation of Human Diploid Cell Strains." *Experimental Cell Research* 25:585–621.

9   Haynes, Suzanne G., Anthony J. McMichael, and H.A. Tyroler.
1977 "The Relationship of Normal Involuntary Retirement to Early Mortality Among U.S. Rubber Workers." *Social Science and Medicine* 11:105–14.

15   Health and Welfare Canada
1977a *Medical Education in Geriatrics, Health Manpower Report No. 1/77.* Ottawa: Minister of Supply and Services.

9, 10, 11   Health and Welfare Canada
1977b *Social Security Research Reports. Retirement in Canada: Summary Report (Report No. 03).* Ottawa: Long Range Planning Directorate, Policy Research and Long Range Planning Branch (Welfare), National Health and Welfare.

6   Health and Welfare Canada
1977c *Who Commits Suicide in Old Age and Why?* Ottawa: Health and Welfare Canada.

1, 9   Health and Welfare Canada
1979 *Retirement Age.* Ottawa: Minister of Supply and Services.

8   Health and Welfare Canada
1982a *Better Pensions for Canadians: Highlights.* Ottawa: Minister of Supply and Services.

1, 3, 7, 8, 9, 10, 11, 14   Health and Welfare Canada
1982b *Canadian Governmental Report on Aging.* Ottawa: Minister of Supply and Services.

7   Health and Welfare Canada
1982c *National Health Expenditures in Canada, 1970–1982: With Comparative Data for the United States. Provincial Data and Sectoral Analysis.* Ottawa: Minister of Supply and Services.

11   Health and Welfare Canada
1982d *New Horizons: First Decade.* Ottawa: Minister of Supply and Services.

13   Health and Welfare Canada
1982e *Palliative Care in Canada.* Ottawa: Minister of Supply and Services.

8   Health and Welfare Canada
1982f *Summary of Submissions: National Pensions Conference, Ottawa, March 31–April 2, 1981.* Ottawa: Minister of Supply and Services.

1, 3, 4, 7, 8, 9, 10, 11, 12, 14, 15   Health and Welfare Canada
1983 *Fact Book on Aging in Canada.* Ottawa: Minister of Supply and Services.

5   Health and Welfare Canada
1984 *Alzheimer's Disease: A Family Information Handbook.* Ottawa: Minister of Supply and Services.

15   Health and Welfare Canada, Health Information Division
1985a *Canada Health Manpower Inventory 1985.* Ottawa: Minister of Supply and Services.

8   Health and Welfare Canada
1985b *Child and Elderly Benefit, Consultation Paper.* Ottawa:

Minister of Supply and Services. National Health and
Welfare.

8   Health and Welfare Canada
         1986a *Canada Pension Plan, Family Allowance, Old Age Security,*
         Canada Pension Plan, Statement on Current Benefits. Ottawa:
         Minister of Supply and Services.

8   Health and Welfare Canada
         1986b *The Canadian Pension Plan* (pamphlet). Ottawa:
         Minister of Supply and Services.

3, 4, 5, 7, Health and Welfare Canada and Statistics Canada
11   1981 *The Health of Canadians* (The Canada Health Survey).
         Cat. No. 82–538E. Ottawa: Minister of Supply and Services.

2   Hendricks, Jon
         1982 "The Elderly in Society: Beyond Modernization." *Social*
         Science History 6:321–45.

1   Hendricks, Jon, and C. Davis Hendricks
         1981 *Aging in Mass Society: Myths and Realities*, 2nd ed.
         Cambridge, Massachusetts: Winthrop.

5, 14   Hendricks, Jon, and C. Davis Hendricks
         1986 *Aging in Mass Society: Myths and Realities*, 3rd ed. Boston:
         Little Brown.

3   Henripin, J.
         1972 *Trends and Factors of Fertility in Canada*. Ottawa: Statistics
         Canada (Dominion Bureau of Statistics).

3   Henripin, J., and Y. Peron
         1972 "The Demographic Transition of the Province of
         Quebec." In *Population and Social Change*, ed. D. Glass and
         R. Revelle. London: Edward Arnold.

13   Henteleff, Paul D.
         1978 "Decisions in the Care of the Dying." *Essence* 2:15–17.

5   Herchak, Gail, and Brian Wilford
         1983 "The Therapy of Pets." *Alberta Report*, November 28.

12   Hess, Beth B., and Beth J. Soldo
         1985 "Husband and Wife Networks." In *Social Support*
         Networks and the Care of the Elderly, ed. W.J. Sauer and
         R.T. Cowards. New York: Springer.

12   Hess, R.
         1982 "Self-help as a Service Delivery Strategy." *Prevention in*
         Human Services 1:1–2.

10   Heumann, L., and D. Boldy
         1982 *Housing for the Elderly*. New York: St. Martin's Press.

12   Hickey, Tom, and Richard L. Douglass
            1981 "Neglect and Abuse of Older Family Members:
            Professionals' Perspectives and Case Experiences." *The
            Gerontologist* 21:171–76.

5   Hirshfield, R.M., and C.K. Cross
            1982 "Epidemiology of Affective Disorders: Psychosocial Risk
            Factors." *Archives of General Psychiatry* 39:35–46.

11   Hobart, C.
            1975 "Active Sports Participation Among the Young, the
            Middle-aged and the Elderly." *International Review of Sports
            Sociology* 10:27–40.

10   Hodge, Gerald
            1984a *Shelter and Services for the Small Town Elderly: The Role
            of Assisted Housing*. Ottawa: Canada Mortgage and Housing
            Corporation.

11   Hodge, Gerald
            1984b "Time and the Environment of the Small Town
            Elderly." Paper presented at the Canadian Association on
            Gerontology 13th Annual Scientific and Educational Meeting,
            Vancouver, B.C.

7   Hogan, David B.
            1984 "Exercise in the Elderly." *Geriatric Medicine Today*
            3:47–48.

6, 12   Holmes, T.H., and R.H. Rahe
            1967 "The Social Readjustment Rating Scale." *Journal of
            Psychosomatic Research* 11:213–18.

12   Holzberg, Carol S.
            1981 "Cultural Gerontology: Toward an Understanding of
            Ethnicity and Aging." *Culture* 1:110–22.

12   Holzberg, Carol S.
            1982 "Ethnicity and Aging: Anthropological Perspectives on
            More than Just the Minority Elderly." *The Gerontologist*
            22:249–57.

5   Horn, J.L.
            1978 "Human Ability Systems." In *Life-Span Development and
            Behavior, Vol. 1*, ed. P.B. Baltes. New York: Academic Press.

5   Horn, J.L., and R.B. Cattel
            1966 "Age Differences in Primary Mental Ability Factors."
            Journal of Gerontology 21:210–20.

5   Horn, J.L., and R.B. Cattell
            1967 "Age Differences in Fluid and Crystallized
            Intelligence." *Acta Psychologica* 26:107–29.

12   Horowitz, Amy
            1985 "Sons and Daughters as Caregivers to Older Parents:

Differences in Role Performance and Consequences." *The Gerontologist* 25:612–17.

12   Horowitz, Amy, and L.W. Shindelman
1981 "Reciprocity and Affection: Past Influences on Current Caregiving." Paper presented at the 34th Annual Scientific Meeting of the Gerontological Society of America.

10   Hough, George S.
1981 *Tenant Receptiveness: Family and Senior Citizen Mixing in Public Housing.* Toronto: Policy and Program Development Secretariat, Ministry of Municipal Affairs and Housing.

8   House of Commons Canada
1983 *Report of the Parliamentary Task Force on Pension Reform* (Frith Commission). Ottawa: Supply and Services Canada.

5   Howard, D.V., M.P. McAndrews, and M.I. Lasagna
1981 "Semantic Priming of Lexical Decisions in Young and Old Adults." *Journal of Gerontology* 36:707–14.

2   Howells, W.W.
1960 "Estimating Population Numbers Through Archaeological and Skeletal Remains." In *The Application of Quantitative Methods to Archaeology*, ed. R.F. Heizer and C.F. Cook. Chicago: Quadrangle.

11   Huang, J.
1974 "Aging and Information." *Journal of Communication* 3:558–61.

2   Hufton, O.
1975 *The Poor in Eighteenth Century France.* Oxford, England: Oxford University Press.

12   Hughes, E.C., and H.M. Hughes
1952 *Where Peoples Meet.* Glencoe, Illinois: Free Press.

5   Hulicka, I.M., and J.L. Grossman
1967 "Age-Group Comparisons for the Use of Mediators in Paired-Associate Learning." *Journal of Gerontology* 22:46–51.

5   Hulicka, I.M., and R.L. Weiss
1965 "Age Differences in Retention as a Function of Learning." *Journal of Consulting Psychology* 29:125–29.

5   Hultsch, David F.
1971 "Adult Age Differences in Free Classification and Free Recall." *Developmental Psychology* 4:338–42.

1, 5, 11   Hultsch, David F., and Francine Deutsch
1981 *Adult Development and Aging: A Life-Span Perspective.* New York: McGraw-Hill.

2   Human Behavior Magazine
1977 "Retirement to the Porch." In *Readings in Aging and*

Death: Contemporary Perspectives, ed. Steven H. Zarit. New York: Harper and Row.

7   Hurwitz, Joel S.
1984 "A Geriatric Day Hospital — The Seven Oaks Experience." Poster display at the Canadian Association on Gerontology 13th Annual Scientific and Educational Meeting, Vancouver, B.C.

5   Iglauer, Edith
1980 "The Unsinkable Hubert Evans." *Today Magazine*, December 20: 16–18.

2   Ikels, C.
1981 "The Coming of Age in Chinese Society: Traditional Patterns and Contemporary Hong Kong." In *Dimensions: Aging, Culture, and Health*, ed. C.L. Fry and contributors. New York: Praeger.

7   Jackson, Marilyn F.
1983 "Day Care for Handicapped Elders: An Evaluation Study." *Canadian Journal of Public Health* 74:348–51.

14   Jacobs, Ruth Harriet, and Beth B. Hess
1980 "Panther Power: Symbol and Substance." In *Aging, the Individual and Society*, ed. Jill S. Quadagno. New York: St. Martin's Press.

5   Jacquish, G.A., and R.E. Ripple
1981 "Cognitive Creative Abilities and Self-Esteem Across the Adult Life-Span." *Human Development* 24:110–19.

11   Jahn, Penelope
1982 "Good Old." *Today Magazine*, January 9: 11–14, 16.

6   Jarvis, George K., and Menno Boldt
1980 "Suicide in the Later Years." *Essence* 4:145–58.

5   Jones, H.E., and H.S. Conrad
1933 "The Growth and Decline of Intelligence." *Genetic Psychology Monographs* 12:223–98.

6   Jung, C.G.
1976 "The Stages of Life." In *The Portable Jung*, ed. Joseph Campbell. Harmondsworth, England: Penguin.

7   Kaban, Leona, and Jeanette Block
1984 "Variations Between a Day Hospital's Team Assessments and Needs Perceived by Referral Source." *Canadian Journal on Aging* 3:147–50.

12   Kahana, B., and E. Kahana
1970 "Grandparenthood from the Perspective of the Developing Grandchild." *Developmental Psychology* 3:98–105.

10   Kaill, Robert C.
1980 "Housing Canada's Aging." *Essence* 4:79–86.

3, 12   Kalbach, Warren E., and Wayne W. McVey
1979 *The Demographic Bases of Canadian Society*, 2nd ed.
Toronto: McGraw-Hill Ryerson.

13   Kalish, R.A.
1963 "An Approach to the Study of Death Attitudes."
American Behavioral Scientist 6:68–70.

13   Kalish, R.A.
1981 *Death, Grief and Caring Relationships*. Monterey,
California: Brooks/Cole.

7   Kane, Robert L., and Rosalie A. Kane
1985 *A Will and a Way: What the United States Can Learn from
Canada about Caring for the Elderly*. New York: Columbia
University Press.

13   Kane, R.L., J. Wales, L. Bernstein, A. Leibowitz, and S. Kaplan
1984 "A Randomized Controlled Trial of Hospice Care."
Lancet 1:890–94.

9   Kaplan, M.
1979 *Leisure: Lifestyles and Lifespan*. Philadelphia: W.B.
Saunders.

4   Kart, Cary S., Eileen S. Metress, and James F. Metress
1978 *Aging and Health: Biologic and Social Perspectives*. Menlo
Park, California: Addison-Wesley.

2   Kastenbaum, R., and B. Ross
1975 "Historical Perspectives on Care." In *Modern Perspectives
in the Psychiatry of Old Age*, ed. J.G. Howells. New York:
Brunner/Mazel.

2   Katz, Michael B.
1975 *The People of Hamilton, Canada West: Family and Class in
a Mid-Nineteenth-Century City*. Cambridge, Massachusetts:
Harvard University Press.

5   Kausler, D.H.
1982 *Experimental Psychology and Human Aging*. New York:
Wiley.

5   Kausler, D.H., and C.V. Lair
1966 "Associative Strength and Paired-Associate Learning in
Elderly Subjects." *Journal of Gerontology* 21:278–80.

9   Keating, Norah, and Barbara Jeffrey
1983 "Work Careers of Ever Married and Never Married
Retired Women." *The Gerontologist* 23:416–21.

12   Keith, Patricia M., Kathleen Hill, Willis J. Goudy, and Edward
A. Powers
1984 "Confidants and Well-Being: A Note on Male
Friendship in Old Age." *The Gerontologist* 24:318–20.

1   Kennedy, Leslie W., and Robert A. Silverman
     1984–85 "Significant Others and Fear of Crime Among the
     Elderly." *International Journal of Aging and Human Development*
     20:241–56.

14   Kernaghan, Kenneth
     1982 "Politics, Public Administration and Canada's Aging
     Population." *Canadian Public Policy* 8:69–79.

14   Kernaghan, Kenneth, and Olivia Kuper
     1983 *Coordination in Canadian Governments: A Case Study of
     Aging Policy*. Toronto: Institute of Public Administration of
     Canada.

9   Kettle, John
     1982 "Forewatch." *Executive* 24:12.

11   Kidd, J.R.
     1973 *How Adults Learn*. New York: Associated Press.

13   Klug, Leo F., and Earle H. Waugh
     1982 "Survey of Credit Courses in Thanatology Offered by
     Canadian Universities: 1971–80." *Essence* 5:227–33.

12   Kneem, Robert
     1963 "Sample Study of Estonian Old Age Population in
     Toronto." Unpublished paper.

1   Knox, V.J., W.L. Gekoski, and E.A. Johnson
     1984 "The Relationship Between Contact with and
     Perceptions of the Elderly." Paper presented at the Canadian
     Association on Gerontology 13th Annual Scientific and
     Educational Meeting, Vancouver, B.C.

5   Koch, Kenneth
     1977 *I Never Told Anybody: Teaching Poetry Writing in a Nursing
     Home*. New York: Random House.

5   Koch, Kenneth
     1982 "Teaching Poetry Writing in a Nursing Home." In
     Readings in Aging and Death: Contemporary Perspectives, 2nd ed.,
     ed. Steven H. Zarit. New York: Harper and Row.

1   Koenig, Daniel, C. Doyle, and P. Debeck
     1977 *The Golden Years in British Columbia: How They are Seen by
     Senior Citizens*. Victoria, B.C.: Department of Human
     Resources, Province of British Columbia.

2   Koty, J.
     1933 *Die Behandlung der Alten und Kranken bei den
     Naturvolkern*. Stuttgart.

9   Koyl, L.F.
     1974 *Employing the Older Worker: Matching the Employee to the
     Job*, 2nd ed. Washington: National Council on the Aging, Inc.

410   *References*

6   Kozma, Albert, and M.J. Stones
           1978 "Some Research Issues and Findings in the Study of
           Psychological Well-being in the Aged." *Canadian Psychological
           Review* 19:241–49.

11   Kraus, H., and W. Raab
           1961 *Hypokinetic Disease*. Springfield, Illinois: Charles C.
           Thomas.

13, 15   Kubler-Ross, Elisabeth
           1969 *On Death and Dying*. New York: Macmillan.

13   Kunz, Phillip, and Jeffrey Summers
           1979–80 "A Time to Die: A Study of the Relationship of
           Birthdays and Time of Death." *Omega* 10:281–89.

6, 15   Kuypers, J.A., and V.L. Bengtson
           1973 "Social Breakdown and Competence: A Model of
           Normal Aging." *Human Development* 16:181–201.

9   Labour Canada
           1986 *Women in the Labour Force, 1985–1986*. Cat. No. L38–30/
           1986. Ottawa: Minister of Supply and Services.

8   *Labour Gazette*
           1924

5   Labouvie-Vief, G.
           1977 "Adult Cognitive Development: In Search of
           Alternative Interpretations." *Merrill Palmer Quarterly*
           23:227–63.

5   Labouvie-Vief, G.
           1985 "Intelligence and Cognition." In *Handbook of the
           Psychology of Aging*, 2nd ed., ed. James E. Birren and
           K. Warner Schaie. New York: Van Nostrand Reinhold.

13   Labovitz, S.
           1974 "Control Over Death: The Canadian Case." *Omega*
           5:217–21.

5   Lachman, J.L., and R. Lachman
           1980 "Age and the Actualization of World Knowledge." In
           *New Directions in Memory and Aging: Proceedings of the George A.
           Talland Memorial Conference*, ed. L.W. Poon, J.L. Fozard, L.S.
           Cermak, D. Arenberg, and L.W. Thompson. Hillsdale, N.J.:
           Lawrence Erlbaum Association.

5   Lachman, J.L., R. Lachman, and C. Thronesbery
           1979 "Metamemory Through the Adult Life Span."
           Developmental Psychology 15:543–51.

6   Lacy, William B., and Jon Hendricks
           1980 "Developmental Models of Adult Life: Myth or
           Reality." *International Journal of Aging and Human Development*
           11:89–110.

9   Laframboise, Josette
           1975 *A Question of Need*. Ottawa: Canadian Council on Social
           Development.

5   Lair, C.V., W.H. Moon, and D.H. Kausler
           1969 "Associative Interference in the Paired-Associate
           Learning of Middle-Aged and Old Subjects." *Developmental
           Psychology* 1:548–52.

7   Lalonde, Marc
           1974 *A New Perspective on the Health of Canadians: A Working
           Document*. Ottawa: Minister of Supply and Services.

12   Lam, Leatrice
           1985 "The Implications of Multicultural Reality for Person
           Care Home Development: A Chinese Canadian Case Study."
           Paper presented at the Canadian Asian Studies Association
           Meeting, Montreal, Quebec.

4   Lane, N., D.A. Block, H.H. Jones, W.H. Marshall, P.D. Wood,
           and J.F. Fries
           1986 "Long-Distance Running, Bone Density, and
           Osteoarthritis." *Journal of the American Medical Association*
           255:1147–51.

11   LaRocque P., and P.D. Campagna
           1983 "Physical Activity through Rhythmic Exercise for
           Elderly Persons Living in a Senior Citizen Residence."
           Activities, Adaptations and Aging 4:77–81.

14   Laskin, Richard, and Richard Baird
           1970 "Factors in Voter Turnout and Party Preference in a
           Saskatchewan Town." *Canadian Journal of Political Science*
           3:450–62.

2   Laslett, P.
           1965 *The World We Have Lost*. New York: Charles Scribner's
           Sons.

2, 3   Laslett, P.
           1976 "Societal Development and Aging." In *Handbook of
           Aging and the Social Sciences*, ed. R.H. Binstock and E. Shanas.
           New York: Van Nostrand Reinhold.

13   Law Reform Commission of Canada
           1982 *Euthanasia, Aiding Suicide and Cessation of Treatment*.
           Working Paper 28. Ottawa: Minister of Supply and Services.

10   Lawton, M. Powell
           1976 "The Relative Impact of Enriched and Traditional
           Housing on Elderly Tenants." *The Gerontologist* 16:237–42.

10   Lawton, M. Powell
           1982 "Environmental Research: Issues and Methods." In
           Research Issues in Aging: Report of a Conference, 1980, ed.

Ronald Bayne and Blossom Wigdor. Hamilton, Ontario: Gerontology Research Council of Ontario.

10   Lawton, M. Powell
      1985 "Housing and Living Environments of Older People." In *Handbook of Aging and the Social Sciences*, ed. Robert H. Binstock and Ethel Shanas. New York: Van Nostrand Reinhold.

6, 10, 15   Lawton, M. Powell, and Lucille Nahemow
      1973 "Ecology and the Aging Process." In *The Psychology of Adult Development and Aging*, ed. Carl Eisdorfer and M. Powell Lawton. Washington, D.C.: American Psychological Association.

10   Lazarowich, Michael
      1986 "The Perspective of the User in the Ontario Granny Flat Demonstration Project." In *Granny Flats: A Housing Option for the Elderly*, Report No. 13, ed. Susan Corke, Gregory S. Romanick, Michael Lazarowich, and Joan Simon. Winnipeg: Institute of Urban Studies.

10   Lazarowich, M., and B.W. Haley
      1982 *Granny Flats: Their Practicality and Implementation.* Ottawa: Canada Mortgage and Housing Corporation.

3   Leacy, F., ed.
      1983 *Historical Statistics of Canada*, 2nd ed. Ottawa: Minister of Supply and Services.

5   LeBlanc, Julia
      1985 "Combined Medical Psychiatric Day Centre." Paper presented at the Canadian Association on Gerontology 14th Annual Scientific and Educational Meeting, Hamilton, Ontario.

5   Leech, S., and K.L. Witte
      1971 "Paired-Associate Learning in Elderly Adults as Related to Pacing and Incentive Conditions." *Developmental Psychology* 5:180.

3   Legare, J., and B. Desjardins
      1976 "La Situation des Personnes Agées au Canada." *Canadian Review of Sociology and Anthropology* 13:321–36.

5   Lehman, Harvey C.
      1953 *Age and Achievement*. Princeton, N.J.: Princeton University Press.

5   Lehman, Harvey C.
      1968 "The Creative Production Rates of Present versus Past Generations of Scientists." In *Middle Age and Aging*, ed. Bernice L. Neugarten. Chicago: University of Chicago Press.

6   Lemon, B., V. Bengtson, and J. Peterson
         1972 "Activity Types and Life Satisfaction in a Retirement
         Community." *Journal of Gerontology* 27:511–23.

4   Leo, John, and Barbara Blonarz
         1981 "Fighting Off Old Age." *Time*, February 16.

2   Lerner, M.
         1970 "When, Why and Where People Die." In *The Dying
         Patient*, ed. O.G. Brim, Jr., H.E. Freeman, S. Levine, and
         N.A. Scotch. New York: Russell Sage Foundation.

5   Leroux, Charles
         1981 "Alzheimer's Disease Steals Aging Mind." *Chicago
         Tribune*, September 21.

6, 15   Levinson, D.J.
         1978 *The Seasons of a Man's Life*. New York: Knopf.

14   Lewis, Doris
         1986 "The Role of Interest Groups in Canadian Pension
         Plans." Paper presented at the Canadian Sociology and
         Anthropology Association 21st Annual Meeting, Winnipeg,
         Manitoba.

13   Ley, Dorothy C.H.
         1985 "Palliative Care in Canada: The First Decade and
         Beyond." *Journal of Palliative Care* 1:32–34.

7   Librach, Gershon, Clair Davidson, Abraham Peretz
         1972 "A Community Home Care Program." *Journal of the
         American Geriatrics Society* 20:500–504.

6   Lieberman, M.A.
         1975 "Adaptive Processes in Late Life." In *Life-Span
         Developmental Psychology: Normative Life Crises*, ed. N. Datan
         and L.H. Ginsberg. New York: Academic Press.

13   Lindemann, E.
         1944 "Symptomatology and Management of Acute Grief."
         American Journal of Psychiatry 101:141–48.

6   Linton, Ralph
         1936 *The Study of Man*. New York: Appleton-Century-Crofts.

14   Long, Cathy, and Carol Shelton, researchers and compilers
         1982 *The Directory: Programs for Senior Citizens Across Canada*.
         Toronto: Canadian Pensioners Concerned, Ontario Division.

5   Longfellow, Henry Wadsworth
         "Morituri Salutamus."

6   Lopata, H.Z.
         1969 "Loneliness: Forms and Components." *Social Problems*
         17:248–61.

6   Lowenthal, M.F.
           1975 "Psychosocial Variations Across the Adult Life Course:
           Frontiers for Research and Policy." *The Gerontologist* 15:6–12.

12   Lowenthal, M.F., and C. Haven
           1968 "Interaction and Adaptation: Intimacy as a Critical
           Variable." In *Middle Age and Aging*, ed. B.L. Neugarten.
           Chicago: University of Chicago Press.

6   Lowenthal, M.F., M. Thurner, and D. Chiriboga
           1975 *Four Stages of Life*. San Francisco: Jossey-Bass.

9   McConnell, Stephen R., Dorothy Fleisher, Carolyn E. Usher,
           and Barbara H. Kaplan
           1980 *Alternative Work Options for Older Workers: A Feasibility
           Study*. Los Angeles: Ethel Percy Andrus Gerontology Centre.

5   McCormack, P.D.
           1982 "Coding of Spatial Information by Young and Elderly
           Adults." *Journal of Gerontology* 37:80–86.

3   McDaniel, Susan A.
           1986 *Canada's Aging Population*. Toronto: Butterworths.

9   McDonald, P. Lynn, and Richard A. Wanner
           1984 "Socioeconomic Determinants of Early Retirement in
           Canada." *Canadian Journal on Aging* 3:105–16.

5   Mace, Nancy L., and Peter V. Rabins
           1981 *The Thirty-Six Hour Day*. Baltimore: Johns Hopkins
           University Press.

3   McInnis, R.M.
           1977 "Childbearing and Land Availability: Some Evidence
           from Individual Household Data." In *Population Patterns in
           the Past*, ed. R. Lee. New York: Academic Press.

6   MacLean, Michael
           1982 "Personal Major Events and Individual Life Satisfaction
           in Old Age." *Essence* 5:119–26.

10   MacLean, M.J., and R. Bonar
           1983 "The Normalization Principle and the
           Institutionalization of the Elderly." *Canada's Mental Health*
           31:16–18.

10   MacLennan, Barbara A.
           1983 "Some Possible Implications for Adapting the Milieu in
           Nursing Homes." *Activities, Adaptation and Aging* 4:33–38.

11   McPherson, Barry D.
           1983 *Aging as a Social Process*. Toronto: Butterworths.

11   McPherson, Barry D.
           1985 "The Meaning and Use of Time Across the Life-Cycle:
           The Influence of Work, Family and Leisure." In *Canadian*

Gerontological Collection V: The Challenge of Time, ed. Ellen M. Gee and Gloria M. Gutman. Winnipeg: Canadian Association on Gerontology.

11   McPherson, Barry D., and Carol Kozlik
1980 "Canadian Leisure Patterns: Disengagement, Continuity or Ageism." In *Aging in Canada*, ed. Victor W. Marshall. Toronto: Fitzhenry and Whiteside.

9   McVeigh, Frank J.
1980 "Mandatory vs. Flexible Retirement and the Functions of Counselling." *Canadian Counsellor* 14:102–9.

2, 3   McVey, Wayne W.
1987 Personal communication.

3   McWhinnie, J., and B. Ouellet
1981 "Health Trends." In *Health and Canadian Society: Sociological Perspectives*, ed. D. Coburn, C. D'Arcy, P. New, and G. Torrance. Toronto: Fitzhenry and Whiteside.

6   Maddox, George
1970 "Fact or Artifact: Evidence Bearing on Disengagement Theory." In *Normal Aging*, ed. Erdman Palmore. Durham, N.C.: Duke University Press.

13   Manitoba Health Organizations
No date. *Bulletin*. Winnipeg: Manitoba Health Organizations.

4   Manitoba Health Services Commission
1980 *Planning Guide for Personal Care Homes in Manitoba*. Winnipeg: Manitoba Health Services Commission.

15   Marcus, Lotte
1978 "Ageing and Education." In *The Social Challenge of Ageing*, ed. David Hobman. London: Croom Helm.

15   Marcus, Lotte
1980 "The Education of the Practitioner in Gerontology." Personal communication.

12   Marcus, Lotte, and Valerie Jaeger
1984 "The Elderly as Family Caregivers." *Canadian Journal on Aging* 13:33–43.

12   Maris, R.W.
1969 *Social Forces in Urban Suicide*. Homewood, Illinois: Dorsey Press.

11   Marmel, Bernice, Susan Sawyer, and Donna Shell
1983 *A Study of the Needs of Tenants of Willow Centre Elderly Persons' Housing. Study #1*. Winnipeg: Nor'West Co-op Health and Social Services Centre, Inc.

13   Marshall, Victor W.
1974 "The Last Strand: Remnants of Engagement in the Later Years." *Omega* 5:25–35.

13   Marshall, Victor W.
      1975 "Age and Awareness of Finitude in Developmental
      Gerontology." *Omega* 6:113–29.

1   Marshall, Victor W., ed.
      1980a *Aging in Canada.* Toronto: Fitzhenry and Whiteside.

13   Marshall, Victor W.
      1980b *Last Chapters: A Sociology of Aging and Dying.* Monterey,
      California: Brooks/Cole.

6   Marshall, Victor W.
      1983 "Generations, Age Groups and Cohorts." *Canadian
      Journal on Aging* 2:51–61.

1   Marshall, Victor W., ed.
      1986 *Aging in Canada,* 2nd ed. Toronto: Fitzhenry and
      Whiteside.

12   Marshall, Victor W., Carolyn J. Rosenthal, and Jane Synge
      1981 "The Family as a Health Service Organization for the
      Elderly." Paper presented at the Annual Meeting of the
      Society for the Study of Social Problems, Toronto.

12   Masters, W., and V. Johnson
      1970 *Human Sexual Inadequacy.* Boston: Little, Brown.

12   Matthews, Anne Martin
      1982 "Canadian Research on Women as Widows: A
      Comparative Analysis of the State of the Art." *Resources for
      Feminist Research* 11:227–30.

12   Matthews, Anne Martin
      1985 "Support Systems of Widows in Canada." In *Widows:
      Other Countries/Other Places,* ed. Helena Z. Lopata.
      Forthcoming. Durham, N.C.: Duke University Press.

12   Matthews, Anne Martin
      1986 "Widowhood as an Expectable Life Event." In *Aging in
      Canada,* 2nd ed., ed. Victor W. Marshall. Toronto: Fitzhenry
      and Whiteside.

12   Matthews, Anne Martin, Kathleen H. Brown, Christine K.
      Davis, and Margaret A. Denton
      1982 "A Crisis Assessment Technique for the Evaluation of
      Life Events: Transition to Retirement as an Example."
      Canadian Journal on Aging 1:28–39.

1   Matthews, Anne Martin, Joseph A. Tindale, and Joan E. Norris
      1985 "The Facts on Aging Quiz: A Canadian Validation and
      Cross-Cultural Comparison." *Canadian Journal on Aging*
      3:165–74.

2   Matthews, C., and J.V. Thompson
      1985 "The Aged in Canadian Fiction: No Longer Tragic

Figures." Paper presented at the Canadian Association on Gerontology 14th Annual Scientific and Educational Meeting, Hamilton, Ontario.

7   Maxwell, Robert J.
        1981 *Health and Wealth.* Lexington, Massachusetts: Lexington Books.

2   Maxwell, Robert J., and Philip Silverman
        1977 "Information and Esteem: Cultural Considerations in the Treatment of the Aged." In *Human Aging and Dying: A Study in Sociocultural Gerontology*, ed. Wilbur H. Watson and Robert J. Maxwell. New York: St. Martin's Press.

2   Mays, H.J.
        1983 "A Place to Stand: Families, Land and Permanence in Toronto Gore Township, 1820–1890." In *The Social Development of Canada: Readings*, ed. W.P. Ward. Richmond, B.C.: Open Learning Institute.

9   Meier, E.L., and E.A. Kerr
        1976 "Capabilities of Middle-aged and Older Workers." *Industrial Gerontology* 3:147–56.

13   Metzger, Anne M.
        1979–80 "A Q-Methodological Study of the Kubler-Ross Stage Theory." *Omega* 10:291–301.

14   Milbrath, Lester W.
        1965 *Political Participation: How and Why Do People Get Involved in Politics?* Chicago: Rand McNally.

5   Miles, C.C., and W.R. Miles
        1932 "The Correlation of Intelligence Scores and Chronological Age from Early to Late Maturity." *American Journal of Psychology* 44:44–78.

6   Miller, Marv
        1979 *Suicide After Sixty: The Final Alternative.* New York: Springer.

11   Milton, B.
        1975 *Social Status and Leisure Time Activities: National Survey Findings for Adult Canadians.* Monograph 3. Montreal: Canadian Sociology and Anthropology Association.

10   Minuk, M., and K. Davidson
        1981 *A Report on the Research Findings on the MHRC 1981 Shelter Allowance Program Review.* Winnipeg: Manitoba Housing and Renewal Corporation.

14   Montgomery, Charlotte
        1985 "Tories Retreat on De-Indexing Pensions." *Globe and Mail*, June 28.

2   Moodie, S.
           1853 *Life in the Clearings Versus the Bush.* New York: DeWitt
           and Davenport.

12   Morris, John N., and Sylvia Sherwood
           1983–84 "Informal Support Resources for Vulnerable
           Elderly Persons: Can They Be Counted on, Why Do They
           Work?" *International Journal of Aging and Human Development*
           18:81–98.

13   Moss, Miriam S., and Sidney Z. Moss
           1984–85 "Some Aspects of the Elderly Widow(er)'s Persistent
           Tie with the Deceased Spouse." *Omega* 15:195–206.

7   Mossey, Jana M., Betty Havens, Noralou P. Roos, and Evelyn
           Shapiro
           1981 "The Manitoba Longitudinal Study on Aging:
           Description and Methods." *The Gerontologist* 21:551–58.

13   Mount, B.F., and J.F. Scott
           1983 "Whither Hospice Evaluation." *Journal of Chronic
           Diseases* 36:731–36.

13   Mount, R.M., A. Jones, and A. Patterson
           1974 "Death and Dying: Attitudes in a Teaching Hospital."
           Urology 4:741.

12   Mullens, Harry J.
           1983 "Love, Sexuality, and Aging in Nursing Homes and
           Public Housing." Paper presented at the Canadian
           Association on Gerontology 12th Annual Scientific and
           Educational Meeting, Moncton, New Brunswick.

4   Murrell, F.H.
           1970 "The Effect of Extensive Practice on Age Differences in
           Reaction Time." *Journal of Gerontology* 25:268–74.

5   Murrell, S.A., S. Himmelfarb, and K. Wright
           1983 "Prevalence of Depression and Its Correlates in Older
           Adults." *American Journal of Epidemiology* 117:173–85.

11   Myers, A.M., and N. Hamilton
           1985 "Evaluation of the Canadian Red Cross Society's Fun
           and Fitness Program for Seniors." *Canadian Journal on Aging*
           4:201–12.

8   Myles, John
           1981 "The Trillion Dollar Misunderstanding." *Working Papers
           Magazine*, July–August.

3, 8   Myles, John
           1982 "Social Implications of a Changing Age Structure." In
           Canada's Changing Age Structure: Implications for the Future, ed.
           Gloria Gutman. Burnaby, B.C.: Simon Fraser University
           Publications.

8, 9, 14, 15   Myles, John
1984 *Old Age in the Welfare State: The Political Economy of Public Pensions*. Boston: Little, Brown and Co.

3, 7, 11, 15   Myles, John F., and Monica Boyd
1982 "Population Aging and the Elderly." In *Social Issues: Sociological Views of Canada*, ed. Dennis Forcese and Stephen Richer. Scarborough, Ontario: Prentice-Hall.

3   Nagnur, Dhruva
1986 *Longevity and Historical Life Tables 1921–1981 (Abridged) Canada and the Provinces*. Statistics Canada Cat. No. 89–506. Ottawa: Minister of Supply and Services.

11   Nahmiash, Daphne
1985 "Intergenerational Relationships." Paper presented at the Canadian Association on Gerontology 14th Annual Scientific and Educational Meeting, Hamilton, Ontario.

2   Nason, J.D.
1981 "Respected Elder or Old Person: Aging in a Micronesian Community." In *Other Ways of Growing Old: Anthropological Perspectives*, ed. P.T. Amoss and S. Harrell. Stanford, California: Stanford University Press.

15   National Advisory Council on Aging
1981 *Priorities for Action: A Report of the National Advisory Council on Aging*. Ottawa: Health and Welfare Canada.

8   National Advisory Council on Aging
1985b *Expression* 2 (1). Ottawa: National Advisory Council on Aging.

14   National Advisory Council on Aging
1985c *"Listen to Me!": The Technical Evaluation Report of The National Advisory Council on Aging's Consultation with Seniors. News Release*. Ottawa: National Advisory Council on Aging.

14   National Advisory Council on Aging
1985d *Seniors and Decision-Making*. Ottawa: Minister of Supply and Services.

10   National Advisory Council on Aging
1985e *Expression* 2 (4). Ottawa: National Advisory Council on Aging.

12   National Advisory Council on Aging
1986b *Expression* 3 (1). Ottawa: National Advisory Council on Aging.

10   National Advisory Council on Aging
1986c *Expression* 3 (3). Ottawa: National Advisory Council on Aging.

7   National Advisory Council on Aging
1986d "Toward a Community Support Policy for Canadians." Ottawa: National Advisory Council on Aging.

8   National Council of Welfare
1979 *Women and Poverty*. Ottawa: Minister of Supply and Services.

8   National Council of Welfare
1984a *1984 Poverty Lines*. Ottawa: Minister of Supply and Services.

8   National Council of Welfare
1984b *A Pension Primer*. Ottawa: Minister of Supply and Services.

8   National Council of Welfare
1984c *Pension Reform*. Ottawa: Minister of Supply and Services.

8   National Council of Welfare
1984d *Sixty-five and Older*. Ottawa: Minister of Supply and Services.

8   National Council of Welfare
1985a *Giving and Taking: The May 1985 Budget and the Poor*. Ottawa: Minister of Supply and Services.

8   National Council of Welfare
1985b *Poverty Lines: Estimates by the National Council of Welfare*. Ottawa: Minister of Supply and Services.

8   National Council of Welfare
1985c *Poverty Profile*. Ottawa: Minister of Supply and Services.

8   National Health and Welfare
1973 *Working Paper on Social Security in Canada*, 2nd ed. Ottawa: Queen's Printer.

6   Neugarten, B.L.
1964 *Personality in Middle and Late Life*. New York: Atherton Press.

6   Neugarten, B.L., ed.
1968 *Middle Age and Aging*. Chicago: University of Chicago Press.

6   Neugarten, B.L.
1969 "Continuities and Discontinuities of Psychological Issues into Adult Life." *Human Development* 12:121–30.

2, 9   Neugarten, B.L.
1980 "Acting One's Age: New Rules for Old" (Interview with Elizabeth Hall). *Psychology Today*, April: 66–80.

4, 14   Neugarten, B.L., and R.J. Havighurst
1979 "Aging and the Future." In *Dimensions of Aging: Readings*, ed. J. Hendricks and C.D. Hendricks. Cambridge, Massachusetts: Winthrop.

6   Neugarten, B.L., R.J. Havighurst, and S. Tobin
1968 "Personality and Patterns of Aging." In *Middle Age and Aging*, ed. Bernice L. Neugarten. Chicago: University of Chicago Press.

6   Neugarten, B.L., and Joan W. Moore
1968 "The Changing Age-status System." In *Middle Age and Aging*, ed. Bernice L. Neugarten. Chicago: University of Chicago Press.

6   Neugarten, B.L., J.W. Moore, and J.C. Lowe
1968 "Age Norms, Age Constraints, and Adult Socialization." In *Middle Age and Aging*, ed. Bernice L. Neugarten. Chicago: University of Chicago Press.

12   Neugarten, B.L., and Karol K. Weinstein
1964 "The Changing American Grandparent." *Journal of Marriage and the Family* 26:199–204.

12   Neysmith, Sheila M.
1982 "The Social Contributions of Old People: A Description and Assessment." Revised version of a paper presented at the Canadian Association on Gerontology 11th Annual Scientific and Educational Meeting, Winnipeg, Manitoba.

14   Neysmith, Sheila M.
1986 "Social Policy Implications of an Aging Society." In *Aging in Canada*, 2nd ed., ed. Victor W. Marshall. Toronto: Fitzhenry and Whiteside.

2   Neysmith, Sheila M., and Joey Edwardh
1983 "Ideological Underpinnings of the World Assembly on Aging." *Canadian Journal on Aging* 2:125–36.

10   Nicklin, Robert L.
1985 "The Role of the Canada Mortgage and Housing Corporation in the Development Process." In *Innovations in Housing and Living Arrangements for Seniors*, ed. Gloria Gutman and Norman Blackie. Burnaby, B.C.: Gerontology Research Centre, Simon Fraser University.

12   Norris, J.
1980 "The Social Adjustment of Single and Widowed Older Women." *Essence* 4:134–44.

12   Norris, Joan E., Kenneth H. Rubin, Janice Cohen, and Lily Both
1983 "Assessing Qualitative Dimensions of Adult Social Interaction: Examining Peer Relationships." Paper presented at the Canadian Association on Gerontology 12th Annual Scientific and Educational Meeting, Moncton, N.B.

1, 6   Northcott, Herbert C.
1982 "The Best Years of Your Life." *Canadian Journal on Aging* 1:72–78.

3   Northcott, Herbert C.
           1984 "The Interprovincial Migration of Canada's Elderly:
           1956–61 and 1971–76." *Canadian Journal on Aging* 3:3–22.

6, 13   Novak, Mark
           1985 *Successful Aging: The Myths, Realities and Future of Aging
           in Canada.* Markham, Ontario: Penguin.

6   Novak, Mark
           1985–86 "Biography After the End of Metaphysics."
           International Journal of Aging and Human Development
           22:189–204.

11   Novak, Mark
           1987 "The Canadian New Horizons Program." *The
           Gerontologist* 27:353–55.

13   Novak, Mark, and Charles Axelrod
           1979 "Primitive Myth and Modern Medicine: On Death and
           Dying, by Elisabeth Kubler-Ross." *The Psychoanalytic Review*
           66:443–50.

5   Novak, Mark, and C. Guest
           1985 "Social Correlates of Caregiver Burden." Paper
           presented at the Canadian Association on Gerontology 14th
           Annual Scientific and Educational Meeting, Hamilton,
           Ontario.

12   Novak, Mark, and Leroy O. Stone
           1985 "Changing Patterns of Aging." Paper presented at the
           annual meeting of the Canadian Sociology and Anthropology
           Association, Montreal, Quebec.

12   O'Brien, J.E., and D.L. Wagner
           1980 "Help-seeking by the Frail Elderly: Problems in
           Network Analysis." *The Gerontologist* 20:78–83.

5   Okun, M.A., I.C. Siegler, and L.K. George
           1978 "Cautiousness and Verbal Learning in Adulthood."
           Journal of Gerontology 33:94–97.

10   Ontario Advisory Council on Senior Citizens
           1978 *Through the Eyes of Others.* Toronto: Ontario Advisory
           Council on Senior Citizens.

10   Ontario Advisory Council on Senior Citizens
           1980–81 *Seniors Tell All.* Toronto: Ontario Advisory Council
           on Senior Citizens.

7   Ontario Council of Health
           1978 "Health Care for the Aged: A Report of the Ontario
           Council of Health." Toronto: Ontario Council of Health.

10   Ontario Ministry of Municipal Affairs and Housing, Research
           and Special Projects Branch
           1983 *Towards Community Planning for an Aging Society.*
           Toronto: Queen's Printer for Ontario.

3   Ontario Ministry of Treasury and Economics
           1979 *Issues in Pension Policy: Demographic and Economic Aspects
           of Canada's Ageing Population*. Ontario Treasury Studies 16.
           Toronto: Ministry of Treasury and Economics, Taxation and
           Fiscal Policy Branch.

7   Ontario Public Health Association
           1983 "Creating a Healthy Ontario: Health Care in the 80's
           and Beyond." Toronto: Ontario Public Health Association.

9   Orbach, Harold L.
           1969 *Trends in Early Retirement*. Ann Arbor, Michigan:
           University of Michigan, Wayne State University Institute of
           Gerontology.

9   Orbach, Harold L.
           1981 "Mandatory Retirement and the Development of
           Adequate Retirement Provisions for Older Persons." In
           Canadian Gerontological Collection II: Retirement Income Systems,
           ed. George Gasek. Winnipeg: Canadian Association on
           Gerontology.

1   Orris, Milton
           1970 *Factors Which Contribute to the Social and Economic
           Independence of People Over 60*. Saskatoon: Joint Advisory
           Committee on Aging.

5   Owens, W.A.
           1972 "Army Alpha Scores at 19, 50 and 61." In *Human
           Ageing*, ed. Sheila M. Chown. Harmondsworth, England:
           Penguin.

4   Paffenbarger, R.S., R.T. Hyde, A.L. Wing, and C. Hsieh
           1986 "Physical Activity, All-Cause Mortality, and Longevity
           of College Alumni." *The New England Journal of Medicine*
           314:605–13.

6   Palmore, Erdman B.
           1970 "The Effects of Aging on Activities and Attitudes." In
           Normal Aging, ed. Erdman Palmore. Durham, N.C.: Duke
           University Press.

1   Palmore, Erdman B.
           1971 "Attitudes Toward Aging as Shown in Humor." *The
           Gerontologist* 11:181–86.

1   Palmore, Erdman B.
           1977 "Facts on Aging: A Short Quiz." *The Gerontologist*
           17:315–20.

1   Palmore, Erdman B.
           1979 "Advantages of Aging." *The Gerontologist* 19:220–23.

12   Palmore, Erdman B.
           1981 *Social Patterns in Normal Aging: Findings from the Duke
           Longitudinal Study*. Durham, N.C.: Duke University Press.

4   Palmore, Erdman B.
             1984 "Longevity in Abkhazia: A Re-evaluation." *The
             Gerontologist* 24:95–96.

1   Palmore, Erdman B., G. Fillenbaum, and L.K. George
             1984 "Consequences of Retirement." *Journal of Gerontology*
             39:109–16.

2   Palmore, Erdman B., and K. Manton
             1974 "Modernization and the Status of the Aged:
             International Correlations." *Journal of Gerontology* 29:205–10.

2   Palmore, Erdman B., and F. Whittington
             1971 "Trends in the Relative Status of the Aged." *Social
             Forces* 50:84–91.

11   Parks Canada
             1973 "Trends in Participation in Outdoor Recreational
             Activities." *CORD Technical Note No. 22.* Ottawa: National and
             Historic Parks Branch, Parks Canada.

6, 13, 15   Peck, Robert C.
             [1955] 1968 "Psychological Aspects of Aging." In *Proceedings
             of a Conference on Planning Research*, Bethesda, Maryland,
             April 24–27, 1955, ed. John E. Anderson. Washington, D.C.:
             American Psychological Association. Excerpted as
             "Psychological Developments in the Second Half of Life." In
             Middle Age and Aging, ed. Bernice L. Neugarten. Chicago:
             University of Chicago Press, 1968.

12   Penning, Margaret J.
             1983 "Multiple Jeopardy: Age, Sex, and Ethnic Variations."
             Canadian Ethnic Studies 15:81–105.

10   Penning, Margaret J., and Neena L. Chappell
             1980 "A Reformulation of Basic Assumptions about
             Institutionalization for the Elderly." In *Aging in Canada*, ed.
             Victor W. Marshall. Toronto: Fitzhenry and Whiteside.

10   Penning, Margaret J., and Neena L. Chappell
             1982 "Mental Health Status: A Comparison of Different
             Socio-Cultural Environments for the Elderly." *Essence*
             5:169–82.

6   Perlman, Daniel, Ann C. Gerson, and Barry Spinner
             1978 "Loneliness Among Senior Citizens: An Empirical
             Report." *Essence* 2:239–48.

5   Perlmutter, M.
             1978 "What Is Memory Aging the Aging Of?" *Developmental
             Psychology* 14:330–45.

11   Perri, Samuel II, and Donald I. Templer
             1984–85 "The Effects of an Aerobic Exercise Program on

Psychological Variables in Older Adults." *International Journal of Aging and Human Development* 20:167–72.

9   Perry, Glenys
        1980 "The Need for Retirement Planning and Counselling."
        Canadian Counsellor 14:97–98.

9   Pesando, James
        1979 *The Elimination of Mandatory Retirement: An Economic Perspective.* Toronto: Ontario Economic Council.

9   Pesando, James, and S. Rea
        1977 *Public and Private Pensions in Canadian Economic Analysis.* Toronto: University of Toronto Press.

12   Pfeiffer, E., A. Verwoerdt, and H.S. Wang
        1968 "Sexual Behavior in Aged Men and Women, I: Observations on 254 Community Volunteers." *Archives of General Psychiatry* 19:753–58.

13   Phillips, D.P., and K.A. Feldman
        1973 "A Dip in Deaths Before Ceremonial Occasions: Some New Relationships Between Social Integration and Mortality." *American Sociological Review* 38:678–96.

3   Philpot, H.J.
        1871 *Guide Book to the Canadian Dominion Containing Full Information for the Emigrant, the Tourist, the Sportsman and the Small Capitalist.* London: n.p.

12   Pihlblad, C.T., D.L. Adams, and D.L. Rosencranz
        1972 "Socio-economic Adjustment to Widowhood." *Omega* 3:295–305.

4   Pitskhelauri, G.Z.
        1982 *The Longliving of Soviet Georgia.* Trans. and ed. G. Lesnoff-Caravaglia. New York: Human Sciences.

9   Pitts, Gordon
        1983 "Getting Ready to Retire Can Be Full-Time Job." *The Financial Post*, May 21.

2   Plath, D.W.
        1972 "Japan: The After Years." In *Aging and Modernization,* ed. D.O. Cowgill and L.D. Holmes. New York: Appleton-Century-Crofts.

12   Podnieks, Elizabeth
        1985 "Case Management of the Abused Elderly." Paper presented at the Canadian Association on Gerontology 14th Annual Scientific and Educational Meeting, Hamilton, Ontario.

5   Poon, Leonard W.
        1985 "Differences in Human Memory with Aging: Nature, Causes, and Clinical Implications." In *Handbook of the*

Psychology of Aging, 2nd ed., ed. James E. Birren and K. Warner Schaie. New York: Van Nostrand Reinhold.

5   Poon, Leonard W., J.L. Fozard, D.R. Paulshock, and J.C. Thomas
1979 "A Questionnaire Assessment of Age Differences in Retention of Recent and Remote Events." *Experimental Aging Research* 5:401–11.

5   Poon, Leonard W., L. Walsh-Sweeney, and J.L. Fozard
1980 "Memory Skill Training for the Elderly: Salient Issues on the Use of Imagery Mnemonics." In *New Directions in Memory and Aging: Proceedings of the George A. Talland Memorial Conference*, ed. L.W. Poon, J.L. Fozard, L.S. Cermak, D. Arenberg, and L.W. Thompson. Hillsdale, N.J.: Lawrence Erlbaum Association.

2   Population Reference Bureau, Inc.
1980 *1980 World Population Data Sheet*. Washington, D.C.: Population Reference Bureau, Inc.

12   Porter, John
1965 *The Vertical Mosaic: An Analysis of Social Class and Power in Canada*. Toronto: University of Toronto Press.

9   Poser, Ernest G., and Mary-Louise Engels
1983 "Self-Efficacy Assessment and Peer Group Assistance in a Pre-Retirement Intervention." *Educational Gerontology* 9:159–69.

14   Pratt, Henry J.
1979 "Politics of Aging." *Research on Aging* 1:155–86.

14   Pratt, Henry J.
1983 "National Interest Groups Among the Elderly: Consolidation and Constraint." In *Aging and Public Policy*, ed. William P. Browne and Laura Katz Olson. Westport, Connecticut: Greenwood Press.

14   Pratt, Henry J.
1984 "Aging in Canada: The Challenge to Political Science." *Canadian Journal on Aging* 3:55–61.

5   Pressey, S.L., and Pressey, A.D.
1967 "Genius at 80; and Other Oldsters." *The Gerontologist* 7:183–87.

12   Priest, Gordon
1985 "Living Arrangements of Canada's Elderly: Changing Demographic and Economic Factors." Occasional Paper Series 85–1. Burnaby, B.C.: Simon Fraser University, Gerontology Research Centre.

10   Pritchard, David C.
1983 "The Art of Matchmaking: A Case Study in Shared Housing." *The Gerontologist* 23:174–79.

1   Proby, Joscelyn
           1984 "Combat Skills Put to Use." *Winnipeg Free Press*, April 10.

14   Pross, A. Paul
           1975 "Canadian Pressure Groups in the 1970's: Their Role
           and Their Relations with the Public Service." *Canadian Public
           Administration* 18:121–35.

7   Psychogeriatric Clinic
           no date "A Telephone Reassurance Service: An Evaluation."
           Ottawa: Ottawa General Hospital.

2   Quadagno, J.
           1980 "The Modernization Controversy: A Socio-historical
           Analysis of Retirement in Nineteenth Century England."
           Paper presented at the meeting of the American Sociological
           Association, New York.

9   Quinn, Joseph F.
           1981 "The Extent and Correlates of Partial Retirement." *The
           Gerontologist* 21:634–43.

9   Quirk, Daniel A., and J.H. Skinner
           1973 "IHCS: Physical Capacity, Age, and Employment."
           Industrial Gerontology 19:49–62.

11   Radcliffe, David
           1982 "U3A: A French Model for the Later Years." Working
           paper prepared for the Annual Conference of
           the Comparative and International Education Society,
           New York, N.Y.

10   Rapelje, Douglas H.
           1985 "A Canadian Example: The Home Sharing Program
           for Older Adults in Regional Niagara." In *Innovations in
           Housing and Living Arrangements for Seniors*, ed. Gloria
           Gutman and Norman Blackie. Burnaby, B.C.: Gerontology
           Research Centre, Simon Fraser University.

11   Rapelje, Douglas H., Bev Goodman, and Pamela Swick
           1986 "Volunteer Opportunities for Senior Citizens: Part of
           the Continuum of Care." Paper presented at the Canadian
           Association on Gerontology 15th Annual Scientific and
           Educational Meeting, Quebec City, Quebec.

5   Read, Donald E.
           1984 "Things Remembered: Places Forgotten." Paper
           presented at the Canadian Association on Gerontology 13th
           Annual Scientific and Educational Meeting, Vancouver, B.C.

7   Rechnitzer, Peter A.
           1982 "Specific Benefits of Postcoronary Exercise Programs."
           Geriatrics 37:47–51.

14   Regenstreif, Peter
           1965 *The Diefenbaker Interlude: Parties and Voting in Canada.*
           Toronto: Longmans.

12   Rempel, Judith
            1985 "Childless Elderly: What Are They Missing?" *Journal of Marriage and the Family* 47:343–48.

7   Research and Planning Unit, Family and Community Support Services Division, Social Services Department
            1983 "A Profile of the Elderly in Calgary: A Demographic Profile and Needs Assessment." Calgary: City of Calgary.

12   Resnick, H., and J. Cantor
            1970 "Suicide and Aging." *Journal of the American Geriatric Society* 18:152–58.

8   Revenue Canada
            1983 *Taxation Statistics*. Ottawa: Minister of Supply and Services.

5   Rhodes, Ann
            1983 "Five Women Who Defy the Stereotypes of Aging." *Chatelaine*, February: 57 and 162.

6   Riegel, Klaus F.
            1975 "Adult Life Crises: A Dialectic Interpretation of Development." In *Life-span Developmental Psychology: Normative Life Crises*, ed. Nancy Datan and Leon H. Ginsberg. New York: Academic Press.

6   Riegel, Klaus F.
            1976 "The Dialectics of Human Development." *American Psychologist* 31:689–700.

4, 6   Riley, M.W., and A. Foner, eds.
            1968 *Aging and Society. Volume I: An Inventory of Research Findings*. New York: Russell Sage Foundation.

6   Riley, M.W., M.E. Johnson, and A. Foner, eds.
            1972 *Aging and Society: A Sociology of Age Stratification*. New York: Russell Sage Foundation.

9   Rix, Sara E., and Paul Fisher
            1982 *Retirement-Age Policy*. New York: Pergamon Press.

9, 11   Roadburg, Alan
            1985 *Aging: Retirement, Leisure and Work in Canada*. Toronto: Methuen.

15   Robertson, Duncan
            1981 "Undergraduate Medical Education in Geriatric Medicine." *Annals Royal College of Physicians and Surgeons of Canada* 14:371–73.

5   Robertson, Duncan, K. Rockwood, and P. Stolee
            1982 "Prevalence of Cognitive Impairment in an Elderly Population." Paper presented at the Canadian Association on Gerontology 11th Annual Scientific and Educational Meeting, Winnipeg, Manitoba.

6   Robertson, Ian
        1981 *Sociology*, 2nd ed. New York: Worth.

12   Robertson, Joan F.
        1977 "Grandmotherhood: A Study of Role Conceptions."
        Journal of Marriage and the Family 39:165–74.

9   Robinson, Pauline K., Sally Coberly, and Carolyn E. Paul
        1985 "Work and Retirement." In *Handbook of Aging and the
        Social Sciences*, 2nd ed., ed. Robert H. Binstock and Ethel
        Shanas. New York: Van Nostrand Reinhold.

4   Rockstein, Morris, and M. Sussman
        1979 *Biology of Aging*. Belmont, California: Wadsworth.

10   Romanick, Gregory S.
        1986 "Municipal Mechanisms for the Implementation of
        Granny Flats." In *Granny Flats: A Housing Option for the
        Elderly*, Report No. 13, ed. Susan Corke, Gregory S.
        Romanick, Michael Lazarowich, and Joan Simon. Winnipeg:
        Institute of Urban Studies.

3   Romaniuc, Anatole
        1984 *Current Demographic Analysis: Fertility in Canada: From
        Baby-Boom to Baby-Bust*. Statistics Canada Cat. No. 91–524E
        Occasional. Ottawa: Minister of Supply and Services.

11   Romsa, G.H., and Ronald Johnson
        1983 "A Preliminary Analysis of Retirement Satisfaction and
        Leisure Patterns in Canada." In *Proceedings of the Third
        Canadian Congress on Leisure Research*, ed. Thomas L. Burton
        and Jan Taylor. Canadian Association for Leisure Studies.

7   Roos, Noralou P., and Evelyn Shapiro
        1981 "The Manitoba Longitudinal Study on Aging." *Medical
        Care* 19:644–57.

7   Roos, Noralou P., Evelyn Shapiro, and Leslie L. Roos, Jr.
        1984 "Aging and the Demand for Health Services: Which
        Aged and Whose Demand?" *The Gerontologist* 24:31–36.

10   Rose, Albert, and J. Grant Macdonald
        1984 *Factors Influencing the Quality of Life of Community-Based
        Elderly, Part II: Housing Conditions of the Elderly in Ontario,
        Research Paper No. 152*. Toronto: Centre for Urban and
        Community Studies, University of Toronto.

4   Rose, M.R., and B. Charlesworth
        1981a "Genetics of Life History in *Drosophila melanogaster*, I.
        Sib Analysis of Adult Females." *Genetics* 97:173–86.

4   Rose, M.R., and B. Charlesworth
        1981b "Genetics of Life History in *Drosophila melanogaster*, I.
        Explanatory Selection Experiments." *Genetics* 97:187–96.

9   Rosen, Benson, and Thomas H. Jerdee
     1982 "Effects of Employee Financial Status and Social
     Adjustment on Employers' Retention/Retirement
     Recommendations." *Aging and Work* 5:111–18.

12   Rosenmayr, L., and E. Kockeis
     1963 "Propositions for a Sociological Theory of Aging and
     the Family." *International Social Science Journal* 15:410–26.

12   Rosenthal, Carolyn J.
     1983 "The Anglo-Canadian Family: A Perspective on
     Ethnicity and Support to the Elderly." Paper presented at the
     Canadian Association on Gerontology 12th Annual Scientific
     and Educational Meeting, Moncton, N.B.

12   Rosenthal, Carolyn J.
     1986 "Family Supports in Later Life: Does Ethnicity Make a
     Difference?" *The Gerontologist* 26:19–24.

12   Rosenthal, Carolyn J., Victor W. Marshall, and Jane Synge
     1980 "The Succession of Lineage Roles as Families Age."
     Essence 4:179–93.

2   Rosow, Irving
     1965 "And Then We Were Old." *Transaction* 2:20–26.

6   Rosow, Irving
     1976 "Status and Role Change Through the Life Span." In
     Handbook of Aging and the Social Sciences, ed. R.H. Binstock
     and E. Shanas. New York: Van Nostrand Reinhold.

9   Ross, David
     1979 "Statement on Retirement Age Policies." Ottawa:
     Canadian Council on Social Development.

5   Ross, E.
     1968 "Effects of Challenging and Supportive Instructions in
     Verbal Learning in Older Persons." *Journal of Educational
     Psychology* 59:261–66.

7   Ross, Val
     1983 "The Coming Old Age Crisis." *Maclean's*,
     January:24–29.

8   Royal Commission on the Status of Pensions in Ontario
     1980 *Report. Vol. II. Design for Retirement.* Toronto:
     Government of Ontario.

12   Rushing, W.A.
     1968 "Individual Behaviour and Suicide." In *Suicide*, ed.
     J. Gibbs. New York: Harper and Row.

2   Salas, Rafael
     1982 "Aging: A Universal Phenomenon." *Populi* 9:3–7.

13   Salmon, C., and P. McGee
     1980 *Palliative Care.* Toronto: Institutional Planning Branch,
     Ontario Ministry of Health.

13   Sanders, Catherine M.
    1980–81 "Comparison of Younger and Older Spouses in
    Bereavement Outcome." *Omega* 11:217–32.

5   Sanders, R.E., M.D. Murphy, F.A. Schmitt, and K.K. Walsh
    1980 "Age Differences in Free Recall Rehearsal Strategies."
    Journal of Gerontology 35:550–58.

5   Sanders, R.E., and J.A. Sanders
    1978 "Long-Term Durability and Transfer of Enhanced
    Conceptual Performance in the Elderly." *Journal of
    Gerontology* 33:408–12.

10   Saskatchewan Housing Corporation
    1984 *Housing Needs in Saskatchewan*. Regina: The
    Corporation.

13, 15   Saunders, Cicely
    1984 "St. Christopher's Hospice." In *Death: Current
    Perspectives*, 3rd ed., ed. Edwin S. Shneidman. Palo Alto,
    California: Mayfield.

5   Schaie, K. Warner
    1959 "Cross-Sectional Methods in the Study of Psychological
    Aspects of Aging." *Journal of Gerontology* 14:208–15.

1, 6   Schaie, K. Warner
    1968 "Age Changes and Age Differences." In *Middle Age and
    Aging*, ed. Bernice L. Neugarten. Chicago: University of
    Chicago Press.

5   Schaie, K. Warner
    1975 "Age Changes in Adult Intelligence." In *Aging: Scientific
    Perspectives and Social Issues*, ed. Diana S. Woodruff and
    J.E. Birren. New York: D. Van Nostrand.

1, 5   Schaie, K. Warner, and G. Labouvie-Vief
    1974 "Generational Versus Ontogenetic Components of
    Change in Adult Cognitive Behavior: A Fourteen-Year
    Cross-Sequential Study." *Developmental Psychology* 10:305–20.

5   Schaie, K. Warner, F. Rosenthal, and R.M. Perlman
    1953 "Differential Deterioration of Functionally 'Pure'
    Mental Abilities." *Journal of Gerontology* 8:191–96.

5   Schaie, K. Warner, and C.R. Strother
    1972 "A Cross-Sequential Study of Age Changes in Cognitive
    Behaviour." In *Human Aging*, ed. Sheila M. Chown.
    Harmondsworth, England: Penguin.

8   Schiele, Michael
    1985 "Pension Plan Reform: It's Here at Last!" *Financial Post*,
    June 1.

4   Schneider, Edward L., and John D. Reed
    1985 "Modulations of Aging Processes." In *Handbook of the*

432   *References*

Biology of Aging, 2nd ed., ed. Caleb E. Finch and Edward L. Schneider. New York: Van Nostrand Reinhold.

13   Schneidman, Edwin S., ed.
1984 *Death: Current Perspectives*, 3rd ed. Palo Alto, California: Mayfield.

1   Schonfield, David
1982 "Who Is Stereotyping Whom and Why?" *The Gerontologist* 22: 267–72.

12   Schorr, A.
1980 "'... thy father and thy mother ...' A Second Look at Filial Responsibility and Social Policy." Social Security Administration Publication 13–11953. Washington, D.C.: U.S. Department of Health and Human Services.

10   Schull, Christiane
1981 "Bag Ladies." *Today Magazine*, April 15: 15–16.

2, 9   Schulz, James
1980 *The Economics of Aging*, 2nd ed. Belmont, California: Wadsworth.

13   Schulz, Richard
1978 *The Psychology of Death, Dying, and Bereavement*. Reading, Massachusetts: Addison-Wesley.

12   Schwartz, A.N.
1979 "Psychological Dependency: An Emphasis on the Later Years." In *Aging Parents*, ed. P.K. Ragan. Los Angeles: University of Southern California.

1, 7, 10   Schwenger, Cope, and M. Gross
1980 "Institutional Care and Institutionalization of the Elderly in Canada." In *Aging in Canada*, ed. Victor W. Marshall. Toronto: Fitzhenry and Whiteside.

1   Senate of Canada
1966 *Final Report of the Special Committee of the Senate on Aging*. Ottawa: Queen's Printer.

1, 8, 9, 14   Senate of Canada
1979 *Retirement Without Tears: A Report of the Special Senate Committee on Retirement Age Policies* (Croll Commission). Ottawa: Minister of Supply and Services.

9   Senior Citizens' Job Bureau
1986 *Report to the Board of Directors*. Winnipeg: Senior Citizens' Job Bureau.

10   Senior Citizens' Provincial Council
1980 *Choosing a Special Care Home in Saskatchewan*. Regina: Senior Citizens' Provincial Council.

10   Senior Citizens' Provincial Council
1981 *Regina Social Support Survey*. Regina: Senior Citizens' Provincial Council.

10   Senior Citizens' Provincial Council
1982 *A Survey of the Transportation Needs of the Rural Elderly*. Regina: Senior Citizens' Provincial Council.

7, 11   Senior Citizens' Provincial Council
1983 *Profile '83: The Senior Population in Saskatchewan. 3: Social Resources*. Regina: Senior Citizens' Provincial Council.

6   Sermat, Vello
1978 "Sources of Loneliness." *Essence* 2:271–76.

12   Shanas, Ethel
1967 "Family Help Patterns and Social Class in Three Societies." *Journal of Marriage and the Family* 29:257–66.

12   Shanas, Ethel
1979 "The Family as a Social Support System in Old Age." *The Gerontologist* 19:169–74.

12   Shanas, Ethel, Peter Townsend, Dorothy Wedderburn, Henning Friis, Poul Milhoj, and Jan Stehouwer
1968 *Older People in Three Industrial Societies*. New York: Atherton Press.

13   Shapiro, Evelyn
1983 "Impending Death and the Use of Hospitals by the Elderly." *Journal of the American Geriatrics Society* 31:348–51.

7   Shapiro, Evelyn, and Leslie L. Roos
1984 "Using Health Care: Rural/Urban Differences Among the Manitoba Elderly." *The Gerontologist* 24:270–74.

9   Shapiro, Evelyn, and Noralou P. Roos
1982 "Retired and Employed Elderly Persons: Their Utilization of Health Care Services." *The Gerontologist* 22:187–93.

7, 10   Shapiro, Evelyn, and Robert B. Tate
1985 "Predictors of Long Term Care Facility Use Among the Elderly." *Canadian Journal on Aging* 4:11–19.

2   Sharp, H.S.
1981 "Old Age Among the Chipewyan." In *Other Ways of Growing Old: Anthropological Perspectives*, ed. P.T. Amoss and S. Harrell. Stanford, California: Stanford University Press.

13   Shedletsky, Ralph, and Rory Fisher
1986 "Terminal Illness: Attitudes in Both an Acute Care and an Extended Care Teaching Hospital." *Journal of Palliative Care* 2:16–21.

13   Shedletsky, Ralph, Rory Fisher, and Grant Nadon
        1982 "Assessment of Palliative Care for Dying Hospitalized
        Elderly." *Canadian Journal on Aging* 1:11–15.

12   Shell, Donna J.
        1982 *Protection of the Elderly: A Study of Elder Abuse.* Winnipeg:
        Manitoba Council on Aging.

11   Shephard, R.J.
        1978 *Physical Activity and Aging.* London: Croom Helm.

13   Shneidman, Edwin S.
        1984 "Malignancy: Dialogues with Life-Threatening
        Illnesses." In *Death: Current Perspectives*, 3rd ed., ed. Edwin S.
        Shneidman. Palo Alto, California: Mayfield.

4   Shock, N.W.
        1962 "The Physiology of Aging." *Scientific American*
        206:100–111.

4   Shock, N.W.
        1977 "Systems Integration." In *Handbook of the Biology of
        Aging*, ed. C.E. Finch and L. Hayflick. New York: Van
        Nostrand Reinhold.

3   Shulman, Norman
        1980 "The Aging of Urban Canada." In *Aging in Canada*, ed.
        Victor W. Marshall. Toronto: Fitzhenry and Whiteside.

11   Sijpkes, Peter, Michael MacLean, and David Brown
        1983 "Hanging Around the Mall." *Recreation Canada*,
        February:44–46.

2   Simmons, L.W.
        1960 "Aging in Preindustrial Societies." In *Handbook of Social
        Gerontology: Societal Aspects of Aging*, ed. C. Tibbitts. Chicago:
        University of Chicago Press.

2   Simmons, L.W.
        1970 *The Role of the Aged in Primitive Society.* New Haven,
        Connecticut: Yale University Press.

5   Simonton, D.K.
        1977 "Creative Productivity, Age, and Stress: A Biographical
        Time-Series Analysis of 10 Classical Composers." *Journal of
        Personality and Social Psychology* 35:791–804.

9   Simpson, Ida H., Kurt W. Back, and John C. McKinney
        1966 "Continuity of Work and Retirement Activities, and
        Self-Evaluation." In *Social Aspects of Aging*, ed. Ida H.
        Simpson and John C. McKinney. Durham, N.C.: Duke
        University Press.

10   Sinclair, Douglas
        1984 "A New Approach to Geriatric Institutional Care."
        Canadian Family Physician 30:1373–76.

13   Skelton, David
      1982 "The Hospice Movement: A Human Approach to Palliative Care." *Canadian Medical Association Journal* 126:556–58.

5   Smith, A.D.
      1977 "Adult Age Differences in Cued Recall." *Developmental Psychology* 13:326–31.

5   Smith, A.D.
      1980 "Age Differences in Encoding, Storage, and Retrieval." In *New Directions in Memory and Aging: Proceedings of the George A. Talland Memorial Conference*, ed. L.W. Poon, J.L. Fozard, L.S. Cermak, D. Arenberg, and L.W. Thompson. Hillsdale, N.J.: Lawrence Erlbaum Association.

11   Smith, E.L.
      1982 "Exercise for Prevention of Osteoporosis: A Review." *Physician and Sportsmedicine* 10:72–83.

4   Smith, E.L., W. Reddan, and P.E. Smith
      1981 "Physical Activity and Calcium Modalities for Bone Mineral Increase in Aged Women." *Medical Science Sports Exercise* 13:60–64.

10   Smith, Wendy
      1979 *Single Old Men on Main Street: An Evaluation of Jack's Hotel*. Winnipeg: Canada Mortgage and Housing Corporation.

12   Snider, Earle L.
      1981 "The Role of Kin in Meeting Health Care Needs of the Elderly." *Canadian Journal of Sociology* 6:325–36.

10   Sokolovsky, J., and C. Cohen
      1981 "Measuring Social Interaction of the Urban Elderly: A Methodological Synthesis." *International Journal of Aging and Human Development* 12:233–44.

9   Solem, Per Erik
      1976 *Paid Work After Retirement Age, and Mortality in Retirement: Norwegian Experience*. Oslo: Norwegian Institute of Gerontology.

1   Solicitor General of Canada
      1983 *Canadian Urban Victimization Survey. Bulletin 1: Victims of Crime*. Ottawa: Minister of Supply and Services.

1   Solicitor General of Canada
      1985 *The Canadian Urban Victimization Survey. Bulletin 6: Criminal Victimization of Elderly Canadians*. Ottawa: Minister of Supply and Services.

13   Southall, H.
      1982 *A Survey of Palliative Care Programs and Services in Canada*. Toronto: Palliative Care Foundation.

11   Stacey, C., A. Kozma, and M.J. Stones
        1985 "Simple Cognitive and Behavioral Changes Resulting from Improved Physical Fitness in Persons over 50 Years of Age." *Canadian Journal on Aging* 4:67–74.

9   Stagner, Ross
        1985 "Aging in Industry." In *Handbook of the Psychology of Aging*, 2nd ed., ed. James E. Birren and K. Warner Schaie. New York: Van Nostrand Reinhold.

10   Stark, A.J., E. Kliewer, G.M. Gutman, and B. McCashin
        1984 "Placement Changes in Long-term Care — 3 years Experience." *American Journal of Public Health* 74:459–63.

1, 3   Statistics Canada
        1968 *1966 Census of Canada*, Vol. 1(1–11). Ottawa: Queen's Printer.

9   Statistics Canada, Labour Division
        1972 *The Labour Force — January, 1972*. Cat. No. 71–001. Ottawa: Minister of Supply and Services.

3   Statistics Canada
        1973a *Census of Canada. Bulletin 1: 2–3* (1971 Census). Ottawa: Information Canada.

3   Statistics Canada
        1973b *Vital Statistics: Vol. 3. Deaths*. Ottawa: Information Canada.

3   Statistics Canada
        1975 *Technical Report on Population Projections for Canada and the Provinces. 1976–2001*. Cat. No. 91–516. Occasional. Ottawa: Statistics Canada.

11   Statistics Canada
        1976a *Culture Statistics. Recreational Activities*. Cat. No. 87–501. Ottawa: Minister of Supply and Services.

8   Statistics Canada
        1976b *Pension Plans in Canada 1976*. Cat. No. 74–401. Ottawa: Minister of Supply and Services.

11   Statistics Canada
        1977 *Perspective Canada II*. Ottawa: Minister of Supply and Services.

10   Statistics Canada
        1978a *Family, Expenditure in Canada. Volume I. Preliminary Estimates: Eight Cities*. Cat. No. 62–549. Ottawa: Minister of Supply and Services.

3   Statistics Canada
        1978b *1976 Census of Canada. Advanced Release*. Ottawa: Minister of Supply and Services.

3   Statistics Canada
1978c *Social Security*. Cat. No. 86–201. Ottawa: Minister of Supply and Services.

3   Statistics Canada
1978d *Vital Statistics. Vol. I. Births. 1975 and 1976*. Cat. No. 84–204. Ottawa: Statistics Canada.

13   Statistics Canada
1978e *Vital Statistics. Vol. III. Death. 1976*. Ottawa: Health Division, Vital Statistics and Diseases Registries Section, Minister of Supply and Services.

3, 9   Statistics Canada
1979a *Canada's Elderly*. Cat. No. 98–800E. Ottawa: Minister of Supply and Services.

9   Statistics Canada, Labour Force Survey Division
1979b *The Labour Force — January, 1979*. Cat. No. 71–001. Ottawa: Minister of Supply and Services.

3   Statistics Canada
1979c *Life Tables. Canada and Provinces. 1975–77*. Cat. No. 84–532. Ottawa: Minister of Supply and Services.

10   Statistics Canada
1980a *Expenditure Patterns and Income Adequacy for the Elderly. 1969–1976*. Cat. No. 13–575. Ottawa: Minister of Supply and Services.

12   Statistics Canada
1980b *Perspectives Canada III*. Cat. No. 11–511E. Ottawa: Minister of Supply and Services.

7   Statistics Canada
1980c *Surgical Procedures and Treatments 1976*. Cat. No. 82–208. Ottawa: Minister of Supply and Services.

3   Statistics Canada
1981a *Canada Year Book 1980–81*. Ottawa: Minister of Supply and Services.

7   Statistics Canada
1981b *Surgical Procedures and Treatments 1977*. Cat. No. 82–208. Ottawa: Minister of Supply and Services.

3   Statistics Canada
1981c *Vital Statistics. 1: Births and Deaths*. Cat. No. 84–204 Annual. Ottawa: Statistics Canada.

8   Statistics Canada
1982 "Social Security National Programs, Vol. 5." *Old Age Security, Guaranteed Income Supplement and Spouse's Allowance*. Ottawa: Minister of Supply and Services.

3   Statistics Canada
               1983 *Canada Update* (1981 Bulletin). Ottawa: Statistics
               Canada.

3, 12   Statistics Canada
               1984a *Canada's Immigrants*. Cat. No. 99–936. Ottawa: Minister
               of Supply and Services.

3, 6, 8, 10,   Statistics Canada
12   1984b *The Elderly in Canada*. Cat. No. 99–932. Ottawa:
               Minister of Supply and Services.

10   Statistics Canada
               1984c *Household Facilities by Income and Other Characteristics.
               1983*. Cat. No. 13–567. Ottawa: Minister of Supply and
               Services.

3, 12   Statistics Canada
               1984d *Life Tables. Canada and Provinces. 1980–82*. Cat. No.
               84–532. Ottawa: Minister of Supply and Services.

12   Statistics Canada
               1985a *Language in Canada*. Cat. No. 99–935. Ottawa: Minister
               of Supply and Services.

12   Statistics Canada
               1985b *Vital Statistics. Volume II: Marriages and Divorces*. Cat.
               No. 84–205. Ottawa: Minister of Supply and Services.

12   Statistics Canada
               1985c *Women in Canada: A Statistical Report*. Cat. No.
               89–503E. Ottawa: Minister of Supply and Services.

11   Statistics Canada
               1986a *Canadian Social Trends*. Cat. No. 11–008E. Ottawa:
               Minister of Supply and Services.

8   Statistics Canada
               1986b *Infomat*. September 26. Cat. No. 11–002E. Ottawa:
               Minister of Supply and Services.

9   Statistics Canada
               1986c *The Labour Force — August, 1986*. Cat. No. 71–001.
               Ottawa: Minister of Supply and Services.

3   Statistics Canada
               1987 *Special Projections 1991–2031*. Unpublished data.
               September. Supplied to Statistics Canada, Health Division,
               Social Security Section. Ottawa: Minister of Supply and
               Services.

2   Stearns, Peter N.
               1967 *European Society in Upheaval*. New York: Macmillan.

2   Stearns, Peter N.
               1977 *Old Age in European Society: The Case of France*. London:
               Croom Helm.

11   Stewart, G.
          1982 "Programme Principles." In *National Conference on
          Fitness in the Third Age: Workshop Discussion Papers*, ed. Fitness
          and Amateur Sport. Ottawa: Government of Canada.

7   Stockwell, H., and E. Vayda
          1979 "Variations in Surgery in Ontario." *Medical Care*
          17:390–96.

5   Stone, Leroy O.
          1986 "Demography and Dementia." Paper presented at a
          conference on Alzheimer's Disease and Other Dementias,
          Toronto, Ontario.

12   Stone, Leroy O.
          1987 "Cohort Aging and Support Network Help Capacity."
          In *Aging: The Universal Human Experience*, ed. George
          Maddox and E.W. Busse. New York: Springer.

3   Stone, Leroy O., and Susan Fletcher
          1980 *A Profile of Canada's Older Population*. Montreal: Institute
          for Research on Public Policy.

12   Stone, Leroy O., and Susan Fletcher
          1986a "The Hypothesis of Age Patterns in Living
          Arrangement Passages." In *Aging in Canada*, 2nd ed., ed.
          Victor W. Marshall. Toronto: Fitzhenry and Whiteside.

4, 7, 12, 14   Stone, Leroy O., and Susan Fletcher
          1986b *The Seniors Boom*. Statistics Canada Cat. No. 89–515E.
          Ottawa: Minister of Supply and Services.

8   Stone, Leroy O., and Michael MacLean
          1979 *Future Income Prospects for Canada's Senior Citizens*.
          Toronto: Butterworths.

11   Stones, M.J., and A. Kozma
          1980 "Adult Age Trends in Record Running Performances."
          Experimental Aging Research 6:407–16.

11   Stones, M.J., and A. Kozma
          1982 "Cross-Sectional, Longitudinal, and Secular Age Trends
          in Athletic Performance." *Experimental Aging Research*
          8:185–88.

12   Strain, Laurel A., and Neena L. Chappell
          1982 "Confidants: Do They Make a Difference in Quality of
          Life?" *Research on Aging* 4:479–502.

12   Strain, Laurel A., and Neena L. Chappell
          1984 "Social Support Among Elderly Canadian Natives: A
          Comparison with Elderly Non-Natives." Paper presented at
          the Canadian Association on Gerontology 13th Annual
          Scientific and Educational Meeting, Vancouver, B.C.

4   Strehler, B.
          1977 *Time, Cells and Aging*, 2nd ed. New York: Academic
          Press.

4   Strehler, B.
           1982 "A New Age for Aging." In *Readings in Aging and
           Death: Contemporary Perspectives*, 2nd ed., ed. Steven H. Zarit.
           New York: Harper and Row.

1   Streib, Gordon, and Clement Schneider
           1971 *Retirement in American Society*. Ithaca, N.Y.: Cornell
           University Press.

7   Sturdy, Catherine, and Joseph A. Tindale
           1985 "The Social Organization of Health Care Provision to
           the Elderly in Ontario." Paper presented to the Canadian
           Association on Gerontology 14th Annual Scientific and
           Educational Meeting, Hamilton, Ontario.

12   Sugiman, Pamela, and Harry Nishio
           1983 "Socialization and Cultural Duality Among Aging
           Japanese Canadians." *Canadian Ethnic Studies* 15:17–35.

4   Surwillo, W.
           1963 "The Relation of Simple Response Time to Brain-wave
           Frequency and the Effects of Age." *Electroencephalography and
           Clinical Neurophysiology* 15:105–14.

2   Synge, Jane
           1980 "Work and Family Support Patterns of the Aged in the
           Early Twentieth Century." In *Aging in Canada*, ed. Victor W.
           Marshall. Toronto: Fitzhenry and Whiteside.

12   Synge, Jane
           No date. "Women as Telephoners: On the Importance of
           Phoning and Writing in Maintaining Kin and Friendship
           Ties in Middle and Old Age." Personal communication.

12   Synge, Jane, and M. Luxton
           1984 "Patterns of Sociability and Companionship Among the
           Middle Aged and the Aged with Special Reference to Elderly
           Women." Paper presented at the Annual Meeting of the
           Canadian Sociology and Anthropology Association.

12   Szasz, George
           1980 "The Sexual Consequences of Aging." In *The Family in
           Later Life: Canadian Gerontological Collection III. Selected Papers
           1980*, ed. John Crawford. Winnipeg: Canadian Association
           on Gerontology.

9   Szinovacz, M.
           1982 "Introduction: Research on Women's Retirement." In
           Women's Retirement, ed. M. Szinovacz. Beverly Hills,
           California: Sage.

9   T. Eaton Company
           1958 Correspondence.

5   Taub, H.A.
1979 "Comprehension and Memory of Prose Materials by Young and Old Adults." *Experimental Aging Research* 5:3–13.

13   Thompson, Edward H.
1985–86 "Palliative and Curative Care: Nurses' Attitudes Toward Dying and Death in the Hospital Setting." *Omega* 16:233–42.

4   Thompson, L.W., and G.R. Marsh
1973 "Psychophysiological Studies of Aging." In *The Psychology of Adult Development and Aging*, ed. C. Eisdorfer and M.P. Lawton. Washington, D.C.: American Psychological Association.

12   Thorman, George
1980 *Family Violence*. Springfield, Illinois: Charles C. Thomas.

7   Thurston, Norma E., Donald E. Larsen, Alfred W. Rademaker, and Janet C. Kerr
1982 "Health Status of the Rural Elderly: A Picture of Health." Paper presented at the Canadian Association on Gerontology 11th Annual Scientific and Educational Meeting, Winnipeg, Manitoba.

4   *Time*
1986a "Extra Years for Extra Effort." March 17.

4   *Time*
1986b "Milestones: Died: Shigechiyo Izumi." March 3.

6   Tindale, J.
1980 "Identity Maintenance Processes of Old Poor Men." In *Aging in Canada*, ed. Victor W. Marshall. Toronto: Fitzhenry and Whiteside.

1, 3   Tindale, J., and V.W. Marshall
1980 "A Generational Conflict Perspective for Gerontology." In *Aging in Canada*, ed. Victor W. Marshall. Toronto: Fitzhenry and Whiteside.

14   *Today Magazine*
1980 "Heroes of 1980." *Today Magazine*, December 27.

3   Torrance, G.
1981 "Introduction: Socio-Historical Overview: The Development of the Canadian Health System." In *Health and Canadian Society: Sociological Perspectives*, ed. D. Coburn, C. D'Arcy, P. New, and G. Torrance. Toronto: Fitzhenry and Whiteside.

4   Toufexis, Anastasia
1986 "New Rub for the Skin Game." *Time*, March 31.

9   Tournier, Paul
        1972 *Learning to Grow Old*. London: SCM Press.

1   Towler, John C.
        1983 "Ageism in Children's Popular Literature and
        Television." Paper presented at the Canadian Association on
        Gerontology 12th Annual Scientific and Educational Meeting,
        Moncton, N.B.

12   Treas, J.
        1977 "Family Support Systems for the Aged: Some Social
        and Demographic Considerations." *The Gerontologist*
        17:486–91.

3   Treasury Board Secretariat
        1977 *Changing Population and the Impact on Government Age-
        Specific Expenditures*. Ottawa: Planning Branch Effectiveness
        Evaluation Division, Treasury Board Secretariat.

14   Trela, James
        1976 "Status Inconsistency and Political Action in Old Age."
        In *Time, Roles, and Self in Old Age*, ed. Jaber Gubrium. New
        York: Human Sciences Press.

2   Turnbull, Colin
        1961 *The Forest People*. New York: Simon and Schuster.

10   Turner, L., and E. Mangum
        1982 *Report on Housing Choice of Older Americans. Summary of
        Survey Findings and Recommendations for Practitioners*. Bryn
        Mawr, Pennsylvania: Graduate School of Social Work and
        Social Research, Bryn Mawr College.

12   Ujimoto, V.K.
        1983 "Introduction: Ethnicity and Aging in Canada."
        Canadian Ethnic Studies 15:iii–vii.

3   United Nations
        1956 *The Aging of Populations and Its Economic and Social
        Implications*. Population Studies No. 26. New York: United
        Nations.

3   United Nations
        1975 *Economic Survey of Europe in 1974. Part II: Post-War
        Demographic Trends in Europe and the Outlook Until the Year
        2000*. New York: United Nations.

10   United Senior Citizens of Ontario
        1985 "Elderly Residents in Ontario: Their Current Housing
        Situation and Their Interest in Various Housing Options."
        Ontario: Minister for Senior Citizen Affairs.

9   U.S. Congressional Budget Office
        1982 *Work and Retirement: Options for Continued Employment of
        Older Workers*. Washington, D.C.: U.S. Government Printing
        Office.

12   Vachon, M.L.S.
        1981 "The Importance of Social Relationships and Social
        Support in Widowhood." Paper presented to the Joint
        Meeting of the Canadian Association on Gerontology and the
        Gerontological Society of America, Toronto, Ontario.

12   Vachon, M.L.S., A. Formo, K. Freedman, A. Lyall, J. Rogers,
        and S. Freeman
        1976 "Stress Reactions to Bereavement." *Essence* 1:23–33.

7   Van Horne, Ron
        1986 *A New Agenda*. Toronto: Government of Ontario.

14   Van Loon, R.
        1970 "Political Participation in Canada: The 1965 Election."
        Canadian Journal of Political Science 3:376–99.

12   Veevers, Jean E.
        1987 "The 'Real' Marriage Squeeze: Mate Selection, Mortality
        and the Mating Gradient." Paper presented at the Annual
        Meeting of the Pacific Sociological Association.

14   Verba, Sidney, and Norman H. Nie
        1972 *Participation in America: Political Democracy and Social
        Equality*. New York: Harper and Row.

14   Verba, Sidney, Norman H. Nie, and Jae-on Kim
        1971 *The Modes of Democratic Participation*. Beverly Hills,
        California: Sage.

12   Verwoerdt, A., E. Pfeiffer, and H.S. Wang
        1969 "Sexual Behavior in Senescence — Changes in Sexual
        Activity and Interest of Aging Men and Women." *Journal of
        Geriatric Psychiatry* 2:163–80.

11   Vigoda, Debby, Lawrence Crawford, and John Hirdes
        1985 "The Continuity Theory: Empirical Support." In *Aging,
        Mirror of Humanity: Canadian Gerontological Collection IV*, ed.
        Norman K. Blackie, Sister Anne Robichaud, and Shawn
        MacDonald. Winnipeg: Canadian Association on
        Gerontology.

4   Walford, R.L.
        1969 *The Immunologic Theory of Aging*. Copenhagen:
        Munksgaard.

7   Wallace, Marilyn M., and Wendy J.A. Thompson
        1985 "The Seniors' Well-Being Activation Team and Society:
        Annual Report." Vancouver: SWAT.

5   Walsh, D.A.
        1976 "Age Differences in Central Perceptual Processing: A
        Dichoptic Backward Masking Investigation." *Journal of
        Gerontology* 31:178–85.

5   Walsh, D.A., R.E. Till, and M.V. Williams
        1978 "Age Differences in Peripheral Perceptual Processing:

A Monoptic Backward Masking Investigation." *Journal of Experimental Psychology: Human Perception and Performance* 4:232–43.

13   Walton, Douglas N., and W.H. Fleming
1980 "Responsibility for the Discontinuation of Treatment." *Essence* 4:57–61.

12   Wanner, Richard A., and P. Lynn McDonald
1986 "The Vertical Mosaic in Later Life: Ethnicity and Retirement in Canada." *Journal of Gerontology* 41:662–71.

5   Waugh, Nancy C., and Robin A. Barr
1982 "Encoding Deficits in Aging." In *Aging and Cognitive Processes*, ed. F.I.M. Craik and Sandra Trehub. New York: Plenum Press.

5   Wechsler, D.
1939 *A Measurement of Adult Intelligence*, 1st ed. Baltimore: Williams and Wilkins.

5   Wechsler, D.
1981 *WAIS-R Manual (Wechsler Adult Intelligence Scale)*, revised. New York: Harcourt, Brace, Jovanovich.

4   Weg, R.B.
1974 "Discussion Summary." In *Theoretical Aspects of Aging*, ed. Morris Rockstein, M.L. Sussman, and J. Chesky. New York: Academic Press.

13   Weisman, Avery
1972 *On Dying and Denying*. New York: Behavioral Press.

6   Weiss, R.S., ed.
1973 *Loneliness: The Experience of Emotional and Social Isolation*. Cambridge, Massachusetts: MIT Press.

5   Welford, A.T.
1958 *Aging and Human Skill*. London: Oxford University Press.

4   Welford, A.T.
1977 "Motor Performance." In *Handbook of the Psychology of Aging*, ed. J.E. Birren and K.W. Schaie. New York: Van Nostrand Reinhold.

3   Weller, Robert H., and Leon F. Bouvier
1981 *Population: Demography and Policy*. New York: St. Martin's Press.

11   Werner, Lawrence
1976 "Functional Analysis of Viewing for Older Adults." *Journal of Broadcasting* 20:77–87.

10   Wershow, H.
1976 "The Four Percent Fallacy: Some Further Evidence and Policy Implications." *The Gerontologist* 16:52–55.

11   Wessel, J.A., and W.D. Van Huss
          1969 "The Influence of Physical Activity and Age on
          Exercise Adaptation of Women Aged 20–69 Years." *Journal
          of Sport Medicine* 9:173–80.

13   Wilcox, Sandra G., and Marilyn Sutton
          1985 *Understanding Death and Dying*, 3rd ed. Palo Alto,
          California: Mayfield.

4   Williams, G.C.
          1957 "Pleiotropy, Natural Selection and the Evolution of
          Senescence." *Evolution* 11:398–411.

12   *Winnipeg Sun*
          1985 "Volunteer Granny Becomes 'Friend' to All of the
          Family." December 22.

5   Winocur, Gordon
          1982 "Learning and Memory Deficits in Institutionalized and
          Non-institutionalized Old People: An Analysis of
          Interference Effects." In *Aging and Cognitive Processes*, ed.
          F.I.M. Craik and Sandra Trehub. New York: Plenum Press.

12   Wister, Andrew V.
          1985 "Living Arrangement Choices Among the Elderly."
          Canadian Journal on Aging 4:127–44.

12   Wister, Andrew V.
          1986 "Living Arrangements and Informal Social Support
          Among the Elderly." Personal communication.

12   Wister, Andrew V., and Laurel A. Strain
          1986 "Social Support and Well-Being: A Comparison of
          Older Widows and Widowers." Paper presented at the 21st
          Annual Meeting of the Canadian Sociology and
          Anthropology Association, Winnipeg, Manitoba.

5   Witte, K.L.
          1975 "Paired-Associate Learning in Young and Elderly
          Adults as Related to Presentation Rate." *Psychological Bulletin*
          82:975–85.

12   Woehrer, C.E.
          1978 "Cultural Pluralism in American Families: The
          Influence of Ethnicity on Social Aspects of Aging." *The
          Family Coordinator*, October: 328–39.

12   Wong, Paul T.P., and Gary T. Reker
          1985 "Stress, Coping, and Well-Being in Anglo and Chinese
          Elderly." *Canadian Journal on Aging* 4:29–38.

6   Wood, Linda A.
          1978 "Loneliness, Social Identity and Social Structure."
          Essence 2:259–70.

6   Wood, Linda, and A. Guest
           1978 "Editorial: Perspectives on Loneliness." *Essence*
           2:199–201.

1   Woodruff, D.S.
           1975 "Introduction: Multidisciplinary Perspectives of Aging."
           In *Aging: Scientific Perspectives and Social Issues*, ed. D.S.
           Woodruff and J.E. Birren. New York: D. Van Nostrand.

4   Woodruff, Diana S.
           1982 "The Life Expectancy Test: Can You Live to Be 100?"
           In *Readings in Aging and Death: Contemporary Perspectives*, 2nd
           ed., ed. Steven H. Zarit. New York: Harper and Row.

5   Wurtman, Richard J.
           1985 "Alzheimer's Disease." *Scientific American*, January:
           62–74.

12   Wylie, Betty Jane
           1981 "Coping with Survival: The Quiet Agony of the
           Widower." *Quest*, Spring: 34–38.

14   Yelaja, Shankar A.
           1981 "Gray Power: A Study on Political Attitudes and
           Behaviour of Older People in a Canadian City." Paper
           presented at the 12th International Congress of Gerontology,
           Hamburg, Germany.

10   Zamprelli, Jim
           1985 "Shelter Allowances for Older Adults: Programs in
           Search of a Policy." In *Innovations in Housing and Living
           Arrangements for Seniors*, ed. Gloria Gutman and Norman
           Blackie. Burnaby, B.C.; Gerontology Research Centre, Simon
           Fraser University.

1   Zarit, Steven H.
           1977 "Gerontology — Getting Better All the Time." In
           Readings in Aging and Death: Contemporary Perspectives, ed.
           Steven H. Zarit. New York: Harper and Row.

12   Zarit, S.H., K.E. Reever, and J. Bach-Peterson
           1980 "Relatives of the Impaired Elderly: Correlates of
           Feelings of Burden." *The Gerontologist* 20:649–55.

12   Zay, Nicholas
           1978 "Old Age and Aging in Canada's Ethnic Population."
           Paper presented at a National Symposium on Aging, Ottawa.

13   Zorza, Victor, and Rosemary Zorza
           1979 "Hospice — Death with Dignity? Or Giving Up on
           Life?" *Texas Medicine* 75:35–37.

5   Zuckerman, H.
           1977 *Scientific Elite: Studies of Nobel Laureates in the United
           States*. New York: Free Press.

INDEX OF NAMES

INDEX OF SUBJECTS